New Frontiers in Translation Studies

Series Editor

Defeng Li, Center for Studies of Translation, Interpreting and Cognition, University of Macau, Macao SAR, China

Translation Studies as a discipline has witnessed the fastest growth in the last 40 years. With translation becoming increasingly more important in today's glocalized world, some have even observed a general translational turn in humanities in recent years. The New Frontiers in Translation Studies aims to capture the newest developments in translation studies, with a focus on:

- Translation Studies research methodology, an area of growing interest amongst translation students and teachers;
- Data-based empirical translation studies, a strong point of growth for the discipline because of the scientific nature of the quantitative and/or qualitative methods adopted in the investigations; and Asian translation thoughts and theories, to complement the current Eurocentric translation studies.

Submission and Peer Review:

The editor welcomes book proposals from experienced scholars as well as young aspiring researchers. Please send a short description of 500 words to the editor Prof. Defeng Li at Springernfits@gmail.com and Springer Senior Publishing Editor Rebecca Zhu: Rebecca.zhu@springernature.com. All proposals will undergo peer review to permit an initial evaluation. If accepted, the final manuscript will be peer reviewed internally by the series editor as well as externally (single blind) by Springer ahead of acceptance and publication.

Ting Yin · Ling Xu · Defeng Li
Editors

AI Through LLMs

Transforming Translation Practice and Teaching

Springer

Editors
Ting Yin
Guangdong Polytechnic Normal University
Guangzhou, China

University of Macau
Macau, China

Ling Xu
Guangdong Polytechnic Normal University
Guangzhou, China

University of Macau
Macau, China

Defeng Li
University of Macau
Macau, China

ISSN 2197-8689 ISSN 2197-8697 (electronic)
New Frontiers in Translation Studies
ISBN 978-981-95-4797-5 ISBN 978-981-95-4798-2 (eBook)
https://doi.org/10.1007/978-981-95-4798-2

This Springer imprint is published by the registered company Springer Nature Singapore Pte Ltd.
The registered company address is: 152 Beach Road, #21-01/04 Gateway East, Singapore 189721, Singapore

Contents

Re-imagining the Classroom: Resources, Tasks, Engagement

Contributors

Chongyu Chen Beijing Language and Culture University, Beijing, China

Lintao Han Beijing Language and Culture University, Beijing, China

Wenzhong He School of International Studies, Zhejiang University, Hangzhou, China

Hui Jiao Xi'an Jiaotong-Liverpool University, Suzhou, China

Tong King Lee University of Hong Kong, Pok Fu Lam, Hong Kong

Kanglong Liu The Hong Kong Polytechnic University, Hong Kong SAR, China

Sirui Peng Chengdu Sport University, Chengdu, China

Yanfang Su Lingnan University, Hong Kong SAR, China

Kizito Tekwa Shenzhen Technology University, Shenzhen, China

Huashu Wang Graduate School of Translation and Interpretation, Beijing Foreign Studies University, Beijing, China

Zixuan Wang Xi'an Jiaotong-Liverpool University, Suzhou, China

Ying Wu Graduate School of Translation and Interpretation, Beijing Foreign Studies University, Beijing, China;
School of Foreign Languages, Wenhua College, Wuhan, China

Bin Xu Shandong Normal University, Jinan, China

Ling Xu Guangdong Polytechnic Normal University, University of Macao, Guangdong, China

Simin Xu The Hong Kong Polytechnic University, Hong Kong SAR, China

Ting Yin Guangdong Polytechnic Normal University, University of Macao, Guangdong, China

Jing Zhang Sichuan Normal University, Chengdu, China

Chuyi Zheng Beijing Language and Culture University, Beijing, China

Xiaojun Zhang Xi'an Jiaotong-Liverpool University, Suzhou, China; Anhui Provincial Key Laboratory of Multimodal Cognitive Computation, Anhui University, Hefei, China

Re-mapping the Landscape: From Practice to Paradigm

Large Language Model-Driven Intelligent Translation: How New Technologies Are Reshaping Translation Practices?

Huashu Wang and Ying Wu

Abstract Amid accelerating globalization and digital transformation, traditional translation practices are increasingly challenged by limitations in efficiency, semantic depth, domain adaptability, and multimodal integration. Large language models (LLMs) have emerged as a disruptive force in intelligent translation, offering advanced capabilities in contextual understanding, semantic reasoning, multilingual generalization, and adaptive learning from human feedback. This study examines how LLMs transcend the constraints of conventional neural machine translation (NMT) and drive a systematic reconfiguration of the translation workflow—from intelligent pre-translation planning and context-aware generation to post-editing and quality assurance. It further explores the evolving translation ecosystem, highlighting shifts in technological infrastructures, professional roles, service paradigms, and data governance. In addressing these transformations, the study examines how these shifts fundamentally impact translation education and training, analyzing pedagogical adaptations including curriculum redesign, competency reconstruction, and the integration of human-machine collaborative learning approaches. The research outlines the trajectory of human–AI collaboration in translation, emphasizing the redefinition of translator competencies, the restructuring of service value models, and the emergence of standardized data ethics. While acknowledging limitations in LLM capabilities, particularly in processing low-resource languages and highly creative texts, this study provides both theoretical foundations for intelligent translation transformation and practical frameworks for educational adaptation, exploring future development trends and collaborative paradigms that will define human-machine translation in the digital humanities context.

H. Wang (✉) · Y. Wu
Graduate School of Translation and Interpretation, Beijing Foreign Studies University, Beijing, China
e-mail: wanghuashu@bfsu.edu.cn

Y. Wu
e-mail: wuying_wy@whc.edu.cn

Y. Wu
School of Foreign Languages, Wenhua College, Wuhan, China

T. Yin et al. (eds.), *AI Through LLMs*, New Frontiers in Translation Studies,
https://doi.org/10.1007/978-981-95-4798-2_1

Keywords Large language models · Intelligent translation · Translation education · Human-machine collaboration · Paradigmatic transformation

1 Introduction

In the context of continuously deepening globalization and informatization, translation has evolved beyond traditional "language conversion" into a practice of cross-cultural and cross-domain information reconstruction. In the face of vast, multilingual, and specialized translation demands, traditional translation practices have exposed significant efficiency and quality bottlenecks, with excessive dependence on translators' linguistic abilities and experience, making it difficult to meet the requirements of large-scale production (Pym, 2013). Particularly in specialized fields such as technology, medicine, and law, the complexity of knowledge integration and the difficulty of contextual conversion further exacerbate the limitations of traditional methods (Jiménez-Crespo, 2013).

In recent years, the rise of Artificial Intelligence (AI), particularly Large Language Models (LLMs), has brought about a structural transformation in translation practices. Models such as GPT-5, Claude, and Gemini have demonstrated unprecedented capabilities in semantic understanding, contextual processing, and language generation, gradually overcoming the bottlenecks in contextual understanding and linguistic naturalness that characterized early Neural Machine Translation (NMT) (Bowker, 2023). These models not only perform complex language conversion but also offer auxiliary functions in multiple stages, including terminology recognition, style adaptation, and translation refinement, driving the evolution of translation workflows toward a systematically intelligent, collaborative model.

This technological revolution extends beyond industry transformation to fundamentally challenge existing paradigms in translation education and training. Traditional translation pedagogy, which has long emphasized linguistic competence and cultural knowledge acquisition, must now grapple with the integration of AI literacy, human-machine collaboration skills, and critical evaluation capabilities. The emergence of LLM-driven translation tools necessitates a comprehensive reevaluation of curriculum design, competency frameworks, and pedagogical approaches to prepare students for an increasingly AI-augmented professional landscape.

Against this backdrop of technological and educational transformation, translation activities are undergoing a profound shift from a human-centered traditional model to an intelligent collaborative system supported by large language models. Focusing on this emerging trend of "LLM-driven intelligent translation," this paper will address the following core questions: **What technical advantages do LLMs hold over traditional translation methods? How do these technologies reshape the pre-translation, translation, and post-translation processes? How will the translation industry ecosystem be transformed as a result? How do these transformations impact translation education and training? And what developmental trajectories will the future human–machine collaborative translation paradigm**

follow? To this end, the article will systematically examine the interrelationships among technological mechanisms, workflow innovations, educational adaptation, and industry transformation, aiming to provide a reference for both theoretical exploration and practical application of intelligent translation while offering guidance for educational reform in the digital age.

2 Systematic Limitations of Traditional Translation Practices

The accelerating process of globalization has led to rapidly increasing translation needs, revealing various challenges and limitations inherent in traditional translation practices (Biau Gil & Pym, 2015). As illustrated in Fig. 1, traditional translation practices are typically constrained by multiple systemic challenges and structural bottlenecks that impede effective translation delivery. These underlying issues manifest in four specific operational dimensions that underscore the need for paradigmatic transformation.

2.1 *Efficiency Bottlenecks in Large-Scale Translation Production*

Global markets and the expansion of digital economies have driven translation demand to levels of both scale and complexity never seen before. Yet traditional

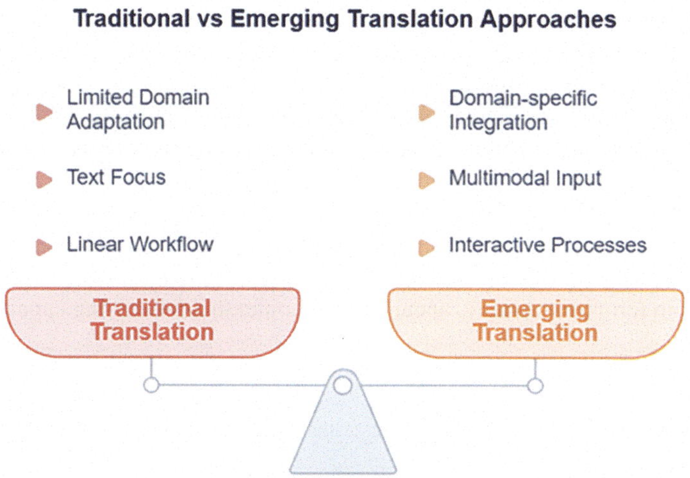

Fig. 1 Systemic challenges in traditional translation practices

translation practices demonstrate obvious efficiency bottlenecks in large-scale, multilingual projects. Even for experienced professional translators, daily output rarely exceeds 3000–5000 words (Drugan, 2013), a rate insufficient to match the rapid expansion of content volume. Meanwhile, critical processes such as terminology extraction and management primarily rely on manual expertise, making them time-consuming and error-prone, while also compromising consistency in terminology and style. At the same time, the construction and maintenance of terminology databases and translation memory systems incur high costs, placing a significant financial burden on small and medium-sized translation agencies, and further exacerbating overall capacity constraints. In such projects, quality assurance and process control also consume substantial human and time resources. According to an industry survey (ELIA, 2019), terminology management and quality assurance processes can account for a significant proportion—frequently reported at 20% to 30% of total working hours in some cases—thereby hindering translation services' ability to meet the real-time responsiveness required by the global market.

2.2 Cognitive Limitations in Semantic Processing

In practical translation processes, traditional approaches exhibit significant shortcomings in comprehending complex semantics and handling cross-cultural information. While human translators can generally ensure accuracy and fidelity, their throughput cannot keep pace with the rapid circulation of content today. Conversely, traditional machine translation systems, though more efficient, possess limited ability to interpret contextual subtleties, frequently resulting in semantic ambiguity, improper handling of polysemy, or mistranslation of culturally loaded concepts, issues that become particularly pronounced in long sentences or texts with heavy cultural encoding (Läubli et al., 2018; Toral & Sánchez-Cartagena, 2017). Furthermore, translations in specialized domains or between low-resource language pairs often suffer from high terminology error rates due to insufficient training data and lack of domain knowledge (Naveen & Trojovský, 2024). For example, Studies have demonstrated that translation inconsistencies disproportionately impact low-resource languages, with machine-translated texts showing significantly larger performance gaps in cross-lingual tasks for low-resource language pairs compared to high-resource ones (Agrawal et al., 2024). Faced with such complex demands for cross-contextual and expert-level knowledge exchange, traditional models prove inadequate in terms of semantic accuracy and contextual processing capabilities.

2.3 Systemic Difficulties in Domain Knowledge Integration

The refinement of the social division of labor and the intensification of knowledge specialization have increasingly brought translation activities into highly technical domains, imposing greater demands on knowledge integration and information management than traditional practices can fulfill. Domain-specific translation requires exceptional precision in terminology and standardized expressions. However, in practice, the manual construction and maintenance of terminology databases remain time-consuming and labor-intensive, with outcomes highly dependent on the accumulated experience of individual participants, making it difficult to dynamically adapt to the pace of knowledge updates (Jiménez-Crespo, 2013). As a result, many small and medium-sized agencies are unable to afford the systematic development of terminology and translation memory resources, so they are forced to rely on the expertise of project managers or a few senior translators to maintain consistency, which is neither scalable nor risk-free. In multi-translator collaborations or large projects, inconsistencies in terminology and style stemming from differing expression habits and understanding become more prominent. For example, in large-scale projects, such as annual report translations for multinational corporations, terminology inconsistencies can become prominent due to differing expression habits and understanding among multiple translators, highlighting the persistent challenges in terminology management (CSA Research, 2020). Meanwhile, although quality evaluation frameworks such as MQM are methodologically rigorous, their complexity often prevents their widespread implementation in high-pressure, fast-paced scenarios (Lommel et al., 2014), making it difficult to establish quality assurance mechanisms that are objective, automated, and quantitatively robust.

2.4 New Demands for Multimodal Translation

In the age of digitalization and multimedia, translation is no longer confined to pure text. A proliferation of multimodal content, including videos, images, and interactive interfaces, has introduced fundamentally new challenges to traditional workflows. Traditional human–machine collaboration models often manifest as a "mechanically segmented" process: machines generate a draft first, followed by human post-editing, with shallow interaction between the two. Crucially, such systems typically lack the ability to learn from human feedback and optimize accordingly (O'Brien, 2011). That is, post-editing in traditional workflows is often constrained by the absence of sustainable and systematic feedback mechanisms. Revisions are typically linear and one-off, making it hard to achieve full-process upgrading through continuous knowledge accumulation (Garcia, 2011; Moorkens & O'Brien, 2017). Translating multimodal content requires translators to possess understanding and transformation capabilities across textual, visual, and interactive domains, abilities that are severely underdeveloped in traditional translation training and professional practice, further limiting the innovation and adaptability potential of translation products in contemporary media environments.

In summary, traditional translation practices face structural constraints across four key dimensions: production efficiency, semantic comprehension, domain-specific knowledge integration, and adaptability to emerging content types. These structural challenges not only increase project costs and risks but also seriously restrict translation quality and industry development. Against this backdrop, emerging AI technologies, especially LLMs offer a critical opportunity to overcome these long-standing limitations and catalyze a paradigm shift within the translation industry.

3 Technological Advantages of LLMs in Intelligent Translation

The rapid advancement of AI technologies has positioned large language models (LLMs) as transformative forces in the field of translation, fundamentally reshaping traditional paradigms of language conversion. This paradigm shift not only advances translation mechanisms on a technical level but also profoundly reshapes the foundational logic of language comprehension, knowledge integration, and human–machine interaction. As illustrated in Fig. 2, LLMs demonstrate multifaceted strengths across four core dimensions: semantic analysis, knowledge integration, multilingual coordination, and adaptive refinement. These capabilities position LLMs as the next-generation technological engine driving intelligent translation toward greater precision and adaptability.

3.1 Deep Semantic Understanding and Contextual Awareness

One of the most significant advantages of LLMs lies in their superior capacity for deep semantic understanding and contextual awareness. Traditional translation models primarily rely on word-to-word mapping mechanisms, often neglecting the influence of contextual factors on meaning. In contrast, LLMs are trained on vast and

Fig. 2 Key strengths of LLMs in translation

diverse datasets, enabling them to capture more nuanced and complex semantic relationships, which allows the models to grasp intricate contextual dependencies and deliver more accurate translations. For instance, deep language models such as BERT leverage both preceding and following textual elements to form bidirectional contextual representations—a mechanism that allows the model to simultaneously consider both the words before and after a given term in a sentence when determining its meaning. This is similar to how a human translator reads an entire sentence (or even the next one) before deciding how to translate an ambiguous word. Such representations help maintain semantic and contextual coherence in the translation of extended texts, reducing misinterpretations of polysemous words or phrases and thus significantly enhancing translation quality (Devlin et al., 2019). The breakthroughs made by LLMs in semantic recognition and context modeling are most evident in their ability to identify multi-layered semantic relationships. Unlike traditional systems that tend to focus on isolated linguistic units, LLMs are capable of establishing semantic continuity across sentences and even entire paragraphs. In this way, LLMs can better handle ambiguity and polysemy in language, providing more precise translation results.

3.2 Knowledge Integration and Reasoning Capabilities

Another major advantage of LLMs lies in their capacities for knowledge integration and reasoning. By incorporating extensive encyclopedic knowledge with advanced inferential mechanisms, LLMs can perform complex semantic reasoning across a wide range of domains and tasks. For example, the SemComLLM model proposed by Pokhrel and Walid (2024), which combines Llama-2 with Joint Source-Channel Coding (JSCC), significantly enhances semantic accuracy and transmission efficiency, demonstrating the potential of LLMs in handling intricate reasoning tasks. Furthermore, LLMs can understand and analyze complex causal relationships more deeply through causal inference frameworks, leading to more precise predictions and decisions (Liu et al., 2024). These capabilities mean LLMs can go far beyond basic syntactic parsing, offering robust support for complex decision-making scenarios that demand high-level reasoning and domain awareness.

3.3 Multilingual Coordination and Cross-Linguistic Generalization

LLMs also exhibit strong advantages in multilingual processing and cross-linguistic generalization. Traditional translation systems are typically fine-tuned for specific language pairs, limiting their scalability and adaptability. In contrast, LLMs, trained on large-scale multilingual corpora, can achieve fluid transfer across languages and promote semantic consistency while accounting for cultural nuances. This allows LLMs to handle multilingual content with enhanced fidelity and authenticity. In practice, LLMs can improve multilingual translation quality through techniques such as multilingual fine-tuning and prompt-based translation, a capability that extends even to language pairs not included in the training data. Recent findings by Li et al. (2024) further confirm that LLMs exhibit exceptional generalization in both prompt comprehension and syntactic adaptation across languages. Even in the absence of parallel training data for certain language pairs, LLMs maintain remarkable cross-linguistic flexibility, providing a solid technological foundation for translation services in multi-linguistic environments.

3.4 Adaptive Capacity for Human Feedback and Self-Refinement

The self-refinement capabilities of LLMs constitute a critical advantage in the context of intelligent translation, one that merits close attention. Just as students improve their writing by understanding and acting on a teacher's suggestions, LLMs optimize their performance over time by incorporating human feedback. By incorporating human feedback mechanisms, LLMs can continuously optimize their performance over time. This iterative optimization process not only improves the model's adaptability but also enables it to respond more flexibly to various new tasks and dynamic environments. A comprehensive review by Fernandes et al. (2023) demonstrates that integrating human feedback into the training of language models substantially improves output quality and better aligns model behavior with human preferences and values, continuously enhancing models' semantic understanding and reasoning capabilities through multi-round interactions. Building upon the improvements brought by human-in-the-loop training, LLMs further incorporate feedback from both users and developers, which helps them adapt to diverse linguistic environments and cultural contexts, and optimize for specific tasks such as machine translation. The presence of a sustained self-refinement mechanism allows LLMs to gradually refine their response accuracy and user satisfaction in multilingual, cross-cultural translation scenarios. Over time, this change leads to enhanced levels of professionalism and efficiency in translation tasks.

Through their capabilities in deep semantic comprehension, knowledge integration and reasoning, multilingual collaboration, and human-in-the-loop self-optimization, LLMs are showing great promises in advancing the field of intelligent translation. These strengths are enabling LLMs to transcend linguistic and cultural barriers, delivering more precise and contextually appropriate translation outputs across increasingly complex scenarios.

4 LLMs-Driven Reconstruction of the Translation Process

LLMs have spurred iterations of translation tools, beginning with intelligent support for pre-translation preparation, progressing to context-aware generation during translation, and culminating in quality enhancement during post-translation refinement. As illustrated in Fig. 3, this comprehensive framework demonstrates how these developments, in turn, have triggered a systematic reconstruction of the entire translation process with the rise of intelligent translation technologies.

4.1 Intelligent Integration in Pre-Translation Preparation

The pre-translation preparation stage plays a crucial role in shaping both the quality and efficiency of the overall translation process. With the widespread use of large language models (LLMs), there is a deeper, more intelligent integration across key areas such as terminology management, source text processing, and project analysis.

In the intelligent applications in terminology management, particularly for terminology extraction and domain knowledge management, it has been well recognized that traditional rule-based matching and statistical approaches suffer from limitations in accuracy and efficiency (Kageura & Umino, 1996). Recent advances in LLMs have significantly improved performance in these areas, overcoming many of the longstanding challenges associated with earlier methods. Owing to their deep semantic understanding capabilities, LLMs can not only accurately identify multi-word and ambiguous terms but also construct relational networks among terms,

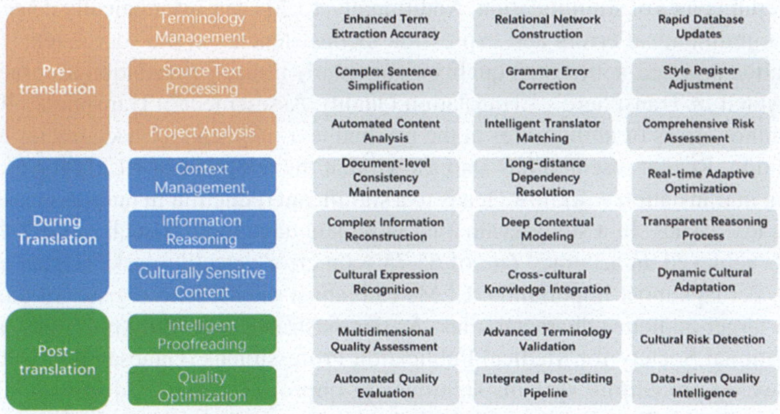

Fig. 3 LLM-enhanced translation workflow framework

forming comprehensive domain-specific knowledge graphs. Research by Żmudka et al. (2024) shows that ChatGPT achieved impressive accuracy rates on the Polish Medical Final Examination, reaching up to 67.86% and exceeding the official threshold of 56% (Żmudka et al., 2024). An empirical study by Woo et al. (2025) confirms that, in orthopedic care, custom LLMs incorporating Retrieval Augmented Generation (RAG)—a technique where models retrieve relevant external information during generation to improve accuracy—and AI agents are capable of achieving up to 95% accuracy in information delivery, representing an average improvement of 39.7% and substantially surpassing the below 60% accuracy of noncustom LLM models. Moreover, driven by technological advancements, certain LLMs-based terminology management systems have demonstrably improved terminology extraction efficiency and significantly shortened the update cycle of terminology databases. For instance, research has shown that implementing LLM-based systems in terminology management can significantly enhance efficiency; one study reported a remarkable 58% reduction in annotation time when LLMs were integrated into a human-annotated workflow for legal terms extraction (Breton et al., 2025). These technological advancements collectively create a richer reference environment for translators, ultimately contributing to greater consistency and accuracy in specialized terminology translation.

In the intelligent optimization of source text preprocessing, LLMs have greatly enhanced the translatability and consistency of texts through their application in sentence structure simplification, grammar error correction, and style adjustment. Sentence structure is a key factor affecting translation quality, with complex and nested long sentences often posing significant obstacles (Naveen & Trojovský, 2024). LLMs can intelligently identify and break down complex syntactic structures. For instance, recent work by Wu and Arase (2024) demonstrates that GPT-4-based models can often transform complex sentences into structurally clear and simple ones while generally preserving the original meaning, although challenges remain with certain types of simplification. Additionally, LLMs can automatically detect and correct grammatical errors and expression inconsistencies in the source text. From translation practice, source text quality significantly impacts translation accuracy; as highlighted in Transphere's "Translation Quality Assessment" (Transphere, 2024), even minor errors or ambiguities in the original text may lead to inaccuracies in the translation. Recent research has also shown that the adoption of LLMs for preprocessing in translation workflows leads to a significant reduction in queries caused by source text issues. In a study evaluating large language models such as GPT-4, the models achieved an accuracy rate of 65.75% on error detection tasks (Uguet et al., 2024). Perhaps most importantly, LLMs can adjust the stylistic register of the text to suit target-audience characteristics. As demonstrated in a study presented at the International Society for Medical Publication Professionals (Ganesan et al., 2024), AI-powered pre-editing systems significantly improved technical documentation's compliance with Plain English standards, with AI-generated content showing a 71% improvement in readability scores (from 20.8 to 35.5) and reducing the required reading grade level from 15.9 to 12.9. Such AI-based source-text preprocessing thus effectively boosts the translatability of the source texts, paving the way for more accurate and efficient translation.

In the intelligent scheduling of project analysis, LLMs have realized the intelligent and precise automation of requirement analysis and resource allocation. In traditional project management, text-feature analysis and resource allocation heavily relied on project managers' personal experience (Dunne & Dunne, 2013), whereas LLMs have significantly improved project analysis efficiency through automatic identification of document types, subject domains, and difficulty levels. According to a comprehensive industry analysis by SEAtongue (2025), businesses implementing AI-driven localization workflows experienced a 60% increase in content delivery speed compared to traditional project management approaches. For translator assignments, AI-driven solutions have significantly improved content-translator matching efficiency, with Smartling's "State of Translation Report" (Smartling Inc, 2024) revealing that AI technologies have reduced per-word translation costs by up to 40% while maintaining quality standards, enabling companies to translate more content and achieve better results. Moreover, LLM-based workload-estimation tools not only perform traditional word-count calculations but also transcend the limitations of count-only approaches by comprehensively evaluating multidimensional factors such as text complexity, terminology density, and structural features (Croxford et al., 2025), providing more precise workload and delivery-time predictions and offering a more reliable basis for project planning. Particularly noteworthy is that LLMs demonstrate a significant capability in automated error analysis. A recent study by Chirkova et al. (2025) on automating error analysis in natural language generation, which includes machine translation, reveals that LLM-as-a-qualitative-judge correctly identifies instance-specific issues in approximately two-thirds of cases, producing error-type reports comparable to those generated by human annotators. This capability is crucial for proactive risk management in translation projects, allowing for early identification and mitigation of potential quality issues.

From the above-mentioned advances in intelligent integration during pre-translation preparation, the demands for information retrieval, contextual judgment, and terminology comprehension highlight the need for educators to guide students in mastering cross-domain preprocessing skills. The teacher can design task-based learning activities, such as using actual medical device manual translation projects to guide students through client requirement analysis (e.g., FDA certification requirements), resource collection (medical regulatory documents, specialized terminology databases), and terminology preparation (establishing multilingual correspondences for professional terms like "cardiac pacemaker" and "biocompatibility") as pre-translation tasks, thereby cultivating their information literacy and contextual construction abilities in practice. Furthermore, guiding students to use medical terminology databases (such as UMLS), knowledge graphs, or AI tools to assist pre-translation analysis when handling complex medical concepts like drug interactions and surgical procedures also helps them adapt to new translation preparation workflows empowered by technology.

4.2 Context-Driven Translation Production

The essence of the translation process lies in accurately comprehending the context of the source-language text and reconstructing that context in the target language. The advent of LLMs has revolutionized context-driven capabilities during the translation phase, shifting the activity from mechanical substitution to deep semantic understanding and reconstruction. This paradigm shift has reshaped modern translation practice primarily through three dimensions: linguistic, informational, and cultural.

From a linguistic perspective, LLMs demonstrate unprecedented contextual comprehension and expression capabilities. Traditional neural machine translation systems were typically limited by shorter context windows, making it difficult to capture long-distance dependencies and maintain document-level consistency (Bahdanau et al., 2015). In contrast, LLMs can process longer text inputs and understand the logical structure and semantic coherence across paragraphs or even entire documents. For instance, in genres such as scientific articles, where preserving native formatting and accommodating domain-specific vocabulary are paramount, LLMs demonstrate the ability to produce context-aware, customized outputs. They can be specifically tailored to the requirements of the scientific community, ensuring consistency of both terminology and style throughout the document (Calzi Kleidermacher & Zou, 2025). Empirical findings demonstrate that LLM-based translation systems significantly improve the translation of long sentences, including those containing approximately 80 words, and even entire documents up to 512 words, showing their superior accuracy over traditional machine translation engines when handling long-distance dependencies (Lyu et al., 2025). Additionally, LLMs can adjust their output based on translators' real-time feedback through human-in-the-loop pipelines, enabling rapid personalized optimization of translations. This human-machine collaboration mechanism, leveraging in-context learning, greatly enhances the linguistic quality of translations (Yang et al., 2023). By continuously refining word choice, sentence fluency, and stylistic consistency, LLMs help produce translations that are more natural and better aligned with the nuances of the target text.

At the information processing level, LLMs, with their powerful capabilities in knowledge integration and reasoning, are highly effective in handling complex information structures and ambiguous expressions. Traditional machine translation systems often suffer from distortions or loss of information when dealing with polysemous words, complex syntactic structures, or domain-specific terminology, struggling to capture contextual information and disambiguate meanings (Naveen & Trojovský, 2024). In contrast, LLMs can accurately reconstruct source information through deep modeling of context and background knowledge. In fields like medicine, LLMs show significant potential in accurately identifying and preserving key terminology, and understanding and reconstructing complex logical relationships embedded in source texts (Alkalbani et al., 2025). Furthermore, LLMs' breakthrough advantages in information processing are also reflected in their transparent thinking processes and decision-making reasoning capabilities. The 'chain-of-thought' (CoT) reasoning exhibited by LLMs allows them not only to generate translation outputs but also to elucidate their decision-making pathways, enhancing their ability to reason and translate complex linguistic puzzles (Lin et al., 2025). This transparency and diversity in information processing significantly enhance translators' ability to comprehend and manage complex semantics. In practical applications, LLM-based translation systems can employ long chain-of-thought reasoning to manage complex linguistic structures through iterative translation processes. They often operate within multi-agent frameworks—collaborative systems where specialized AI agents focus on different subtasks such as terminology analysis, cultural adaptation, and quality assessment. This setup enables LLMs to explore, reflect, and self-improve their reasoning during translation, much like a team of expert translators working together to refine a draft. As a result, these systems achieve more accurate semantic reconstruction (Wang et al., 2025). Such advanced information processing transforms the translation from a single-output process into a multidimensional task of semantic analysis and reconstruction.

Contextual understanding from a cultural perspective represents another critical breakthrough in the translation generation capabilities of LLMs. Culture-specific expressions and metaphors have long been recognized as bottlenecks in improving the quality of cross-linguistic translation, as cultural and linguistic contexts often render direct translation inadequate for effectively conveying intended meanings (Li et al., 2023). Through large-scale pretraining on diverse corpora, LLMs have internalized extensive world knowledge and cross-cultural backgrounds, enabling them to perform notably better when handling culturally sensitive content. Empirical studies show that GPT-4 achieves a 94–98% accuracy rate in understanding multilingual idioms and culturally embedded expressions, significantly outperforming traditional systems such as Google Translate by 17(German)–92%(Hebrew) across five different languages (Mudrik et al., 2023). This capability is particularly evident in literary translation, as shown in the TransAgents project by Monash University, where LLMs supported human translators through a multi-agent system. AI editorial teams preserved stylistic tone, while localization and proofreading agents provided culturally adaptive translations for rhetorical devices, dialects, and references (Wu et al., 2024). In the translation of children's literature, LLMs have further demonstrated their capacity to render complex classical texts into culturally authentic, child-friendly styles, as shown in Ahn and Lim's (2025) study where ChatGPT, Claude, and Gemini adapted English and American classics, with Claude 3.5 Sonnet yielding the most accessible versions and significantly enhancing comprehension and cultural resonance. As such, LLMs drive translation generation not only at the linguistic encoding level but also through dynamic adaptation to deep cultural contexts, empowering translators with greater expressive flexibility and accuracy in cross-cultural communication.

It is worth noting that LLM-driven translation generation goes beyond unidirectional machine output, placing growing emphasis on **interaction and collaboration with human translators**. The interactive translation experience enabled by natural language interfaces allows translators to question the generated output, request explanations, or demand stylistic adjustments at any point in the process, to which the system can respond and adapt in real time (Jiménez-Crespo, 2025). This bidirectional interaction enhances the translator's sense of engagement and control while providing greater flexibility in managing complex translation tasks, as demonstrated with emerging research showing that LLMs demonstrate exceptional capabilities in handling complex tasks through advanced text generation and interactive human-machine collaboration, significantly enhancing translation accuracy and efficiency, especially in low-resource language scenarios. (Wang et al., 2024).

Moreover, the application of LLMs in **adaptive translation systems** further advances the intelligence of the translation generation phase. By learning from translation demonstrations and stylistic patterns, LLMs can automatically adjust subsequent translation suggestions to achieve both personalization and project-specific customization through steering techniques that exploit latent concepts and inference-time interventions (Scalena et al., 2025), while translation memory integration enables LLMs to better understand and respond to domain-specific terminology and style preferences (Mu et al., 2023). Compared with traditional adaptive machine translation, LLM-based systems can quickly learn translator preferences from minimal examples through few-shot learning approaches that demonstrate superior adaptation capabilities in specialized domains (Tang et al., 2025). In specialized domains, this capability has proven especially valuable, with adaptive LLM approaches showing promising results in real-time translation improvement through in-context learning mechanisms (Moslem et al., 2023). These adaptive capabilities represent a significant advancement in personalized translation technology, offering the potential for sustained quality improvements across diverse translation scenarios.

Given the revolutionary context-driven capabilities demonstrated by LLMs in the translation production phase, human-machine collaboration has increasingly become an important form of translation practice. The teacher can employ simulation-based instruction or introduce AI-assisted translation platforms (such as Trados, DeepL Write, or ChatGPT) to allow students to experience collaborative workflows with machines in simulated real translation environments. For example, they can organize multi-round prompt design tasks for legal contract translation, having students process clauses in Software License Agreements while training them to optimize prompts (such as "Please translate the following legal clauses, paying attention to maintaining the accuracy of legal terminology and the logical rigor of the provisions") to improve output quality, and conduct analysis and discussion by comparing the expression of key legal concepts like "breach of contract liability" and "intellectual property rights" in original versus revised texts, enhancing their human-machine interaction awareness and dynamic response capabilities. This teaching strategy not only improves technical operational skills but also promotes students' critical understanding of the translation process.

4.3 Quality Optimization in Post-Translation

Post-translation processing is a key stage for ensuring that the final translation product meets predefined standards and satisfies end-user requirements. Traditional post-editing workflows, such as manual proofreading and review, often face challenges related to inefficiency, subjectivity, and the lack of unified quality benchmarks (Drugan, 2013). The emergence of LLMs has revitalized this stage by leveraging their advanced capabilities in language understanding, generation, and analysis to systematically reconfigure proofreading, evaluation, and overall quality management.

From the perspective of quality assurance, LLMs substantially expand the scope and depth of post-translation checks. LLM-powered intelligent proofreading systems go beyond the limitations of traditional tools that focus only on spelling and basic grammar (Qian et al., 2024), offering comprehensive evaluations through multi-stage processes that include pre-translation research, drafting, refining, and proofreading phases, resulting in significant translation quality improvements across multiple language pairs (Briakou et al., 2024). Moreover, LLMs demonstrate remarkable capabilities in systematic self-correction of their own translation outputs through frameworks that employ error estimation and refinement processes, with studies showing successful improvements in translation quality across a wide range of languages from high-resource to low-resource language pairs (Feng et al., 2024). Additionally, advanced quality assurance mechanisms enable LLMs to maintain cross-lingual consistency in their translation outputs, with research revealing that systematic evaluation frameworks can effectively measure translation behavior across multiple languages, though consistency varies significantly depending on language families and training data exposure (Gupta et al., 2025).

From the perspective of efficiency enhancement and workflow optimization, LLMs have transformed traditional post-translation processes through systematic automation and intelligent integration. The automation of quality evaluation and post-editing workflows represents a significant advancement in operational efficiency, with empirical studies demonstrating substantial reductions in editing time compared to traditional approaches. Research on literary translation post-editing shows that LLM-generated translations require significantly less editing time, with GPT-4 requiring only 64.33 minutes compared to 115.68 minutes for human translation from scratch, representing a 44.4% reduction in processing time. Notably, GPT-4 significantly outperformed other models, requiring 35.4% less time than Mistral-60 k (87.12 minutes) and 86.2% less time than GPT-3.5 (119.74 minutes) (Castaldo et al., 2025). Beyond individual task efficiency, large-scale experimental evidence reveals that LLM assistance in translation workflows produces substantial productivity gains across professional translators, with every 10x increase in model compute resulting in 12.3% faster task completion and 16.1% higher earnings per minute, demonstrating scalable efficiency improvements that extend beyond simple time savings to encompass overall economic productivity (Merali, 2024). Additionally, LLMs have demonstrated competitive performance in cross-domain post-editing tasks by streamlining the correction process itself, enabling translators to achieve higher productivity rates while maintaining acceptable quality standards across various specialized domains (Algaraady & Mahyoob, 2025). This systematic approach to workflow optimization represents a fundamental shift toward AI-augmented translation processes that achieve measurable efficiency improvements while preserving translation quality.

Building upon the systematic reconfiguration of post-translation processes through LLM-driven quality optimization, the focus on quality assessment and text refinement requires students to possess meticulous linguistic judgment and proofreading skills. The teacher can adopt reflective teaching methods, encouraging students to review and document their revision logic (such as consistency checks for terms like "balance sheet"), language choices (such as appropriate tone modulation for risk disclosures and investment warnings), and problem-solving strategies (such as accuracy verification of exchange rate conversion explanations) after completing post-editing tasks for, say, financial report translations. Meanwhile, peer review mechanisms can be introduced, allowing students to discuss and provide feedback on post-editing results for financial texts such as Annual Financial Reports, with particular attention to the consistency of financial terminology and accuracy of data presentation, enhancing their linguistic awareness and editing strategy capabilities. Additionally, by analyzing error types in machine translation when processing financial texts (such as misuse of terms like "equity dilution," inappropriate financial data formatting, and inadequate stylistic expression of investment risks), the teacher can guide students to establish systematic evaluation frameworks and deepen their post-editing capabilities.

5 LLMs-Driven Ecosystem Transformation of the Translation Industry

The continuous evolution of industrial structures is fostering cross-sector integration and sustained innovation within the translation industry. Technological breakthroughs, particularly the rise of large language models (LLMs), are inevitably catalyzing industrial restructuring. From technological systems and professional roles to service models and data ecosystems, every facet reflects the profound shifts shaping the AI-driven translation industry landscape. These transformations present unprecedented opportunities and challenges for translation education, requiring educators to reexamine talent development objectives and curriculum design.

5.1 *Shifting of Technological Systems*

Translation technology is undergoing a paradigm shift from auxiliary tools to intelligent primacy. Traditional computer-assisted translation (CAT) tools primarily offered terminology databases and translation memory functions, serving only as support systems for human translators. The emergence of LLMs has fundamentally disrupted this pattern by achieving breakthroughs in automated translation quality through deep semantic understanding. As demonstrated by Lyu et al. (2023), LLM-based translation systems not only maintain cross-sentence and cross-paragraph coherence, but also handle complex linguistic phenomena such as implicit references and complex rhetorical devices that traditional systems often fail to capture, elevating translation generation from isolated sentence processing to holistic discourse comprehension. This intelligent-led transformation is fundamentally reshaping translation workflows and decision-making mechanisms, marking the elevation of translation technology from auxiliary attachment to production core.

Facing this fundamental paradigm shift in technology, translation education must find a new balance between traditional language skills and AI collaboration capabilities. Educators should redesign curriculum systems by incorporating courses such as "AI-Assisted Translation Theory and Practice" into core modules, enabling students to master effective human-machine collaboration strategies based on understanding LLM working principles. For example, through "Intelligent Translation Project Training," students can experience the complete AI-driven translation process from text preprocessing to quality assessment, cultivating their adaptability and critical thinking in intelligent-led environments while emphasizing the irreplaceable value of human translators in cultural adaptation and creative expression.

5.2 *Transformation of Professional Roles*

LLMs have precipitated a profound transformation in the role of translation professionals. Traditionally, translators primarily served as language conversion specialists, with their work centered on complete text translation. With the advancement of LLM capabilities, translator responsibilities are shifting from full-text translation toward higher value-added tasks. Recent translation research commonly argues that in the new technological environment, translators are evolving into the nexus of human-machine collaboration, with their core value extending beyond linguistic competence to encompass prompt engineering, cultural adaptation, and cross-linguistic information integration (Chen & Guo, 2024). This transformation requires translators to master new digital literacies, enabling them to precisely guide LLMs in generating content that meets specific domain and audience requirements, forming a collaboratively enhanced working model.

This transformation of professional roles directly impacts the talent development specifications of translation programs, requiring educators to construct a "compound human-machine collaborator" training system. Course offerings should include modules such as "Translation Project Management" and "Cross-Cultural Communication Strategies" to cultivate students' diverse capabilities and strategic thinking. For example, a "Translation Consulting Practice" course can be designed to have students simulate developing multilingual content strategies for enterprises, experiencing the transition from language experts to technical consultants through role-playing, and understanding the new positioning and value creation methods of modern translators in digital environments.

5.3 Restructuring of Service Models

LLMs have driven translation services to shift from traditional project-based outsourcing structures toward embedded, platform-based, and real-time solutions. Previously, translation services were typically organized around documents or projects as units, with fragmented processes and lengthy delivery cycles. Now, API-based translation services and microservice architectures enable translation capabilities to be deeply embedded into various aspects of enterprise content management, product development, and customer service, achieving on-demand, real-time language services (Vasiļjevs et al., 2024). For example, industries such as e-commerce, news, and education have widely adopted embedded translation, integrating functions like text generation, terminology unification, and content review into business processes, dramatically improving the circulation efficiency and consistency of multilingual content, marking the fundamental transformation of the translation industry from "outsourced service providers" to "language technology enablers."

This restructuring of service models presents new challenges for translation education: how to prepare students to adapt to API-driven, real-time response work environments? Educators should simulate real technological work scenarios in teaching, helping students understand the operational mechanisms of embedded services. For example, through an "Case Analysis on Enterprise Language Services" course, students can conduct in-depth research on AI-driven multilingual strategies of platforms like Amazon, analyzing the design concepts and implementation effects of embedded translation services such as automatic product description translation and real-time user review localization, cultivating students' working capabilities and service awareness in distributed, real-time environments.

5.4 Emergence of Data Ecosystems

In the LLM-driven translation industry, data has leaped from auxiliary resources to core strategic assets. High-quality bilingual parallel corpora, domain-specific terminology collections, and stylistic repositories are no longer merely translation references but have become key resources for training and fine-tuning LLMs, directly determining system performance ceilings. Research by Roussis et al. (2024) demonstrates through constructing scientific domain-specific corpora that enterprises possessing parallel corpora in specialized fields such as energy research and neuroscience can develop more precise professional translation systems, gaining significant advantages in high value-added markets. Meanwhile, the elevation of data value has also triggered rights disputes specific to the translation industry, with corpus data ownership, usage authorization, and value distribution becoming focal points of industry governance, spawning a multi-layered industrial ecosystem centered on translation data.

The elevation of data status requires translation education to cultivate students' data awareness and management capabilities. Educators should integrate data literacy development into curriculum systems by offering courses such as "Translation Corpus Applications" and "Multilingual Resource Management," helping students understand the strategic value of data in the modern translation industry. For example, through "Construction Project of Professional Domain Corpora," students can participate in real corpus collection, organization, and annotation work, mastering corpus construction methods and quality assessment standards in practice while cultivating sensitivity to issues such as data ethics and intellectual property rights, laying the foundation for becoming compound talents who understand both language and data management.

6 Future Development of Human-Machine Collaboration in Translation

Looking ahead, as intelligent technologies become deeply integrated across the entire translation lifecycle, translators' roles and competency frameworks are being continuously redefined; at the same time, service models are being redesigned around value optimization, while increasingly stringent data-governance requirements drive the standardization of industry oversight. These transformations present both unprecedented opportunities and significant challenges for translation education, requiring educators to fundamentally rethink pedagogical approaches and curriculum design.

6.1 Deep Integration of Intelligent Technologies

Future translation technologies will extend beyond breakthroughs in isolated tools, achieving full-chain intelligence from source content to application scenarios. Multimodal translation systems will emerge as the norm, capable of processing various information types including text, speech, and images, meeting translation needs across diverse communication contexts and media formats. Similarly, advances in deep contextual understanding will enable machines both to capture literal meaning and to continually track discourse context, maintaining document-level semantic coherence and producing outputs that better align with human cognitive patterns. Industry knowledge graphs and domain-specific intelligence are expected to become core components of the technological system, significantly improving translation accuracy and reliability across various fields by structuring specialized knowledge and embedding it into reasoning processes. Furthermore, systems with real-time self-learning capabilities will become widespread, continuously optimizing model performance through user feedback and driving personalized, dynamic, and high-quality development of translation outcomes, as demonstrated by recent case studies of human-machine collaborative workflows (Chen & Guo, 2024).

In this process, human-machine collaboration exhibits distinct process-oriented characteristics: translator-LLM interaction is not a one-time input-output operation, but rather a dynamic cycle of "prompt-output-evaluation-prompt adjustment." Experienced translators can guide AI to produce more accurate translations through multi-round dialogues, while beginners often accept results after the first prompt. Teaching should focus on cultivating students' iterative optimization awareness, using screen recording and other methods to document student-AI interaction processes and establish best practice case libraries for collaboration.

6.2 Reconstruction of Translator Competencies

In the era of human-machine collaboration, the structure of translation professionals is undergoing a profound "competency reconstruction." Going forward, "Translator+" hybrid talents will become mainstream: they will not only possess solid linguistic skills but also command cross-domain knowledge and related technologies such as data analysis, MT post-editing, and prompt engineering. As AI-empowered workflows proliferate, the traditional language expert's role will shift toward post-translation quality control, pre-translation data preparation, and innovative content planning. Translators will no longer be passive adapters but leaders in training, optimizing, and innovating intelligent systems. Professional competency standards will be updated accordingly, with digital literacy, systematic problem-solving ability, and human–machine collaboration communication skills all incorporated into the core competency framework. Among these, cross-verification capability serves as a crucial component of competency reconstruction, requiring translators to employ strategies such as comparing multiple AI tools, consulting specialized terminology databases, and seeking expert advice to ensure translation quality, reflecting practitioners' emphasis on maintaining control and autonomy in AI-enhanced workflows (Jiménez-Crespo, 2025).

In collaborative workflow teaching practice, educators should focus on helping students address specific challenges, such as how to identify and correct "confident but incorrect" translations produced by LLMs (e.g., mistranslations of culturally specific terms) using cross-verification strategies. Through designing such case exercises, educators can cultivate students' critical thinking and quality control abilities in human-machine collaborative environments.

6.3 Value Reshaping of Service Model

Translation services are rapidly evolving into global communication consultancy. Leading language service providers have begun to integrate translation into broader strategic advisory offerings that cover language conversion, audience analysis, cultural adaptation, and communication effectiveness assessment. The rise of embedded translation services facilitates direct multilingual integration across diverse application scenarios, from e-commerce to telemedicine, transforming multilingual communication into core infrastructure rather than an external add-on. Deep customization in vertical domains is another prominent trend: sectors such as finance, life sciences, and law demand ultra-high-quality translations, giving rise to "boutique translation" service models highly specialized for each field. Also, the maturation of platform-based ecosystems is redefining industry collaboration by uniting AI systems, professional translators, domain-specific experts, and end users on a single platform, forming efficient, flexible translation production networks. These service-model innovations redraw the boundaries of translation's value while also propelling the entire industry's transformation from traditional language providers into strategic enablers of global communication.

Facing the reality of uneven technological resource distribution, educators should help students understand and adapt to diverse technological environments. For situations where advanced models like GPT-4 are not accessible, educators should guide students in mastering the use of open-source LLMs (such as LLaMA, ChatGLM) and designing hybrid human-machine collaborative workflows, ensuring students maintain competitiveness under different technological conditions.

6.4 Standardization of Data Governance

The widespread adoption of AI-driven translation has brought the industry face-to-face with multiple challenges: data security, intellectual property rights, cultural sensitivity, and professional ethics. To address these issues, regulations have emerged successively around the world: the EU's "General Data Protection Regulation" and "AI Act"; the U.S. "Algorithmic Accountability Act"; and China's "Data Security Law" and "Personal Information Protection Law." Complementing these regulations, the publication of international standards such as ISO 18587 and ISO 17100, alongside China's "Application Guidelines for Generative AI in the Translation Industry (China Daily, 2025)" and related ethical codes, has provided clearer specifications for translation quality assessment, process management, and classification. In practice, LLM developers are continually strengthening scrutiny over data sources and screening, and users are increasingly concerned with privacy protection and intellectual property rights, while translators are actively promoting professional ethics within new collaborative workflows. A multi-stakeholder data-governance mechanism is taking shape across the industry, which enhances interaction and shared responsibility among all parties through collaborative discourse and joint standards development.

Translation education should incorporate data ethics and privacy protection into curriculum systems, cultivating students' professional ethical awareness and regulatory compliance capabilities in the AI era. Teachers should emphasize the importance of responsible AI use, guiding students to engage in discussions about the potential biases in AI models and the societal impact of their applications (Wang & Liu, 2025). Students should actively participate in these discussions and apply their theoretical knowledge through practical case studies and collaborative projects, which will reinforce the necessity of ethical decision-making in their future careers.

7 Conclusion

The rapid advancement of large language models (LLMs) and artificial intelligence technology has brought a paradigm-shifting and profound transformation to the translation industry. This paper analyzes the core technological advantages of LLM-driven intelligent translation compared to traditional translation methods, summarizing breakthroughs in comprehension, generation, and contextual adaptation, and details how LLMs deeply empower the translation process, from pre-translation data preparation to automated generation during translation, and post-translation quality assessment, achieving systematic reconstruction and efficiency improvements. Regarding human-machine collaboration, this research has explored the evolving paradigms set to define the future of translation. The deep integration of technology and human expertise brings about a productivity revolution while also providing new opportunities for innovative development in translation education, and simultaneously driving the industry toward enhanced data governance and ethical standards.

However, LLM technology itself still faces numerous limitations. At the technical level, LLMs perform better than machine translation, but still poorly in processing low-resource languages and highly creative texts, and often struggle with understanding deep cultural connotations (Comic, 2025). Although LLMs have made significant progress in cultural contextual understanding, they still fall short of human translators' sensitivity and accuracy when dealing with complex culture-specific expressions and metaphors. These technical limitations have multiple impacts on translation education: the scarcity of teaching resources for low-resource languages restricts the cultivation of multilingual translation talent; the challenges in processing creative texts bring new complexities to the instructional design of advanced courses such as literary translation; and the limitations in cultural understanding may lead students to over-rely on AI while neglecting the development of cross-cultural communication competencies. Furthermore, the technological equity issues described in Sect. VI are equally prominent in the educational sphere, where uneven distribution of technological resources may exacerbate disparities in educational opportunities. The long-term impact of LLM-assisted workflows on student translator creativity remains unclear, and their effectiveness in complex assessment tasks such as cultural adaptation and stylistic control has yet to be verified.

Despite these challenges, the integration of LLMs and the translation industry extends beyond the industry's transformation and upgrading to reshaping the landscape of global information circulation and cultural exchange, contributing to the construction of a more equal and diverse global language service system. In the field of translation education, this technological revolution is catalyzing fundamental changes in pedagogical approaches: transitioning from traditional skill transmission to human-machine collaborative competency development, upgrading from singular language conversion training to compound translation talent cultivation, and expanding from closed classroom instruction to open practical platforms. LLMs not only provide powerful technological support for translation education but also open broad prospects for cultivating new-generation translators adapted to the AI era. This path of integration is fraught with challenges yet also brims with infinite opportunities. It is hoped that all parties in the industry will join hands to pioneer a new chapter of translation in the era of human-machine collaboration.

References

Agrawal, A. S., Fazili, B., & Jyothi, P. (2024). Translation errors significantly impact low-resource languages in cross-lingual learning. In *Proceedings of the 18th conference of the European chapter of the Association for Computational Linguistics: Short papers* (pp. 319–329). Association for Computational Linguistics. https://doi.org/10.18653/v1/2024.eacl-short.28

Ahn, J. M., & Lim, Y. H. (2025). Transformation of classic English and American literature into children's literature using artificial intelligence. *Asia-Pac J Converg Res Interchange, 11*(5), 17–37.

Algaraady, J., & Mahyoob, M. (2025). Exploring ChatGPT's potential for augmenting post-editing in machine translation across multiple domains: Challenges and opportunities. *Frontiers in Artificial Intelligence, 8*, 1526293. https://doi.org/10.3389/frai.2025.1526293

Alkalbani, A. M., Al-Hadhrami, T., Al-Rashdi, A., et al. (2025). A systematic review of large language models in medical specialties: Applications, challenges and future directions. *Information, 16*(6), 489. https://doi.org/10.3390/info16060489

Bahdanau, D., Cho, K., Bengio, Y. (2015). Neural machine translation by jointly learning to align and translate. In *International conference on learning representations (ICLR)*. arXiv:1409.0473.

Biau Gil, J. R., & Pym, A. (2015). Redefining translation competence in an electronic age. In defence of a minimalist approach. *Meta, 60*(1), 20–35. https://www.erudit.org/en/journals/meta/2015-v60-n1-meta02005/1032403ar.pdf

Bowker, L. (2023). *De-mystifying translation: Introducing translation to non-translators.* Routledge.

Breton, J., Goasdoué, F., Kooli, N., et al. (2025). Leveraging LLMs for legal terms extraction with limited annotated data. *Artifical Intelligence and Law*. https://doi.org/10.1007/s10506-025-09448-8

Briakou, E., Koehn, P., Carpuat, M. (2024) Translating step-by-step: Decomposing the translation process for improved translation quality of long-form texts. In *Proceedings of the ninth conference on machine translation. Association for Computational Linguistics.* 1301–1317. https://aclanthology.org/2024.wmt-1.123/.

Calzi Kleidermacher, H., Zou, J. (2025). *Science across languages: assessing LLM multilingual translation of scientific papers*. arXiv:2502.17882.

Castaldo, A., Ramponi, A., Guerini, M., et al. (2025). *Extending CREAMT: leveraging large language models for literary translation post-editing*. arXiv:2504.03045. https://doi.org/10.48550/arXiv.2504.03045

Chen, R., & Guo, B. (2024). Human-machine collaborative translation based on artificial intelligence technology. *Sci Soc Res, 6*(4), 2963–2970.

China Daily. (2025). *China releases first generative AI translation application guide*. China Daily, 3 May 2025. Retrieved May 24, 2025, from https://cn.chinadaily.com.cn/a/202505/03/WS6815e726a310205377031903.html

Chirkova, N., Aji, A. F., Ruder, S. (2025). *LLM-as-a-qualitative-judge: automating error analysis in natural language generation*. arXiv:2506.09147.

Comic M. (2025). *Can LLM translate text accurately for real-world use? Lokalise Blog*, 6 May 2025. https://lokalise.com/blog/can-llm-translate-text-accurately/

Croxford, E., Zhang, Y., Wang, L., et al. (2025). Current and future state of evaluation of large language models in summarization tasks. *Nat AI, 1*(2), 123–135. https://doi.org/10.1038/s44401-024-00011-2

CSA Research. (2020). *Augmented translation: are we there yet? CSA Research*, 4 Nov 2020. https://csa-research.com/Blogs-Events/Blog/augmented-translation-2020

Devlin, J., Chang, M. W., Lee, K., et al. (2019). *BERT: pre-training of deep bidirectional transformers for language understanding*. arXiv:1810.04805.

Drugan, J. (2013). *Quality in professional translation: Assessment and improvement*. Bloomsbury Academic.

Dunne, K. J., & Dunne, E. S. (Eds.). (2013). *Translation and localization project management: The art of the possible*. John Benjamins Publishing Company.

ELIA. (2019). *2019 language industry survey—Expectations and concerns of the European language industry*. ELIA.

Feng, Z., Zhang, M., Chen, J., et al. (2024). *TEaR: improving LLM-based machine translation with systematic self-refinement*. arXiv:2402.16379.

Fernandes, P., Deutsch, D., Finch, T., et al. (2023). *Bridging the gap: a survey on integrating (human) feedback for natural language generation*. arXiv:2305.00955.

Ganesan, S., Thompson, R., Martinez, L., et al. (2024). Readability of published vs. artificial intelligence (AI)-generated plain-language summaries (PLS). In *International society for medical publication professionals annual meeting*, April 2024.

Garcia, I. (2011). Translating by post-editing: Is it the way forward? *Machine Translation, 25*(3), 217–237.

Gupta, A., Khandelwal, A., Nayak, G., et al. (2025). *Found in translation: measuring multilingual LLM consistency as simple as translate then evaluate*. arXiv: 2505.21999. https://doi.org/10.48550/arXiv.2505.21999

Jiménez-Crespo, M. A. (2013). *Translation and web localization*. Routledge.

Jiménez-Crespo, M. A. (2025). Human-centered AI and the future of translation technologies: What professionals think about control and autonomy in the AI era. *Information, 16*(5), 387. https://doi.org/10.3390/info16050387

Kageura, K., & Umino, B. (1996). Methods of automatic term recognition: A review. *Terminology, 3*(2), 259–289.

Läubli, S., Sennrich, R., Volk, M. (2018). Has machine translation achieved human parity? A case for document-level evaluation. In *Proceedings of the 2018 conference on empirical methods in natural language processing. Association for Computational Linguistics.* 4791–4796.

Li, J., Zhang, Y., Fan, A., et al. (2024). Eliciting the translation ability of large language models via multilingual finetuning with translation instructions. *Trans Assoc Comput Linguist, 12*, 576–592. https://doi.org/10.1162/tacl_a_00655

Li, T., Wang, H., Chen, M., et al. (2023). Semantic transformation and cultural adaptation of metaphor and multimodal metaphor in multilingual communication from the perspective of cognitive linguistics. *Eurasian J Appl Linguist, 9*(1), 161–189. https://doi.org/10.32601/ejal.901015

Lin, Z. L., Chen, H., Wang, J., et al. (2025). *Probing large language models in reasoning and translating complex linguistic puzzles.* arXiv:2502.00817.

Liu, X., Chen, Y., Zhang, L., et al. (2024). *Large language models and causal inference in collaboration: a comprehensive survey.* arXiv:2403.09606.

Lommel, A., Uszkoreit, H., & Burchardt, A. (2014). Multidimensional quality metrics (MQM): A framework for declaring and describing translation quality metrics. *Tradumàtica, 12*, 455–463.

Lyu, C., Yang, W., Zhou, F., et al. (2023). A paradigm shift: the future of machine translation lies with large language models. In *Proceedings of the MT large data and code contributions workshop (MT-LD-CC 2023).* Association for Computational Linguistics. 1. https://arxiv.org/abs/2305.01181

Lyu, Y., Zhang, W., Chen, K., et al. (2025). *Salute the classic: revisiting challenges of machine translation in the age of large language models.* Trans Assoc Comput Linguist. arXiv:2401.03784.

Merali, A. (2024). *Scaling laws for economic productivity: experimental evidence in LLM-assisted translation.* arXiv:2409.02391. https://doi.org/10.48550/arXiv.2409.02391

Moorkens, J., & O'Brien, S. (2017). Assessing user interface needs of post-editors of machine translation. In D. Kenny (Ed.), *Human issues in translation technology* (pp. 109–130). Routledge.

Moslem, Y., Haque, R., Kelleher, J. D., & Way, A. (2023). Adaptive machine translation with large language models. In M. Nurminen, J. Brenner, M. Koponen, S. Latomaa, M. Mikhailov, F. Schierl, T. Ranasinghe, E. Vanmassenhove, S. Alvarez Vidal, N. Aranberri, M. Nunziatini, C. Parra Escartín, M. Forcada, M. Popovic, C. Scarton, & H. Moniz (Eds.), *Proceedings of the 24th Annual Conference of the European Association for Machine Translation* (pp. 227–237). European Association for Machine Translation. https://aclanthology.org/2023.eamt-1.22/

Mu, Y., Li, J., Zheng, C., et al. (2023). Augmenting large language model translators via translation memories. In *Findings of ACL 2023.* arXiv:2305.17367. https://doi.org/10.48550/arXiv.2305.17367

Mudrik, N., Levy, O., Tenney, I., et al. (2023). *Beyond words: a glimpse into comparing LLMs on idiom translation.* AI Mind, 20 July 2023. https://pub.aimind.so/beyond-words-a-glimpse-into-comparing-llms-on-idiom-translation-a463775272e

Naveen, P., & Trojovský, P. (2024). Overview and challenges of machine translation for contextually appropriate translations. *iScience, 27*(7), 110878. https://doi.org/10.1016/j.isci.2024.110878

O'Brien, S. (2011). Towards predicting post-editing productivity. *Machine Translation, 25*(3), 197–215.

Pokhrel, S. R., Walid, A. (2024). On large language model based joint source channel coding for semantic communication. In *2024 2nd international conference on foundation and large language models (FLLM).* IEEE. 322–329.

Pym, A. (2013). Translation skill-sets in a machine-translation age. *Meta, 58*(3), 487–503. https://doi.org/10.7202/1025047ar

Qian, S., Bojar, O., Kocmi, T. (2024). What do large language models need for machine translation evaluation? In *Proceedings of the 2024 conference on empirical methods in natural language processing (EMNLP).* Association for Computational Linguistics. pp 3660–3674.

Roussis, D., Papavassiliou, V., Prokopidis, P., et al. (2024). Enhancing scientific discourse: machine translation for the scientific domain. In *Proceedings of the 25th annual conference of the*

European Association for Machine Translation (Volume 1). European Association for Machine Translation. 229–238.

Scalena, D., Bentivogli, L., Negri, M., et al. (2025). *Steering large language models for machine translation personalization*. arXiv:2505.16612. https://doi.org/10.48550/arXiv.2505.16612

SEAtongue. (2025). *How AI is transforming translation & localisation in 2025*. SEAtongue Blog, 10 Feb 2025. https://seatongue.com/blog/business/how-ai-is-transforming-translation-localisation-in-2025/

Smartling Inc. (2024). *2024 state of translation report*. Smartling, 25 Sept 2024. https://www.smartling.com/company-news/smartling-unveils-2024-state-of-translation-report/

Tang, L., Zhang, Y., Chen, H., et al. (2025). *Adaptive few-shot prompting for machine translation with pre-trained language models*. arXiv:2501.01679. https://doi.org/10.48550/arXiv.2501.01679

Toral, A., Sánchez-Cartagena, V. M. (2017). A multifaceted evaluation of neural versus phrase-based machine translation for 9 language directions. In *Proceedings of the 15th conference of the European chapter of the association for computational linguistics: volume 1*, long papers. Association for Computational Linguistics. 1063–1073.

Transphere. (2024). *Translation quality assessment: a practical guide for 2025*. Transphere, 13 Dec 2024. https://www.transphere.com/translation-quality-assessment/

Uguet, C. S., Bentivogli, L., Negri, M., et al. (2024). LLMs in post-translation workflows: comparing performance in post-editing and error analysis. In *Proceedings of the 25th annual conference of the European Association for Machine Translation (Volume 1)*. European Association for Machine Translation. 373–386.

Vasiļjevs, A., Pinnis, M., Skadiņš, R., et al. (2024). A market study and open-source solutions for multilingual content management in the public sector. In: Proceedings of the 25th annual conference of the European Association for Machine Translation. European Association for Machine Translation. 499–508.

Wang, H., & Liu, S. (2025). From MTPE to AIPE: Evolution of translation modes in the GenAI era and its implications for translation education. *Shandong Foreign Language Teaching, 46*(3), 37–46. https://www.researchgate.net/publication/393461258_congMTPEdaoAIPEGenAIshidaifanyimoshiyanbianjiqiduifanyijiaoyudeqishi_From_MTPE_to_AIPE_Evolution_of_Translation_Modes_in_the_GenAI_Era_and_Its_Implications_for_Translation_Education

Wang, J., Zhang, Y., Mu, Y., et al. (2025). *DRT: deep reasoning translation via long chain-of-thought*. arXiv:2412.17498. https://doi.org/10.48550/arXiv.2412.17498

Wang, Y., Caswell, I., Bapna, A., et al. (2024). Recent advances in interactive machine translation with large language models. *IEEE Access, 12*, 179353–179382. https://doi.org/10.1109/ACCESS.2024.3487352

Woo, J. J., Chen, L., Zhang, H., et al. (2025). Custom large language models improve accuracy: Comparing retrieval augmented generation and artificial intelligence agents to noncustom models for evidence-based medicine. *Arthroscopy, 41*(3), 565–573.e6.

Wu, M., Abdul-Mageed, M., Klyueva, N., et al. (2024). *(Perhaps) beyond human translation: harnessing multi-agent collaboration for translating ultra-long literary texts*. arXiv:2405.11804. https://doi.org/10.48550/arXiv.2405.11804

Wu, X., Arase, Y. (2024). *An in-depth evaluation of large language models in sentence simplification with error-based human assessment*. arXiv:2403.04963. https://doi.org/10.48550/arXiv.2403.04963

Yang, X., Wang, J., Duh, K., et al. (2023). Human-in-the-loop machine translation with large language model. In *Proceedings of the 19th machine translation summit (MT Summit 2023)*. Vol. 2. user track. ACL Anthology, 88–98.

Żmudka, K., Małecki, K., Biernat, P., et al. (2024). ChatGPT—A tool for assisted studying or a source of misleading medical information? AI performance on polish medical final examination. *Ann Acad Med Siles, 78*, 94–103.

Huashu Wang is a full professor, doctoral supervisor, and postdoctoral co-supervisor at the Graduate School of Translation & Interpretation, Beijing Foreign Studies University. He also serves as Executive Director of the ATI AI-Powered Translation Lab; Secretary-General of the Translation Technology Committee of the Translators Association of China; Deputy Secretary-General of the Foreign Language Educational Technology Committee of the China Association for Comparative Studies of English and Chinese; member of the Technical Committee of the International Federation of Translators (FIT); expert on Terminology Resource Management for ISO TC 37/ SC 3; and committee member of the Theoretical and Applied Terminology Sub-Technical Committee (TC 62/SC 1) of the National Language and Terminology Standardization Technical Committee. His research focuses on translation technology, foreign-language educational technology, and language-service management. He has published extensively in journals such as *Chinese Translators Journal*, *Shanghai Journal of Translators*, *Foreign Language Education*, *Computer-Assisted Foreign Language Education*, and *The Interpreter and Translator Trainer*, with over 90 published papers. He is the author of more than 10 books, including *Research in Translation Technology*, *Translation Technology for Everyone*, *A Guide to Translation Search*, *Introduction to Computer-Assisted Translation*, *Application Localization*, and *Project Management in Translation and Localization*. He has led more than 10 national and provincial research projects and sits on the editorial boards of multiple academic journals.

Ying Wu is a full professor and Director of the Computer-Assisted Translation Research Center at the Faculty of Foreign Languages, Wenhua College, a CATTI-II Translator, and a doctoral student at the Graduate School of Translation & Interpretation, Beijing Foreign Studies University. Her research focuses on computer-assisted translation, translation technology applications, and corpus-based translation studies. She has published more than 20 academic papers and led over 10 research projects at provincial, ministerial, and institutional levels. She is the author of *English Major Thesis Writing Tutorial for Applied Universities* (Chief Editor) and *Research on Translation Teaching and Talent Development Paths in Applied Universities* (Associate Editor). Her course "Computer-Assisted Translation" was recognized as a Provincial-Level First-Class Course in 2023. She serves as a council member of the Hubei Translators Association and the Future Education Committee of the Chinese Society of Educational Development Strategy.

Hybrid Translation Production: The Whole-Process AI-Empowerment

Wenzhong He

Abstract The advent of large language models (LLMs) has fundamentally reshaped the translation paradigm, transitioning from traditional human-centered workflows to a human-AI collaborative model. Advanced LLMs now support translators throughout the entire translation pipeline, encompassing pre-translation planning, drafting, post-editing, and evaluation. These generative AI systems augment human cognitive capabilities, rendering the translation process increasingly AI-driven. Accordingly, the translator's role is redefined—from that of a linguistic executor to a strategic mediator who orchestrates, refines, and critically evaluates machine-generated content. This transformation not only improves efficiency and quality but also reconfigures the core professional competencies required, emphasizing AI literacy, prompt engineering, and collaborative problem-solving. As a result, translation education must adapt to equip future professionals with the skills necessary to thrive within emerging human–machine translation ecosystems.

Keywords Large language models · Hybrid translation production · Whole process AI empowerment · Human AI synergy

1 Introduction

1.1 Background: The Emergence of LLMs

Recent advances in language processing have been driven by the development of large language models (LLMs) such as the GPT series and BERT. These models have significantly enhanced natural language understanding and generation. GPT's autoregressive architecture enables the production of coherent, contextually appropriate text, supporting applications from conversational agents to content generation. In parallel, BERT's bidirectional encoding has advanced semantic comprehension by

W. He (✉)
School of International Studies, Zhejiang University, Hangzhou, China
e-mail: donhwz@zju.edu.cn

T. Yin et al. (eds.), *AI Through LLMs*, New Frontiers in Translation Studies,
https://doi.org/10.1007/978-981-95-4798-2_2

capturing context from both preceding and following text. Collectively, these innovations have improved the fluency and accuracy of language tasks and broadened their application domains.

In contrast, traditional translation models, typically rule-based or statistical, struggle with the inherent complexity and ambiguity of human language. Their limited contextual understanding often results in inaccurate translations, particularly with idiomatic and nuanced expressions. Furthermore, such models require extensive manual effort in data preparation, feature engineering, and rule construction, rendering the translation process labor-intensive and less efficient.

1.2 Paradigm Evolution in Translation

Throughout most of human history, translation had been a domain of entirely human creativity. It was not until the latter half of the twentieth century that digital tools began to assist in this process. The emergence of statistical machine translation (SMT) in the 1990s marked the beginning of a shift in the translation production paradigm and initiated a transformation in the translator's role (Table 1).

The quality leap from NMT to LLM translation can be seen from the following Example 1.

Table 1 Evolution of translation production and human–machine roles

Translation mode	Human role	Machine role	Key features
FHT	Translator handles all aspects: comprehension, interpretation, writing, revision	None	Deep contextual understanding, high cultural sensitivity, creative style; slow and labor-intensive
SMT	Pre- and post-editing; maintains terminology databases; quality assurance	Phrase-based translation using probability and alignment models	Fast but literal; lacks fluency and deep contextual awareness; high need for human post-editing
NMT	Post-editor; quality controller; custom trainer (domain-specific tuning)	Sentence-level translation using neural networks; captures syntax and semantics	More fluent and accurate than SMT; still struggles with idioms, ambiguity, and style
LLM	Prompt designer; editor; decision-maker; cultural/contextual consultant	Generates, refines, localizes, and adapts translation with contextual awareness and stylistic control	Capable of nuanced, audience-specific output; supports collaborative human-AI workflows

Note Rule-based machine translation is excluded due to its limited usability in real translation production

Example 1 ST: As the school principal Lung-Hsing Yang admired the shishuan tree towering over a place of worship, he eagerly sought its scientific name. The deciduous bright-green leaves congregated in small branchlets, seed-bearing cones, and fissured dark-grey bark flaking away in ribbons revealing inner brown hues were unlike any other tree in the area. When he met Chan Wang, an employee of the Bureau of Forest Research conducting fieldwork in the forests of Enshi, western China, in 1943, Yang hoped he might finally have an answer, but he was disappointed. Intrigued by news of this strange tree, Wang visited Moudao, in Sichuan province, where he found the tree and collected specimens he later identified as a cypress. Three years later he gave a specimen to a colleague, who showed the herbarium sheet to his botanical colleague Wan-Chun Cheng at the National Central University. Convinced the species was not a common conifer, Cheng examined the original specimens collected by Wang, arranged for a student to collect further specimens, and shared his suspicions with his colleague Hsen-Hsu Hu, Director of Beijing's Fan Memorial Institute of Biology. Hu reclassified the tree within the Metasequoia genus first described by Shigeru Miki at Kyoto University in 1941. Miki had worked from fossils widely believed to represent an extinct species over 100 million years old. Hu first described the species as a living fossil in print in 1946 without formally naming the species. Two years later, Hu and Cheng formally named Metasequoia glyptostroboides, making headlines around the world.

GNMT: 当校长杨隆兴欣赏到这棵耸立在礼拜场所的石斛树时，他急切地想知道它的学名。这种落叶的鲜绿色叶子聚集在小枝上，结有种子的球果，裂开的深灰色树皮呈带状剥落，露出内部的棕色色调，与该地区的其他树木都不一样。1943 年，当他遇到在恩施州西部森林进行实地考察的林业研究局员工陈王时，杨希望他最终能找到答案，但他失望了。这棵奇怪的树的消息引起了王的好奇，他去了四川省牟道，在那里他发现了这棵树并收集了标本，后来他鉴定为柏树。三年后，他将一个标本交给了一位同事，这位同事将标本展示给了他在国立中央大学的植物学同事郑万春。程教授确信该物种不是普通的针叶树，他检查了王教授收集的原始标本，安排一名学生收集更多标本，并与他的同事、北京范纪念生物研究所所长胡汉旭分享了他的怀疑。胡汉旭将该树重新归类为水杉属，该属由京都大学的三木茂于 1941 年首次描述。三木研究的化石被广泛认为代表了一种超过 1 亿年前的灭绝物种。胡汉旭于 1946 年首次在印刷品中将该物种描述为活化石，但并未正式命名该物种。两年后，胡汉旭和程教授正式将其命名为水杉，引起全球关注。

DeepL: 当校长杨隆兴欣赏这棵耸立在祭祀场所的石杉树时，他急切地想知道它的学名。它的叶子落叶后呈鲜绿色，小枝上聚集着结籽的球果，深灰色的树皮裂纹呈带状剥落，露出褐色的内层，与当地的其他树木截然不同。1943 年，杨振宁在中国西部恩施的森林里遇到了正在进行实地考察的林业研究局雇员王昌龄，他希望自己最终能找到答案，但他失望了。由于对这种奇特树木的消息感到好奇，王昌龄来到四川省谋道，在那里他发现了这种树，并采集了标本，后来他确认这是一种柏树。三年后，他将标本交给了一位同事，同事将标本表给他在国立中央大学的植物学同事程万春看。程万春确信该树种不是常见的针叶树，他检查了王氏采集的原始标本，安排一名学生进一步采集标本，并将自己的怀疑告诉了他的同事、北京范文澜纪念生物学研究所所长胡先煦。胡先骕将水杉重新归入水杉属。三木的研究对象是被普遍认为已有一亿多年历史的灭绝物种化石。胡先骕于 1946 年首次以活化石的形式将水杉描述出来，但并未正式命名该物种。人们普遍认为，三木所研究的化石代表了一种灭绝物种，距今已有一亿多年的历史。1946 年，胡先骕首次以活化石的形式描述了水杉，但没有正式命名。两年后，胡先骕和郑万钧将水杉正式命名为“石杉”，成为世界新闻的头条。

Deepseek: 杨龙兴校长伫立在一处庙宇前，仰望着高耸入云的“shishuan”古树，迫切想要探明它的学名。这棵落叶乔木的翠绿枝叶在小枝上簇拥成团，暗灰色树皮裂成条片剥落，露出内层褐色，枝头还结着球果——周围再没有第二棵这样的树。1943年，他在鄂西森林考察时偶遇林业研究所技术员王战，原以为能解开谜团，却再度失望。听闻这株奇树的消息，王战专程赴四川谋道溪考察，采集标本后暂定其为柏木新种。三年后他将标本转交国立中央大学郑万钧教授，后者察觉这绝非普通针叶树，遂组织学生补充采集，并联系北平静生生物调查所所长胡先骕共研。胡先骕敏锐意识到，这极可能是日本学者三木茂1941年基于化石建立的水杉属现存物种。该属化石当时被学界公认为一亿年前灭绝的古老类群。1946年，胡先骕率先在学术刊物上将其确认为活化石，两年后与郑万钧联名发表《水杉新科及生存之水杉新种》，正式赋予其"水杉(Metasequoia glyptostroboides)"的学名,这一发现随即轰动国际学界。

1.3 Capabilities of LLMs in Translation

The integration of large language models (LLMs) into translation workflows represents a transformative advancement in language technology. Unlike traditional rule-based or statistical systems, LLMs offer context-aware, semantically rich processing that enables more adaptive and intelligent translation.

Multilingual Competence and Zero-Shot Translation: LLMs such as ChatGPT, Gemini, Claude, Deepseek, Doubao, Kimi and Qwen are trained on extensive multilingual datasets, enabling them to support a broad range of language pairs, including those with limited resources. Many LLMs are capable of zero-shot or few-shot translation, requiring minimal task-specific training. This expands translational reach and reduces dependence on large parallel corpora.

Contextual Understanding and Semantic Coherence: LLMs operate with wide context windows, allowing for improved handling of long texts, idiomatic expressions, and discourse-level cohesion. This facilitates more accurate and stylistically appropriate document-level translation, in contrast to earlier models that often failed to preserve semantic consistency.

Domain Adaptability and Prompt-Based Customization: LLMs can be tailored to specific domains (e.g., legal, medical, technical) through prompt engineering or fine-tuning. Translators can embed terminological or stylistic constraints within prompts, enabling outputs that align with specialized conventions and target audience expectations.

Interactive and Iterative Translation Workflows: Unlike static translation engines, LLMs support interactive refinement. Translators can engage in iterative prompting to resolve ambiguities, explore alternatives, or improve phrasing, fostering a collaborative human–machine translation process.

Multimodal Translation Capabilities: With integration into vision and speech models, LLMs are increasingly capable of multimodal translation, handling text from images, audio, and video. This enables applications such as caption translation, transcription, and subtitling, facilitating cross-media, cross-lingual communication.

Quality Estimation and Self-Evaluation: Some LLMs can assess their own outputs by offering quality scores or generating alternative versions for comparison. This supports translators in identifying errors and refining translations, positioning LLMs as both generative and evaluative tools.

However, it is important to underscore that, at present, neither human translation nor fully automated AI translation alone is capable of consistently delivering high-quality output across all contexts. Human translators continue to face challenges in maintaining uniform quality at scale, while AI-generated translations often fall short in fully automatically handling semantic nuance, cultural adaptation, and domain-specific complexity without human intervention (Table 2). Consequently, a human–machine coupled translation model is essential, one that strategically combines the efficiency and consistency of AI with the interpretive, contextual, and decision-making capabilities of human translators. Notably, many critical decisions, particularly those involving ambiguity, tone, or pragmatic appropriateness, still require human judgment and cannot yet be reliably automated. Thus, in this setting, human-LLM hybrid translation production would be the prevailing paradigm of translation production.

Table 2 contrasts the strengths and limitations of fully human translation and LLM translation, emphasizing key considerations such as context sensitivity, scalability, and ethical implications.

The following excerpt illustrates why full LLM translation is not ready for delivery.

Example 2 ST: Kubrick contacted Malcolm McDowell, asking him to read the book, before offering him the lead role, and filming began in September 1971, lasting twenty-three weeks, until February 1971. *A Clockwork Orange* was made using a small mobile crew, on location, with only a few sets built where suitable locations couldn't be found, resembling the shoots of his earliest feature films (*Fear and Desire* through to *The Killing*). He did all of the handheld shooting himself, which, combined with the film's lack of stars, made it a relatively cheap production at just $2 million. During the shoot Kubrick extensively rewrote the dialogue during long rehearsals with the actors, especially McDowell. He worked on Alex's voice-over until March 1971, when he began postproduction. Working seven days a week, he completed the film by the end of the year. The film premiered in New York City on December 20, 1971, and in Britain on January 13, 1972. Two years later Kubrick himself withdrew the film in the United Kingdom and it was not rereleased there until after his death, on March 17, 2000.

Deepseek: 库布里克联系了马尔科姆·麦克道威尔,在邀请其出演主角前先请对方阅读原著。影片于 1971 年 9 月开拍,历时二十三周,至 1972 年 2 月杀青。整部《发条橙》采用小型流动摄制组进行实景拍摄,仅当找不到合适场地时才搭建少量布景,这种工作方式延续了库布里克早年从《恐惧与欲望》到《杀手》等

Table 2 Comparison of fully human translation and Large Language Model (LLM) translation

Aspect	Fully Human Translation	LLM Translation
Accuracy	High, especially in nuanced and context-rich texts	High in general contexts; may falter in highly specialized or ambiguous passages
Cultural Sensitivity	Strong; informed by lived experience and deep intercultural understanding	Moderate; based on training data and prompt specificity
Contextual Judgment	Excellent; integrates broader discourse and pragmatic cues	Improving; infers context but lacks experiential judgment
Speed	Slower; time-consuming due to research and quality assurance	Very fast; delivers instant results
Cost	High; requires skilled professionals, especially for specialized domains	Low; cost-effective for routine or high-volume tasks
Consistency	May vary due to individual translator styles or fatigue	High; maintains uniform terminology and phrasing with proper configuration
Creativity and Style	Strong; adapts tone, rhetorical style, and literary nuance	Moderate; style control is possible but often formulaic
Scalability	Limited; constrained by time and labor availability	Excellent; easily handles large-scale projects
Error Types	Human errors (e.g., mistranslations, omissions, subjective bias)	AI errors (e.g., hallucinations, factual inaccuracies, overgeneralization)
Ethical Considerations	Clear authorship, accountability, and traceability	Raises issues related to bias, data provenance, and responsibility
Interdisciplinary Integration	Strong; can draw on subject-matter expertise and real-world experience	Variable; performance depends on training corpus coverage
Adaptability to Feedback	High; responsive to revisions and collaborative processes	Moderate; adaptable through prompting or fine-tuning, but less intuitive

作品的拍摄传统。所有手持镜头均由他亲自掌镜,加之影片未启用明星阵容,最终制作成本仅 200 万美元,堪称相对低廉。拍摄期间,库布里克通过与演员(尤其是麦克道威尔)的长时间排练,对台词进行了大量重写。他为亚历克斯的旁白配音工作一直持续到 1971 年 3 月,随后便投入后期制作。以每周七天连轴转的工作强度,终于在当年年底完成全片。该片于 1971 年 12 月 20 日在纽约首映,1972 年 1 月 13 日登陆英国银幕。两年后,库布里克亲自将本片从英国院线下架,直至 2000 年 3 月 17 日其逝世后才得以重新公映。

This excerpt presents four key challenges for human translators as well as LLMs:

Chronological inconsistency: The sentence "filming began in September 1971, lasting twenty-three weeks, until February 1971" contains a temporal error—filming could not end before it began. The mistake lies in "February 1971," not in the duration.

Film title translation: The movie The Killing should be rendered as "杀手," its conventional Chinese title. Many models fail to recognize this.

Premiere date accuracy: The film's New York premiere is often incorrectly translated. Authoritative sources (IMDB, Douban, Wikipedia) confirm it was December 19, 1971—not December 20.

Incorrect attribution of death date: A third of tested models incorrectly interpret "March 17, 2000" as Stanley Kubrick's death date without understanding the function of the comma. In fact, he died on March 7, 1999; the former refers to the rerelease date.

Since the release of ChatGPT-3.5 in November 2022, I have tested nearly every major LLM version. Most, including Deepseek, performed poorly on this passage. Common issues include failure to detect factual errors, lack of verification of established translations, and misinterpretation of dates, highlighting the importance of fact-checking and contextual awareness in AI-assisted translation and reaffirming the indispensable role of experienced translators.

1.4 Human-LLM Hybrid Translation Production

Human-LLM hybrid translation production refers to a translation paradigm that seamlessly integrates large language models (LLMs), AI-powered search engines, and computer-assisted translation (CAT) tools, such as Trados and MemoQ, with the cognitive, cultural, and evaluative competencies of human translators, all underpinned by AI technologies.

At its core, this model aims to achieve synergistic optimization of both translation efficiency and quality through a dynamic and collaborative workflow characterized by a two-phase structure: LLM pre-processing with human prompts followed by human refinement with LLM help. In this workflow, LLMs are primarily responsible for standardized and large-scale tasks, including high-speed text conversion, initial translation polishing, quality assessment, consistency check, and so on under the guidance of proper prompts carefully crafted by human translators (For the design of prompt for LLMs, refer to Gao et al. 2023). Human translators, in turn, contribute by performing semantic disambiguation, cultural adaptation, logical restructuring, stylistic enhancement, verification of proper nouns, terminologies as well as other critical decision-making in complex or ambiguous contexts, all of which are then revised with the help of LLMs and AI search engines.

Generative AI does not merely automate translation; it collaborates:

It supports creative decision-making throughout the translation process, including stages traditionally considered the exclusive domain of human translators, such as pre-translation planning.

It reduces dependence on human post-editing, subject matter expert and native speaker review, and traditional tools such as CAT systems, bilingual aligners, term extractors, and QA checkers.

It can rewrite source texts, surpassing the capabilities of conventional translation software, making it well-suited for poorly written content or texts not adapted to target audiences or media. This is what translation insiders often call "carving on the shit" to avoid "garbage in, garbage out."

It can analyze and summarize multiple documents, making it effective for non-literal translation tasks such as abridged, selective, compiled, or extracted translation.

It can clarify language, logic, terminology, and culturally specific elements, aiding translators in understanding the source text, conveying intended meaning, adapting culturally, and ensuring accurate knowledge transfer.

In summary, unlike traditional translation tools, generative AI functions as a copilot or co-author, not merely a technical aid.

Under this paradigm of hybrid production, not only is translation efficiency greatly enhanced, but the quality of translated texts is also significantly improved, reducing the workload of manual post-editing and proofreading. Translation has entered a new era of human–machine hybrid production, in which LLMs are playing an increasing part thanks to the iteration of GAI technologies.

2 Technological Foundations and AI Tools for Translation

2.1 Technological Foundations of LLMs

The success of modern large language models (LLMs) in translation stems primarily from the Transformer architecture and its attention mechanism. Introduced in *Attention Is All You Need*, the Transformer replaced earlier recurrent neural network (RNN) and long short-term memory (LSTM) models, overcoming limitations related to long-term dependencies and training efficiency. The attention mechanism enables the model to dynamically focus on relevant parts of the input sequence during output generation (Vaswani et al., 2017). In translation, this allows for more accurate alignment between source and target language elements, enhancing coherence and contextual fidelity, particularly in complex sentences.

American LLMs, such as the GPT series, Gemini, Claude typically adopt general-purpose pre-training on large-scale, diverse internet corpora, followed by task-specific fine-tuning. In contrast, Chinese models like Deepseek, Doubao and Qwen often incorporate pre-training strategies tailored to the linguistic and cultural features of Chinese, leveraging domain-specific corpora to improve performance on Chinese-centric translation tasks, as shown in Example 3.

Example 3 ST: The term "Three Masters of Sinology" generally refers to three North American scholars who succeeded John K. Fairbank–Philip A. Kuhn of Harvard University, Frederic E. Wakeman of UC Berkeley, and Jonathan D. Spence of Yale

University. Spence distinguished himself through narrative artistry, Kuhn through methodological innovation, while Wakeman excelled in selecting groundbreaking research topics and archival mastery. These three sinologists are widely considered the third generation in North American China studies, following the first generation represented by Fairbank and the second generation including Joseph R. Levenson, Benjamin I. Schwartz, and Mary C. Wright. This generational framework can be traced back to historian Paul A. Cohen's Discovering History in China (1984) and even earlier academic discussions.

ChatGPT: "汉学三杰"一词通常指三位在约翰·费尔班克 (John K. Fairbank) 之后崭露头角的北美汉学家:哈佛大学的菲利普·A·孔 恩 (Philip A. Kuhn) 、加州大学伯克利分校的魏斐德(Frederic E. Wakeman),以及耶鲁大学的史景迁 (Jonathan D. Spence) 。三人各具特色:史景迁以叙事艺术见长,孔恩以方法论创新著称,而魏斐德则擅长选题前沿,精通档案资料。这三位汉学家被普遍视为北美中国研究的第三代学者,承继第一代以费正清为代表,第二代包括列文森(Joseph R. Levenson) 、施耐德 (Benjamin I. Schwartz) 与玛丽·赖特 (Mary C. Wright) 等人。这一代际划分可以追溯到历史学家柯文(Paul A. Cohen)于1984年出版的《在中国发现历史》一书,甚至更早的学术讨论。

Doubao: "汉学三杰" 这一术语通常指的是三位继承了费正清 (John K. Fairbank) 学术衣钵的北美学者,即哈佛大学的孔飞力 (Philip A. Kuhn) 、加州大学伯克利分校的魏斐德 (Frederic E. Wakeman) 和耶鲁大学的史景迁 (Jonathan D. Spence) 。史景迁以其叙事艺术脱颖而出,孔飞力以其方法论创新著称,而魏斐德则擅长选择具有开创性的研究课题,并精通对档案资料的运用。这三位汉学家被广泛认为是北美中国研究领域的第三代学者,在他们之前,第一代以费正清为代表,第二代则包括列文森 (Joseph R. Levenson) 、史华慈 (Benjamin I. Schwartz) 和芮玛丽 (Mary C. Wright) 。这一学术代际框架可以追溯到历史学家柯 文(Paul A. Cohen) 于 1984 年所著的《在中国发现历史》(Discovering History in China) 以及更早的学术讨论。

LLMs exhibit strong multilingual processing through cross-lingual alignment mechanisms that map semantic and syntactic structures across languages. These mechanisms enable the recognition of equivalent expressions and facilitate accurate translation between diverse language pairs. For low-resource languages, LLMs utilize transfer learning, drawing on knowledge from high-resource languages to improve translation quality despite limited training data.

LLMs are also good at domain adaptation, primarily through prompt engineering and fine-tuning. Prompt engineering involves crafting domain-specific instructions to guide output generation. For example, prompts enriched with legal terminology can steer the model toward translations that align with legal discourse norms.

Fine-tuning further refines the model by training it on domain-specific corpora, such as medical literature, enabling accurate translation of specialized vocabulary and complex concepts.

The combination of prompt engineering and fine-tuning allows LLMs to deliver high-quality, contextually appropriate translations tailored to specific domains.

2.2 *Recommended Tools and LLMs*

The AI arsenal is quite eye-dazzling, evolving at a speed never seen before. However, a simple combination of tools and LLMs suffices in most translation projects.

Table 3 summarizes the key components of AI-human hybrid translation production and highlights the complementary roles of AI and human translators.

Despite the growing capabilities of generative AI, TMS remains indispensable, particularly in large translation projects, where consistency, accuracy, and workflow management are paramount. The use of a TMS offers a range of advantages, as shown in Table 4.

2.3 *Deploying Local LLMs and Building Local Knowledge Bases*

Though American models are not accessible for most people in China, there are many leading models available online for translators either through API at a very low cost or free of charge through Apps or web services. However, in some cases, translators are not allowed to use online machine translation or LLM services as stipulated in the contracts. In such cases and more, translators should consider deploying local large language models (LLMs) and building localized knowledge bases to enhance autonomy, professionalism, and data security. The benefits are as follows (Table 5):

In short, local LLM deployment transforms translators from tool users into knowledge managers, fostering improvements in translation quality, efficiency, and data security through technological autonomy and domain knowledge integration.

Below is a table of the platforms, models and assistants for personal local deployment. Large LSPs or TSPs may consider deploying full-sized Deepseek. For instructions of deployment, please refer to related tutorials online (Table 6)..

3 Hybrid Translation Workflow

3.1 *Strategy Design and Workflow Design*

Simon Sinek's renowned "Golden Circle" model conceptualizes human behavior and decision-making through a framework of three concentric circles that represent different levels of purpose and action. At the outermost layer is the "What", referring to the tangible products, services, or specific actions undertaken by an organization or individual. The middle layer, the "How", encapsulates the methods, processes, and strategies employed to realize goals. At the core, however, lies the "Why", the most fundamental and powerful layer, which pertains not to surface-level motivations such

Table 3 Major tools and LLMs

Category	Name	Description	Roles in hybrid production
LLMs	Doubao*, Deepseek*, Kimi*, Qwen, ERNIE	App, web (Free) or API (at low cost)	Helping understand author, text, background, generating initial translation, automatic post-editing, suggesting translations, proofreading
	ChatGPT, Gemini, Claude, Grok	Not accessible in China	
	Deepseek*, Qwen*, Gemma*, Llama	Local, free, deploying through Ollama	
AI search engines	Metaso (秘塔搜索)*; iflow (心流AI)*;	App or web; free	Checking and verifying proper nouns, terminologies, knowledge
	ThinkAny; Perplexicity	Not accessible in China	
TMS	RWS Trados Studio*; MemoQ*	Suitable for personal use and small TSPs; commercial	Managing translation projects, ensuring quality and consistency
	RWS Trados Studio + Groupshare MemoQ + MemoQ server	Costly, not suitable for personal use or small TSPs; commercial	
	YiCAT, LanguageX, Phrase	Online TMS	
Terminology management	MultiTerm Desktop*; Glossary Converter*	Must-have for term base building; free	Converting and managing term bases
File translator	GT4T*	Powerful tool for translation, supporting multiple ST formats; commercial	Generating initial translations

Note Items marked with * are highly recommended for freelance translators, students, and educators in China. These users need not be concerned about access restrictions to American LLMs or AI tools, as Chinese alternatives offer comparable performance in translation tasks

Table 4 Benefits of TMS

Benefits	Description
Reuse of Language Assets	A TMS enables the reuse of previously translated content through translation memory, thereby minimizing redundant work and enhancing productivity in future projects
Increased Translation Efficiency	By leveraging completed translations and pre-translated segments, a TMS accelerates project timelines, allowing greater output with reduced time and human resources
Enhanced Consistency	Through automated matching with translation memories and terminology databases, a TMS ensures terminological and stylistic consistency, reducing the likelihood of inconsistent renderings of identical content
Improved Translation Quality	Quality assurance is strengthened through structured processes that include translation, revision, and approval stages, supplemented by automated QA (Quality Assurance) and TQA (Translation Quality Assessment) tools
Streamlined Formatting	The automatic preservation and application of source document formatting reduces the time and effort required for layout adjustments, enabling translators to concentrate on linguistic tasks
Optimized Project Management	A TMS supports project planning by facilitating workflow design, resource allocation, and progress tracking, thereby ensuring systematic and timely project execution
Facilitated Team Collaboration	In multi-translator environments, a TMS promotes efficient collaboration through centralized task assignment, version control, and integrated communication tools, fostering better coordination and productivity

as profit, but to the deeper sense of purpose, belief, and values that drive actions: why an organization exists, and why it does what it does. (Sinek: 2009).

While conventional motivation often proceeds from the outside in, beginning with "What," moving to "How," and seldom reaching "Why", exceptional leaders and communicators operate from the inside out. They start by articulating a clear sense of purpose ("Why"), then determine the appropriate methods ("How"), and finally express the outcomes or deliverables ("What") as a natural result of their foundational vision.

This model is particularly instructive when applied to translation as a communicative practice. Translation is not merely the mechanical transfer of content from one language to another; rather, it is a purpose-driven, cross-cultural communication process that entails critical decision-making before, during, and after the act of translation.

Adopting the Golden Circle approach in translation and communication requires us to first clarify the underlying purpose ("Why") of a translation project, why this content needs to be translated, and what communicative or strategic objectives it is intended to fulfill. Only after establishing this rationale should we move on to

Table 5 The benefits of deploying local LLMs

Benefits	Details
Data Security and Privacy	Sensitive information in the translation data remains within the local environment, reducing the risk of data leakage to external servers or third-party cloud services. This is especially crucial for organizations handling confidential documents, such as government agencies, law firms, and financial institutions
Customization	Users can train the local LLM on specific domain—specific datasets, such as legal, medical, or technical terminology. This enables the model to provide more accurate and specialized translations tailored to the specific needs of the user's industry or field
Offline Capability	Once deployed, local LLMs can operate without an internet connection. This is beneficial in situations where there is limited or no network access, such as in remote areas, during emergencies, or in environments with strict network restrictions
Lower Latency	The translation process can be faster as there is no need to send data to and receive results from remote servers. This is particularly advantageous for real—time translation applications, such as instant messaging or live video captioning, where low latency is crucial for a seamless user experience
Cost—Effectiveness	For organizations that handle a large volume of translation tasks, deploying a local LLM can be cost—effective in the long run. Although there may be significant upfront costs for hardware and software installation, it can save on the recurring fees associated with using cloud—based translation services
Regulatory Compliance	In some industries, there are strict regulations regarding data storage and processing. Deploying a local LLM allows organizations to ensure compliance with these regulations, as they have full control over the data and the computing environment

Table 6 Deployment of local LLMs and knowledge bases

LLM platform	LLMs	LLM assistant
Ollama	Deepseek	Cherry Studio
LM Studio	Qwen	Anything LLM
	Gemma	
	Llama	

consider the methods and strategies ("How") for achieving those goals, and finally, the specific content to be translated ("What").

Translation efforts that focus solely on the outer layer, the "What", without addressing the "Why" or "How" often result in superficial or failed outcomes. By contrast, aligning translation processes with a clear sense of purpose and strategy enhances both effectiveness and impact.

Based on content strategy in technical communication, I once proposed the concept of a "translation strategy":

> A translation strategy is a deliberate communicative initiative in which an organization (Who) delivers purposeful and context-relevant content (What) to a specific audience (Whom), at an appropriate time and within a relevant sociocultural or institutional setting (Which Context), in order to fulfill defined organizational objectives (Why), utilizing suitable translators (on behalf of the organization) and media channels (Which Channel) in the right way (Which Way), with the aim of producing intended communicative and strategic outcomes (With What Effect).

This is essentially an extension of the 5W Communication Model (Lasswell, 1948), adapted to contemporary needs based on Getto (2022). The purpose of this 8W Model is very different from the 6W1H proposed in Li Changshuan (2022).

Translation failure often stems from a combination of strategic, procedural, and communicative oversights. Many projects begin without a clear understanding of the target audience or communicative purpose, rendering the translation redundant. Key stakeholders, namely clients, commissioners, and translators, frequently neglect essential factors such as audience expectations, delivery channels, narrative voice, and content timing. Moreover, translation strategies are often chosen arbitrarily, with little consideration of whether full, selective, summary, or rewritten translation best aligns with the communicative goals. Workflow design, tool selection, and resource integration are similarly underdeveloped.

These shortcomings typically result in poor linguistic quality and ineffective communication. In some cases, the translation undermines the original message or damages credibility; in others, it fails to generate any meaningful impact. Furthermore, post-project evaluation is rarely conducted, leaving critical questions about outcomes, deficiencies, and improvements unaddressed.

Traditional translation education reinforces these issues by prioritizing linguistic transfer over strategic and contextual awareness. This narrow focus is particularly limiting in the age of artificial intelligence, where mechanical aspects of translation are increasingly automated. Ironically, the most essential components of successful translation, those involving critical judgment, purpose-driven strategy, and audience engagement, remain the most overlooked (Fig. 1).

3.2 LLM-Empowered Translation Preparation

Careful translation preparation is one of the key factors ensuring translation success. Taking book translation as an example, with the help of large language models, translators can quickly gain insights into the author, the work, its background, the audience, and other related aspects, which aids in making appropriate translation decisions (Table 7).

Terminology extraction or generation is another vital task in the preparation stage. It not only ensures the accuracy and consistency of terminology in subsequent translation but also helps translators understand domain knowledge. LLM term extraction and generation capability has rendered previous methods and technologies obsolete. For comparison of terms extraction methods refer to Chan (2017).

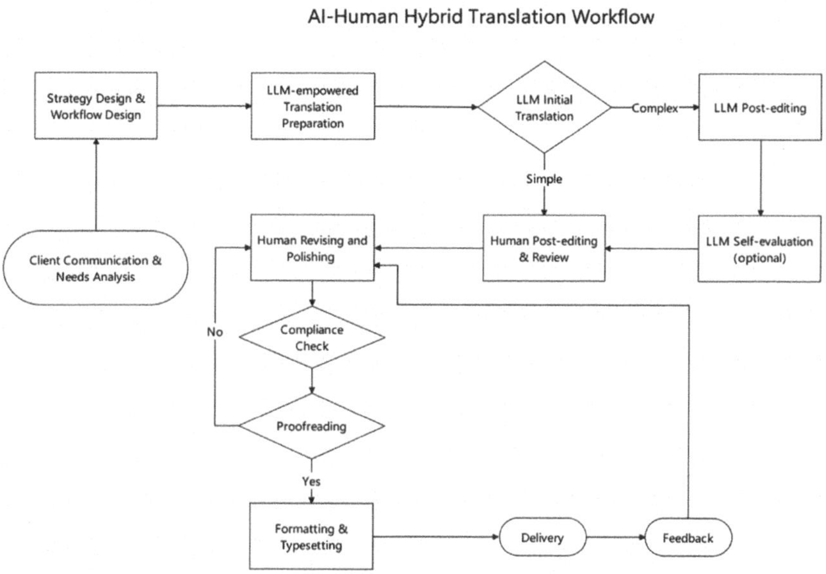

Fig. 1 AI-human hybrid translation workflow

For convenience, proper nouns and domain-specific terms are collectively categorized as terminology (Table 8).

With the bilingual table generated by LLMs, the base of a term base is ready. It can be easily converted into an SDLTB terminology database by following these steps:

- Copy the content of the glossary table;
- Paste it into a new spreadsheet;
- Change the first row of the spreadsheet to the corresponding English names of the languages (Chinese, English) and delete any columns other than the English-Chinese terms;
- Save the spreadsheet under an easily identifiable file name;
- Upload the spreadsheet to another large language model to have it check the accuracy and authority of the translated names of specialized terminology;
- Launch the glossary converter, set the input file as the spreadsheet, select SDLTB as the output format, and convert the spreadsheet into an SDLTB terminology database.

For the LLM verification of the bilingual terms (step 5 above), input a prompt like this:

> You are a technical expert and terminology specialist in the new energy vehicle field. I have uploaded a spreadsheet containing English-Chinese terms in this field, with the first column being Chinese terms and the second column being English terms. Please carefully check whether the translations of these terms are accurate and authoritative. The output should

Table 7 What translators need to know before translating

Category	Sample Prompts
Author Profile	Provide the author's full name, nationality, lifespan, and primary professional identity (e.g., writer, scholar, industry expert). List other representative works, and note any distinctive writing style or academic approach What motivated the author to write this book? (e.g., industry debates, personal experience, theoretical construction). Are there prefaces, interviews, or afterwords that clarify the author's core intent? Identify the author's linguistic traits (e.g., long sentences, metaphor use, minimalist style). How does their cultural background influence the text? (e.g., regional dialects, religious or ethnic imagery)
Textual Analysis	What is the book's central theme? Summarize core topics in 3–5 keywords. Are there multiple or intersecting themes? Outline the structural logic (e.g., linear narrative, parallel structure, problem–solution model) Does the text include special formats (e.g., poetry, charts, formulas, epistolary style)? What function do these forms serve in the source language? What high-frequency terms appear? Are multiple terms used for the same concept (e.g., slang vs. academic terms)? Is a glossary required?
Domain Knowledge	Which disciplines are involved (e.g., medicine, law, computer science, art history)? What theoretical background is needed? Should original literature be consulted? Does the text reference historical events, organizations, or niche cultural elements? Assess their familiarity to source culture readers and determine the need for explanatory notes How is professional data presented (e.g., chart conventions, units, citation norms)? Are there disciplinary or regional differences (e.g., British vs. American usage)?
Context	When and where was the book first published? What was the prevailing sociocultural context? How might historical language shifts (e.g., semantic changes, taboo evolution) affect interpretation? Which regional cultural references appear (e.g., festivals, local vocabulary, historical sites)? Are equivalents available in the target culture, or is free translation needed? Are there ideologically sensitive expressions (e.g., political, religious, or value-laden content)? What cultural sensitivities might affect target readers?
Stylistic Features	Identify the overall language style (e.g., academic, colloquial, literary, satirical). Analyze average sentence length and rhetorical device frequency (e.g., metaphor, parallelism, irony) Describe features of dialogue, if applicable (e.g., dialects, jargon, unique grammar) What is the emotional tone (e.g., passionate, solemn, objective)? How is it conveyed linguistically (e.g., diction, syntax, punctuation)?
Audience Analysis	Who is the book's intended audience (e.g., specialists, general readers, youth)? Does it assume prior knowledge or cultural literacy? How do the target readers' cultural and knowledge backgrounds differ from those of the source audience? Identify potential comprehension challenges (e.g., conceptual leaps, cultural references) What is the intended function of the translated text (e.g., academic, popular, educational)? How does this influence translation style and annotation requirements?

Table 8 Extracting and generating terminologies and proper nouns

Task	Sample Prompt
Term Extracting	*You are an expert English–Chinese translator and terminology specialist with in-depth knowledge of artificial intelligence, large language models, and key figures and institutions in the U.S. technology and investment sectors. I have uploaded a Word document on Sam Altman and OpenAI. Please extract all proper nouns (e.g., names of people, places, organizations) and domain-specific terms related to AI and large language models, translate them into Chinese, and compile a bilingual English–Chinese table in a single unified format*
Term Generating	*I have been invited to serve as an English-Chinese simultaneous interpreter at an upcoming international seminar on new energy vehicle technology. As a technical expert and terminology specialist in this field, could you please compile a glossary of 100 commonly used and authoritative terms, presented in an English-Chinese table? The terms should be professional, representative, and aligned with standard industry usage*

only list the terms with translation errors and their correct translations, presented in a table format.

Besides, the preparation stage also involves the preparation of documents to be translated, which includes conversion of media types, file formats and splitting of large-sized documents into manageable smaller ones. Generative AI also greatly helps in all such tasks.

3.3 *Generation of Initial Translation with LLM*

Although it is technically feasible to upload documents directly to large language models (LLMs) for initial translation, it is recommended that translators first establish a translation project within a computer-assisted translation (CAT) tool such as Trados Studio or MemoQ. This approach enables the effective utilization of translation management system (TMS) functionalities, including translation memory, terminology management, and quality assurance features. For detailed guidance on project setup and operation, consult relevant instructional videos available online.

To effectively leverage large language models (LLMs) in the translation workflow, the process begins with "Export for Bilingual Review" in the "Batch Tasks" menu of Trados. Once the bilingual document is generated, it can be used as input for the LLM to assist in producing the initial draft translation. By doing so, translators are freed from the trouble of installing MT plugins and applying for API.

Below is a sample prompt for the translation task in the previous section:

> You are a highly proficient English-Chinese translator with expertise in artificial intelligence, large language models, and familiarity with key figures and institutions within the U.S. technology and investment sectors. I have uploaded a document structured into four columns: the first indicates the segment number, the second shows the segment status, the third contains the English source text, and the fourth–currently blank–is designated for the

> corresponding Chinese translation. I request that you act as a professional translator, beginning with segment 1 (Row 2) and proceeding sequentially according to the segment numbers. Please translate the English source text in the third column into fluent, accurate, and contextually appropriate Chinese, preserving technical terminology and ensuring high readability. Present your translations in table format, row by row, maintaining the original structure: segment number, segment status, English source text, and the Chinese translation. If it is not feasible to complete all translations in a single output, please divide the content into multiple parts until the full document is translated.

For translation projects without using CAT, upload the documents to online or local LLM one by one and input the modified version of the above prompt.

Large language models (LLMs) are driving significant innovation in interdisciplinary translation by breaking down traditional knowledge barriers and reducing reliance on manual intervention. Pre-trained on diverse, cross-domain corpora, LLMs can effectively integrate concepts from fields such as medicine, law, and technology, enabling accurate translation of complex, hybrid topics like gene editing or the metaverse. Their zero-shot learning capabilities allow them to handle emerging interdisciplinary content without domain-specific training, while still producing fluent, contextually appropriate translations that align with target language norms.

3.4 LLM Post-Editing

Upon completion of the initial translations generated by the large language model (LLM) for all bilingual review files, it is advisable to initiate a AI refinement phase using the LLM prior to commencing manual review and revision. This intermediate step is intended to enhance translation accuracy, minimize residual errors, and improve overall linguistic quality, thereby reducing the cognitive load and time investment required for subsequent human post-editing.

This is done by uploading the updated bilingual review documents (with LLM-generated initial translation) one by one to online or local LLMs and inputting the following prompt:

> I have uploaded a document consisting of four columns: the first contains the segment number, the second indicates its status, the third presents the original English text, and the fourth provides the corresponding machine-translated Chinese version. I now request that you assume the role of a professional English–Chinese translator and English-language editing specialist. Beginning with segment 1 (Row 2), and proceeding sequentially by number, please review and refine the Chinese translations in the fourth column line by line. The output should be formatted as a table, preserving the original structure: segment number, status, English source text, and the polished Chinese translation. Please ensure that the final Chinese version demonstrates fluency, accuracy in terminology, and high readability. If it is not feasible to complete the full document in a single output, please divide the task into multiple batches until all segments have been fully revised.

3.5 LLM Self-Evaluation of Translation Quality

LLMs can rapidly scan through large volumes of translations to identify consistency errors, terminology mismatches, or grammatical issues that might be time-consuming for humans to detect manually. This serves as a guide for latter human post-editing and revision.

For instance, the following framework may be employed as a prompt for large language models (LLMs) to assess translation quality and generate revision suggestions. This evaluation model is designed to ensure both linguistic accuracy and contextual appropriateness, while also promoting professional standards in translation quality assurance (Table 9).

It is important to note that while powerful, LLM self-evaluation is not a substitute for human expertise. It may overlook contextual or cultural subtleties (e.g., humor, regional idioms), and it requires domain-specific fine-tuning to accurately evaluate niche content (e.g., legal, medical translations). Combining LLM self-evaluation with human oversight creates a hybrid model that maximizes both efficiency and accuracy.

Table 9 LLM self-evaluation framework

You are to act as a professional translation quality evaluator and conduct a systematic assessment of the English source text and its corresponding Chinese translation. Follow the procedure below:
Step 1: Evaluation Criteria
Assess the translation across five core dimensions, scoring each from 0 to 10 and providing justification:
Accuracy: Does the translation faithfully convey the original meaning, including technical terms, numbers, and proper nouns?
Fluency: Is the Chinese natural, grammatically correct, and idiomatic, avoiding literal or awkward phrasing?
Terminology Consistency: Are key terms translated uniformly?
Cultural Adaptation: Are idioms and culturally specific elements appropriately localized to avoid misinterpretation?
Logical Clarity: Are sentence structures and transitions coherent, logical, and aligned with Chinese discourse norms?
Step 2: Evaluation Procedure
Comparative Review: Conduct a sentence-by-sentence comparison of the source and translation, identifying problematic segments (e.g., Segments 1–3)
Improvement Suggestions: Provide clear, actionable revision advice, such as restructuring, rewording, or adding annotations
Step 3: Output Format
Present the evaluation results in a structured table with the following 4 columns: segment number, source segment, target segment, problems, suggestions for improvement

3.6 Human Post-Editing and Review

Traditional post-editing is labor-intensive, requiring human translators to correct errors, refine style, and ensure overall quality. In contrast, large language models (LLMs) enable iterative optimization through adaptive feedback and continuous refinement, improving efficiency and consistency. For detailed discussion of post-editing and revision, refer to Koponen (2021).

To enhance output quality, a three-layer verification framework is proposed, integrating AI-driven processing with human expertise. The latter two layers—human validation and final review—are especially critical. Experienced translators provide irreplaceable value in interpreting complex contexts, emotional subtleties, and culturally embedded meanings often missed by AI. In specialized fields such as law and medicine, they ensure terminological precision and logical clarity. Their adaptability supports context-sensitive decision-making, while their creative and ethical judgment allows for customized, secure, and high-quality translations tailored to client needs (Table 10).

Although large language models (LLMs) demonstrate strong cross-lingual translation capabilities, their performance is inherently constrained by algorithmic limitations and the quality and scope of their training data. As a result, various types of translation errors may occur in practical applications. Even after post-editing by LLMs, certain inaccuracies often persist, underscoring the need for human oversight in ensuring translation quality (Table 11).

Example 4 ST: “郡县治,则天下安。”县是国家治理的基本单元,在国家治理体系中具有承上启下的地位。

AI: “If governance is effective at the county level, the whole world will be at peace.” The county serves as the fundamental unit of national governance and holds a pivotal role in linking higher-level administration with grassroots implementation.

HPE: “When counties are well governed, the nation thrives.” The county is the basic unit of national governance and plays a critical intermediary role in the country’s governance system.

Example 5 中国人民是崇尚正义、不畏强暴的人民,中华民族是具有强烈民族自豪感和自信心的民族。中国人民从来没有欺负、压迫、奴役过其他国家人

Table 10 Three-layer verification framework

No	Layer	Task
1	LLM post-editing	The LLM conducts an initial review for fluency, accuracy and consistency
2	Human-AI Collaborative post-editing and review	Human editors provide feedback, which the AI uses to further improve the translation
3	Final Human revising and polishing	Experienced translators perform a comprehensive review to ensure cultural relevance and domain-specific accuracy

Table 11 Major problems of LLM-generated translation

Error Type	Manifestations
Terminology and Proper Noun error	Inconsistency between professional terminology translation and disciplinary standards (e.g., "The North-China Daily News" being mistranslated as "《华北每日新闻》" instead of "《字林西报》")
Semantic deviation	Insufficient contextual understanding leading to semantic errors (e.g., "奴役" in example 5)
Grammar/ Syntax error	Violations of the target language's grammatical rules (e.g., missing subject, tense confusion, unclear reference)
Information loss or redundancy	Key content omissions or the inclusion of meaningless information (such as untranslated sentences or phrases, or unnecessary summarization or elaboration)
Cultural adaptation error	Cultural adaptation error leading to ambiguity, misunderstanding or conflicts
Logical confusion	The translation is contradictory or nonsensical, for example, with reversed causality
Blended style	A blend of formal style and colloquial expressions (e.g., slang in academic reports)

民,过去没有,现在没有,将来也不会有。同时,中国人民也绝不允许任何外来势力欺负、压迫、奴役我们,谁妄想这样干,必将在14亿多中国人民用血肉筑成的钢铁长城面前碰得头破血流!

Deepseek: The Chinese people are a people who uphold justice and are not afraid of tyranny. The Chinese nation is a nation with strong national pride and confidence. The Chinese people have never bullied, oppressed, or enslaved people of other countries—not in the past, not now, and never in the future. At the same time, the Chinese people will never allow any external forces to bully, oppress, or enslave us. Anyone who dares to try will be met with the Great Wall of steel forged with the flesh and blood of over 1.4 billion Chinese people, and will surely break their heads and bleed!

Authorized version: We Chinese are a people who uphold justice and are not intimidated by threats of force. As a nation, we have a strong sense of pride and confidence. We have never bullied, oppressed, or subjugated the people of any other country, and we never will. By the same token, we will never allow any foreign force to bully, oppress, or subjugate us. Anyone who would attempt to do so will find themselves on a collision course with a great wall of steel forged by over 1.4 billion Chinese people (Table 12).

The errors in large language model translation stem from multiple causes:

Example 6 ST: See **Example 1**

Doubao: 1943 年,校长杨龙兴在欣赏一棵高耸于礼拜场所的水杉树时,急切地想知道它的学名。这棵树的落叶鲜绿色叶子聚集在小枝上,有种子球果,开裂的深灰色树皮呈带状剥落,露出内部的棕色色调,与该地区的其他树都不同。当他遇到在四川恩施森林进行实地考察的林业研究局工作人员王战,希望能得到

Table 12 Major causes of errors

Causes	Explanation
Bias and Data quality defects	The training data contains noise or lacks specialized content (e.g., missing medical corpus)
Context modeling limitations	The attention mechanism only captures local context (unable to comprehend correlations across paragraphs)
Differences in language characteristics	Morphological richness and differences in word order result in structural misalignment, such as the absence of tense markers in Chinese
Lack of knowledge reasoning	Unable to perform basic reasoning (such as the association between "heart attack" and "chest pain")
Terminology database dynamic lag	Delayed updates of specialized domain terminology (e.g., COVID-19-related neologisms)
Incomplete cultural symbol database	Lack of cultural background knowledge, such as religious taboo lexicons
Failure to generate translation	LLMs refuse to respond to your question due to value alignment or other sensitive issues

答案,但却失望了。王战对这棵奇怪的树很感兴趣,于是前往四川谋道,在那里他发现了这棵树并收集了标本,后来他将其鉴定为柏树。三年后,他将一个标本交给了一位同事,这位同事将标本展示给了中央大学的植物学同事郑万钧。郑万钧确信这不是一种常见的针叶树,于是检查了王战收集的原始标本,并安排一名学生收集更多标本,同时与北京静生生物调查所所长胡先骕分享了他的怀疑。胡先骕将这棵树重新归类到水杉属,该属由日本京都大学的三木茂于1941年首次描述。三木茂是根据被广泛认为代表1亿多年前已灭绝物种的化石进行研究的。胡先骕在1946年首次在出版物中将该物种描述为活化石,但没有正式命名。两年后,胡先骕和郑万钧正式将其命名为水杉,这一消息轰动了全世界。

Doubao PE: 1943 年,校长杨龙兴在校园礼拜堂前见到一株挺拔的树木,其形态迥异于当地常见树种 —— 叶片鲜绿,簇生于小枝;球果饱满,深灰色树皮呈带状开裂剥落,露出内层的棕褐色纹理。他迫切想知道这棵树的学名,却苦于无人可询。恰在此时,他偶遇正在四川恩施林区考察的林业研究局工作人员王战,遂上前请教,却未得到答案。王战对这株奇特的树木产生浓厚兴趣,专程前往四川谋道现场考察,不仅找到了该树种,还采集了标本,并初步将其鉴定为柏科植物。三年后,王战将标本转交给同事,后者又将其带给中央大学植物学家郑万钧。郑万钧一眼便断定这绝非普通针叶树,他仔细研究了王战采集的原始标本,一面安排学生前往原产地补充采集样本,一面将自己的怀疑告知北京静生生物调查所所长胡先骕。胡先骕查阅资料后发现,这株树的形态特征与日本京都大学三木茂教授 1941 年根据化石描述的水杉属植物高度吻合——该属植物此前一直被认为是一亿多年前灭绝的化石物种。1946 年,胡先骕首次在学术文献中称其为 "活化石",但尚未正式命名。直到 1948 年,胡先骕与郑万钧联名发表论文,正式将其命名为 "水杉",这一发现随即震惊世界植物学界。

HPE: 1943 年,万县农校校长杨龙兴在一处祭祀场所旁发现一棵参天古树,迫切想知道它的学名。这棵树有着独特的生物特征:鲜绿色的叶子密集生长在细枝上,结出带种子的球果,深灰色树皮呈带状剥落,露出内层的棕色纹理,与当地其他树种截然不同。当时,农林部中央林业实验所的技工王战正在湖北恩施进行野外考察,杨龙兴闻讯赶来请教,却未得到确切答案。王战被这棵奇树吸引,专程前往利川谋道镇实地探访。他不仅找到了这种树,还采集了标本,并初步鉴定为柏科植物。三年后,王战将一段枝条和两枚果实标本交给同事吴中伦。吴中伦又将其转交给中央大学植物学教授郑万钧。郑万钧敏锐察觉这并非普通针叶树,立即查阅原始标本,并安排学生补充采集。他同时联系了北平静生生物调查所所长胡先骕,分享了自己的发现。胡先骕研究后确认,这种树正是日本京都大学学者三木茂 1941 年根据化石建立的水杉属物种。此前科学界普遍认为水杉是一亿年前灭绝的古生物。1946 年,胡先骕首次在学术刊物上称其为"活化石",但未正式命名。直到 1948 年,胡先骕与郑万钧联名发表论文《水杉新科及生存之水杉新种》,正式将其命名为"水杉"。这一发现震惊了全球植物学界,被誉为"20 世纪植物学最重要发现之一"。

We have shown that LLMs translate much better than previous machine translation engines (DeepL and GNMT) and Chinese models perform better than American models in tasks that are China-related (compare the proper nouns in the SL excerpt and all the TL versions). However, even so, the AI post-edited translation is still problematic. The author used mixed spelling systems for Chinese names (*Lung-Hsing Yang*, *Chan Wang*, *Wan-Chun Cheng*, and *Hsen-Hsu Hu* in Wade-Giles spelling) and places (*Enshi*, *Moudao*, *Sichuan*, and *Beijing* in Chinese pinyin) and outdated or wrong information about administrative regions (Moudao was allocated to Lichuan, Hubei Province from Wanxian, Sichuan Province in 1952; and Enshi is not in the west of China, but the west of Hubei), which are probably the causes of all the errors in the MT and LLM translations. I don't know why it is so for a book written in 2025 (Table 13).

Fidelity in translation is a "Priority Game". In actual translation practice, conflicts often arise between various dimensions of fidelity, necessitating the establishment of priority hierarchies based on text type to achieve a Dynamic Equilibrium of Fidelity (Table 14).

The core principles of fidelity emphasize that there is no such thing as "absolute fidelity", only fidelity that is adapted to context. Translators, much like sound engineers, must skillfully balance multiple dimensions, making translation a "dance in shackles": bound by the constraints of accuracy, yet requiring creative transformation.

Understanding the nuances of fidelity is crucial in the age of AI, where machine translation often excels at reproducing semantic content and textual form. However, it continues to fall short in areas that demand cultural sensitivity, interpretation of authorial intent, and alignment with communicative purpose. These dimensions require nuanced judgment and cultural literacy that only human translators can provide. Recognizing these limits helps prevent the mechanical rigidity that often characterizes AI-generated translations.

Another important aspect in translation is consistency. However, previous understanding of consistency is somewhat limited. Much emphasis has been put on the document-internal and project-internal consistency with little attention paid to other levels of consistency (Table 15).

Human Post-Editing and Review (PER) imprints the human signature in hybrid Translation. Transcending mere error correction; it is where linguistic expertise,

Table 13 Levels of fidelity in applied translation

Dimensions	Descriptions
Fidelity to knowledge	Ensuring the translation accurately conveys the specialized knowledge, factual information, and logical relationships, avoiding knowledge-related errors. Correcting such errors in the original text
Fidelity to communicative goal	Aligning with the functional purpose of the original text (such as persuasion, information dissemination, entertainment, etc.), ensuring the target text achieves equivalent communicative effects in the target context
Fidelity to culture	Striking a balance between preserving the cultural characteristics of the original text and the acceptability in the target culture when dealing with culturally loaded elements (such as idioms, religious symbols, social norms)
Fidelity to author's intention	Restoring the author's creative intent, emotional orientation, and stylistic features, particularly suitable for literary, academic, and other texts emphasizing "authorial authority."
Semantic fidelity	Ensuring the literal meaning of vocabulary and sentences remains accurate in cross-language conversion, with emphasis on the correspondence between linguistic signs and their referents
Textual fidelity	Preserving the textual formal features of the original text (such as stylistic structure, format, rhythm, punctuation marks) to achieve the unity of form and content

Table 14 Priority game of fidelity

Text type	Priority fidelity	Secondary fidelity
Literary works	Authorial intent, culture, textual form	Semantics (moderate paraphrasing is acceptable)
Scientific works	Knowledge, Semantics	Culture (simplifying non-core elements)
Commercial advertisements	Communication objectives, culture	Text form (reconstructable sentence structure)
Legal documents	Semantics, knowledge, textual forms	Communication goal (prioritizing accuracy)

Table 15 Levels of consistency

Level	Description
Document-internal Consistency	Consistency within a single document
Project-internal Consistency	Consistency within all the documents of a translation project
Inter-project Consistency	Consistency with previous projects
Consistency with the Knowledge System or Discourse System	Consistency with the existing knowledge or discourse systems
Consistency with the Real World	Linking language expressions with the real world entities or events

cultural intuition, and domain knowledge converge to produce contextually nuanced translations. Unlike AI's pattern-based or probability-based outputs, PER enables translators to interpret meaning, preserve authorial voice, and align the translation with the intended communicative function. For example, human reviewers detect and adjust culturally bound expressions, restore stylistic integrity in literary or legal texts, and resolve ambiguity using contextual clues AI often overlooks.

PER also serves as an ethical checkpoint, correcting AI-generated content that may perpetuate bias or insensitivity. From maintaining terminological consistency across serialized texts to adapting metaphors for different markets, human editors ensure coherence at both micro and macro levels. Ultimately, PER is a creative and interpretive act: balancing fidelity, functionality, and cultural resonance. As AI automates routine tasks, PER becomes the defining contribution of human translators, embodying the judgment, empathy, and critical thinking machines cannot replicate.

3.7 The Human Touch that Inputs Translation with Vitality

The Human Post-Editing and Review, Human Revising and Polishing, Compliance Check and Final Proofreading constitute the so-called human touch, which functions as the magic that removes the AI flavor and input human vitality into the translation.

The "final human touch" in AI-human hybrid translation is not merely a corrective step but a transformative act that elevates technical output to human-centric communication. While AI excels at speed, scale, and basic linguistic conversion, it lacks the nuanced understanding of context, culture, and intent that defines effective translation.

Human intervention is indispensable for the following reasons:

Resolving Ambiguity Through Contextual Intelligence: AI processes language statistically, often missing the pragmatic meaning embedded in context. Humans, however, decode hidden layers.

Preserving Cultural and Emotional Nuance: AI struggles with culture-bound concepts and emotional tone, whereas human intuition reigns in cultural adaptation and emotional resonance. Experienced human translators adjust the connotation based on the target audience and capture the author's intended mood.

Ensuring Ethical and Inclusive Representation: AI's training data can perpetuate biases, but humans act as ethical gatekeepers, mitigating bias and aligning to power dynamics.

Aligning with Authorial Intent and Stylistic Consistency: AI struggles with authorial voice and genre-specific conventions, areas where human expertise shines in literary fidelity and Brand tone consistency.

Adding Creative and Strategic Adaptation: Human translators don't just edit—they reimagine content for the target audience, a process rooted in creativity, especially in transcreation and audience-specific translation.

Safeguarding Against Systemic Errors: AI is prone to hallucinations (inventing information) or context drift in long texts, which humans detect and correct.

Empathy and Relatability: Human translators infuse translations with empathy, making them resonate on a human level.

In an AI-human hybrid model, the machine handles the "what" (translation of words), but humans determine the "why" and "how." This final touch is about humanizing language—ensuring that translations don't just convey information but respect the cultural, ethical, and emotional realities of the people who will read them. As AI advances, the role of humans shifts from laborious translation to curators of meaning, using their experience, judgment, and creativity to turn AI outputs into tools for connection, understanding, and impact. In short, the human touch is where technology meets humanity—and that's where translation truly comes alive.

The human touch can be divided into three categories, each including several aspects which call for specific human actions.

Information Verification

In applied translation contexts—such as business, technology, law, and healthcare—rigorous verification of information and knowledge is essential to ensuring the accuracy, professionalism, and reliability of translated texts. This process not only prevents the serious consequences of factual inaccuracies, such as financial loss or safety hazards, but also safeguards the precision of specialized terminology and upholds the authority and credibility of the translation. Moreover, it enables the interpretation of implicit cultural and contextual meanings, reduces risks related to intellectual property, accommodates the rapid evolution of domain-specific knowledge, and facilitates effective interdisciplinary communication. Verification functions as both cross-contextual knowledge transfer and a form of risk management. By confirming factual accuracy, standardizing terminology, accounting for cultural nuance, and aligning with updated cognitive models, it ensures that translations are functional, credible, and contextually appropriate. Ultimately, the human capacity for critical thinking and knowledge curation is indispensable in preventing the amplification of errors and ensuring the faithful transmission of meaning across languages and domains (Table 16).

Table 16 Information verification

Aspects	Actions
Terms and Proper Nouns	Accuracy Verification of Terminology and Proper Nouns (Domain Adaptation of Professional Terms; Standardized Processing of Proper Nouns)
Culture	Accurate transmission of cultural and contextual information (interpretation of culture-specific concepts; coherence verification of contextual logic)
Knowledge, facts, and data	Verification of knowledge-based, factual, and data-driven information (accuracy of numerical and quantitative data; authenticity of events, individuals, and timelines)
Logic	Cross-linguistic Logic and Expression Adaptation (Compensation for Linguistic Structural Differences; Equivalence Verification of Pragmatic Functions)

Cultural Adaptation

Cultural adaptation plays a critical role in the success of translation projects. When poorly managed, it can not only undermine the intended communicative goals but may also result in unintended negative consequences. This process entails nuanced decisions about whether certain culturally sensitive content should be translated at all, and if so, how it should be rendered to ensure appropriateness and impact. AI's mechanistic processing often lacks the cultural sensitivity required for such tasks, potentially leading to serious misinterpretations. Effective cultural adaptation thus relies not only on the translator's cultural awareness and judgment but also on a robust quality assurance framework—one that assesses the potential risks of content handling, guides the selection of appropriate strategies, and ensures iterative review by experienced translators and editors. Specifically, human editorial interventions for cultural adaptation may involve the following practices (Table 17).

Many translation projects entail engagement with political positions, ideological perspectives, and value systems. Addressing ideology in translation demands that translators adopt flexible, context-sensitive strategies tailored to the specific goals of the translation task, the expectations of the target audience, and the cultural and sociopolitical environment. Such nuanced treatment is essential not only for ensuring the accurate transmission of information but also for fostering meaningful cross-cultural dialogue and minimizing the risk of misinterpretation or conflict.

Language Improvement

Language conversion is among the core strengths of large language models (LLMs). When followed by basic post-editing, LLM-generated translations often exceed the output of translators with average language proficiency. However, for experienced translators and discerning readers, the pursuit of translation excellence is continuous—there is always room for improvement. Despite their impressive capabilities, LLMs still face challenges in capturing subtle linguistic nuances and fulfilling complex pragmatic functions. Therefore, high-level human intervention remains essential to elevate the translation to advanced standards of linguistic precision and stylistic appropriateness. Specifically, linguistic post-editing and revision in language conversion typically involve the following aspects (Table 18).

Table 17 Cultural adaptation

Aspects	Actions
Value alignment	Political stance translation, social values balancing, religious philosophy adaptation
Handling of culture-specific items	Historical allusions explanation, customs conversion, taboo avoidance, loaded words translation
Pragmatic Cultural Adaptation	Politeness level adaptation, humor reconstruction, social norm conversion
Reconstruction of cross-cultural contexts	Background supplementation, symbol substitution, scenario rewriting

Table 18 Language improvement

Aspects	Actions
Logic adjustment	The expression aligns more closely with perceptual and cognitive logic; the logical focus shifts
Sentence re-structure	English sentences exhibit strong hierarchical structures, resembling grape clusters, while Chinese sentences tend to follow a flowing, bamboo-joint-like pattern. Syntactic restructuring is required
Smoothness of expressions	Making the expression more smooth, coherent and precise
Clarity of reference	Chinese prefers concrete references, while English favors pronominal references. References should be adjusted accordingly
Unnecessary words	Eliminating redundant words that do not compromise the expression of meaning
Prosody beautification	Make the translation sound more beautiful
Stylistic duplication	The translation better reflects the linguistic style of the original text
Style guide compliance	Following the provided style guide throughout the project

4 Institutionalizing Artificial Intelligence in Translation Education

The rapid rise of large-language models (LLMs) has disrupted the traditional workflow of translation production. In turn, translation education—historically organized around the "trad-pedagogy" of human expertise and generational apprenticeship—must evolve to prepare students for the realities of human-AI co-creation. This section presents a concrete, actionable roadmap for universities that wish to embed AI into their curricula, faculty development programs, and research agendas.

4.1 The Levels of AI Literacy

Translators vary in their translation competence, and likewise in their levels of AI literacy. When all other factors are held constant, these differences can lead to substantial disparities in translation performance, affecting not only output efficiency but also overall quality.

Since the release of Deepseek R1 in the spring, it has become difficult to find individuals who do not engage with AI in some form—and rarer still to find those entirely unfamiliar with it. Nevertheless, it is apparent that most users interact with large language models primarily through web or mobile applications. Such modes of engagement seldom leverage the full capabilities of AI (Fig. 2).

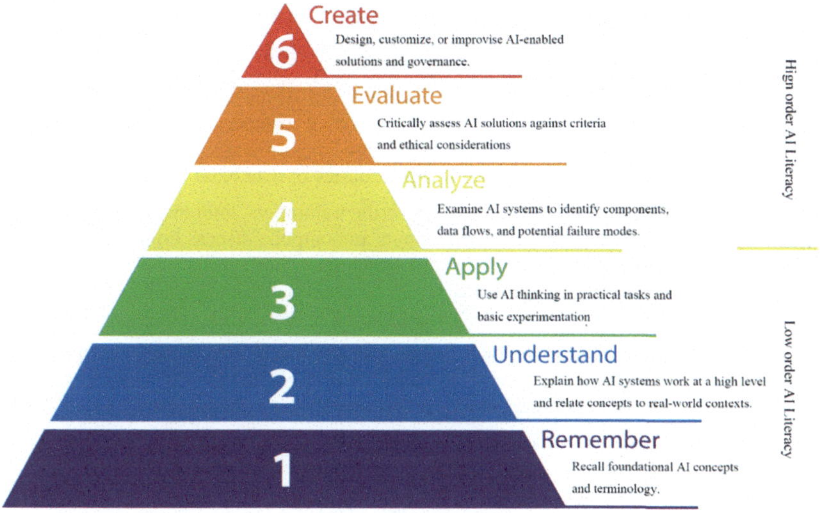

Fig. 2 Levels of AI literacy (adapted from Bloom's Taxonomy)

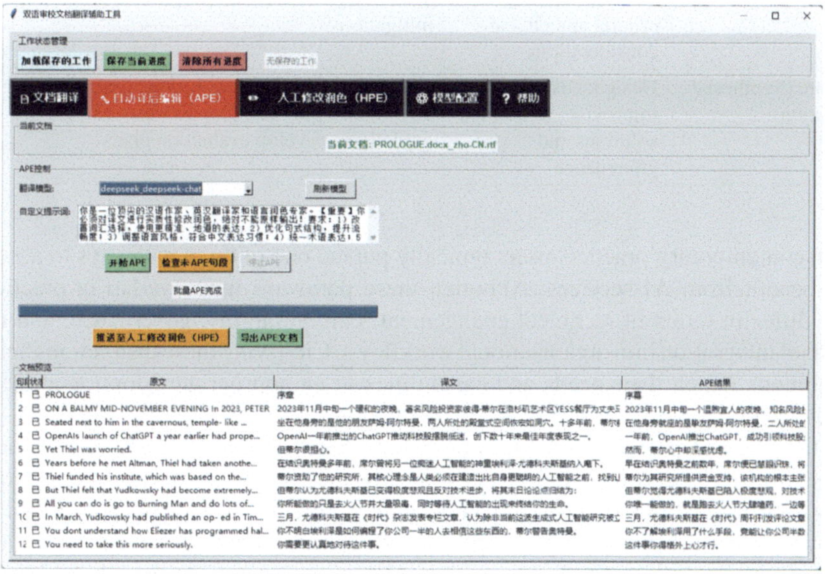

Fig. 3 Bilingual traslator interface

The following diagram presents an adaptation of Bloom's taxonomy for AI literacy.

The table below delineates the scope of each level and specifies corresponding AI-related competencies and applications (Table 19).

Table 19 Levels of AI literacy

Level	Definition	Examples
Remember (Knowledge)	Recall foundational AI concepts and terminology	Definitions of AI and machine learning; supervised vs. unsupervised learning; common algorithms (e.g., linear regression, decision trees); basics of data bias
Understand (Comprehension)	Explain how AI systems work at a high level and relate concepts to real-world contexts	Describe training vs. inference; explain model inputs and outputs; discuss limitations and assumptions
Apply (Application)	Use AI thinking in practical tasks and basic experimentation	Run a simple model on a dataset; interpret outputs; apply evaluation metrics (e.g., accuracy, precision/recall) to a small problem
Analyze (Analysis)	Examine AI systems to identify components, data flows, and potential failure modes	Distinguish data sources; assess feature importance; identify bias indicators; perform error analysis; compare performance across subgroups
Evaluate (Evaluation)	Critically assess AI solutions against criteria and ethical considerations	Compare models; discuss trade-offs (e.g., accuracy vs. fairness); assess risks; propose mitigations
Create (Synthesis/ Creation)	Design, customize, or improvise AI-enabled solutions and governance	Architect a simple AI workflow; draft data governance policies; propose responsible AI guidelines; develop evaluation plans

In contemporary practice, users typically pursue one of three pathways to access and benefit from AI services. Although these pathways may overlap in practice, they differ in terms of technical engagement, configurability, governance, and the depth of integration into organizational workflows. Clarifying these distinctions helps institutions match their needs and capabilities to an appropriate adoption strategy (Table 20).

Direct use of provider interfaces prioritizes accessibility; API-enabled applications prioritize operationalization and workflow fit; and custom development prioritizes control and differentiation. Selecting among these pathways should be guided by task criticality, data sensitivity, compliance obligations, required speed to value, and the organization's capacity for ongoing engineering and governance. A deliberate, staged approach—beginning with provider interfaces, advancing to API-enabled tools, and progressing to custom applications—often yields the most balanced combination of agility, safety, and strategic impact. This three-tiered pathway can likewise serve as a scaffold for developing AI literacy.

Recently, Dr. Han Lintao adapted the well-known CAT tool, Swordfish, for the Chinese context by integrating nearly all available large language models into its machine translation module and augmenting it with additional capabilities such as

Table 20 Three pathways to utilize AI services

Pathway	Typical Users/ Examples	Key Advantages	Primary Limitations	Best-Fit Scenarios
Provider Interfaces (Web/ App)	Individuals; educators; students; rapid one-off tasks	Lowest barrier to entry; Seamless updates and polished UX; Fast prototyping and just-in-time assistance	Limited customization and observability; Opaque parameters/ context management; Weak systems integration; manual workflows	Exploratory use, ad hoc drafting/ summarization, low-governance contexts
API-Enabled Tools (Third-Party Apps)	Teams using office suites, support platforms, analytics with LLM features	Versioned prompts and logging; Pipeline integration and audit trails; Configurable safeguards (filters, rate limits)	Indirect control over models/ configs; Constraints on pricing, latency, context by vendor	Operational efficiency with moderate governance, without heavy engineering
Custom Applications (Direct API/ Custom Models)	Orgs with engineering/ data teams; high-stakes or sensitive domains	Maximum architectural and governance control RAG, tool orchestration, multi-step workflows Fine-grained security, telemetry, and compliance	High engineering and maintenance costs; Ongoing evaluation, red-teaming, and risk management required	Differentiated products, sensitive data, strict compliance, scalable workflows

terminology extraction and an AI assistant. These enhancements address the tool's limitations in the contemporary AI era and position it as a compelling platform for AI-assisted translation production.

I have also developed a suite of AI-enabled applications to address concrete challenges in translation workflows. Notably, BilingualTranslator integrates large language model (LLM) translation, automated LLM-based post-editing, and human review into a unified pipeline for processing bilingual review files from Trados and memoQ (which are not fully adapted to AI age), thereby substantially reducing manual effort and accelerating turnaround. In addition, Smart TermExtractor leverages LLMs to identify, extract, translate, and verify terminology across multiple file formats, exporting validated termbases in TBX, SDLTB, CSV, or XLSX. Collectively, these tools operationalize human–AI collaboration to enhance efficiency, consistency, and delivery speed in professional translation settings (Fig. 3).

4.2 Learning to Design Good Prompts for Superior Translation Outcomes

Human interact with AI through prompts. In contemporary AI-human hybrid translation production, the quality of the prompt is a primary determinant of output fidelity, consistency, and efficiency. Well-crafted prompts explicitly define communicative intent, domain, audience, register, and constraints (e.g., terminology, style guides, length, and citation format), thereby reducing ambiguity and aligning model behavior with task specifications. By encoding disambiguation cues, error-avoidance rules, and evaluation criteria, high-quality prompts enhance terminological coherence, mitigate hallucinations and literalism, and improve handling of polysemy, idioms, and culturally bound expressions. Conversely, underspecified prompts shift interpretive burden to the model, increasing variance, propagation of source-language interference, and sensitivity to spurious context. Empirical practice further indicates that structured prompting—such as exemplars, stepwise reasoning instructions, and verifiable checklists—yields measurable gains in adequacy and fluency while decreasing post-editing effort. Accordingly, systematic prompt engineering constitutes a critical competency for achieving reliable, high-quality translation with large language models. Table 21 below gives a brief summary of the features of good prompts.

At the initial stage of training, learners may appropriately emulate established prompting frameworks—such as CRISPE, CO-STAR, or CRAFT—to internalize core principles of goal specification, role assignment, constraints, and evaluation criteria. However, sustainable gains in translation quality require progression beyond formulaic templates toward the principled design of task-specific prompts. This entails articulating communicative intent; specifying domain, register, and audience; constraining terminology and style guides; defining error tolerances and quality metrics; and encoding procedural steps for reasoning, verification, and post-editing. As learners' methodological awareness matures, they should iteratively refine prompts through empirical evaluation—A/B testing variants, logging outputs, and analyzing failure modes such as literalism, omission, terminological drift, or cultural misalignment. An effective strategy is meta-prompting: providing the model with the draft prompt and asking it to critique and revise for clarity, coverage, and enforceability, while justifying the modifications. This reflexive loop leverages the model as a prompt co-designer, producing prompts that are both operationally robust and context-sensitive. Ultimately, expertise in prompt engineering for translation is demonstrated not by adherence to a single framework, but by the capacity to synthesize constraints from the workflow, adapt to domain-specific risks, and codify them in prompts that yield reliable, auditable, and high-fidelity outputs with minimal human post-editing.

Table 21 Features of good prompts

Section	Subsection	Content
Clarity and Specificity	Clear objective	State exactly what you want (e.g., "Summarize this document in three bullets.")
	Defined scope	Limit the topic, length, or depth (e.g., "200–250 words" or "focus on financial impacts.")
	Concrete details	Provide explicit constraints, examples, formats, or required elements
Context and Relevance	Background information	Offer necessary context, audience, purpose, and assumptions
	Known constraints	Mention items the AI should avoid or prioritize (tone, formality, jargon level)
Structure and Predictability	Explicit structure	If a specific format is required, specify it (e.g., bullets, sections, YAML/JSON)
	Step-by-step expectations	For complex tasks, request a plan or approach first, followed by results
Realism and Feasibility	Feasible requests	Align prompts with the model's capabilities (e.g., avoid requesting real-time data unless provided or a retrieval method is specified)
	Checkpoints	Divide tasks into stages and request interim outputs to verify alignment
Testability and Debuggability	Edge cases	Instruct the model to consider potential edge cases or alternative interpretations
	Validation criteria	Specify how the answer will be evaluated (accuracy, completeness, consistency)
Safety and Ethics	Sensitive content handling	Indicate whether the prompt should avoid unsafe, biased, or harmful content
	Privacy considerations	Avoid sharing or requesting private or sensitive data unless necessary and appropriate
Reproducibility and Traceability	Source requests	Request sources or citations when appropriate
	Rationale	For explanations, provide a brief reasoning path

(continued)

Table 21 (continued)

Section	Subsection	Content
Style and Tone	Voice and audience	Specify tone (professional, formal, technical) and the target audience
	Format preferences	State preferences for formatting, e.g., headings, code blocks, or diagrams

5 Rethinking Translation Training: From Technique-Centered Pedagogy to Process-Oriented Human–AI Co-Creation

Traditional translation pedagogy—organized around discrete techniques (e.g., amplification, omission, transposition, modulation)—is increasingly misaligned with the realities of contemporary practice. The emergence of large language models (LLMs), integrated CAT ecosystems, and data-centric quality assurance has reconfigured translation as a socio-technical pipeline rather than a sequence of isolated textual maneuvers. A process-oriented, project-driven model centered on human–AI co-creation better reflects professional workflows and more effectively cultivates comprehensive translator competencies.

5.1 Limitations of Technique-Centered Training

Contemporary translator training faces critical gaps: by emphasizing discrete technique drills over end-to-end project reasoning, it overlooks how real workflows are shaped by tools, data, and teams. The result is a narrow skill set that struggles to transfer across tasks, align with instrumented practice, adapt to shifting contexts, produce valid assessments of professional performance, or prepare graduates for collaborative delivery. The table below outlines these limitations (Table 22).

5.2 Rationale for a Process-Oriented, Human–AI Co-Creation Model

Modern translator training should pivot from isolated techniques to process-aware, AI-augmented practice. The table below outlines five core principles that align education with real industry workflows, elevate human–AI collaboration, embed data governance, cultivate transferable, future-proof skills, and anchor quality management in measurable evidence (Table 23).

Table 22 Limitations of technique-centered training

Limitation	Key Issues
Narrow skill transferability	–Technique drills optimize for local textual operations, not for end-to-end problem solving across heterogeneous tasks (e.g., corpus preparation, terminology governance, risk assessment) – They underemphasize upstream (brief analysis, scoping, domain research) and downstream (QA, stakeholder feedback, delivery) stages that determine real-world quality and cost
Insufficient alignment with tool-mediated practice	– Modern translation is instrumented: termbases, TMs, quality frameworks (MQM/DQF), and LLM-assisted modules (RAG, auto post-editing) mediate decisions. Technique-centric syllabi marginalize data stewardship, prompt design, and metrics literacy
Static view of competence	– Emphasis on prescriptive moves (e.g., fixed equivalence strategies) neglects adaptive expertise needed to handle domain shift, multimodality, and evolving client constraints (style guides, regulatory requirements, privacy)
Limited assessment validity	– Assessments focused on micro-edits and "correctness" at sentence level fail to capture throughput, consistency, traceability, and risk management—key dimensions of professional performance
Underpreparedness for collaboration	– Contemporary translation is collaborative (PMs, reviewers, engineers, subject experts, and AI systems). Technique drills rarely cultivate coordination, communication, and role-based accountability

5.3 Core Components of the Proposed Pedagogy

This framework shifts translator training from technique drills to project-grounded, AI-enabled, end-to-end practice. It emphasizes real client contexts, deliberate human–AI collaboration, workflow literacy across pre/in/post stages, quantifiable quality management, and team discipline through role rotations—building skills that transfer across tools and evolving industry standards (Table 24).

5.4 Expected Learning Outcomes

By implementing this new pedagogy, we can expect outcomes that would prepare students for human-AI co-creation. These outcomes integrate tool fluency, empirical methods, strategic decision-making, and responsible practice to cultivate translators who can operate across end-to-end, AI-enabled workflows. Together, they emphasize not only how to deliver quality but how to scope, measure, optimize, and govern work in ways aligned with modern industry standards. Even if they do not engage in translation industry, such qualities will be transferable and beneficial to their future career (Table 25).

Table 23 Rationale for a process-oriented, human–AI co-creation model

Principle	Key Issues
Authentic alignment with industry workflows	Translation is now an integrated pipeline: intake → scoping → data prep → MT/LLM prompting → post-editing → terminology consolidation → QA → delivery → retro. Training should mirror this lifecycle
Augmented cognition over manual optimization	LLMs excel at first-pass generation, variant exploration, and routine consistency checks. Human expertise should shift toward prompt architecture, critical evaluation, error forensics, and context-sensitive decision making
Data—and governance-centric competence	Effective practice depends on terminology governance, version control, privacy/compliance, and quality telemetry. Process training embeds these literacies, which technique drills overlook
Transferable, future-proof skills	Process skills (requirements elicitation, experiment design, evaluation, tooling orchestration) generalize across tools and models, mitigating vendor lock-in and technological churn
Evidence-based quality management	Process frameworks support measurable KPIs (adequacy, fluency, consistency, turnaround, cost), enabling A/B testing of prompts, post-editing effort estimation, and continuous improvement

Table 24 Core components of the proposed pedagogy

Principle	Components & Focus
Project-driven learning	Students execute full-cycle projects with real or simulated client briefs, deliverables, timelines, and acceptance criteria, fostering accountability and professional realism
Human–AI collaboration by design	Prompt engineering for task, domain, and audience alignment; LLM-assisted workflows (MT + automatic post-editing + human review); retrieval-augmented generation using proprietary corpora; risk controls (hallucination detection, privacy, bias mitigation)
End-to-end workflow literacy	Pre-translation: scope definition, corpus curation, termbase seeding; In-translation: segmentation strategies, TM leverage, LLM orchestration; Post-translation: MQM/DQF evaluation, regression checks, terminology consolidation, packaging and delivery
Measurement and telemetry	Use of structured rubrics and metrics (e.g., HTER, BLEU/COMET with human adjudication), error typologies, and cost–quality trade-off analysis
Team roles and accountability	Rotations through roles (PM, lead translator, post-editor, terminologist, QA analyst, prompt designer), with version control and audit trails to cultivate collaborative discipline

Table 25 Expected learning outcomes

Outcome Category	Description
Technical fluency	Proficiency with CAT/MT/LLM tools; termbase management; secure data pipelines
Methodological rigor	Ability to design, test, and iterate prompts and workflows using empirical evidence and risk criteria
Strategic judgment	Task scoping; resource allocation; quality–cost–time optimization in contextually constrained scenarios
Ethical and compliance awareness	Data residency; confidentiality; attribution; responsible-AI practices (documentation; human-in-the-loop checks)

5.5 Implementation Suggestions

In the context of adapting translation practice to the AI era, the most crucial driver is cognitive innovation. This entails rethinking how translators understand, generate, validate, and integrate machine-assisted processes, so that human and artificial agents collaborate productively rather than compete for primacy (Table 26).

Cognitive innovation carries profound implications for curriculum and professional practice. Pedagogically, it necessitates the systematic integration of metacognitive training, decision-making under uncertainty, and human-AI workflow design across courses rather than confining these competencies to isolated modules. Practically, it demands redesigned processes that foreground critical evaluation of AI outputs, collaborative role reconfiguration between human and machine agents, and continuous, data-informed quality assurance. Together, these shifts realign learning objectives, assessment criteria, and organizational routines to support sustainable, high-fidelity human-AI co-creation in translation (Table 27).

Ensuring equitable access to AI in translation education requires institution-level provisioning that places instructors and students on symmetrical footing. This includes sandboxed CAT/LLM environments that safeguard data privacy while enabling experimentation with prompt engineering, post-editing, and workflow design; shared, version-controlled terminological resources and style guides to standardize usage and facilitate reproducible learning; and lightweight pedagogical MLOps that support prompt and evaluation versioning without imposing full DevOps complexity. Such infrastructure reduces capability gaps, establishes common pedagogical baselines, and enables rigorous, replicable inquiry into human–AI collaboration.

Equally vital is a supervisory and assessment regime that verifies students' critical engagement with AI outputs. A multidimensional framework should blend product quality metrics—such as MQM-based adequacy and fluency scores—with process indicators, including throughput and revision density, and corroborating collaboration evidence drawn from issue tracking and commit logs. Assignments must require transparent AI-use documentation (e.g., prompt histories and parameter settings),

Table 26 Key Dimensions of cognitive innovation for human–AI co-creative translation

Dimension	Core Idea	Practical Focus	Expected Outcomes
Cognitive reorientation over mere tool adoption	Merely adding AI tools is insufficient; a fundamental shift in cognitive frameworks is required	Reframe the role of automation; interpret AI outputs critically; appraise uncertainty and error systematically	Translators leverage AI as an augmenting partner rather than a replacement; improved judgment and reliability
Conceptual integration of humans and machines	Build a cohesive conception of work that fuses human cognitive strategies with algorithmic capabilities	Combine error detection, source-text analysis, and cultural adjudication with post-editing heuristics, terminology alignment, and data-driven QA	Higher efficiency and fidelity; smoother, integrated workflows
Metacognitive competencies as enablers	Higher-order skills enable calibrated use of AI suggestions	Develop metacognition, strategic planning, and reflective practice to decide when to trust, modify, or reject AI outputs	Robust decision-making under ambiguity; consistent quality control
Learning ecosystems and organizational cognition	Move beyond individual skills to systemic, culture-level modernization	Cultivate organizational and educational environments for iterative learning, AI-in-the-loop experimentation, and best-practice dissemination	Sustainable adaptation; continuous improvement and knowledge sharing

rationalized acceptance/modification/rejection of system suggestions, and provenance controls to ensure authorship integrity. By weighting both outcomes and the sophistication of underlying cognitive strategies, programs can foster accountable, reflective, and auditable human–AI translation practice.

Technique-centered training is a necessary but insufficient foundation in a field now defined by instrumented, collaborative, and data-driven workflows. A process-oriented, human–AI co-creation pedagogy, implemented through project-based learning and comprehensive workflow literacy, offers a more valid, scalable, and future-ready model for cultivating translators who can deliver reliable, auditable, and efficient outcomes in real-world settings.

Table 27 Implications for curriculum and practice in AI-augmented translation

Dimension	Core Directive	Illustrative Practices	Intended Outcomes
Curriculum design	Embed cognitive innovation as a core objective across modules	Integrate units on translation workflows, collaboration with nonhuman agents, and quality assessment that explicitly cultivate metacognitive and strategic thinking	Coherent, program-wide development of human–AI literacy and decision-making competence
Pedagogical approaches	Use active, reflective, and decision-focused learning methods	Scenario-based learning, reflective journals, and decision-making simulations requiring justification of AI-mediated choices, confidence calibration, and acceptability criteria	Calibrated judgment, transparent reasoning, and transferable evaluation heuristics
Assessment paradigms	Evaluate both outputs and underlying cognitive strategies	Rubrics that reward error analysis, rationale for AI acceptance/ modification/rejection, and adaptive workflow design	Higher-quality outcomes with demonstrable, auditable thought processes
Professional development	Sustain practitioner growth in AI-critical competencies	Ongoing training to cultivate discerning evaluation of AI outputs, continuous improvement, and responsible deployment of translation technologies	Mature professional practice, accountability, and sustainable adoption

6 Outlook of LLM Translation Agent

In the near future, LLM translation agent will further automate the translation workflow. Actually, Andrew Ng has already designed an experimental agent and open sourced on Github (For detail, visit https://github.com/andrewyng/translation-agent).

The foundational architecture of a large language model (LLM)-driven translation agent typically comprises the following core components:

Perception Module: This module is responsible for acquiring and interpreting input from various modalities, including text, images, and speech. It enables the agent to perceive its external environment and gather the contextual information necessary for translation tasks.

Core Processing Module (LLM): Functioning as the agent's "brain," the LLM serves as the central unit for natural language understanding, reasoning, decision-making, and output generation. It provides the linguistic competence and cognitive flexibility required for sophisticated language interactions.

Memory Module: Designed to store and retrieve information, this module manages both short-term and long-term memory. It allows the agent to retain prior interactions and apply contextual knowledge to enhance translation consistency and coherence.

Planning Module: This component decomposes user instructions into executable actions and dynamically adjusts strategies based on environmental feedback. It is essential for orchestrating the agent's workflow and ensuring efficient task completion.

Table 28 Competency framework in AI age

Layer	Traditional translation competence	New capabilities in the AI era	Characteristics of capability evolution
Core	Bilingual conversion capability; Cultural sensitivity	Human-LLM collaborative thinking; Critical Assessment; Multimodal processing capability	Shifting from monolingual conversion to cultural decoding and re-creation
Technical	Terminology Management; Basic CAT Tool Usage	Techniques AI Prompt Engineering; Information Mining with AI Search Engines; Deployment of LLMs and Open Source Tools; LLM Training and Fine-tuning; AI Agent Building	Technological tools have transitioned from auxiliary roles to symbiotic partners
Strategic	Fundamentals of Project Management	Translation strategy; Data security governance	Evolving from an executor to a decision-making participant

Action Module: Responsible for implementing the agent's decisions, this module generates translated output, operates external tools, or interacts with users. It directly connects the agent's internal processes with external task execution.

Tool Integration Module: This module provides access to external tools—such as search engines, databases, and code interpreters—that augment the agent's problem-solving and information-retrieval capabilities, especially for complex or domain-specific tasks.

Collaboration Module: In multi-agent systems, this module facilitates coordination, information exchange, and collaborative task-solving among agents, thereby enhancing overall system efficiency and performance.

Self-Reflection Module: Enabling introspection and performance evaluation, this module generates feedback on task execution and supports continual learning and optimization. It is vital for adaptive improvement and error correction over time.

This is called Multi-agent translation, a translation approach or system in which multiple autonomous agents—often AI models or modules—collaborate to complete translation tasks (Fig. 4). These agents may specialize in different subtasks or operate across different layers of the translation workflow, working together to improve overall quality, efficiency, and adaptability. Refer to Wu et al. (2024) for more details.

Such multi-agent translation will be the dominant paradigm of translation production, which will be the Industrial Revolution 4.0 in translation. In this paradigm,

Table 29 Concentric circles of translation craftsmanship

Aspect	Details	Interrelation with other components
Cognition	Foundational understanding, including what translation is, why it's done, and its complexities (e.g., meaning, emotion, culture). Shapes decision-making, tool selection, and ethics	Underpins competence by providing the knowledge base; influences operation by guiding methods and strategies; essential for achieving effective outcomes
Competence	Integration of linguistic, cultural, and technical skills, modeled as an expert knowledge system with sub-competences (e.g., bilingual, strategic)	Built on cognition, as skills are developed from understanding; enables effective operations by providing the necessary abilities; contributes to outcomes through quality and appropriateness
Operation	Practical methods and tools, such as bilingual transformation, cultural adaptation, and LLMs. Includes process-oriented activities like decision-making and problem-solving	Shaped by cognition (guiding approach) and competence (enabling execution); directly impacts outcomes by determining how the translation is carried out
Outcome	Communicative effectiveness, meeting client needs, resonating with audiences, and adhering to standards. Examples: commercial translations convey brand tone; literary translations retain cultural flavor	Result of cognition, competence, and operation working together; feedback from outcomes can refine cognition and competence, creating a dynamic system

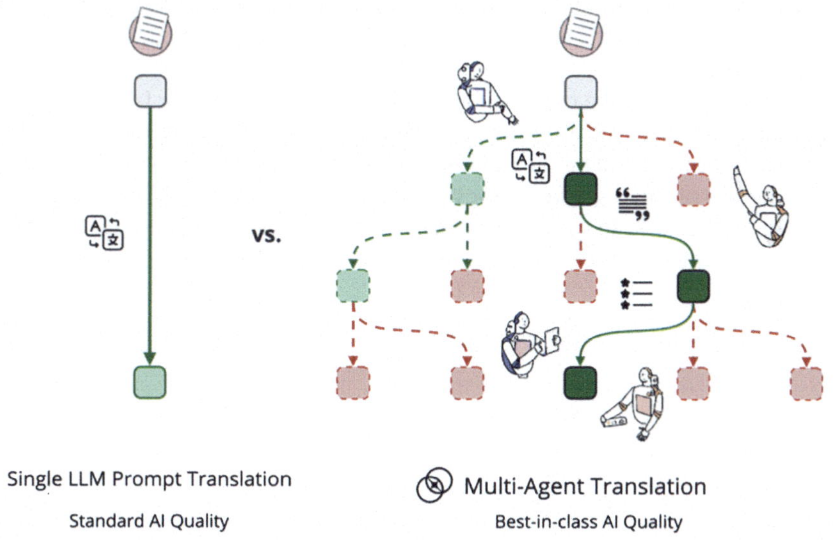

Fig. 4 Single LLM prompt translation versus Multi-Agent translation. (*Source* https://www.onesky.ai/)

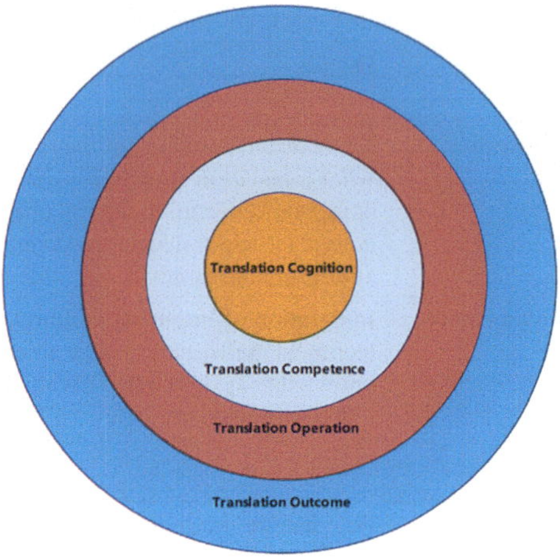

Fig. 5 Translation craftsmanship

the requirement for human intervention is even more considerably reduced, further compressing the room of employment for average translators.

Single-agent translation is simpler and may suffice for straightforward, low-volume tasks, such as basic document translation. However, it can struggle with complexity, scalability, and handling cultural nuances, particularly in AI-driven systems. Multi-agent collaborative translation, on the other hand, offers superior performance for complex, high-volume, or culturally sensitive tasks due to its ability to leverage specialization, collaboration, and parallel processing. This makes it particularly effective for literary translation and ultra-long texts, as evidenced by recent research (Wu et al., 2024).

The choice between the two approaches depends on factors like task complexity, budget, and scalability needs. For instance, businesses seeking high-quality localization for marketing content might prefer multi-agent systems, while those with limited budgets and simple texts might opt for single-agent AI solutions. The evolving nature of AI, with frameworks like AutoGen and CrewAI, suggests that multi-agent systems will continue to gain traction, especially as computational resources become more accessible.

7 Transformation of Roles and New Competency Framework

7.1 Shift in Core Tasks and Redefinition of the Translator's Roles

The emergence of Human-LLM translation paradigm leads to two major transformations: a shift in the translator's core tasks and a redefinition of their professional role. Traditionally, translators acted as text generators, focused on direct source-to-target linguistic transfer with an emphasis on lexical fidelity and grammatical accuracy.

In the new paradigm, routine translation tasks are increasingly automated, repositioning human translators as evaluators and quality controllers. Their primary responsibilities now involve assessing the semantic accuracy, terminological consistency, and contextual appropriateness of AI-generated outputs. This evaluative role requires not only bilingual competence, but also cross-cultural and cross-domain expertise.

Translators are also becoming strategic decision-makers. Rather than solely converting text, they now integrate and assess multiple linguistic resources, such as LLM outputs, translation memory (TM), and terminology databases, making context-sensitive choices aligned with communicative goals. For example, choosing between "非同质化代币" and "NFT" depends on the technical literacy of the target audience, just as literary translation involves strategic decisions between foreignization and domestication based on cultural reception.

In addition to micro-level editing, translators now engage in macro-level planning: determining what content to translate, when, and by which method (e.g., full human translation, post-editing, or selective translation). This broader scope aligns translation workflows with organizational objectives and user needs.

Parallel to this shift, the translator's role is expanding from linguistic mediator to intercultural communicator. Particularly in domains like international marketing, translators adapt AI-generated content to resonate with local audiences, recontextualizing cultural references, adjusting rhetorical strategies, and modifying formats to suit local norms and expectations. This requires not only linguistic precision but also cultural sensitivity, market insight, and strategic communication skills.

The translator's evolving role, as evaluator, strategist, and communicator, signals a fundamental transformation in the profession. Translation is no longer a mechanistic act of linguistic substitution but a hybrid, creative process that merges technological efficiency with human judgment. Translators must now master not only language, but also AI tools, quality assurance protocols, and intercultural dynamics.

Ultimately, this shift redefines the value of translation as a socially consequential activity. The translator's competitive advantage lies in their ability to critically engage with AI: leveraging its strengths while compensating for its limitations through contextual discernment, emotional intelligence, and cultural intuition. This human–AI synergy affirms the continued relevance of translators and elevates translation as a key facilitator of global communication.

7.2 *Competency Framework in AI Age*

Much has been discussed about the translation competence (Schaffner & Adab, 2000) and several frameworks have been proposed, such as PACTE model (PACTE, 2003) or EMT model (EMT, 2017). However, the new hybrid translation production requires a new set of skills. Combining AI literacy with traditional translation craftsmanship while developing a set of skills adapted to new translation production methods can make you a super translator.

The Competency in AI age is a 3-layered hierarchy (Table 28).

Echoing Sinek's golden circle, I conceptualized translation craftsmanship as a dynamic interplay of four concentric circles in 2024: cognition, competence, operation, and outcome. This framework positions translation not merely as linguistic transfer but as a cognitively grounded, professionally enacted, and socially evaluated communicative act (Fig. 5).

Cognition is the core, competence is the externalization of cognition, operation is the implementation of competence and outcome is the realization of the operation. These four form an interdependent, evolving system in translation. Cognition provides the foundation, competence and operation implement this understanding, and the outcome reflects their success, judged by communicative effectiveness. In the AI era, translators must navigate this system while leveraging technology to enhance their work, ensuring that cognitive depth and human touch remain central to achieving high-quality translations. This framework not only clarifies the translator's role but also highlights the need for continuous learning and adaptation in a rapidly evolving field (Table 29).

7.3 *Training Qualified "Human-AI Coupled Translators" in the AI Era*

The disruption of translation paradigm puts great pressure on current translation education, which devotes too much time and energy into the teaching of language transfer skills. Such techniques of the Paleolithic Age are not suitable for the AI era. Today's translators need a new set of skills adapted to the new production paradigm.

To train competent translators in the AI era, translation education must move beyond traditional paradigms and adopt an integrated framework that combines linguistic and cultural depth, technological proficiency, and cognitive collaboration. Central to this approach is reinforcing the translator's irreplaceable role in interpreting nuanced cultural and linguistic meanings. This involves cultivating refined bilingual sensitivity, understanding implicit language structures, and engaging with authentic, real-world discourse to move beyond mechanical translation patterns.

Equally important is the development of technological literacy, whereby translators evolve from passive tool users to strategic collaborators. This includes mastering AI-powered tools, designing effective prompts, recognizing the limitations of large language models, and establishing rigorous quality control processes throughout the translation workflow. For a basic AI competency, refer to the UNESCO frameworks (UNESCO, 2024a, 2024b).

Human-AI collaboration also requires a fundamental shift in translator identity, from language producer to orchestrator of meaning, where humans handle cultural adaptation and rhetorical choices, while AI supports data-intensive tasks such as terminology retrieval and draft generation. Critical engagement with AI outputs is essential, as is familiarity with common system errors and a working knowledge of AI's underlying principles. Translators must also possess interdisciplinary awareness, enabling them to assess AI-generated content within specialized domains.

A progressive, practice-based training model supports this transformation, beginning with controlled human-AI interaction and advancing to full project management in real-world settings. Mentorship, reflective practice, and adherence to ethical standards further reinforce professional development. Evaluation frameworks should assess not only cultural and linguistic appropriateness, but also technological fluency and the effectiveness of human–machine coordination. For instance, translation challenges that simulate high-pressure, mixed-method tasks can help gauge both efficiency and quality.

Ultimately, human-AI translation is not about replacement but augmentation, leveraging AI to broaden the scope and scale of translation while relying on human insight to preserve depth, nuance, and creative agency. The ideal translator acts as the conductor of this human–machine symphony, skillfully aligning technological tools with the interpretive power of human intelligence.

8 Conclusion

The transformation of translation production can be understood along four key dimensions.

First, on the technological front, the field has shifted from NMT to large language models (LLMs), which empower the whole process of translation and offer context-aware, high-quality translations that surpass earlier approaches.

Second, workflow processes have evolved from linear, human-led models to dynamic human–AI collaboration. Human–AI interactions enhance both quality and efficiency and support iterative refinement and quality assurance.

Third, the professional role of translators has expanded from linguistic executors to strategic collaborators. Modern translators now act as prompt engineers and workflow coordinators, requiring new competencies in AI literacy, prompt engineering, and interdisciplinary collaboration.

To remain competitive amid technological disruption, translators should consider engaging in continuous professional development by acquiring up-to-date knowledge of large language models (LLMs), prompt engineering, and data literacy.

Fourth, large language models (LLMs) help eliminate interdisciplinary barriers while reducing reliance on domain experts and native-language reviewers. By autonomously generating dynamic terminology and ensuring structural coherence in technical texts, LLMs effectively bridge knowledge gaps across specialized fields. They also exhibit strong command of pragmatic language use and cultural localization, accurately rendering idiomatic expressions and metaphors.

However, LLMs continue to face challenges when dealing with highly specialized jargon and culturally nuanced content, such as dialects and internet slang. Therefore, an optimal translation workflow integrates LLM-generated drafts with expert human refinement, balancing machine-driven efficiency with the depth, accuracy, and contextual sensitivity that only human insight can provide. As Steve Jobs remarked, "Technology alone is not enough. It's the marriage of technology and the liberal arts that yields the results that make our hearts sing." In the era of artificial intelligence, the essence of translation lies not in technological advancement but in the enduring value of human craftsmanship and cultural insight.

Unlike the rapid acquisition of AI tool proficiency, the core skills of professional translation, linguistic mastery, cultural literacy, strategic thinking, and critical analysis, require long-term cultivation. These enduring capabilities are essential for navigating AI-enhanced translation workflows and for maintaining professional excellence in a competitive environment.

Ultimately, translation is not a mechanical act of symbol substitution but a process of cross-cultural meaning reconstruction. While AI excels at replicating known patterns, it falters in the face of ambiguity, contextual complexity, and cultural depth. In the foreseeable future, translation will continue to rely on human–machine collaboration, where algorithmic efficiency supports, but cannot replace the cultural intuition and ethical judgment of human translators.

References

Chan, S. (Ed.). (2018). *The Human Factor in Machine Translation*. Routledge.

Changshuan, L. (2022). *Theory and Practice of Non-Literary Translation* (非文学翻译理论与实践(理解 表达 变通 上\下)). China Translation and Publishing House.

EMT Expert Group. (2017). *Competences for Professional Translators, Experts in Multilingual And Multimedia Communication* [White paper]. European Commission. https://ec.europa.eu/emt

Gao et al. (2023). *How to Design Translation Prompts for ChatGPT: An Empirical Study*. https://arxiv.org/pdf/2304.02182v2

Getto, G., Labriola, J., Ruszkiewicz, S. (2022). Content Strategy: A How-to Guide. Routledge.

Koponen, M., Mossop, B., Robert, I., & Scocchera,G. (2021). *Translation Revision And Post-Editing: Industry Practices and Cognitive Processes*. Routledge.

Lasswell, H. D. (1948). The structure and function of communication in society. In L. Bryson (Ed.), *Communication and public policy* (pp. 95–100). Wiley.

PACTE Group. (2003). Building a translation competence model. *Meta: Translators' Journal*, *48*(2), 127–138.

Schaffner, C., & Adab, B. (2000). *Developing Translation Competence*. John Benjamins Publishing Company.

Sinek, S. (2009). *Start With Why: How Great Leaders Inspire Everyone to Take Action*. Penguin.

UNESCO. (2024). *AI Competency Framework for Students*. United Nations Educational, Scientific and Cultural Organization.

UNESCO. (2024). *AI Competency Framework for Teachers*. United Nations Educational, Scientific and Cultural Organization.

Vaswani, A., Shazeer, N., Parmar, N., Uszkoreit, J., Jones, L., Gomez, A. N., Kaiser, Ł., & Polosukhin, I. (2017). Attention is all you need. In I. Guyon et al. (Eds.), *Advances in Neural Information Processing Systems* (Vol. 30, pp. 5998–6008).

Wu et al. (2024). *Beyond Human Translation: Harnessing Multi-Agent Collaboration for Translating Ultra-Long Literary Texts*. https://arxiv.org/pdf/2405.11804

Wenzhong He is an associate professor of linguistics and translation studies at Zhejiang University, China. His research focuses on corpus-based linguistic and translation studies, translation technologies and technical communication. He is the author of *A Cognitive Account of Middle Constructions* (2007) and *Explorations in AI Translation* (forthcoming) has published extensively in journals such as *Foreign Language Teaching and Research*.

Postdigital Translation in the Age of Algorithms: Implications for Practice and Pedagogy

Tong King Lee

Abstract This chapter addresses the nature and scope of translation in the advent of generative artificial intelligence (GenAI). It argues for a conception of translation which exceeds the act of transferring content from one language into another and encompasses an entire transaction from the commission of an assignment to its consumption by the end-user. This enlarged view is pertinent today as platforms like ChatGPT are demonstrating enhanced translation competencies on the level of meaning transfer. Drawing on key rubrics from Australia's National Accreditation Authority for Translators and Interpreters (NAATI), the American Translators Association's (ATA) job task analysis, and the European Masters in Translation (EMT), the chapter proposes a paradigm shift in translator training and translation quality assessment—one which pivots away from language competency toward intercultural competency, research competency, technological competency, and service provision competency.

Keywords Postdigital translation · Paradigm shift · Translation certification · Total language solution

This chapter argues that in light of techno-capitalist imperatives in the present age, translation as practice, profession, and pedagogy is at the crux of what philosophers of science call a model crisis, and must experience a paradigm shift to manage and thrive on developments in generative artificial intelligence (GenAI). A few terms need unpacking here. In his classic *The Structure of Scientific Revolution* Thomas Kuhn postulates that when a "normal" science drifts to a point where its prevailing paradigm— "the key theories, instruments, values and metaphysical assumptions that comprise the disciplinary matrix" (Bird, 2018: n.p.)—is unable to cope with cumulative challenges or "anomalies", a "crisis" or failure in confidence can occur (Kuhn, 1970: 66–76). As Bird (2018: n.p.) explains:

T. K. Lee (✉)
University of Hong Kong, Pok Fu Lam, Hong Kong
e-mail: leetk@hku.hk

T. Yin et al. (eds.), *AI Through LLMs*, New Frontiers in Translation Studies,
https://doi.org/10.1007/978-981-95-4798-2_3

> A particularly troublesome anomaly is one that undermines the practice of normal science. For example, an anomaly might reveal inadequacies in some commonly used piece of equipment, perhaps by casting doubt on the underlying theory. If much of normal science relies upon this piece of equipment, normal science will find it difficult to continue with confidence until this anomaly is addressed. A widespread failure in such confidence Kuhn calls a "crisis".

Now when a paradigm-in-crisis is overridden by a competing paradigm, the disciplinary matrix of the field would come to be revised. This is the stage of "revolution", which eventually results in the emergence of a new paradigm. According to Kuhn, the worldview (comprising taxonomies and lexical networks) ensuing from this new paradigm is "incommensurable" with that under the preceding one. This is the Kuhn Cycle.

1 Evidence of Crisis and Potential for Paradigm Shift

Although machine translation (MT) has been around with us for many decades, the surge in interest in GenAI has "rocked the boat", so to speak, to an extent hitherto unseen. On this view, GenAI can be seen as an anomaly in the history of MT, and of translation more generally. If we regard, for the sake of argument, translation as a "normal science" in the Kuhnian sense of the term, then the anomaly that is GenAI has begun to undermine the confidence of the practitioners of this science. But has this failure in confidence come to such a widespread degree as to constitute a "crisis"?

The answer is probably yes; and if not yet, then soon enough. I would suggest that the immediate reaction of the translation community to the onset of GenAI in November 2022 is indicative of a model crisis in translation. In November 2023, the American Translators Association issued a statement with a similar tenor, listing several potential problems with using AI and stressing the importance of involving "expert translators and interpreters" in decisions about when and how to employ AI:

> As the latest language technology tools gain traction, stakeholders need to be aware of when AI is being used and its limitations. That starts with transparency about AI-generated translations, with appropriate disclaimers about the potential for suboptimal results, such as miscommunication, AI hallucinations, gender bias, inconsistencies across language pairs, and potential disclosure of confidential information. ATA believes that additional safeguards addressing these concerns are warranted and encourages their development and enforcement. A good first step for all interested parties is to ensure that whenever AI tools are being used, *expert translators and interpreters—who have the language skills, training, and experience to determine how and when to employ them*—are involved in this process. (ATA, 2023a)

A similar tenor is struck when Société française des traducteurs warns that using free AI tools for translating incurs tangible and intangible costs. Among other things, these include "foregoing confidentiality" as well as "legal, economic, liability, security, reputational, manipulation; as well as error risks"; "misinformation, falsification and data manipulation"; "mind-numbing fatigue" from postediting of machine translations; accentuation of cultural inequalities due to the dominance of global languages in AI; and, due to AI's "phenomenal consumption of energy and natural resources (electricity to power data centers, water to cool them, etc.)", environmental depletion in contravention of the Paris Agreement on Climate Change and the UN sustainable development goals (Steering Committee of the Société française des traducteurs, 2024).

Witness again a statement put forth by the European Council of Literary Translators' Associations on the matter. Premised on the maxim Machines Are Not Translators, the statement puts out demands to anchor the legal rights, professional integrity, and humanistic values of (human) translators. Inter alia, it urges for accountability and transparency on the part of content producers by declaring GenAI usage on the final output, and for fair compensation to translators for their role in the commodity chain. It warns of the standardization of translation under GenAI, with the consequence of "impoverishing written cultures and languages in general through, among other things, priming bias (the tendency to be influenced by the first option given to us by the machine) and self-pollution (the machine learning from itself)". And it reminds us that translation is essentially a creative enterprise that should be protected as "a national and international literary treasure" and as part of "humanity's cultural heritage" (CEATL, 2022). A rather different kind of manifesto is set out by UK's Institute of Translation and Interpreting—a Slow Translation Manifesto (in the style of such similar movements as slow food and slow tourism) that offers the antidote to the pitfalls of GenAI. Thus, as opposed to the instancy of machine translation, Slow Translation advocates "artistry over automation", "quality", "high ethical standards", and demonstrable "cross-cultural competence" to caution against the temptation of using GenAI a quick fix in translation (ITI, 2024).

It is not difficult to infer from these statements and manifestos that GenAI has aroused a high degree of anxiety among professional translation communities. This is symptomatic of Kuhn's crisis stage insofar as it indicates a siege mentality, resulting in a confidence crunch in human translation that is now in need of defence. All of this is very understandable in light of the proliferation of software and mobile applications purporting to deliver high quality translations at the mere click of a button. More pertinent, however, is the nature of our response to GenAI. Going by the Kuhn Cycle, is translation headed toward the stage that comes after crisis, namely, revolution and change? Or back to where it came from the stage of so-called normal science? Based on the manifestos, it appears that translators are clutching on to the last vestiges of the humanist paradigm of translation—the stage of "normal science" in the field. As a corollary, the potential revolution that GenAI is engendering is pushed against, or at least cautioned against. This chapter argues for a reversal of such a move. It advocates a Kuhnian paradigm shift under which the translator's professional persona and the ontology of translation itself would need to be changed. This shift would herald what I call Postdigital Translation Studies, where translating would evolve into a total language solution with implications for both practice and pedagogy.

2 Leveraging: The Certification Model vs the Multicompetence Model

My central argument revolves around the term "leveraging", used in financial circles to mean using financial instruments or borrowed capital to amplify potential returns on investments. In present usage leveraging means pivoting from the Certification model to the Multicompetence model by proactively tapping into the translation capacities of GenAI to extend the translator's spectrum of literacies beyond language per se. The Certification model refers to the assessment model that informs institutionalized translator certification or accreditation programs; it is also a dominant pedagogical model underpinning translator training programs in tertiary institutions. Generally speaking, this model privileges translating as a linear process with reference to some preexisting text. The Multicompetence model, on the other hand, entails a wide spectrum of knowledge, skills, and abilities/attributes (KSAs) that do not directly pertain to the linear translating act but may nonetheless implicate translation as part of a broader enterprise. These include project management, service provision, practical research, intercultural competence, and digital literacy, which together form a constellation or assemblage into which linear translating may be inserted.

Going from the Certification model to the Multicompetence model means leveraging on GenAI potentialities to pivot from KSAs relating to linear translating toward KSAs relating to a broader notion called the translational—a penumbra of things including but not limited to translating. This leveraging thus involves shifting from a narrow conception of translating as "moving words across papers" 搬字過紙 (a Cantonese expression for literal translation) to an enlarged conception that conceives of translation as an entire transaction—or what I call a total language solution—as opposed to a discrete linguistic act. As we will see in a moment, some of the ingredients for such a paradigm shift already exist in various established reference standards for translation. What we need is a *discourse* (in the Foucauldian sense) that allows us to pivot away from the nuts and bolts of translating toward key competencies that are hitherto relatively marginal, for it is these marginal competencies that will provide multilingual professionals with the niche they need in the age of GenAI. The paradigm shift mentioned earlier is geared toward the generation of such a discourse.

Let us look at one case in point. In 2009, ATA conducted a Job Task Analysis (JTA) as part of a comprehensive review of its translator certification program. The aim of the exercise was to identify KSAs needed to perform professional translation services competently and which will dovetail into their certification scheme. 13 knowledge areas, 13 skills, and 10 abilities, for a total of 36 KSAs were identified, among which the following were found to be most salient (Koby & Melby, 2013: 183 with minor adaptations).

Knowledge: Grammar and vocabulary knowledge for a language pair have the highest importance

Skills: Terminology research and general writing skills have the highest importance

Abilities/Attributes: Ability to read a source language and write in a target language has the highest importance. Thoroughness, meticulousness, and attention-to-detail

These KSAs exemplify the Certification model, which is premised on a notion of translation as a linear process going from one end to the other. This manifests in more concrete terms in the Framework for Standardized Error Marking adopted by the ATA Certification Program updated in 2023 (ATA, 2023b). This is a set of grading rubrics that operates on a demerit-point system for translation errors. These errors, grouped under the three categories, are given abbreviated forms. Under "target language mechanics", we have **G** (Grammar), **SYN** (Syntax), **WF/PS** (Word Form/ Part of Speech), **SP/CH** (Spelling/Character), **C** (Capitalization), **D** (Diacritical marks/Accent), **P** (Punctuation). Under "meaning transfer", there is **A** (Addition), **O** (Omission), **T** (Terminology), **FA** (Faux ami), **V** (Verb form), **AMV** (Ambiguity), **COH** (Cohesion), **F** (Faithfulness), **MU** (Misunderstanding of source text), **IND** (Indecision), **UNF** (Unfinished). And under "writing quality" are **U** (Usage), **TT** (Text Type, failure to follow Translation Instructions), **R** (Register), and **ST** (Style).

These abbreviations resemble a system of codes; indeed, the grading sheet puts them under the heading "Code". Examiners are required to indicate the number of marks to be deducted for each item. To do this, they tick one out of five boxes preset in neat gradations of 1, 2, 4, 8, and 16—it is not possible to deduct 7 marks or 12.5 marks. Restrictions pertain to different categories. A ceiling of four points is set for target language mechanics as well as for writing quality; presumably, this means for each item under these two categories, the maximum number of points that may be demerited is 4, whereas for items under meaning transfer, that number can go up to 16. Three further instructions are given: "A grader may stop marking errors when score reaches 40 error points (mark such exams 40+)"; "A grader may award a quality point for each of up to three instances of exceptional translation"; "Quality points are subtracted from the error point total to yield a final score. A passage with a score of 18 or more points receives a grade of Fail".

For translation assessment purposes this is a very well-designed rubric. It achieves what all good rubrics should do, which is to facilitate rigorous and uniform marking by setting down tight parameters and precise restrictions. And in virtue of this rigour, it is easy to imagine how this set of metrics can be coded into an algorithm. The point becomes clearer when we turn to another related document titled "Flowchart for Error Point Decision" (ATA, 2023b), in which micro-decisions undertaken by a marker of translations are mapped into a several tiers of "yes" and "no" options culminating in deductible points. Hence, for example, in terms of mechanics, if the answer to the question "Error apparent to any attentive reader" is yes, this leads on to "Error apparent to a typical target reader? (text still intelligible)"; and if the answer to the latter is still yes, the marker is led to the question "Error disruptive to a typical target reader? (effort required for understanding)". Answering the last question to the affirmative leads to a deduction in four points. At each tier, a "no" answer will lead the marker in the other direction, leading to different result. A similar flowchart is designed for the metric "translation transfer/strategy error (identifiable by comparing to source text)", with layers of parameters coding different severities of transfer error, for instance, whether the transfer error leads to a "slight effect"; a "marked difference in meaning" whose effect is "limited in scope"; or a "glaring difference in meaning" whose effect is "limited to the immediate context of the error"; or if the text is rendered altogether "unusable" by a serious transfer error. One may argue that each of the micro-decisions still entails human judgment, and therefore that human intervention is indispensable. This argument is weakened by the fact that GenAI has been shown to be able to annotate text for the purposes of foreign language teaching simply through the felicitous use of prompts. It does not seem at all far-fetched to suggest that each of the micro-decisions in ATA's error point schema could be encoded in an algorithm, given that they are already conceived in the format of a decision flowchart.

Assuming, for the sake of argument, that we can fully encode these error point decisions into an algorithm. The immediate consequence is that translations can now be graded by machines. More than that: it is not implausible that an intelligent system can use these parameters, initially designed for human markers, to produce translations of the desired quality by automation. This kind of machinic reflexivity, so integral to deep learning, is not the stuff of fantasy. Lest it be misunderstood, I am not suggesting that the KSAs pertaining to mechanics and language transfer no longer need to be learnt by human translators; what I am saying, rather, is that they are *necessary but no longer sufficient*, given that they can partially if not substantially be executed by algorithmic systems. In other words, the Certification model, in particular the salient KSAs pertaining to transfer and stylistic competences, can potentially be delegated to GenAI, giving space for human translators to develop other competencies beyond translating.

3 Pivoting: From Translation to Total Language Solution

What are these other competencies? Despite the wording here, my argument is that these "other" competencies are not peripheral but core. As a case in point, let us turn to another translation quality assessment framework: the European Master's of Translation (EMT) Competence Framework 2022 (EMT, 2022).

The framework comprises five components. The first two components, labelled Language and Culture (transcultural and sociolinguistic awareness and communicative skills) and Translation (strategic, methodological and thematic competence), share a list of 14 learning objectives ("Students know how to …") which, for present purposes, are coextensive with KSAs. These include knowledge and transfer competencies familiar to applied translation studies, for instance, "Summarise, rephrase, restructure, and shorten a message and adapt it to market needs rapidly and accurately in at least one target language, using written and/or spoken communication". But aspects of functionalist approaches to translation are evident in the list; for instance, the notion of "fit for purpose", which aligns with Skopos theory, is invoked in the KSA that reads: "Translate general and domain-specific material in one or several fields from one or several source languages into their target language(s), producing a 'fit for purpose' translation". In connection with this functionalist perspective, the need to develop pre-translation preparatory skills is emphasized, for instance: "Carry out research to evaluate the relevance and reliability of information sources with regard to translation needs". The more advanced concept of translation as adaptation appears to underpin the KSA "Translate and mediate in specific intracultural and intercultural contexts, for example, those involving public service translation (and interpreting), website or video-game localisation and accessibility, community management, etc." Interestingly, the last KSA for the two competencies relates to postediting MT output: "Post-edit MT output using style guides and terminology glossaries to maintain quality standards in MT-enhanced translation projects". It is important to appreciate that some of these KSAs exceed the usual concern with informational accuracy and mechanical felicity. It is these KSAs that need foregrounding in the GenAI age. Whereas hitherto things like research, media adaptation, and postediting are seen as auxiliary, they should now be seen as essential, for these are the areas that—for now, at least—require a degree of creative and critical intervention.

The next several KSAs in the EMT framework pertain to the category Technology, which includes "all the knowledge and skills used to implement and advise on the use of *present and future translation technologies* within the translation process. It also includes basic knowledge of machine translation technologies and the ability to implement machine translation according to potential needs" (EMT, 2022; emphasis added). This theme is obviously relevant to translating to the topic at hand; it will conceivably feature in the curricula and pedagogies of translation training programs, including those not exclusively designed around MT. Adapting and updating the KSAs drawn up by EMT (2022) under this category to a GenAI context would yield learning objectives along the following lines:

- Use the most relevant GenAI applications, and adapt rapidly to emerging resources having critically assessed their relevance and the impact of change on their work practices
- Make effective use of GenAI, search engines, corpus-based tools, text analysis tools, computer-assisted translation (CAT), and quality assurance (QA) tools where appropriate
- Pre-process, process and manage files and other media/sources as part of the translation workflow, e.g., outputs from different GenAI platforms and multimedia files
- Understand the basics of GenAI and other networked systems and their impact on the translation process, and integrate GenAI into a translation workflow where appropriate
- Recognise the importance and value of networked models, demonstrating GenAI literacy
- Apply other tools in support of language and translation technology, such as workflow management tools mediated by GenAI

The points on adapting to emerging language technologies and managing translation workflows, already present in the original EMT framework, are especially key. They relate to the networked logistics around translating at the frontline that will be subject to many contingencies in the age of GenAI. In my view, these KSAs should constitute a salient skillset for professional translation training more generally, at least on par with if not more privileged than language and meaning transfer competencies.

Advanced digital literacy, in other words, is a prerequisite, not a mere good-to-have, in the new order of things in translating. It is a cornerstone in the pivoting from the Certification model toward the Multicompetence model.

It is in this connection that the last two sets of competencies under the EMT deserve special attention. These are labeled Personal and Interpersonal and Service Provision. The former pertains to "soft skills" to enhance one's adaptability and employability in the workplace (EMT, 2022):

- Plan and manage time (including complying with deadlines)
- Manage workload, cognitive load, stress and critical professional situations
- Work both autonomously and in virtual, multicultural and multilingual teams, using appropriate communication technologies
- Use social media responsibly for professional purposes
- Take account of and adapt the organisational and physical ergonomics of the working environment
- Continuously self-evaluate, update and develop competences and skills through personal strategies and collaborative learning and acknowledge the importance of lifelong learning

These skills are formulated in such a generic way as to be applicable to any field and industry; and by dint of this genericity they generally do not feature in the curricula of academic translation programmes. It is hard to imagine that ergonomics, for instance, would be expressly taught as a topic in a translation course. It is therefore significant that the EMT expressly includes these workplace survival skills as learning objectives, suggesting that they should have a role in the translator training. Yet the placement of Personal and Interpersonal after Language and Culture, Translation, and Technology also implies that they are relatively backgrounded. Such prioritization needs to be changed in the wake of GenAI, which should prompt us to leverage algorithmic platforms such as LLMs (large language models) and pivot toward personal and interpersonal skills that require *affective and embodied nuance*—something that cannot yet be converted into computational formulae and therefore deserves investment on the part of human translators.

Exactly the same point applies to Service Provision. This final set of KSAs under the EMT encompasses skills "relating to the implementation of translation and, more generally, to language services in a professional context", ranging from "awareness of clients, commissioners and users and negotiation through to project management and quality assurance" (EMT, 2022).

- Monitor and take account of new societal and language industry demands, new market requirements and emerging job profiles
- Approach existing clients and find new clients through prospecting and marketing strategies using the appropriate written and oral communication techniques
- Clarify the requirements, objectives and purposes of the client, recipients of the language service and other stakeholders and offer the appropriate services to meet those requirements

- Interact at all stages with the client (negotiate deadlines, rates/invoicing, working conditions, access to information, contracts, rights, responsibilities, language service specifications, tender specifications, offer feedback, etc.)
- Organise, budget and manage translation projects involving single or multiple translators and/or other service providers
- Understand and implement the standards applicable to the provision of a language service
- Apply the quality management and quality assurance procedures required to meet pre-defined quality standards and manage client feedback and complaints
- Critically assess and work within the ethical principles (such as confidentiality, fair competition, impartiality) defined in codes of ethics and guides of good practice
- Network with other translators and language service providers, including via professional associations, events and social media so as to improve individual and collective professional visibility
- Analyse and critically review language services and policies and suggest improvement strategies as an extension to their social and economic responsibility

Ethics does occupy a place in translator training, and would obviously come to the forefront, as evidenced by debates on the ethics of using GenAI since the inception of LLMs. However, things like client management, budgeting, and networking are less obvious topics for standard pedagogies in the translation classroom. In my opinion, service provision capacities such as those stipulated by EMT above would be increasingly important with the intensification of techno-capitalism, whereby technology and commodification go hand in hand in penetration of all aspects of everyday life. The implication of this is that these KSAs, prima facie unrelated to translating, will now need to be integrated into a more holistic paradigm for translator training that focuses on the concept of total language solution. This is the paradigm shift alluded to at the beginning of this chapter, namely the shift from an instrumentalist framework that prioritizes language transfer skills to a multicompetency framework that emplaces translating practices within the context of entire transactions from commission to delivery. This entire transaction view entails that translators are not merely or even primarily word-workers; they do not operate on the level of language alone, but participate within a network of actions and follow through the whole transaction, such as a localization project, in which translation partakes of as a component.

The concept of total language solution therefore hinges on current frameworks of translation assessment but subverts the hierarchy of KSAs in these frameworks. With the EMT framework, while Technology will conceivably attract more attention from practitioners and educators than ever, Personal and Interpersonal and Service Provision would also need to be given more premium with a view to developing translators' multicompetency beyond the domain of language transfer. This does not mean eradicating the first two sets of KSAs altogether; as mentioned earlier, they are still necessary but no longer sufficient, as an increasing proportion of work on the level of language transfer can be coded into algorithms and delegable to automated platforms. Instead of responding to this crisis negatively, we should leverage this development and pivot toward multicompetency, which necessitates the foregrounding of KSAs that already figure in current competency frameworks like the EMT but are relatively marginalized.

Let me illustrate this last point with another case example, the competency framework under Australia's National Accreditation Authority for Translators and Interpreters (NAATI). Like the EMT, NAATI's framework comprises a series of KSAs grouped under various heads, listed in linear, non-alphabetical order. The ordering implies a prioritization, with competencies perceived as more important coming up at the top. The following descriptors are for the qualification of NAATI Certified Advanced Translator, though the same competency categories apply to Recognised Practising Translator and Certified Translator, with a gradation of requirements (NAATI, n.d.):

Transfer Competency

Transfers highly complex, specialized texts from a source language into a target language text that accurately reflects the meaning.

Language Competency

Comprehends and produces complex texts in two languages across a variety of text types in specialized domains, appropriately using specialized and complex language including technical expressions and jargon.

Intercultural Competency

Understands in detail how culture and language interact in specialized contexts, identifies all significant and nuanced culturally-specific information in texts, is able to apply this to the translation task and account for its use.

Thematic Competency

Knows about and understands a broad range of complex and specialized contexts, topics, and current events. Has a higher-level of knowledge in a specialized domain at the level of experts writing for experts.

Ethical Competency

Has full and detailed knowledge and understanding of the relevant Code of Ethics, and is able to apply this to situations in translation practice, client interactions, and other professional activities.

Research Competency

Can use a variety of research tools and methods to search for information, including highly specialist resources in a variety of domains, and is able to extract and manage specialized and complex information from research and apply it to the translation task.

Service Provision Competency

Operates in the translation industry and manages interactions with clients and other translators to provide services.

Technological Competency

Knows and is able to use technology required for text production and management, including complex visual material (e.g. graphics), and CAT tools, where available.

Typical Domains & Situation Types

All domains and document types a Certified Translator deals with, plus politics (e.g. government submissions), diplomacy (e.g. international agreements), legal (e.g. high court documentation), health (e.g. conference papers), technology and science (e.g. textbooks, scientific works), business (e.g. international business agreements), finance (e.g. academic articles), commerce and economics (e.g. international trade documentation).

One observes a degree of overlap between the NAATI and EMT frameworks, not just in terms of the specific KSAs but also the sequencing. It is no coincidence, for instance, that Transfer Competency and Language Competency come up on top again, which is characteristic of the Certification model. The more important point, however, is this: what we are seeing is in fact a multicompetency framework comprising aspects like Research Competency (which in the EMT framework is embedded under the heads of Language and Culture/Translation), Service Provision Competency, Ethical Competency, and Technological Competency that are at best tangential to the treatment of language per se. To reiterate my argument, these tangential competencies will need to be moved up the metaphorical ladder such as to be on par with the entrenched competencies of language transfer. They need to be moved nearer the centre. This would conceivably trigger an overhaul of the curricula of translation programmes, the relevant pedagogies, and the assessment criteria. Crucially, this would in the longer run transform the translator's persona from a word-worker into a language-oriented professional who is multicompetent—both in terms of possessing the "hard" skills like technology-related expertise (e.g., knowledge about coding) and research skills (beyond search engines and dictionaries), but also the "soft" skills, such as how to negotiate translation fees and datelines with clients; how to engage the materialities of different media platforms (e.g., when translation intersects with the game industry); and how to market one's multilingual skills within broader value chains of commodity distribution or service provision. In a sense, this is the age-old idea of developing well-rounded individuals. But applied pointedly and comprehensively to translation (and any other domain for that matter), this would constitute a paradigm shift in the field.

4 Postdigital Translation Studies

As with all paradigm shifts, the process of moving through the current crisis in translation into a refashioned framework that conceives of the translator as a multicompetent professional will be full of tensions. To facilitate such a shift, what needs to be changed from the outset is the mentality of translation practitioners, educators, and stakeholders toward the ontology of translation itself.

One must come to terms with the fact that human intervention is not a prerequisite for effective translation in some, though by no means all, circumstances. This is a posthumanist approach to translation which I have advocated elsewhere (Lee, 2024), which is absolutely central to the paradigm shift outlined in this chapter. A cursory look at the state of technology at the time of writing points us to why we need to moderate the role of humans in translation—and "at the time of writing" is an important qualification here, for the rate at which new AI products are emerging is so high that any such technology as described here may be dated at the instance of this chapter's publication. At any rate, let us just use as an illustration one of a plethora of AI "translation earbuds" available on the market *at the time of writing*. The W4 Pro AI Interpreter Earbuds, by the company TimeKettle, is acclaimed as the world's "first two-way voice call interpreter earbuds" that seeks to usher in "a new era of seamless global business interactions" with its capacity to perform interpreting across 40 languages in 93 accents. Three modes of interpreting are available, namely real-time simultaneous interpreting, "listen & play translation" (consecutive interpreting), and so-called media translation, or translation "during online meetings, foreign video streaming, or even impromptu video calls". The device can create personal glossaries of terms to tailor-make intercultural communicative experiences and summaries of post-meeting notes as a human secretary might do (TimeKettle, n.d.).

Before we are astounded by this technology and start lamenting that human interpreters will soon lose their jobs (they may), let us remind ourselves that since the advent of neural machine translation (NMT) systems in mid-2010s of which Google Translate is exemplary, translation has never been the same again. The current development is thus not a fundamental change, but a qualitative one in terms of materiality, efficiency, and accuracy of translation output due to the coming on stage of LLMs. Nevertheless, the idea that real-time interpreting can be accomplished without human intervention may be unsettling for some professional interpreters, whose first instinct may be to push against the technology, citing, among other things, its lack of ethical consciousness and inability to deal with cultural nuances. I suggest the inverse approach: how about embracing the technology—which is irresistible anyway—and enabling human interpreters to rise above the technicalities of language transfer? Interpreters, in the new paradigm, would be advocates of interpersonal as well as intercultural communication who have in regard the bigger picture of the interaction at hand, with oversight of the translation output of AI devices such as interpreting earbuds. This means leveraging AI capacities and pivoting to higher level competencies. We must recall at this point Anthony Pym's observation back in 2016 that MT

> has reached the stage where it is frequently more cost-effective to have translators post-edit rather than translate from scratch, *the added value of our work must increasingly be found at higher levels of cross-cultural communication, including text selection and alteration*. The term 'translation' is not anchored to some eternal essence where such things are unthinkable. (Pym, 2016: 231; emphasis added)

We are presently well beyond the point of MT, not to mention CAT, which means to say we are in the age of postdigital translation; but the Pym's point that "the added value of our work must increasingly be found at higher levels of cross-cultural communication" holds today more than ever before. This is why KSAs such as technology, research, (inter)personal skills, and service provision, which are extant but relatively marginalized in the competency frameworks of EMT and NAATI, need to be foregrounded. In a postdigital age where algorithms are no longer merely ancillary to and assistive of human translation but increasingly autonomous operators, human translators need to find their niche at higher orders of communication. This is not limited to post-editing, which GenAI can cover with good prompting; as Pym

(2023) predicts, and to which I concur, project management may fall within the job scope of translators in the very near future, if not already. I would add that with the advent of agentic AI, the prospect of human translators becoming programmers and managers of AI translators has become very real. In a playfully self-reflexive move, let us have Microsoft Co-Pilot—drawing on articles from IBM, Nvidia, and *Harvard Business Review*—explain for us what agentic AI is:

> Agentic AI refers to artificial intelligence systems that can operate autonomously, making decisions and executing tasks with minimal human intervention. Unlike traditional AI models that require predefined instructions, agentic AI exhibits goal-driven behavior, adaptability, and reasoning to solve complex, multi-step problems. These AI agents can perceive, reason, act, and learn, continuously improving their performance through feedback loops. For example, an agentic AI system could not only suggest the best time to climb Mt. Everest but also book flights and accommodations based on your schedule. This technology is expected to revolutionize industries by enhancing productivity, optimizing workflows, and personalizing user experiences. However, it also raises concerns about bias, errors, and ethical considerations in AI deployment. (Microsoft, 2025)

What is the role of the translator in this postdigital context; and as a corollary, what is translation to become? It may be, as I have intimated above, that the translator would become a manager of AI agents performing technical translation tasks—an agent of agents, as it were. An example of this comes from an initiative Max Lee, who conceives of a virtual translation company that "leverages specialized AI agents to deliver professional translation services" (Lee, 2025). Titled "From Manager to Proofreader: An agentic AI translation system built on collaboration, role-based expertise, and full-stack delivery", the initiative generates a series of agentic AI translators across different domains (legal, academic, business, technical, medical, news, literary) who can perform translation tasks autonomously. These AI translators are coordinated by a manager agent, who (and the relative pronoun for human agents is quite appropriate here): (a) analyzes content and selects appropriate translator; (b) coordinates the translation pipeline; (c) provides detailed reasoning for decisions; (d) sets specific guidelines for each translation; (d) ensures quality and consistency across translations; (e) manages terminology and style guidelines; (f) handles complex translation requirements; and (g) makes intelligent decisions about translation approach (Lee, 2025).

In the midst of this type of agentic AI workflow, the human translator is, as with Max Lee, the invisible hand behind the veil, governing but not necessarily doing the substantive work that is translating. Translation then becomes translational, where the ambit of translation broadens beyond the nitty-gritties of language material and into the ever-fluid realm of algorithmic substances; where translating as a hands-on practice is still relevant but not constitutive of translation in its postdigital guise. The upshot of this is that translation education will need to alter its gears to align with the new personae of the translator—as post-editor, as project manager, as the coordinator of AI agents.

Acknowledgements An early version of this chapter was read as a keynote speech at the 10th Anniversary Conference of the National Translation Committee, Singapore on 15 November 2024.

References

ATA (American Translators Association). (2023a). *ATA Statement on Artificial Intelligence*, https://www.atanet.org/advocacy-outreach/ata-statement-on-artificial-intelligence/

ATA (American Translators Association). (2023b). *How The Exam Is Graded*, https://www.atanet.org/certification/how-the-exam-is-graded/

Bird, A. (2018). Thomas Kuhn. In Edward N. Zalta (Ed.), *The Stanford Encyclopedia of Philosophy*, https://plato.stanford.edu/archives/spr2022/entries/thomas-kuhn/

CEATL (European Council of Literary Translators' Associations). (2022). *Statement on Artificial Intelligence*, https://www.dskp-drustvo.si/wp-content/uploads/2023/12/CEATL-AI-statement-EN.pdf

EMT (European Master's of Translation). (2022). *Competence Framework 2022*, https://commission.europa.eu/document/download/b482a2c0-42df-4291-8bf8-923922ddc6e1_en?filename=emt_competence_fwk_2022_en.pdf

ITI (Institute of Translators and Interpreters). (2024). *Slow Translation Manifesto*, https://www.iti.org.uk/discover/policy/slow-translation-manifesto.html

Koby, G. S., & Melby, A. K. (2013). Certification and Job Task Analysis (JTA): Establishing Validity of Translator Certification Examinations. *Translation & Interpreting, 5*(1), 174–210.

Kuhn, T. (1970). *The Structure of Scientific Revolutions* (2nd ed.). University of Chicago Press.

Lee, T. K. (2024). Artificial Intelligence and Posthumanist Translation: ChatGPT Versus the Translator. *Applied Linguistics Review, 15*(6), 2351–2372.

Lee, M. (2025). *From Manager to Proofreader: An Agentic AI Translation System Built on Collaboration, Role-Based Expertise, and Full-Stack delivery*, https://github.com/Max-Lee-explore/agentic-ai-translation-company

Microsoft. (2025). Copilot [Large Language Model]. https://copilot.microsoft.com

NAATI (National Accreditation Authority for Translators and Interpreters). (n.d.). *Skills and Competencies for Translating*, https://www.naati.com.au/resources/skills-and-competencies-for-translating/

Pym, A. (2016). *Translation Solutions for Many Languages: Histories of a Flawed Dream*. Bloomsbury.

Pym, A. (2023). *ChatGPT and the Training of Translators*. Presented at the 60th anniversary of the Faculty of Translation and Interpretation at the Université de Mons, Belgium, https://www.youtube.com/watch?v=b9U_FUaneso

Steering Committee of the Société française des traducteurs. (2024). *Statement on artificial intelligence by the Steering Committee of the Société française des traducteurs*, https://www.sft.fr/global/gene/link.php?doc_id=551&fg=1

TimeKettle. (n.d.). *W4 Pro AI Interpreter Earbuds*, https://www.timekettle.co/products/w4-pro-ai-interpreter-earbuds

Tong King Lee is Professor and Head of the School of English, University of Hong Kong, Fellow of the Hong Kong Academy of the Humanities, and Honorary Professor of Culture, Communication, and Media at University College London, UK. His research interests span intercultural and nonverbal communication for global business, translanguaging in digital media, and artificial intelligence for creative writing and translation. Author of *Hypertranslation* (Cambridge University Press, 2024), *Kongish: Translanguaging and the Commodification of an Urban Dialect* (Cambridge University Press, 2023), *Choreographies of Multilingualism: Writing and Language Ideology in Singapore* (Oxford University Press, 2022), and *Translation as Experimentalism: Exploring Play in Poetics* (Cambridge University Press, 2022), Professor Lee was conferred the University-level Outstanding Researcher Award at the University of Hong Kong in 2024.

Quality, Evaluation and Translationese

Translationese: Can AI Refinement Techniques Completely Eradicate Translational Distortions?

Bin Xu

Abstract In the domain of English-Chinese translation, "translationese" denotes linguistic phenomena where translated texts manifest foreign syntactical structures or deviate from indigenous Chinese communicative norms. This linguistic phenomenon is fundamentally characterized by several critical attributes: linguistic unnaturalness, compromised textual fluency, syntactical rigidity, and potential comprehension challenges. Throughout the evolutionary trajectory of machine translation, these systems have historically been notorious for generating mechanistic translations that uncannily mirror the structural limitations of human-produced translationese. The recent technological advances in artificial intelligence have precipitated a paradigmatic shift. Contemporary AI-driven translation tools now incorporate sophisticated refinement mechanisms, enabling users to strategically enhance translated texts through carefully calibrated linguistic prompts. This development represents a significant methodological evolution in addressing the longstanding challenges of translational artificiality. This research critically examines a pivotal question: Can advanced artificial intelligence effectively eliminate translationese through its refinement mechanisms? Utilizing an authentic proofreading scenario from a professional publishing house, I analyzed translation materials to evaluate AI's linguistic intervention capabilities. The findings reveal a nuanced landscape: Advanced AI systems significantly enhance amateur translations, demonstrating remarkable potential in detecting and mitigating translationese instances. However, critical limitations persist. Compared to professional translators, AI lacks the sophisticated linguistic intuition necessary for navigating complex nuances. Crucially, AI cannot autonomously initiate contextually sensitive linguistic adaptations. Therefore, I propose a human-AI symbiotic model—specifically, a triangulated editing approach—as the optimal translation production paradigm for the foreseeable future. Beyond its professional application, this triangulated framework holds significant pedagogical value. It establishes a curriculum structure for moving translation training beyond simple tool operation toward the cultivation of critical thinking and sophisticated human-AI collaboration.

Keywords Generative AI · Human–Machine cooperation · LLM · Translationese

B. Xu (✉)
Shandong Normal University, Jinan, China
e-mail: binich@outlook.com

T. Yin et al. (eds.), *AI Through LLMs*, New Frontiers in Translation Studies,
https://doi.org/10.1007/978-981-95-4798-2_4

1 Introduction

Translationese refers to the phenomenon in translation where the target text appears rigid and unnatural due to excessive adherence to the source language's structure, vocabulary, or expressive conventions. Although many studies suggest that, according to existing literature, Eugene Nida is one of the earliest scholars to systematically define and discuss Translationese, in practice, translators throughout history have intuitively recognized its existence.[1] In other words, "translationese" is a concept that naturally arises in the minds of translators, and studying this phenomenon does not require deliberate attention to who first coined the term.

From a cognitive perspective, the reason why translationese can be intuitively identified by translators and readers lies in the human brain's innate sensitivity to linguistic patterns. This sensitivity is built upon cognitive schemas, linguistic expectations, and statistical learning abilities developed through long-term exposure to and use of one's native language. Cognitive interference and linguistic transfer during the translation process lead to deviations from prototypical expressions in the target language. Such deviations can be intuitively perceived even by those without specialized training in translation. This explains why "translationese" has been an intuitively recognized phenomenon among translators since ancient times, requiring no formal academic training to identify. During translation, the syntactic structures, expressive patterns, and thought processes of the source language unconsciously transfer into the target language, creating cognitive interference. Prototype theory in cognitive linguistics explains why we can intuitively detect translationese. Each language has its own "prototype"—the most typical and natural way of expression. Translations often contain expressions that, while grammatically correct, deviate from these prototypes, making them perceived as "unnatural" or "non-native" (Tan, 2012).

At its core, the historical debate between *wen* (literary elegance) and *zhi* (literal fidelity) in ancient Chinese Buddhist scripture translation reflects translators' intuitive awareness of the existence of translationese. In the modern era, Lin Yutang (1994, p. 306) proposed three standards for translation (faithfulness, fluency, and beauty) in his essay "On Translation", and criticized the mechanical literal translation phenomenon prevalent in the translation field at that time. The "dead translation" Lin Yutang criticized ("Dead translation can be said to be the extreme result of the literal translation school… its attitude is to worship and revere the original text's words and sentences, not daring to take a single step beyond.") and "Europeanized Chinese" are specific manifestations of translationese. Since the late twentieth century, translators such as Si Guo and Yu Guangzhong have also offered numerous criticisms and discussions about translationese.[2] Shuttleworth and Cowie (2014, p. 187) define

[1] Nida explicitly introduced the term in his 1964 work *The Theory and Practice of Translation*, co-authored with Charles Taber, describing it as a translation phenomenon where over-reliance on the source language's structure results in unnatural target language expressions.

[2] These discussions are scattered throughout works such as Si Guo's *Translation Studies*, *Further Explorations in Translation*, and *Delving into the Art of Translation*, as well as Yu Guangzhong's *Yu Guangzhong on Translation* and other collections of translation discourse.

translationese as "[a] general pejorative term used to refer to TL usage which because of its obvious reliance on features of SL is perceived as unnatural impenetrable or even comical." *The Dictionary of Chinese Translation Studies* (2011, p. 168) identifies three main manifestations of translationese: (1) mediocre translations, (2) unnatural language, and (3) over-translation. This research focuses on the second manifestation in English-to-Chinese translation—namely, rigid and unidiomatic translations that deviate from conventional Chinese style.

The root cause of translationese lies in the cognitive interference exerted by the source language on the target language. In translated works (particularly English-Chinese literary translations in this study), translationese primarily manifests as expressions that remain overly influenced by the source language's structure and conventions, failing to fully transform into idiomatic and natural target language text. The typical manifestations of translationese mainly include:

(1) Mechanical borrowing of source-language collocations or phrases, resulting in stiff word choices or unnatural combinations; and misinterpretation of word meanings, leading to rigid and inappropriate translation choices.
(2) Europenized syntactic structures, where the word order or clause relationships of the source language are directly replicated. Examples criticized by Yu Guangzhong, such as the overuse of "当……时候" (when…) and excessive use of the particle "的" (*de*-laden phrases), fall into this category. Additionally, the rigid adoption of source-language punctuation conventions also constitutes structural Europeanization.
(3) Illogical target-language expressions or unnatural information sequencing, where the translation violates the logical flow or conventional presentation order expected in the target language. For example, information organization, temporal sequencing, and cause-effect relationships may be mechanically arranged according to the source text, significantly deviating from Chinese cognitive patterns.

Additionally, translationese encompasses certain translators' habitual misuse of words and sentence structures. These lexical and syntactic choices exhibit high recurrence rates and are highly stereotypical, yet they fail to conform to the grammatical, pragmatic, or stylistic norms of the target language.

Texts with pronounced translationese often make readers feel the presence of the source text, as the sentence structures visibly retain traces of the original syntax. The existence of such translationese issues renders the translated text rigid and unnatural, creating reading obstacles for the audience. High-quality translation should, while remaining faithful to the original meaning, fully consider the expressive conventions of the target language, allowing readers to perceive the text as if it were not a translation at all. Regarding translationese, Xu (2021, p. 96) notes that "Whether in literary translation practice or the reception of translated literature, resistance to translationese has now become a prevailing trend."

In the era of purely human translation, translationese primarily stemmed from translators' lack of competence, resulting in compromised translation quality.

The translation process involves complex cognitive operations, including source-language decoding, concept extraction, and target-language re-encoding. During this process, translators face high cognitive loads, which may lead to insufficient attention to the naturalness of the target-language expression. This phenomenon can be explained in cognitive psychology as a result of attentional resource allocation—when excessive focus is placed on meaning transfer, the naturalness of language may be compromised. In rare cases, translationese may also arise from deliberate (yet inappropriate) stylistic choices by translators seeking specific rhetorical effects.

With the introduction of machine translation (MT) into translation production, a new source of translationese has emerged: MT-induced unnaturalness. Rule-based machine translation (RBMT), due to its operational mechanism, is particularly prone to producing translationese. Similarly, statistical machine translation (SMT) that followed also exhibited noticeable translationese. Most translationese generated by these two technological approaches consists of grammatical and pragmatic errors. After machine translation entered the neural machine translation (NMT) stage, the fluency of its output improved significantly. However, it still struggles to avoid translationese caused by linguistic, logical, and cultural differences between languages. It can be said that MT-induced translationese is a product of algorithmic limitations.

Today, an increasing number of translators opt for large language models (LLMs) for translation preprocessing. The translation quality of such AI systems has improved markedly in recent years, substantially reducing translationese. Given this reality, many traditional machine translation service providers have begun integrating AI translation and AI text refinement functions to optimize their services.

The latest AI translation and refinement workflows are based on the application of LLMs. Depending on the instructions given, translation and refinement can either operate as two separate processes or be seamlessly integrated. This is because LLMs process language holistically rather than as discrete translation or refinement tasks. Leveraging their contextual awareness, LLMs can better identify pragmatic, cultural, and other nuanced elements in texts, thereby delivering higher-quality translation and refinement outputs. Kornacki and Pietrzak said,

> AI-powered proofreading and editing tools represent a leap forward in assisting students to refine their translations. These tools go beyond simple grammar checks; they analyse the text for style, clarity and fluency, ensuring that translations not only are grammatically correct but also read naturally in the target language. (2024, p. 121)

However, from practical applications of LLMs it can be seen that while AI translation has significantly reduced surface-level translationese (e.g., grammatical errors), deep-level translationese (logical, cultural, and stylistic issues) persists. Additionally, LLMs are constrained by context window limits (varying by model—e.g., ChatGPT-4's 32 K token limit), which may lead to the loss of key contextual information when translating or refining lengthy documents.

Based on these observations, this study seeks to address the following research questions:

Q1: Is monolingual editing/refinement effective for human translated text?

Q2: Can LLM-based editing/refinement eliminate translationese in human translations?

Q3: What is the optimal workflow for LLM-based editing/refinement?

2 Material and Methodology

2.1 Sample Texts

In response to the research questions proposed above, I conducted experiments using selected text segments from one published and one forthcoming translated works. These works are: (1) *A Short History of Nearly Everything*; (2) *Unf*ck Your Stress*. Specifically, three chapters selected from (1) will undergo comprehensive AI editing/refinement to identify translationese phenomena and verify whether AI can effectively detect translationese in full-length translated texts. Additionally, manually selected representative text fragments from the books will be analyzed in depth to evaluate the capabilities of AI editing/polishing.

A Short History of Nearly Everything by Bill Bryson is a highly popular science book distinguished by its vivid narrative style and humorous tone in the original English version. However, its Simplified Chinese translation (translated by Yan Weiming and Chen Yong) exhibits noticeable translationese issues, making it well-suited as experimental material for this study. The translationese problems in this translated version primarily manifest in the following aspects:

1. A tendency to render "be + *adj.*" structures into "是……的" constructions in Chinese. Using AntConc to analyze Chapters 8 and 9 of the Simplified Chinese version, 36 instances of "是……的" structures derived from English "be + *adj.*" constructions were identified—a proportion significantly higher than natural Chinese texts.
2. Inaccurate translations due to misinterpretations of word meanings or overly rigid translations lacking flexibility. For example, the translators rendered "established theory" as "固定的理论" (literal meaning: "fixed theory"), while "figure out" was consistently and erroneously translated as "测算" (literal meaning "to measure and calculate").
3. Europeanized translations featuring excessively long attributives and inverted cause-effect relationships. (Eg. *This means, as Stephen Hawking has observed with a touch of understandable excitement, that one cannot "predict future events exactly if one cannot even measure the present state of the universe precisely!"* 正如斯蒂芬·霍金有点儿激动地 (这可以理解)说, 这意味着, 你无法"确切预知未来的事情, 要是你连宇宙的现状都无法确切测定的话"。)
4. Retaining English punctuation marks (like dashes) without adaptation. The original author of this book frequently employs dashes—a trend in contemporary English non-fiction writing where the use of dashes has become increasingly

common. However, in translation, punctuation marks should not be mechanically transferred, as the punctuation systems of English and Chinese are not entirely equivalent. In the Simplified Chinese translation of this book, it is evident that the handling of punctuation marks is rigid and overly literal. The translators largely transplant the original punctuation marks directly from English to Chinese without adaptive adjustments. This results in unnecessary unnaturalness in the translation, making the text less fluid and readable.

5. Idiosyncratic expressions leading to personalized translationese. For instance, the translators habitually render English modal verbs such as "must" and "have to" as "非得" (*fēiděi*), a somewhat colloquial and stylistically marked choice that may not always align with the original tone or register. This reflects a personal translation quirk that contributes to the overall translationese in the text. (Eg. *For a memorial you must look to the sky and the Hubble Space Telescope, launched in 1990 and named in his honor.* 若要表示纪念，你非得遥望天空，遥望1990年美国发射的、以他的名字命名的哈勃太空望远镜。) Another tendency of the translators is to render the discourse marker "well" uniformly as "哎呀" (*āiyā*), a much stronger and more emotionally charged interjection in Chinese that alters the original text's pragmatic tone and conversational nuance. (Eg. *Undaunted—well, perhaps mildly daunted—Planck turned to other matters.* 普朗克没有泄气——哎呀，也许稍稍有点胆怯，开始把注意力转向别的问题。)

Since this book is a formally published translation with notably prominent translationese, it serves as an ideal test case. Additionally, there is another Chinese version of the book published in Taiwan (translated by Shi Mingrui), which demonstrates significantly higher translation quality, featuring more idiomatic and fluent language. This version can be used as a reference text to verify both the lesser translation version and the editing/polishing results produced by LLMs.

The second book, *Unf*ck Your Stress*, underwent my personal review before publication, during which AI-assisted editing was partially employed. Drawing from firsthand experience, I can cherry-pick representative passages to analyze the effectiveness of AI-based editing and refinement.

By selecting published or forthcoming human translations containing translationese and refining them using LLMs, we can better evaluate the practical efficacy of LLMs in improving real-world translation outputs. Two important points require clarification here: (1) All LLM interaction data was collected in early April 2025; (2) Even with identical prompts and identical input texts, the output generated by LLMs cannot be perfectly replicated. Due to these two factors, the LLM-generated results presented in this research are inherently non-reproducible—a limitation dictated by the stochastic nature of LLMs and their continuous evolution.

2.2 *Methodology*

Refinement

Based on the research questions proposed above, I opted to employ an LLMs-powered editing/refining workflow for the experiment, which focuses on editing and refining existing human-translated texts, rather than tasking the tested LLMs with the translation work simultaneously. During the editing/polishing process, I first adopted a monolingual approach, providing instructions for LLMs to identify translationese and refine the translated text in batches. After completion, I initiated new sessions, requiring LLMs to analyze the English-Chinese bilingual text sentence by sentence or paragraph by paragraph, in order to identify translationese and other errors in the translations, and then offer suggested improved translations.

(1) **Monolingual Refinement**

Due to the token limitations of LLMs in a single processing session, employing monolingual refinement enables stable processing of longer texts in a single instance, resulting in higher overall efficiency. For monolingual refinement, I provided the following prompt to the AI:

> **Prompt (1)**: Based on the "typical characteristics of translationese" that I have provided, please analyze the following text, make refinements and improvements to avoid translationese, and provide the revised text. Please highlight significant modifications in bold characters.

During the actual refinement process, when the style of certain AI-modified translations became excessively formal, I would supplement with additional prompts, instructing the AI to adopt a more flexible or colloquial style.

(2) **Bilingual Refinement**

When conducting bilingual refinement, I initially attempted to upload English-Chinese parallel texts of entire chapters, arranged paragraph by paragraph or sentence by sentence, to the AI, along with the following instructions for processing:

> **Prompt (2)**: I am providing you with a plain text file containing English-Chinese parallel content from Chapter 9 of "A Short History of Nearly Everything," with each translation unit numbered. As a professional translator, please identify instances of translationese and suggest refinements and improvements. When offering suggestions, please reference the original numbering. Strictly analyze the content from the uploaded file without fabricating content.

However, in practice, I discovered that LLMs have limited attention span. When applying this refinement method, the AI often exhibited serious hallucinations after processing 40–60 units. This manifested in two ways: First, the Chinese translation analyzed by the LLMs was authentic, but the English text was not quoted from the uploaded file; rather, it was "back-translated" by the AI itself. Second, both the

English and Chinese texts were fabricated by the AI. Even after I promptly instructed the AI to pause and pointed out the problem in the performance, some LLMs tended to continue to fabricate data in the subsequent rounds.

Consequently, Prompt (2) was abandoned and instead smaller batches were sent to the AI. With the consideration of its attention span and conversation limit, before each processing session, I would initiate a new conversation and provide the following prompt:

> **Prompt (3)**: I will provide the original text and translation of the popular science book "xxx." Each time I will present approximately 3 paragraphs. Please compare the English original and the Chinese translation to determine if the translation contains the following issues:

(1) Obvious translation errors, such as mistranslations resulting from misunderstanding the meaning of words, phrases, or sentences in the original text;
(2) Translationese: excessive adherence to source language structures, vocabulary, or expression habits, leading to rigid and unnatural translations, including Europeanized Chinese expressions influenced by English syntax.

> *Particularly for translationese, please provide refined versions that conform to Chinese expression conventions, ensuring the translation is natural and idiomatic.*

After running several batches, I made adjustments based on actual feedback, adding the following requirement:

> For translationese phenomena, please explicitly indicate where the translation is 'rigid' or 'exhibits translationese'" to the final line of the prompt.

This addition was intended to better identify translationese issues detected by the AI in subsequent statistical analysis.

The design of these prompts was not only a methodological choice for research but was also a potentially powerful pedagogical framework. The value of them in a classroom setting lies in the structured and analytical nature, which makes students see the function of simply "getting a better translation" of an AI and teaches them to engage with it critically. The rationale for their use in education is twofold: first, it models a professional editing workflow by breaking down a complex task into specific, analyzable categories (mistranslations, translationese). Second, by requiring the AI to provide refined versions *and* explain its modifications, it makes the process of revision transparent and justifiable. The students can then further analyze and evaluate the explanations before arriving at their own conclusions.

Data Collecting

Bilingual AI-powered editing/refinement was used for three chapters of *A Short History of Nearly Everything*. After receiving feedback from the AI, I conducted manual verification, tallying the instances where the AI either had effectively identified translationese phenomena or had already corrected them through the provided refined translations, thus obtaining relevant statistical data.

To determine whether the AI effectively identified or modified translationese, I employed manual judgment methods. The following example represents the only instance in Chapter 1 where the AI neither detected nor effectively modified the translationese[3]:

Ex 1: Their names were Arno Penzias and Robert Wilson.

TL1: 他们的名字分别叫做阿诺·彭齐亚斯和罗伯特·威尔逊。

AI: 这两位天文学家名叫阿诺·彭齐亚斯和罗伯特·威尔逊。(DS V3)

The phrase "他们的名字分别叫做" in TL1 represents obvious translationese, and the AI's modified expression (这两位天文学家名叫) is still not sufficiently natural. Idiomatic Chinese would express this as: 这两位天文学家一个叫……, 另一个叫…….

This example also reflects that relatively stringent standards are adopted when identifying translationese. According to these standards, the frequency of translationese in *A Short History of Nearly Everything* is relatively high, which makes an excellent authentic material for verifying the efficacy of AI editing/refinement in eliminating translationese. Apart from this instance of translationese in Chapter 1, after three rounds of examination, I found that all instances of translationese in Chapters 9 and 16 were corrected in the AI-refined drafts.

3 Analysis and Discussion

As shown in Table 1, AI's editing/refinement capabilities are particularly outstanding, and can effectively identify or modify the vast majority of translationese created by human translators. Although some users have pointed out that AI translations still exhibit a certain proportion of mistranslations and translationese phenomena, when performing dedicated editing/refinement tasks, AIs appear to demonstrate a heightened "alertness" to translationese in this study. Next, I used several cherry-picked examples to illustrate and compare the performance differences between LLMs' monolingual and bilingual proofreading.

From a pedagogical standpoint, this heightened "alertness" of AI transforms it into an invaluable teaching tool. Some of the examples that follow are not merely demonstrations of AI's capabilities, but are presented as case studies with teaching notes for a translation classroom. The intention is to show how educators can leverage AI's ability to identify translationese and translation errors as a starting point for

[3] In all examples in this paper, those marked with TL1 represent the original translations, those maked with TL2 represent the human edited version, while those with AI represent translations provided by artificial intelligence. The specific model used is noted in parentheses after the AI translations.

Table 1 Cases of translationese identified

Chapter	Words	Translationese phenomena identified/corrected	Translationese phenomena not identified/corrected
Chapter 1	3775	60	1
Chapter 9	5865	100	0
Chapter 16	5931	60	0

critical discussion. By deconstructing *why* a human translation was flawed, *how* an AI diagnosed the issue, and *why* such translations are flawed, students can develop a more sophisticated understanding of linguistic transfer, cultural nuance, and stylistic appropriateness in a good translation. This section aims to show that AI functions as a "critical partner" both to translators and translation educators.

3.1 AI Monolingual and Bilingual Editing/Refinement

In the actual book translation workflow, at the editing/refinement stage, text editors generally adopt a monolingual editing mode, reading only the printed translated text and correcting issues based on their own language intuition and professional judgement. At this stage, the problems remaining in the manuscript are (presumably) primarily occasional typographical errors, punctuation errors, and a small amount of translationese. Only when encountering sentences with obvious logical inconsistencies would text editors refer to the original text to check for mistranslations. To check the efficacy and the validity of this approach in the case of AI proofreading, this research also employed a monolingual editing/refinement mode for some sample texts, processing them with AI.

Ex 2: As a scholar he was equally proficient, and had no trouble gaining admission to study physics and astronomy at the University of Chicago (where, coincidentally, the head of the department was now Albert Michelson).

TL1: 作为一名学者, 他也是出色得不得了, 不费吹灰之力就考上芝加哥大学, 攻读物理学和天文学(说来也巧, 系主任就是阿尔伯特·迈克尔逊)。

AI: 作为学生, 他也厉害得不得了, 轻轻松松就考上了芝加哥大学, 学物理学和天文学(说来也巧, 系主任正是阿尔伯特·迈克尔逊)。(Claude 3.7 Sonnet)

When conducting monolingual editing/refinement on the translation of Ex2, Claude 3.7 Sonnet successfully changed "学者" (xué zhě, scholar or expert) to "学生" (xué shēng, pupil or student), as according to the context provided in this sentence, Hubble was still in secondary school at that time and could not be referred to as a "xué zhě" in Chinese, meaning a renowned expert in a certain field. In English, the word "scholar" can refer to either a "student" or "a learned person." However, the translator evidently assumed this word only has the latter meaning, resulting in a semantic selection error. In addition, in Claude's refined version, the inappropriate expression "不费吹灰之力" (without expending any effort) was replaced, as it implies that the task is excessively simple. However, when performing monolingual checks on this sentence, several other mainstream LLMs failed to find the translation error of turning "scholar" into "学者."

Ex 3: According to his own accounts, he also managed to fit into his life more or less constant acts of valor—rescuing drowning swimmers, leading frightened men to safety across the battlefields of France, embarrassing world-champion boxers with knockdown punches in exhibition bouts. It all seemed too good to be true. It was. For all his gifts, Hubble was also an inveterate liar.

TL1: 按照他自己的说法, 他生活中还经常做些英雄事迹——救落水的人; 带着吓坏了的人穿过法国战场, 把他们带到安全地方; 在表演赛中几下子就把世界冠军级的拳击手打倒在地, 弄得他们很难堪。这些听起来好得简直让人难以置信, 但都是真的。尽管才华出众, 但哈勃也是个顽固的大骗子。

When conducting monolingual editing/refinement on the translation of Ex3, the AI improved the fluency of the translation to some extent. However, despite obvious logical error in the underlined part (the underlined part), multiple AI systems failed to detect it. For instance, ChatGPT noted that there were "basically no obvious mistranslations, but a certain degree of translationese exists." And the translationese it identified included phrases like "按照他自己的说法" ("according to his own accounts") and "生活中还经常做些英雄事迹" ("to fit into his life more or less constant acts of valor"). Notably, it also pointed out that the part "这些听起来好得简直让人难以置信, 但都是真的" (the underlined part) "reads somewhat awkwardly."

When provided with bilingual text for editing/refinement, all AI systems test identified the obvious mistranslation in the text, pointing out that the original "It was" had been mistranslated as "但都是真的" (meaning "but they are all true"), which constitutes a misunderstanding of the original. Based on contextual logic (the subsequent text reveals him as a fraud) and syntactic analysis ("It was" is a sentence that omits "too good to be true"), the LLMs correctly determined that this sentence should have a negative meaning.

The examples above demonstrate that when using AI's editing/refinement capabilities to identify and improve on translationese, it is preferable to provide bilingual text to avoid missing important mistranslations during the editing and refinement process. Particularly, since LLMs process text at speeds significantly higher than human editors, the additional time required for processing bilingual text is negligible. Therefore, adopting a monolingual AI proofreading mode is not recommended.

Ex 4: It was Einstein who provided the first incontrovertible evidence of atoms' existence with his paper on Brownian motion in 1905, but this attracted little attention and in any case Einstein was soon to become consumed with his work on general relativity.

TL1: 是爱因斯坦在1905年以那篇论布朗运动的论文首次提出了无可争议的证据, 证明原子的存在, 但没有引起多大注意。无论如何, 爱因斯坦很快就忙于广义相对论的研究。

AI: 1905年, 爱因斯坦通过布朗运动研究首次为原子存在提供了确凿证据, 然未获学界重视。彼时他正全力投入广义相对论研究, 无暇他顾。(DS V3)

Regarding this example, DeepSeek V3 pointed out that the translation exhibits problems of Europeanized sentence structure. Additionally, it noted that the term "

忙于" (be busy with) was too colloquial (for the phrase "become consumed with") and inconsistent with the overall style. The edited and refined translation provided by DeepSeek indeed shows significant improvement in terms of expression fluency and stylistic consistency. Specifically, the AI restructured the sentences and also made notable improvements in this aspect.

Ex 5: He was one of the first to see-possibly the very first-that the power inherent in the atom could, if harnessed, make bombs powerful enough to "make this old world vanish in smoke."

TL1: 他是最先的人之一——很可能就是最先的人——发现原子里所固有的能量一旦得到利用可以制造炸弹, 其威力之大足以"使这个旧世界在烟雾中消失"。

AI: 作为最早 (很可能是首位) 洞见者, 他意识到原子蕴含的能量若被利用, 可制成威力足以"令旧世界灰飞烟灭"的炸弹。(DS V3)

For this example, DeepSeek explicitly identified two instances of translationese: First, the expression "最先的人" (the first people) was awkward and inconsistent with modern Chinese linguistic conventions. Second, the handling of direct quotation was inappropriate. The optimized translation provided by DeepSeek achieved a higher level, though it made a small error by translating "old world" as "旧世界" (the Old World). Here, "this old world" does not literally mean a world that is "old" as in "the Old World" (such as Europe in geographical terms), but rather refers to "the existing world" or "the world we live in." The word "old" carries an emotional nuance or an attitude of affection, representing a literary, metaphorical expression. Combined with the latter part of the sentence "make this old world vanish in smoke," it means that the atomic bomb, with its immense explosive power, is capable of reducing the earth or world on which humans depend to ashes.

Ex 6: Dalton was born in 1766 on the edge of the Lake District near Cockermouth to a family of poor but devout Quaker weavers. (Four years later the poet William Wordsworth would also join the world at Cockermouth.)

TL1: 道尔顿的故乡位于英国湖泊地区边缘, 离科克默思不远。他1766年生于一个贫苦而虔诚的贵格会织布工家庭。(4年以后, 诗人威廉·华兹华斯也来到科克默思。)

AI: 道尔顿的家乡位于英国湖区边缘, 距科克默思不远。他1766年出生于一个贫困而虔诚的贵格会织布工家庭。(四年后, 诗人威廉·华兹华斯也来到了科克默思。) (DS V3 Mono Editing)

AI: 1766年, 道尔顿出生于英国湖区科克默思镇, 一个贫寒而虔诚的贵格会织布工家庭。(四年后, 诗人华兹华斯亦诞生于此。) (DS V3 Bilingual Editing)

When using AI to perform monolingual editing/refining on the TL1 in this example, the AI corrected the mistranslation of "the Lake District" from "湖泊地区" (a generic name meaning any district surrounding any lake) to "湖区" (a proper name in geography referring to the specific place in England), but failed to recognize the incorrect interpretation for "William Wordsworth … join the world at Cockermouth"—TL1 rendered it as Wordsworth literally "came to" the place instead of "being born" here; additionally, it is worth noting that the monolingual refinement did not suggest any revisions for the somewhat awkward translation in the second sentence (the modifier for "family" was converted to an overly long modifier in Chinese: "一个贫苦而虔诚的贵格会织布工"). In contrast, after bilingual editing and refinement, the AI pointed out that "the two sentences are connected awkwardly" and identified and corrected the mistranslation regarding Wordsworth (pointing out that "'came to' is inaccurate, and the time description is stiff").

There are also cases that involve both translationese and mistranslation, where simple bilingual editing cannot identify the issues, and instead require more human–machine interaction, with humans providing additional instructions to AI.

Ex 7: Ashcroft relates a story concerning the directors of a new tunnel under the Thames who held a celebratory banquet as the tunnel neared completion. To their consternation their champagne failed to fizz when uncorked in the compressed air of the tunnel. However, when at length they emerged into the fresh air of a London evening, the bubbles sprang instantly to fizziness, memorably enlivening the digestive process.

TL1: 阿什克罗夫特讲了个在泰晤士河底下修建新隧道的故事。隧道快要完工的时候，主管们举行了一个庆祝宴会。他们在隧道的压缩空气里打开瓶盖，只见香槟酒没有泛起泡沫，令他们大吃一惊。然而，当他们最后走进伦敦夜晚的新鲜空气里的时候，香槟立即泛起泡沫，恢复了大家的食欲。

AI-1: 阿什克罗夫特讲述了一个关于泰晤士河下新隧道董事们的故事：在隧道即将竣工之际，他们举办了一场盛大的庆功宴。然而令他们懊恼的是，在隧道压缩空气环境中打开香槟酒时，酒竟然没有冒泡。不过，当他们好不容易回到伦敦夜晚的新鲜空气中后，气泡立刻活跃起来，汩汩冒出——这种突如其来的"起泡"体验令他们的消化过程变得格外难忘。(Claude 3.7 Sonnet)

AI-2: 阿什克罗夫特讲过这样一则轶事：在泰晤士河下修建一条新隧道的工程接近尾声时，几位主管在隧道里举行了庆祝宴会。让他们惊讶的是，在隧道内高压环境下打开香槟时，香槟竟然完全不起泡沫。但等到他们走出隧道、呼吸到伦敦夜晚的新鲜空气时，刚刚喝下肚的香槟却瞬间在体内猛烈起泡，给大家的消化过程带来了令人难忘的"活力"。(Claude 3.7 Sonnet)

In the editing/refinement feedback for this translation, Claude 3.7 Sonnet noted that the translation exhibits "a certain degree of translationese", primarily manifested in the sentence "阿什克罗夫特讲了个……的故事" (Ashcroft relates a story…), which it considered structurally rigid, noting that it was as if converted directly from the English expression. Additionally, Claude pointed out that the most serious error in the translation was in the interpretation of the final part of original text. The original phrase "memorably enlivening the digestive process" referred to champagne suddenly bubbling and making the digestive process memorably vivid, whereas the translation rendered it as "restored everyone's appetite", which was a distortion of the original meaning. In the first revised draft, the AI's observation was correct, but still missed a nuanced layer of understanding. In the story's actual context, the individuals were in a pressurized tunnel beneath the River Thames. The pressure inside the opened champagne bottle was precisely balanced with the surrounding environmental pressure, which was why it did not bubble. However, it's important to note that they still drank the champagne to celebrate the completion of the engineering project. When these people returned to the ground and the atmospheric pressure returned to normal surface conditions, the champagne they had already consumed began to bubble. "Memorably enlivening the digestive process" specifically refers to the result of champagne bubbling in their stomachs. So the story actually depicted a remarkably interesting scenario. After this deeper layer of meaning being pointed out, the AI quickly realized its weakness in the first draft (AI-1) and provided the second version (AI-2).

Moreover, the AI failed to identify a mistranslation related to cultural background knowledge: the expression "打开(香槟)瓶盖" (literally meaning "opening the bottle cap") was inaccurate. Champagne bottles are sealed with a cork, not with a twist-off or crown cap. The expression "when uncorked" in the original text specifically refers to the act of removing the cork, which is far more nuanced than simply "opening the bottle cap." Through human–machine interaction, the AI quickly recognized the mistake of bottle cap, and the more important point with the bubbling of the champagne that it has missed ("This is precisely the key point I missed in my analysis!") and acknowledged this as one of the most significant misunderstandings in the translation. Claude 3.7 Sonnet's analysis after this "sudden realization" was as follows:

1. **The Most Critical Misunderstanding:** The translation failed to capture the crucial point that the champagne began bubbling in people's stomachs. The original text's "digestive process" explicitly indicated the champagne suddenly started bubbling during its digestive process within their bodies, while the translation completely missed this point and erroneously translated it as "restored everyone's appetite".
2. **Causal Relationship Error:** The translation said that the champagne bubbled after returning to ground level in the bottle, whereas the original text's intrigue lies in the fact that the champagne had already been consumed and suddenly bubbled in the drinkers' stomachs—this being the true meaning of "memorably enlivening the digestive process."
3. **Scientific Principle Omission:** This story actually demonstrates the effect of atmospheric pressure on dissolved gases—in high-pressure environments, gases dissolve more easily in liquids and are released when pressure decreases. This scientific principle was completely lost in the translation.

The sensitivity of translators and proofreaders to textual style plays a critically important role in correctly handling texts. In the book *Unf*ck Your Stress*, the following passage is particularly light-hearted and humorous. Unfortunately, neither TL1 nor the TL2 (refined by the editor from the printing house) managed to reproduce this stylistic feature.

> **Ex 8:** And while every single one of my books has some kind of "how to use this book" section, I remain terrible at writing them. Because I am a member of Generation X, which means I fully support you using the book however you see fit. Jump around if you like, the book won't break if you read it backwards (tho watch for accidental spellcasting so you don't accidentally summon a Demogorgon). Read it and use it to drunkenly lecture others at closing time. Or just read what applies to you, find stuff that's helpful, and move on with your life. It's all good.
>
> TL1: 虽然我每本书都有某种"如何使用本书"的部分, ① <u>但我写这部分的能力仍然很差</u>。因为我是X世代的一员, ② <u>这意味着我完全支持你按照自己的方式使用这本书</u>。如果你喜欢跳着读、倒着读,这本书它也不会坏(不过可要当心触发什么咒语,以免不小心召唤出什么恶魔来)。无论你阅读它是为了③ <u>在酒醉时侃侃而谈</u>, 还是只读你需要的部分, 找到有用的东西, ④ <u>然后继续你的生活</u>, <u>这都是可以的</u>。

TL2: 虽然我的每本书都有类似"如何使用本书"的部分, ① 但我仍然不擅长写这部分内容。因为我是X世代的一员, ② 完全支持你按照自己的方式使用这本书, 不管是跳着读, 还是倒着读。此外, 不管你阅读本书的目的是什么, 是 ③ 充当酒桌上的谈资还是寻找对你有价值的内容, 都是没有问题的。

In TL1, the sections marked with numerical and symbolic annotations ①–④ exhibit clear characteristics of translationese, with text that is stiff, static, and lacking in humor. In the human edited version shown in TL2, the content corresponding to ④ was deleted, while ①–③ still suffered from similar rigidity and inflexibility. Specifically, TL2 lost the humorous and playful tone. For instance, the translation of "I remain terrible at writing them" as "不擅长" (back translation: "not skilled at") appears overly formal. The original text's playful comment "tho watch for accidental spellcasting… Demogorgon" was outright omitted in the edited version, significantly reducing its entertainment value. The original text embodied a casual conversational style. The expression in TL2, "不管是跳着读, 还是倒着读" (literal back translation: "whether skimming or reading backwards"), while grammatically smooth, lacks the rhythmic quality of spoken language. The phrase "充当酒桌上的谈资" (literal back translation: "serving as a topic of conversation at the dinner table") is too formal, lacking the interesting quality of "边喝酒边吹牛" (to drunkenly lecture others at closing time).

AI: 虽然我每本书都煞有介事地写了"使用指南", ①但说真的, 这部分我写得烂透了。毕竟我是X世代的人, ②主打一个"爱咋用咋用"——跳着读、倒着读都行, 书又不会散架 (不过小心别念错咒语, 万一召出个恶魔就尴尬了)。你可以③边喝酒边拿它吹牛, 也可以只挑对你有用的部分, ④看完该干嘛干嘛。总之, 随你开心! (DeepSeek V3)

The revised translation demonstrates several key improvements: 1. Enhanced Conversational Style: the text becomes more colloquial and livelier, particularly in sections ① and ④. The language now reflects a more natural, spoken-like rhythm. 2. More Natural Expressions: sections ② and ③ adopt more idiomatic and contextually appropriate phrasing. 3. Humor Restoration: most critically, the improved translation successfully recreates the original text's humorous tone. It captures the playful, irreverent style of the source material while avoiding the stiffness of translationese.

This example illustrates a significant capability of LLMs: not only can they identify and correct instances of translationese, but they can also accurately discern the stylistic nuances of a text and effectively reproduce these stylistic elements during editing and refinement. So they can create translations that are both linguistically accurate and stylistically faithful to the original. The result is a translation that reads more fluently and engagingly, maintaining the original text's communicative intent and emotional resonance.

3.2 A Triangulated Refinement Process

For certain critical texts, a collaborative human–machine triangulation method for editing and revision should be adopted. The concept and methodology of Triangulation originally emerged in the sociological domain. Norman K. Denzin first systematically articulated the concept of Triangulation in his 1970 work *The Research Act: A Theoretical Introduction to Sociological Methods*, defining it as combining multiple methods, data sources, or theoretical perspectives to investigate the same phenomenon, with the aim of enhancing research validity and reliability. Translation cognitive research has borrowed the triangulation concept from social science research, seeking to more comprehensively reveal cognitive mechanisms, translator behaviors, and translation phenomena through multi-perspective and multi-level cross-verification. As Denzin (2017, p. 36) pointed out, the necessity of triangulation stems from the principle that "sociologists must approach the empirical world from as many methodological perspectives as possible."

Given the varied performance of different LLMs and their significantly diverse original training data, it is advisable to adopt a triangulation approach in translation editing and refinement. Such a method involves invoking multiple LLMs for editing and revision and integrating human judgment. This methodological approach ensures a more rigorous and comprehensive translation editing process, leveraging the complementary strengths of machine intelligence and human linguistic expertise.

> **Ex 9:** Basically everything is organized in ways that make sense to me and make it easier to put my hands on it when I need it. My niblings know where their stuff is in the house if they swing by and I'm not there. My clients know where everything is in the back offices in the same way. // Marie Kondo or Martha Stewart would probably weep at all of it, but it all works for me and that's the important thing. And it does help my stress levels in small-but-impactful-over-time ways.
>
> TL1: 基本上, 所有的东西都按照对我有意义的方式组织起来, 使我在需要的时候更容易拿到它。如果我的侄子们来我家, 我不在, 他们知道他们的东西在房子里的哪里。我的客户也知道办公室的所有东西在哪里。//我的两位侄子, 玛丽·康多 (Marie Kondo) 和玛莎·斯图尔特 (Martha Stewart) 可能会为此哭泣, 但这一切对我来说都很有效, 这是最重要的。
>
> TL2: 基本上, 所有的东西都按照对我来说有意义的方式组织起来, 我就可以在需要的时候方便拿到它们。所以如果我不在家, 我也知道侄子们的东西在房间的哪个地方, 客户的东西在办公室的哪里。// 我的两个侄子——玛丽·康多和玛莎·斯图尔特可能会因他们的东西在我家的安排而哭泣, 但这种安排对我来说很有效, 这就够了。
>
> AI: 基本上, 所有的东西都按照我的习惯摆放得井井有条, 需要时随手就能拿到。即使我不在家, 侄子们也知道他们的东西放在哪里; 客户们同样清楚办公室里的物品位置。// 玛丽·康多或玛莎·斯图尔特看到这种布置可能会摇头叹息, 但对我来说非常实用, 这才是最重要的。而且, 这种安排也在潜移默化中缓解了我的压力。(DS V3)

Example 9 is extracted from the book *Unf*ck Your Stress* which I proofread. The refined translation provided by DS V3 addressed multiple instances of translationese, rendering the text in a more fluent way. Several noteworthy modifications include:

(1) Idiomatic Expression Refinement: "make it easier to put my hands on it" was transformed from a literal translation to the more natural Chinese expression "需

要时随手就能拿到"; "按照对我来说有意义的方式组织起来" was revised to "按照我的习惯摆放得井井有条" (organized in ways that make sense to me), better aligning with Chinese linguistic conventions.

(2) Emotional Tone Adjustment: The original translation "因……而哭泣" (meaning "weeping because of…") was perceived as overly dramatic. The refined version "可能会摇头叹息" (meaning "shake their heads and sigh") more subtly captures the emotional nuance, reflecting the characteristic Chinese communicative style of understatement.

(3) Significant Mistranslation Correction: A particularly notable correction addressed a substantial error in the initial translation. The phrase "我的两个侄子——玛丽·康多和玛莎·斯图尔特" (literal back translation: "my two nephews - Marie Kondo and Martha Stewart") was an apparent mistranslation. The original text "Marie Kondo or Martha Stewart" refers to two renowned organizing experts, not the author's relatives.

This example demonstrates the sophisticated capabilities of AI in translation refinement, showing that it can understand cultural communication styles and identify and correct substantive mistranslations. From this we can see that LLMs can play a critical role in the human–machine collaborative translation editing and refinement processes and help humans to achieve high-quality, contextually appropriate textual renderings.

Comparing the text with the edited version (TL2) after human single-language proofreading, it is found that human editors, without maintaining sufficient vigilance, may fail to effectively correct translationese and significant mistranslations due to cognitive limitations and fatigue. The most logically incongruous error in TL1 occurs in the phrase meaning "my two nephews - Marie Kondo and Martha Stewart." Several critical issues are evident in this rendering. The most prominent problem is the logical inconsistency. Both names (Marie Kondo and Martha Stewart) are clearly female names, yet they were inexplicably described as "侄子" (zhí zi, meaning "nephews", who are male relatives). After AI editing, DS noticed that these two individuals were not the "nephews" of the author, and this was a critically important correct interpretation. However, the AI's initial solution of transliterating the names was not the optimal translation, i.e., it did not convert the name of Marie Kondo back to the Japanese script Kanji.

Gemini 2.5 Pro identified multiple conspicuous translation errors and translationese phenomena in TL1, with a particularly significant mistranslation regarding personal identities:

> The erroneous interpretation of Marie Kondo (Kondo Marie) and Martha Stewart as "my two nephews" represents a severe comprehension error. These two are internationally renowned organizing experts and lifestyle coaches. The original meaning is that, although my own organizing method works well for me, these two experts might find it too messy or inconsistent, to the point of "crying" (indicating disapproval or finding it problematic). The recommended translation provided by Gemini is: "像近藤麻理惠或玛莎·斯图尔特这样的整理大师看了(我这套整理方式), 大概会 (被气/愁得) 哭吧"。

During triangulated verification, it can be seen that some LLMs can immediately identify Marie Kondo as "近藤麻理惠", while others failed to do so (such as in ChatGPT Mini and DS V3's analyses, where the name was treated as a purely Western name and transliterated as "玛丽·康多"), resulting in inconsistencies between them. Or, when we are merely uncertain about the name "近藤麻理惠" provided by LLMs—in either of these scenarios, we can further interrogate the AI, asking it to give more information about the two persons mentioned in the original text, or use the good old search engines to verify the AI's response. Regardless of the method employed, triangulated verification can better ensure that translators ultimately find the correct translation.

From this example we can see that human proofreading, despite its perceived reliability, is susceptible to overlooking significant linguistic and logical errors, because fatigue and cognitive constraints can compromise a person's ability. So, AI-assisted editing can provide an additional layer of scrutiny, detecting errors that might escape human reviewers. The example also shows the potential of collaborative human–machine approaches in translation quality assurance, highlighting the complementary strengths of human linguistic intuition and machine systematic analysis. As translation is a nuanced cognitive process, adding more verification layers can significantly enhance textual accuracy and fidelity.

3.3 Methodological and Pedagogical Considerations for Educational Application

While the triangulated refinement process demonstrates significant value for enhancing translation quality, its potential in educational application requires specific methodological considerations. To transition this model from a finding based on practical investigation and research generalization to an effective teaching tool, educators must focus on three key areas: demystifying prompt design, emphasizing the value of bilingual refinement workflows, and actively cultivating critical skepticism toward AI outputs.

Teaching Prompt Engineering for Translation

The effectiveness of an LLM is heavily dependent on the quality of the user's prompt. For students to leverage AI as a learning partner, they must be taught how to craft precise, goal-oriented prompts. The prompts used in this study—to identify "translationese" and "obvious errors" while providing justifications—were deliberately designed to make the AI's reasoning process transparent. Educators can make amendments of the prompts by referring to the following prompt engineering checklist:

1. **Specify the Task and Role:** It is important to assign the AI a specific role. For example: "Act as a professional Chinese-English translator and editor. Your task is to review the Chinese translation against the English source text."
2. **Define Key Error Categories:** Instruct the AI to look for specific translation errors. For Example: "Identify and label instances of: (a) Translationese (unnatural, literal renderings), (b) Mistranslations (factual or comprehension errors), and (c) Cultural Inappropriateness (terms or tones that clash with target culture norms)."
3. **Demand Justification:** The most critical step for learning is to require the AI to explain its changes. For example: "For each suggested change, explain *why* the original was problematic and *why* your alternative is better."

In addition to these three basic principles, one can also control the output format by asking the AI to use either the markdown syntax to make the output clearer. By teaching students to construct such detailed prompts, educators transform the interaction from a passive request for a solution into an active dialogue. Students learn to articulate what constitutes a "good" translation, forcing them to internalize critical standards before engaging with the technology.

The Pedagogical Imperative of Bilingual Refinement

The research design deliberately prioritized a bilingual refinement process—providing both source and target texts—for the AI refinement and the human proofreading. This has pedagogical values because monolingual proofreading, while valuable for final-stage polishing, trains a different skill set and can ingrain bad habits in translation trainees if used prematurely.

The case of Marie Kondo in Example 9 vividly illustrates this point. A human editor working monolingually on TL1 or TL2 might spot the logical incongruity of female names being labeled as "nephews" (侄子). Their cognitive process, constrained by the available information, might lead to a "correction" to "nieces" (侄女), which would still contain a fundamental mistranslation. The core comprehension error—that Kondo and Stewart are not [the author's] relatives but cultural exemplars—is impossible to be detected without consulting the source text.

By enforcing a bilingual workflow with AI, educators achieve a crucial learning outcome: they model and reinforce the professional practice of constant cross-verification in translation. This process teaches students a foundational awareness for professional practice: a translation's validity is always anchored to its source. This principle guards against the very cognitive fatigue and oversight that led to the error being missed in the first place.

Teaching Notes to Key Examples

Educators can use the AI's initial failure as a pedagogical tool. Carefully designed in-class activities integrating the use of AI in the refinement process should show the students that human–machine interaction is not a one-shot command but an iterative dialogue, where human insight is required to guide the AI toward a more appropriate solution.

Analyzing Errors on Multi-Levels

The "champagne in the tunnel" example in Ex7, serves not only as evidence for the efficacy of human–machine collaboration but also as rich, teachable moments. To maximize their educational value, such examples can be framed as structured learning modules. Furthermore, the principles can be extended beyond popular science and self-help texts used as cases in this research to other specialized domains like literary and legal translation.

Ex 7 is an ideal case study for teaching advanced critical thinking skills in translation because its errors operate on multiple levels: linguistic, cultural, and scientific. An educator can use this example to guide a class through a multi-layered analysis so as to show students that a good translator does not just fix errors; they sense "thin ice"—areas where the meaning feels shallow or illogical—and they keep probing until they solve all the uncertainties.

Teaching Module: The Skeptical Translator's Inquiry
Objective:

To cultivate students' critical skepticism by training them to identify points of uncertainty in a translation and to engage in a persistent, iterative dialogue with an AI until the deepest layers of meaning are uncovered.

Step 1: The Initial Briefing—Seeding Doubt

- **Setup:** The instructor provides students with only the source text (Ex. 7) and the flawed human translation (TL1). The AI's analysis is withheld.
- **Instructor's Prompt:** "Read this translation. Don't just look for obvious grammar mistakes or fluency problems. Look for 'thin ice'—any phrase that seems slightly illogical, or makes you pause and think, 'Is that really what happened?' Mark every single point of uncertainty, no matter how small."
- **Goal:** This framing shifts the mindset from "proofreading" to "skeptical inquiry." Students are encouraged to doubt, not just to correct. They will likely mark:
- 打开瓶盖 (Champagne? Bottle cap? Seems odd.)
- 恢复了大家的食欲 (So they didn't eat in the tunnel? How does champagne restore appetite in this context? This feels illogical.)

Step 2: The First Cross-Examination—Confronting the AI Witness

- **Setup:** Students are now given the initial AI translation (AI-1) and the analysis.

- **Instructor's Prompt:** "Here is the testimony from our first expert, an AI. It has identified one of our points of uncertainty—'restored appetite'—and corrected it. Is the AI's explanation fully satisfying? Does it resolve all our doubts? Compare the AI's analysis with your list of doubts."
- **Discussion and Probing Questions:**
- "The AI missed our doubt about 打开瓶盖. Why do you think it overlooked this cultural detail?"
- "The AI's translation of the part about the bubbling 'enlivened the digestive process' is better, but it's still incomplete. The rendered version seems to have failed to convey the element of humor of the original author. Can you provide a better version?"
- **Goal:** Students learn that an AI's correction can still be incomplete. They practice identifying gaps and vagueness in an AI's reasoning, treating it as a new piece of evidence to be questioned.

Step 3: The Iterative Inquiry—Drilling Down with Follow-Up Prompts

- **Setup:** This is the core of the module. Students, working in groups, must now act as relentless interrogators. Their task is to draft a series of follow-up prompts to force the AI to resolve the remaining uncertainties.
- **The Prompting Challenge:** "Your goal is to lead the AI to its 'aha!' moment. You cannot give it the answer directly. You must guide it with skeptical questions. Draft at least two follow-up prompts."
- **Prompt 1 (Targeting the 'Where'):**
- **Student-drafted prompt:** "Let's re-examine the 'digestive process.' Please trace the sequence of events precisely. At which exact step does the 'enlivening' happen?"
- **Desired Outcome:** This forces the AI to confront the logical sequence, leading it to the "in the stomach" conclusion.
- **Prompt 2 (Targeting the cultural elements):**
- **Student-drafted prompt:** "You overlooked the phrase 'when uncorked.' Please analyze the difference in meaning and cultural context between 'uncorking' and 'opening a bottle cap.'"
- **Desired Outcome:** This pushes the AI to connect cultural knowledge (how champagne bottles work) with scientific context (pressure).
- **Goal:** Students learn that a sophisticated user of AI doesn't just ask a question; they conduct a multi-turn conversation, using logic and contextual clues to steer the AI toward a deeper truth.

Step 4: The Final Revelation and Reflection

- **Setup:** The instructor reveals the AI's "final realization" and the improved version (AI-2).
- **Instructor's Prompt for Reflection:** "Let's reflect on the process. Why was our initial skepticism so important? What would have been lost if we had accepted the first translation? What if we had stopped after the AI's first correction? What does this teach you about your responsibility as a human translator when using AI tools?"
- **Key Takeaways (to be summarized by the instructor):**
- **Trust Your "Gut Feeling":** The initial feeling that something is "off" is a critical signal that must be investigated.

- **Question Everything:** Treat every translation, whether human or AI, as a draft hypothesis, not a final fact.
- **Vagueness is a Red Flag:** Vagueness in a human translation is a hint that there is something unresolved; similarly, an incomplete or vague explanation from an AI is a sign of its own uncertainty and a cue for deeper probing. Here, a story which is supposed to be humorous but turns out to be bland is an indication that something is missed in the translation.
- **The Human's Role is to Ask Better Questions:** The ultimate quality of the translation depended not on the AI's initial knowledge, but on the human's persistence in asking precise, skeptical, and logically structured questions.

Such teaching modules places the student in the driver's seat of inquiry, making skepticism an active, powerful tool for discovery rather than a passive state of doubt.

Cultivating Critical Skepticism

A final, crucial step in integrating AI into translation pedagogy is to actively teach skepticism. As demonstrated by the AI's initial failure to reveal the true meaning in the story of Champagne, or its failure to render "Marie Kondo" as 近藤麻理惠, LLMs are fallible. They can miss cultural nuances, misinterpret context, or "hallucinate" information with supreme confidence. To prepare students for this reality, educators can simulate these failures by designing exercises using examples like Ex 7 and 9.

For error detection, teachers can adopt a simple role-playing exercise like the following:

Role-Playing Exercise: The AI Detective

Setup: The instructor provides students with an AI-revised translation that contains a known, subtle error (e.g., a cultural mistranslation, a plausible-sounding but incorrect term).

Task: The students' role is not to translate, but to act as fact-checkers. They must verify every significant change made by the AI using external tools (dictionaries, encyclopedias, search engines, terminology databases, parallel texts).

Goal: The students "win" by finding the AI's error and providing evidence-based reasoning for their correction. This exercise directly trains them to question AI outputs and develops their research and verification skills.

Considering the fact that different LLMs possess unique strengths and weaknesses stemming from their diverse training data, students must be warned of the limitations that a certain LLM can make in refining texts, and learn how to debug AI revisions using logic and domain knowledge. The triangulated method proposed in the proceeding section is an effective way to help students develop their abilities in this aspect.

In-Class Activity: The AI Translation Tribunal

This activity is designed to simulate the triangulated refinement process in translation. Its primary purpose is to move students beyond using a single AI tool and teach them the critical skill of leveraging multiple AI outputs combined with their own human judgment. By acting as "judges" who cross-examine multiple AI "witnesses," students learn to identify conflicting advice, synthesize the best elements from each, and resolve ambiguities, thereby producing a superior final translation. This process demonstrates that the modern translator's value lies not in competing with AI, but in orchestrating a human–machine collaboration to ensure maximum accuracy, cultural appropriateness, and stylistic nuance.

Activity Steps:

The Briefing:

The instructor introduces the activity, framing it as a "Tribunal." Students are the "judges." He then distributes a handout containing: (1) a short English source text with known difficulties, (2) a flawed human translation (the "case"), and (3) pre-generated revisions from two different AIs (e.g., GPT-4 and DeepSeek), who act as the "expert witnesses."

Group Deliberation:

Students form small groups ("judicial panels"). Using a structured worksheet, they compare how each AI model handled specific errors in the human translation (e.g., idioms, cultural references, mistranslations). For each error, they analyze which AI offered a better solution and why, noting any remaining flaws in the AI suggestions.

Synthesize the Verdict:

Based on their comparative analysis, each group synthesizes a new, definitive translation. This final version is not copied from one AI but is a polished hybrid, combining the best suggestions from both models with the group's own editorial judgment.

Announce and Justify:

Each group presents its final translation to the class. Crucially, they must justify one key decision, explaining how comparing the two AIs (the act of triangulation) allowed them to arrive at a superior solution that neither AI alone provided. The instructor concludes by summarizing how this process highlights the modern translator's role as a critical synthesizer and final arbiter of quality.

By incorporating these exercises, educators move students beyond being passive recipients of AI assistance. They become active, critical partners in a human–machine collaboration, equipped to leverage the AI's strengths while vigilantly guarding against its weaknesses. This approach ensures that the ultimate goal of this education process is not merely a better text, but a more capable and discerning translator.

3.4 AI Refinement Across Different Genres

While this paper uses data from texts of popular science and self-help, the human-guided triangulated workflow is also highly adaptable in literary or technical texts. In literary texts, a literal error is often less critical than a failure to capture metaphor, subtext, or authorial voice. The AI's strength lies in its ability to generate multiple alternatives for a single metaphor, but its weakness is its inability to grasp the metaphor's narrative function across the entire work. Realizing this, a translator/trainer/trainee can ask AI to brainstorm and provide several alternative ways to render a metaphor. As for legal and other technical texts, AI refinement can work as a proofreader with specific domain knowledge background and give highly valuable suggestions on the correctness of terminology. It can at least flag those "suspicious" items and alert the human translator to check. Educators can design and provide the genre-specific translation refinement activities to teach students that AI is not a monolithic tool but a versatile instrument. Regardless of text type, the core principles of critical evaluation and iterative prompting endure. What changes is the inquiry's focus, which must align with each type's unique demands.

3.5 Summary

Overall, compared to human editing/refinement, AI demonstrates higher efficiency. In general, due to the time-consuming and labor-intensive nature of bilingual editing/refinement, editors in publishing houses tend to view this as a "mission impossible", especially when faced with manuscripts of substantial volumes. Consequently, in practical work, they often adopt a monolingual working mode. When confronting low-quality translation texts like the one in this example, which are rife with extensive translationese and mistranslations, editors face significant challenges due to their limited cognitive resources, making it arduous to comprehensively address all potential linguistic issues. Their proofreading effectiveness generally falls short of AI's bilingual editing and refinement capabilities. Even when attempting to identify contradictions—such as the mismatch between "nephews" and female names—human editors frequently overlook the nuanced details of individuals' identities, inadvertently introducing subtle inaccuracies into the final translation. Additionally, it is worth noting that even some advanced LLMs, while adeptly recognizing Marie Kondo and Martha Stewart's identities and comprehending the underlying text, may still encounter challenges in employing flexible explanatory translation or strategically placed annotations to elucidate the two individuals' professional status as "organizing experts." Such contextual clarification would significantly enhance readers' understanding of why these renowned home organization professionals would "weep" at such an arrangement. These scenarios underscore the critical importance of human intervention in triangulation verification—seasoned translators can strategically harness the insights provided by AI to expedite and refine the translation process, bridging the gap between machine efficiency and nuanced human understanding.

4 Conclusion

Through the statistical analysis and exemplar-based investigation conducted in this study, we can now comprehensively address the research questions initially posited in the introductory section: (1) AI-driven refinement emerges as a robust methodology for detecting instances of translationese and textual errors in translated works. The remarkable computational capabilities demonstrated by LLMs suggest that integrating AI into translation editing and text refinement can significantly enhance overall linguistic precision and productivity. (2) Leveraging the successful identification of translationese—encompassing grammatical and syntactical anomalies—AI-powered editing and refinement demonstrate remarkable potential in elevating textual quality. Nevertheless, for a nuanced subset of translationese and mistranslations, comprehensive improvement necessitates strategic human intervention, particularly when navigating complex cultural contexts, ensuring logical coherence, and maintaining stylistic integrity. Consequently, contemporary LLMs are optimally positioned as "assistive technologies" for translation editing and refinement, strategically complementing rather than supplanting the expertise of professional translators and editors. (3) In the editing and refinement of translated texts, providing LLMs with bilingual source materials demonstrates superior reliability compared to presenting solely the translated version. (4) Given the recommended human–machine interactive approach in AI-assisted proofreading and refinement, a triangulated methodology emerges as the optimal strategy: utilizing two or more LLMs for cross-validation of translated texts, with strategic human intervention applied when necessary. Moreover, in instances where LLMs exhibit potential hallucination risks, traditional search engines may offer more reliable contextual verification. Ultimately, human expertise remains paramount in translation practice, serving as the critical final arbiter of linguistic accuracy and contextual nuance. It is also important to note that targeted pre-translation editing—strategically refining source materials with consideration of the target language's linguistic and cultural norms—can significantly enhance the quality of the initial translation, thereby substantially mitigating subsequent post-editing demands.

Building upon the pedagogical potential of AI translation refinement investigated in this research, the findings also advocate for a structured curriculum framework for AI-augmented translation education. Such a framework should be designed to cultivate critical thinking rather than mere operational skills. It could be structured around key modules, beginning with "AI Prompt Engineering," where students learn to craft precise instructions to guide AI analysis. This would be followed by a module on "Cultural and Contextual Nuance Debugging" to train students to identify the subtle errors that AIs often miss and to engage in iterative, skeptical inquiry. The curriculum would culminate in a "Triangulated Verification" module, where students learn to synthesize conflicting outputs from multiple LLMs. A suitable capstone assessment would be a final project requiring students to refine a complex text using at least two different AI models, submitting not only the polished translation but also a "Translator's Justification Report" defending their human interventions and final choices.

References

Denzin, N. K. (2017). *The Research Act: A Theoretical Introduction to Sociological Methods*. Routledge.

Fang, M. Z. (2011). 中国译学大辞典 *[A Dictionary of Translation Studies in China]*. Shanghai Foreign Language Education Press.

Kornacki, M., & Pietrzak, P. (2024). Translator–AI Interaction. In *Hybrid Workflows in Translation* (1st ed.). Routledge.

Lin, Y. T. (1994). 语言学论丛 [Essays on Linguistics]. In 林语堂全集 (第19卷) *[The Complete Works of Lin Yutang]* (Vol. 19). Northeast Normal University Press.

Shuttleworth, M., & Cowie, M. (2014). *Dictionary of Translation Studies*. Routledge.

Tan, Y. S. (2012). 翻译教学的认知语言学观 [A Cognitive Linguistics Perspective on Translation Teaching]. 外语界 [*Foreign Language World*], (03), 66–73+88.

Xu, J. (2021). 关于文学翻译的语言问题 [Linguistic Considerations in Literary Translation]. *Foreign Languages (Journal of Shanghai International Studies University)*, *44*(01), 91–98.

Xu Bin (1972–) is a professor from Shandong Normal University. He is now head of the Master of Translation and Interpreting program. He has published over 30 papers in academic journals at home and abroad. He has published more than 60 translated works, covering a wide range of disciplines such as literature, history, (popular) science, etc. The titles include Einstein's Cosmos (Michio Kaku), The Artful Universe (John Barrow), Now: The Physics of Time (Richard Muller), Einstein's Dice and Schrödinger's Cat (Paul Halpern), Pacific Crucible and The Conquering Tide (The Pacific War Trilogy, 1 & 2), etc. He has also translated several books from Chinese into English as well as the subtitles of over 10 episodes of documentaries which has been put on the screen on Discovery Channel, NHK, etc. He is a pioneer in the research of translation technology in China, and has published the first monograph on translation technology in China, New Vision of Translation, as well as other academic monographs such as Guidelines for Writing Computer-Assisted Research Papers. He has completed one project of the National Social Science Foundation (2015) and participated in several other projects of the National Social Science Foundation and the Chinese Academy of Social Sciences.

Comparing Generative AI and Traditional Machine Translation Systems: An Assessment of Computer Errors and the Human Post-Editing Process

Kizito Tekwa

Abstract ChatGPT's release in late 2022 threw generative AI (GenAI) chatbots into the spotlight, significantly disrupting the status quo of numerous fields of study. Translation studies quickly adopted GenAI as researchers compared it with current neural machine translation (NMT) systems and leveraged its multiple potentials. However, despite growing interest, few studies have evaluated and documented GenAI chatbots' translation errors. To bridge this gap, a comparison of translations of a specialized text using ChatGPT and three traditional neural machine translation (NMT) systems is performed, and errors are documented. Furthermore, by recording the screens of posteditors, an analysis of the translation process is performed to: (1) Determine whether posteditors need more or less effort working on ChatGPT-translated texts and (2) Assess posteditors' practices during the editing process. The multiple findings have significant practical and pedagogical implications vis-à-vis human–computer interactions during postediting.

Keywords Generative artificial intelligence · ChatGPT · Neural machine translation · Postediting · Human–computer interaction

1 Introduction

GenAI has emerged as a prominent field of study, completely revolutionizing processes and applications across multiple domains. In the translation field, AI-based chatbots have particularly disrupted established neural machine translation (NMT) systems like Google Translate, Baidu Translate, and DeepL, which dominated translation research and practice before ChatGPT's release in late 2022. The multiplicity of machine translation (MT) systems had ushered in a period of translation research underpinned by comparisons among various systems, especially vis-à-vis efforts

K. Tekwa (✉)
Shenzhen Technology University, Shenzhen, China
e-mail: tekwakizito@outlook.com

T. Yin et al. (eds.), *AI Through LLMs*, New Frontiers in Translation Studies,
https://doi.org/10.1007/978-981-95-4798-2_5

deplored to post-edit machine-translated texts. Aligned with the development of MT systems, research has, for instance, evaluated efforts deplored to post-edit passages translated using rule-based, statistical, example-based, and neural MT systems (Jia et al., 2019; Stasimioti et al., 2020; Zaretskaya et al., 2016). The focus has been on the time spent, keystrokes, with pauses and cognitive effort. Therefore, it has been a natural phenomenon for translation researchers to compare AI-based chatbots like ChatGPT with traditional MT systems (Cady et al., 2023; Khoshfah, 2023; Manakhimova et al., 2023; Omazić & Šoštarić, 2023). Based on many conclusions, GenAI chatbots compete with traditional MT systems, especially in translating general text types.

Despite the conclusions and seemingly massive appetite among translation researchers, GenAI's application as a translation and post-editing tool has not been sufficiently evaluated. More precisely, research on applying GenAI chatbots both as translation and post-editing (PE) tools remains scanty. In other words, research has not sufficiently explained whether GenAI-translated texts contain fewer errors and whether post-editing them poses fewer significant challenges to post-editors, despite research on the ability of chatbots to comprehend language and foster translation (Liu et al., 2024). Some questions requiring investigations include: "Do GenAI-translated texts contain fewer errors than traditional MT-translated texts? Do they require less post-editing effort? How challenging is it for posteditors to employ GenAI chatbots as postediting (PE) tools?" Therefore, this study attempts to answer these questions based on the perception that the findings will, among others, facilitate GenAI chatbot integration into translator training.

The study participants are eight graduate trainees enrolled in a Chinese university's Machine Translation Post-editing (MTPE) course. As part of regular training, the trainee post-editors edited a technical document (users' manual) translated using ChatGPT and three MT systems, including Baidu, DeepL, and LanguageX. Since there were eight post-editors and four post-editing (PE) tools, two post-editors edited texts translated using the same tool. That means there was one source text (ST), one ChatGPT and three MT-translated versions, and eight post-edited versions, as indicated in Fig. 1.

To assess how the PE process differed based on the PE tool, post-editors using ChatGPT were required to utilize the chatbot during the entire translation and post-editing process. This was because, unlike traditional NMT systems, ChatGPT facilitates terminological research and information mining and answers language requests. The entire translation and PE activities were screen-recorded and then analyzed to determine whether ChatGPT produced a translation with fewer errors and facilitated the PE process.

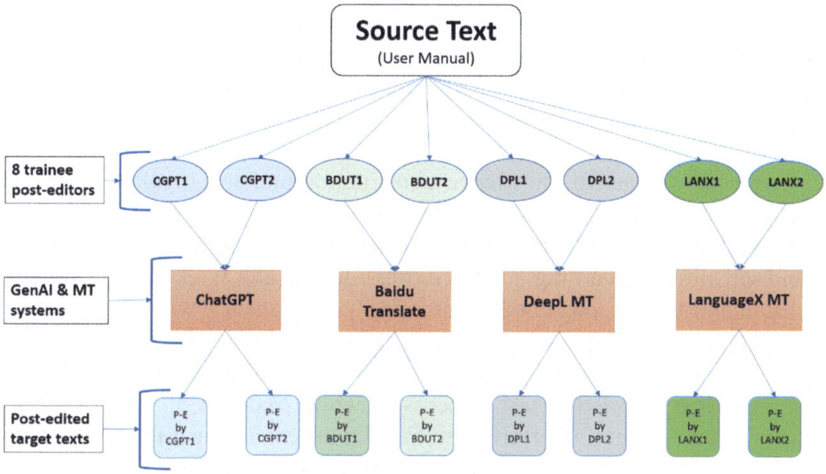

Fig. 1 Translation and post-editing task structure

2 Theoretical Framework and Literature Review

2.1 Theoretical Framework: Process-Oriented Learning Framework

The process-oriented framework provides a structured approach to learning and task execution, emphasizing the analysis and improvement of underlying processes rather than solely focusing on the outcome (Vermunt & Vermetten, 2004). It features a cognitive and metacognitive focus, exploring how individuals process information, manage their learning, and adjust strategies, with Vermunt and Vermetten (2004) introducing tools like the Inventory of Learning Styles (ILS) to track these efforts. This framework also adopts a multidimensional approach, as suggested by Bolhuis (2003), by incorporating social, cultural, emotional, and contextual elements to create a supportive learning environment that fosters self-directed growth. Gijbels et al. (2014) highlight the importance of recognizing diverse learning patterns shaped by cultural and personal differences, calling for customized educational strategies. Meanwhile, Vrieling et al. (2010) advocate for practical design principles, such as scaffolding and feedback, to enhance self-regulation and process improvement across various settings. Together, this framework serves as both a theoretical foundation and a practical tool, guiding the creation of interventions that enhance learning and performance by focusing on the evolving nature of the process rather than just the result.

The process-oriented learning framework has been adeptly applied across various disciplines, prioritizing the enhancement of cognitive and procedural processes over mere outcomes. Initially, in teacher education, Vrieling et al. (2010) utilize scaffolding and structured feedback to cultivate self-regulated learning among primary teachers, thereby strengthening their instructional capabilities. Similarly, Abdous (2011) extends this approach to online teaching, emphasizing processes like strategic planning and adaptation to develop effective virtual instruction competencies. Moreover, in educational psychology, Vermunt and Verschaffel (2000a, 2000b) advocate for active knowledge construction and self-regulation, fostering lifelong learning skills in students. Additionally, Grandbastien et al. (2003) apply the framework to design online learning environments that support cognitive engagement and self-directed learning. Furthermore, Foucrier and Wiek (2019) implement it in sustainability entrepreneurship, aligning competencies with entrepreneurial processes to tackle complex sustainability challenges. In the translation discipline, Tekwa (2024) employs video ethnography to analyze collaborative and individual computer-assisted translation task processes, while Malta et al. (2019) use eye-tracking to examine cognitive effort in (re)translation, enhancing training by focusing on translators' procedural strategies and resource management.

2.2 Literature Review Machine Translation Post-Editing

MT systems, including Google Translate, Baidu Translate, and DeepL, are popular due to their ubiquity. Their use, including by smartphone owners, does not necessarily hinge on their translation or foreign language knowledge. However, MT-translated texts often contain errors that could have far-reaching semantic implications, hence the need for post-editing. According to O'Brien (2022, p. 105), "the identification of such errors and their revision, or correction, is known as post-editing." The PE process involves inputting a text into an MT system, which translates it using a pre-determined translation memory (TM), i.e., a bilingual database of previous translations. The MT system then outputs the texts, obviously with errors, which are corrected by a human, i.e., a post-editor.

Efforts of post-editors have been compared based on the tool or MT system utilized. For instance, in a study comparing the post-editing and human efforts of 16 postgraduate translation students based on three MT systems—statistical MT, generic NMT, and tailored-NMT outputs, Stasimioti et al. (2020) concluded that participants had a higher score for both generic NMT and tailored-NMT outputs. In a study that focused on the technical effort and temporal PE effort spent on post-editing different errors from different MT systems (rule-based, statistical, and hybrid engines), Zaretskaya et al. (2016) found a weak correlation between time and effort though more time was invested in errors that required mistranslations and literal translations. In another study comparing the effort of students post-editing simple and complex texts translated using a phrase-based statistical MT system and a generic NMT system, Jia et al. (2019) concluded that translation by the NMT system led to reduced technical and cognitive PE effort and that "in contrast to HT (human translation), post-editing effort is not necessarily correlated with the source text complexity" (Jia et al., 2019, p. 9). Toral et al.'s (2018) study focused on the post-editing by six translators of a novel translated using two MT systems —phrase-based statistical MT and NMT. The researchers found an increase in productivity, though more for NMT, in terms of reductions in keystrokes and lower cognitive effort, but longer pauses.

MT systems produce different error types, including grammatical, syntactic, omissions, lexical, terminological, collocational, and stylistic. The number of errors produced depends on the MT system, the "language pair and direction, content type, and the data or techniques used to train the MT engine" (O'Brien, 2022, p. 106). The number of MT errors correlates with the effort required to post-edit the texts. For example, Daems et al. (2017) investigated the PE effort, concluding that "machine translation quality has an impact on product and process post-editing effort indicators alike…with coherence issues, grammatical issues and other meaning shifts being good candidates for effort prediction on the basis of MT quality" (p. 14). Though MT errors are predominantly classified as fluency (language-related) or adequacy (meaning-related), it is worthy of note that MT error types also depend on the MT system and language combination (Bojar, 2011; Haque et al., 2020).

Meanwhile, PE effort describes the labor intensiveness of the PE activity. PE effort is often measured using several methods and tools, including keystroke logging (Daems et al., 2017; Toral et al., 2018), eye-tracking, human perception, and time spent (Toral et al., 2018). Simultaneously, efforts have been made to design automated tools that track MT errors to reduce the post-editors' efforts. For instance, Specia and Farzindar (2010) designed the Human-targeted Translation Edit Rate (HTER) to determine sequence-level errors in machine-translated texts to facilitate PE effort. In addition, think-aloud protocols (O'Brien, 2005, p. 37), which "cast light on the temporal, cognitive and technical aspects of post-editing effort," have predicted PE effort. Moreover, PE effort has been determined based on post-editors' perceptions of such effort (Koponen, 2012) and the length of documented pauses during the post-editing process (Jakobsen, 2019).

2.3 Generative AI for Translation and Post-Editing

With the ubiquity of GenAI chatbots, research has focused on their ability to comprehend human language, including summarizing, translating, or enhancing translation. In a study on ChatGPT's understanding ability, Zhong et al. (2023) evaluated the chatbot on the GLUE benchmark and compared it with four representative fine-tuned BERT-style models. It was found that ChatGPT performed comparatively poorly in paraphrasing, had a comparable performance on sentimental analysis, and considerably outperformed all BERT models in inference tasks. With regard to summarization, researchers have had mixed conclusions depending on the AI model and text type summarized. For instance, an experiment by Liu et al. (2024) on the use of three AI models—BART (proposed by Facebook), ChatGPT, and BERTSUM (a summarization AI model based on the BERT model) to summarize medical dialogues generated during online consultations found the results of ChatGPT more reliable and akin to human performance than BART and BERTSUM results. Hence, attempts to propose approaches that address the issue of large language models (LLMs) failing to recall past information and generating inconsistent responses with long texts and lengthy conversations (Wang et al., 2023).

As part of investigations on how AI chatbots can enhance translation, researchers have focused on known shortcomings, including generating prompts in complex tasks that involve low-resource and distant-pair languages. Prompt engineering remains crucial in GenAI's ability to perform effective translations. Therefore, in their study, Peng et al. (2023) assess ChatGPT's translation ability, focusing on temperature, task information, and domain information. Based on these elements, they propose and examine two types of simple but effective prompts—task-specific and domain-specific prompts and their effects on translation output. They conclude that the performance of ChatGPT depends on temperature, with lower temperatures that yield better output. In addition, both task and domain information improve the chatbot's performance, though hallucinations are often generated for non-English-centric MT tasks.

Prompt engineering is the deliberate and systematic crafting of input instructions to guide large language models (LLMs), such as ChatGPT, toward producing precise and contextually appropriate outputs for tasks like text generation and translation. It involves formulating structured prompts that specify linguistic nuances, cultural contexts, or task requirements to customize LLM behavior and optimize performance (White et al., 2023). By addressing complex linguistic challenges, such as idiomatic expressions or cultural specificity, prompt engineering ensures high-quality, relevant results, making it a crucial skill for effectively leveraging AI technologies.

In translation education, prompt engineering aligns with digital competence frameworks, such as those proposed by Korzynski et al. (2023), which emphasize information management, critical thinking, and technology-mediated communication. Accurate prompting enables students to produce contextually precise translations, as demonstrated by Ajai Krishna et al. (2024), who improved English-Tamil and English-Hindi translations using GPT-3.5, as evaluated by BLEU and METEOR scores. Task-based learning (TBL) facilitates this by engaging students in authentic tasks, such as crafting prompts for specialized texts (e.g., medical or legal documents). Through prompt design, execution, and feedback-driven refinement, TBL cultivates critical digital literacy, equipping students to meet real-world translation demands with precision and cultural sensitivity (Korzynski et al., 2023; Ajai Krishna et al., 2024).

Meanwhile, other investigations on GenAI's contribution to translation have underscored discrepancies in models and MT systems, language combinations, and different domains. For instance, Manakhimova et al. (2023) compared ChatGPT's translations in English, German, and Russian, while Cady et al. (2023) compared ChatGPT with NMT leaders in the industry using a Chinese-English patent corpus. For their part, Jiang and Zhang (2024) compared ChatGPT with other influential NMT systems in the industry using a corpus of diplomatic texts, while Omazić and Šoštarić (2023) compared how ChatGPT and major NMT systems differed in their translation of legal texts. The MT output quality, assessed using BLEU and human evaluators, indicated that ChatGPT performed as well as, and in some instances, surpassed other NMT systems and Google Translate (Sanz-Valdivieso & López-Arroyo, 2023). Despite these conclusions, professionals were advised not to rely wholly on GenAI output, cautioning against the limitations of ChatGPT (Khoshafah, 2023). In particular, ChatGPT's shortcomings in handling the language of a technical domain were highlighted by Cady et al. (2023). Khoshafah (2023, p. 1) concluded that "ChatGPT can be used as a translator for simple content, though it struggles with complexities that require human intervention," and Manakhimova et al. (2023) highlighted the chatbot's limitations in translating linguistic nuances.

However, few studies have examined how post-editors simultaneously employ GenAI as a translation and PE tool, presumably because the model is relatively new and may currently not be widely used in the industry. A few studies have investigated GenAI chatbots and PE; however, they have mainly used ChatGPT as an "automatic post-editor of raw output from the pay-for version of DeepL Translator" (Farrell, 2023, p. 108). The conclusion that ChatGPT reached human proficiency levels in automatic monolingual PE and exceeded human translation in automatic bilingual PE was insightful. Unlike comparing how GenAI chatbots can post-edit MT output, Wang (2023) evaluated their usefulness in building a knowledge pool and terminology database to edit texts automatically. Another experiment by Moslem et al. (2023) included utilizing large language models (LLMs) to generate bilingual terminologies for PE machine-translated texts. In other words, the LLM data was infused with specialized terminologies, which were leveraged in performing a terminology-constrained post-editing of the translation. According to Moslem et al., (2023, p. 902), the approach was effective in "improving the integration of pre-approved terms into translations…across language pairs."

2.4 Research Lacunae and Research Questions

Interactions between translators, post-editors, and GenAI chatbots in translation and post-editing have not been adequately studied. First, process-oriented studies investigating how post-editors edit GenAI-generated translation have not been foregrounded. Such studies shed light on details, often overlooked in the PE process, that could inform pedagogical choices and methods. According to Vermunt and Verschaffel (2000a, 2000b), process learning is crucial because it integrates teaching and learning with thinking strategies and "domain-specific knowledge" (p. 209). Second, many questions remain unanswered regarding human interactions with AI-based translation chatbots and other MT systems, and few studies have compared MT output, GenAI-translated output, and human output using humans as evaluators. Third, human–computer interactions that underpin post-editing, like temporality, terminological research, instruction compliance, data mining, and tool design interface (Carl et al., 2011), have not informed discussions regarding translations by AI-based chatbots.

Furthermore, although MT and GenAI-based translations have been compared for specialized texts (Cady et al., 2023), a significant scarcity of research remains on comparing the challenges of post-editing specialized texts using GenAI and MT systems. Furthermore, comparisons between GenAI and traditional MT systems have been scarce within the process-oriented translation framework. In other words, GenAI-based translation processes have not been compared with current post-editing processes that mainly focus on texts translated by traditional MT systems like Google, Baidu, and DeepL. In other words, research has not determined whether GenAI-translated texts are perceptibly easier to post-edit than traditional machine-translated texts. Such comparisons, whether undertaken by professional or trainee translators, remain crucial.

The existence of these lacunae suggests that the pedagogical and practical applications of GenAI are not well understood. Hence, empirical evidence from research is required to understand the practical and pedagogical applications of GenAI in translation. Current researchers have used AI chatbots as translation tools, but have not provided sufficient information on the best pedagogical practices and approaches for trainees to use GenAI. The current study intends to bridge this gap by answering the following research questions:

- RQ1: Do GenAI-translated technical texts contain fewer errors and are easier to PE than traditional machine-translated texts?
- RQ2: Do GenAI-translated texts require less effort to PE than traditional machine-translated texts?
- RQ3: What are post-editors' practices when utilizing GenAI chatbots as PE tools?

This study answers these questions by comparing non-human post-edited errors of a technical text (user manual) translated using ChatGPT and three NMT systems. It then evaluates the post-editing process, which is screen-recorded and analyzed to determine practices that facilitate or inhibit the utilization of ChatGPT as a PE tool.

Translating user manuals is crucial for ensuring product usability, safety, and accessibility across global markets, particularly for technical products like medical devices or electronics, where precise, culturally sensitive instructions prevent misuse and enhance user experience. Therefore, a process-oriented approach (Vermunt & Verschaffel, 2000a, 2000b) supports endeavor by emphasizing cognitive and metacognitive strategies that enable translators to analyze source texts and adapt terminology for diverse audiences. Prompt engineering is complementary in that it facilitates the crafting of targeted inputs for large language models (LLMs), specifying technical jargon and cultural nuances to produce accurate translations, as shown by improved BLEU and METEOR scores in multilingual tasks (Ajai Krishna et al., 2024). Task-based learning (TBL), aligned with digital competence frameworks (Korzynski et al., 2023), facilitates training by engaging students in real-world manual translation tasks, with iterative feedback refining the design of prompts. These approaches could enhance high-quality, user-friendly translations that meet industry standards and foster critical digital literacy.

3 Methodology

3.1 Study Design

The study took place in the 15th week of the course after trainees had post-edited 7 different text types, including formal letters, restaurant menus, user manuals, newspaper articles, general economic texts, resumes, and cover letters. Furthermore, given that participants had no previous experience with MTPE despite informally translating using MT systems, we considered 14 weeks of MTPE training sufficient to prepare them for the study. On Week 13, trainees learned how to write a manual in English, followed by an MT and PE task on manual translation. In Week 14, they received feedback on the PE task and discussed the associated challenges, as outlined in Fig. 2.

The study, therefore, repeated the tasks performed during weeks 13 and 14 of the semester. By this time, the trainees were already familiar with the text type and the translation process, given their previous use of the systems.

Participants

Eight participants (five females and three males) were first-year graduate students. Although the number of participants appears limited, this practice is consistent with translation studies research, often mirroring the industry's practical realities (Toral et al., 2018), where translators work individually (as freelancers) and in teams. For example, the study of whether post-editing influences creativity (Guerberof et al., 2024) involved four students from the University of Groningen and eleven students from Leiden University. Furthermore, it is common practice in the research arena to

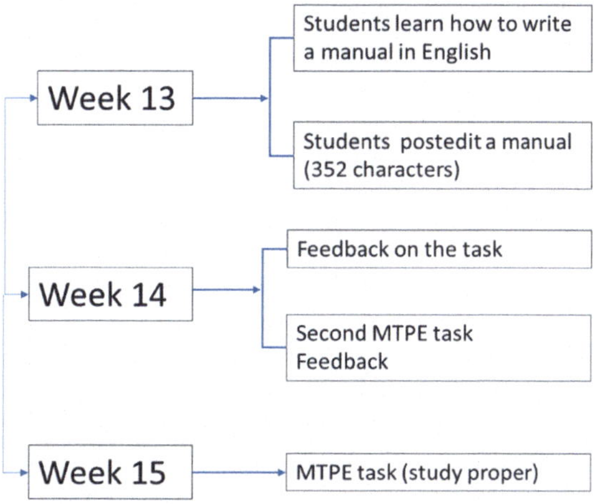

Fig. 2 Activities during the two weeks preceding the study

present the opinions of individual experts (Zhang, 2019) or small groups of experts via interviews or roundtable discussions (Moorkens et al., 2024).

Participants were enrolled in the Masters of Translation and Interpretation (MTI) program at a Chinese university and were required to take the MTPE course. They were all native Chinese speakers and had succeeded in a rigorous entrance examination into the program, during which they translated into English. They also attended two levels of interviews and took an English proficiency test. Trainees were selected after taking an entrance examination assessing their proficiency in Chinese and English and their translation and interpretation levels, as outlined in Table1.

The course lasted for 18 weeks, during which trainees learned about MT systems, identified and corrected MT errors, used CAT tools, and post-edited multiple texts multiple times, sometimes adapting them to audiences with different cultural backgrounds.

Data Collection and Instruments

To answer the research question, we recorded the trainees' screens as machine-translated and post-edited the text. We also required them to answer a few questions on the post-edited texts that they had submitted.

– Video screen recording

The EV Screen recorder, selected because it is easy to download and install on desktop and laptop computers, was utilized in the study. Trainees installed the recorder on their PCs or on desktop computers provided in the CAT laboratory where lessons are generally held. They recorded their screens while performing the MT and PE tasks. In total, eight screen recordings corresponding to the eight trainees were obtained for analysis. The video lengths differed, though none was one hour long (lengths). The screen recordings covered the entire MTPE activity from the beginning to the end. This included the time taken to perform the PE task, the terminological

Table 1 Background of trainees

Item	Explanation
Native Language	Chinese
English level	Level determined after entrance examination into the program. The examination included translation, interpretation, English language tests, and face-to-face interviews in English
Experience with MTPE	No previous knowledge before admission into the program. However, there were 13 weeks of MTPE training prior to the experiment
Familiarity with the source text	Trainees learned (1) How to write a manual in English and (2) How to post-edit a manual text two weeks before the experiment

resources consulted, the time taken to postedit the text, computer interface management, including the number of open tabs/windows, non-task related actions, steps followed in the process, and.

- Machine-translated text

Trainees were requested to machine-translate and postedit a 431-character furniture assembly manual. The text contained 5-step instructions to mark assembly points, assemble embedded components, wheels and other moving parts, screw different components, and attach wheels at the base of the furniture. The text was translated using GenAI and three MT systems – Baidu Translate, DeepL, and LanguageX. Two trainees independently used ChatGPT while two trainees each used the three MT systems.

3.2 Data Analysis

Error Annotation Process

To answer the first research question, we required trainees to extract the number of MT errors identified in each text. The MT errors of the texts were evaluated before they were post-edited. They were evaluated based on two criteria—fluency and adequacy (see Appendix 1). They were rated by the trainees, then by two translator trainers with 23 years of teaching experience and one professional translator with seven years of experience. Considering that all evaluators were translation instructors and professionals who had used the same assessment rubric and fully understood the source text, being Chinese native speakers, we did not deem it necessary to have any formal pre-assessment training. However, a trial assessment was conducted, where each evaluator annotated two target texts, followed by an evaluation by the researchers. A few discrepancies were identified, and a brief online meeting was held to harmonize various perspectives. The inter-rater reliability among the two instructors and a professional translator was significantly high (Cohen's Kappa = 0.89). The differences were mainly in areas requiring subjective scoring, including style (10 points) and naturalness (10 points). To ensure the homogeneity of the scores, we performed a paired-sample T-test to determine statistical differences among the various evaluators' scores. No differences were found.

RQ1: Do GenAI-Translated Technical Texts Contain Fewer Errors and Are Easier to PE Than Traditional Machine-Translated Texts?

First, trainees identified the MT errors in the text before post-editing the texts. That means there were eight MT error reports, two each for ChatGPT and the NMT systems. Each tool's two MT error reports were consolidated into a single report, containing only the errors identified by both trainees (redundant errors were counted as a single instance). Then, the three invited evaluators were handed four unedited texts, one translated using ChatGPT and the others using the three MT systems. The evaluators identified MT errors using the same criteria as the trainees. Ultimately, four MT error reports (one from the trainees and three from the evaluators) were analyzed to compare the performance of ChatGPT with that of other MT systems.

To determine whether the ChatGPT-translated text was easier to post-edit, we asked trainees, after post-editing their texts, to rank the level of difficulty on a scale from 1 (not at all difficult) to 10 (extremely difficult). Also, the three evaluators rated the level of difficulty of the text based on the errors they identified. Then, we found the average difficulty level for each text by adding and dividing the ranking provided by trainees and evaluators.

RQ2: Do GenAI-Translated Texts Require Less Effort to PE Than Traditional Machine-Translated Texts?

We analyzed the screen recordings of trainees to determine the PE effort, focusing on temporality because the "time spent on post-editing can be seen as the most visible and economically most important aspect of post-editing effort (Koponen, 2012, p. 181). Furthermore, trainees scored their perceived post-editing effort, which we used to triangulate the temporal elements evaluated. Accordingly, we coded the videos using the V-Note analysis tool (Tekwa, 2024) to determine the following:

- total time spent on the MTPE activity
- total time spent on conducting terminology research
- total time of pauses (no visible action on the screen)
- total time spent on non-task-related activities, including on social media.

Therefore, the video was coded using several colors, as demonstrated in Table 2.

In addition, we tallied the number of prompts and requests for information while interacting with ChatGPT or accessing online resources (OR). Given that two trainees used the same MT system or ChatGPT, we divided their time by two to obtain the total time for each tool. Once we obtained the time spent on each tool, we performed T-tests and one-way ANOVA to determine the statistical and practical differences among the data of various PE tools. The time spent reflected the efforts trainees exerted on the PE activity.

Table 2 Coded items and their respective color codes

	Item coded	Color code
1	Total MTPE time	Blue
2	Terminology time	Red
3	Pauses	Yellow
4	Non-task-related activities	Orange

RQ3: Do Some Trainees' PE Practices Deserve Particular Attention?

We answered this question by observing trainees' interactions with ChatGPT and how they post-edited their texts. We analyzed the accuracy of trainees' prompts and ChatGPT's responses, computer screen management, including the number of tabs or windows open, the alignment of the source and target text being post-edited, access to OR, and non-task-related activities (for instance, accessing social media sites). In our findings, we focused on practices with pedagogical and practical implications.

4 Findings

In this section, we analyzed data obtained from the video recordings, perception of the level of MTPE difficulty, and assessment of the MTPE output to answer our two research questions. Therefore, our findings are structured based on the RQs.

4.1 RQ1: Do GenAI-Translated Technical Texts Contain Fewer Errors and Are Easier to PE Than Traditional Machine-Translated Texts?

GenAI-Translated Technical Texts Contain Fewer Fluency and Adequacy Errors

We analyzed the MT errors based on fluency and accuracy with rubrics from a combination of translation quality assessment (TQA) models (Lommel, 2018). The MT errors were identified by trainees, two translator trainers, and a professional translator. We computed the average number of errors for texts translated using each tool.

Fluency Errors

We evaluated the generative-AI-translated and machine-translated text based on naturalness, language, style, punctuation, and formatting (see Appendix 1). The errors found are presented in Table 3.

The data indicates that ChatGPT had the lowest number of errors, followed by DeepL, Baidu, and LanguageX. Grammar appeared to have the most significant differences, given that ChatGPT had 2.75 errors, while the MT systems had 4 errors or more (LanguageX = 5.25).

The subjective scoring of the Naturalness and Style categories corroborated the data. The average scores for Naturalness were 8.5, 7, 7.5, and 6.6 for ChatGPT, Baidu Translate, DeepL, and LanguageX, respectively, while the Style scores were 6.1, 2.5, 2.5, and 2 for ChatGPT, Baidu Translate, DeepL, and LanguageX, respectively. The data showed that ChatGPT outperformed MT systems in these two categories.

Table 3 Average number of fluency errors per MTPE tool

	Item	ChatGPT	Baidu	DeepL	LanX
Fluency	Naturalness 10pts (subjective scoring)	–	–	–	–
	Language 25pts(total)				
	Grammar 5pts	***2.75***	4	4	5.25
	Tenses 5pts	***2.75***	2.75	2.75	2.75
	Collocations 5pts	***1.75***	3.5	2.5	3.75
	Prepositions 5pts	***2.75***	2.75	2.75	2.75
	Miscellaneous 5pts	***3.75***	4	4	5.5
	Style 10pts (Subjective scoring)	–	–	–	–
	Punctuation and Formatting 10pts	***1***	1.75	1.25	2.5
Average total errors		*14.75*	18.75	17.25	22.5

The considerable discrepancy in Style may be because ChatGPT was told it was translating a manual into English. Consequently, it followed the convention for writing instructions in English by utilizing the active voice, as demonstrated in the following example in Table 4.

ChatGPT employs an active voice in the clause "install all the screws on the board," and unlike Baidu and DeepL, avoids repeating the words "install" and "mount."

Table 4 Differences in style between ChatGPT and NMT systems

Source text	Tool	Translation
安装螺钉仔细区分板的ab位置，例如嵌入式螺钉上的螺钉，清除ab位置后，板上的所有安装螺钉都是安装	ChatGPT	Carefully distinguish between the **A and B** positions on the board, such as screws on embedded screws. After clearing the A and B positions, **install all the screws on the board**
	Baidu Translate	Carefully distinguish the **AB** position of the board when installing screws, such as the screws on the embedded screws. After removing the AB position, **all installation screws on the board are installed**
	DeepL	Carefully distinguish the **ab** position of the board, for example, on the recessed screws, after clearing the ab position, **all mounting screws on the board are mounted**,…
	LanguageX	Deliberately install screws, distinguishing meticulously the ab position—as with the embedded screws on the surface. Once the ab position is cleared, **all screws installed upon the board are identical in function**;…

Furthermore, unlike in the source text, ChatGPT distinguishes positions A and B and ends the sentence, as is often the case in manuals, with a period. This is crucial because manuals use short, precise, concise, and simple sentences (Končar, 2020).

Adequacy Errors

On average, ChatGPT outperformed the three MT systems based on the number of errors in the adequacy category. The data shows that, overall, ChatGPT made 10.75 adequacy errors, followed by DeepL (12.75), Baidu Translate (15.75), and LanguageX (19.25), as outlined in Table 5.

With an average of 18 errors across all MTPE tools, wrong terms were the most common error type, followed by mistranslations (14.75 errors), semantically inaccurate translations (11 errors), under-translation (8 errors), omissions (6 errors), and additions (0.75 errors). For instance, the term "偏心轮" is sometimes translated by LanguageX into "biased gear" and "bi-convex disc" and by Baidu Translate into "eccentric disc," which, by our estimations, are wrong terms. Besides terminological errors, there were general mistranslation errors, as outlined in Table 6.

Further instances of terminological errors are evident with the Chinese term "板" (board), translated into "place" by Baidu Translate and DeepL. In contrast, though LanguageX maintains the term "board," it performs a near-incomprehensive translation—a mistranslation: "The position of the eccentric wheel is to place correctly within the hole, neither too high nor too low upon the board." We also consider the translation of "以正确的 " + -"方向拧紧连接器以完成" into "Fractured the linker by applying the correct " + " and "-" direction" as a mistranslation. Furthermore, LanguageX erroneously employs the wrong article "a" instead of "the" in the expression "The final step in fixing *a* biased gear...".

ChatGPT outperformed traditional MT systems in all categories except in the wrong term category, where the AI chatbot had an identical number of errors with DeepL. A computation of the mean score and standard deviation of the fluency and adequacy errors of the four tools confirmed the MT error data. In particular, ChatGPT ($M = 2.13$, SD = 1.28) outperformed DeepL ($M = 2.5$, SD = 1.26), Baidu Translate ($M = 2.88$, SD = 1.37), and LanguageX ($M = 3.48$, SD = 1.39) and a T-test indicated

Table 5 Average number of adequacy errors per MTPE tool

	Item	ChatGPT	Baidu T	DeepL	LanX
Adequacy	Mistranslation 10pts	*2.75*	4.25	3	4.75
	Under-translation 10pts	*1.25*	2	1.75	3
	Wrong term 10pts	*4.25*	4.75	4.25	4.75
	Omission 5pts	*0.5*	1.5	1.5	2.5
	Semantically inaccurate 10pts	*2*	3.25	2.25	3.5
	Addition 5pts	*0*	0	0	0.75
		10.75	15.75	12.75	19.25

Table 6 Terminological and mistranslation errors by NMT systems

Original text	ChatGPT	Baidu Translate	DeepL	LangaugeX
偏心轮固定最后一步是将偏心轮放入孔中。偏心轮的位置可以正确地放置在孔中，不高于板或低于板。这是正确的孔深度。以正确的 " + -"方向拧紧连接器以完成。	The final step to fix the eccentric wheels is to insert them into the holes. The position of the eccentric wheels can be correctly placed in the hole, not higher or lower than the board. This is the correct hole depth. Tighten the connector in the correct " + - "direction to complete	The final step in fixing the eccentric wheel is to place the eccentric wheel into the hole. The position of the eccentric disc can be correctly placed in the hole, not higher or lower than the plate. This is the correct hole depth. Tighten the connector in the correct " + -" direction to complete	The final step in fixing the eccentric wheel is to place the eccentric wheel into the hole. The eccentric wheel can be positioned correctly in the hole, not above or below the plate. This is the correct hole depth. Tighten the connector in the correct " + -" direction to finish	The final step in fixing a biased gear is to place the bi-convex disc within the hole. The position of the eccentric wheel is to place correctly within the hole, neither too high nor too low upon the board. This is the correct aperture depth. Fractured the linker by applying the correct " + " and "-" direction

that the data was statistically significant ($p = < .001$), with a large effect size (i.e., a significant practical impact) of Cohen's d over 1.0.

GenAI-Translated Texts Were Perceived to Be Easier to Post-Edit

The task's difficulty level was assessed by trainees (individually) and the three invited evaluators. They were required to score the difficulty level on a scale from one (not at all difficult) to ten (extremely difficult). Trainees assessed the difficulty level after post-editing the text, while the evaluators assessed it after evaluating the MT errors of each tool. Our finding was based on the presumption that the higher the difficulty level, the harder it was to post-edit the text.

Based on the analysis, ChatGPT-translated texts were perceived to be less challenging to post-edit than texts translated using other MT systems. This perception was shared by all trainees and the three evaluators, as outlined in Table 7.

The data analysis shows that trainees rated the texts as more difficult to PE, given that their mean score was $M = 8.19$, compared to $M = 7.62$, $M = 7.87$, and $M = 6.87$ for evaluators 1 and 2 (translator trainers) and 3(professional translator),

Table 7 Perceived difficulty levels of the text per evaluator

	ChatGPT	Baidu translate	DeepL	LanguageX
Trainees	7.25	8.25	8.5	8.75
Evaluator 1	6	8	7.5	9
Evaluator 2	6.5	9	8	8
Evaluator 3	5	7.5	7	8

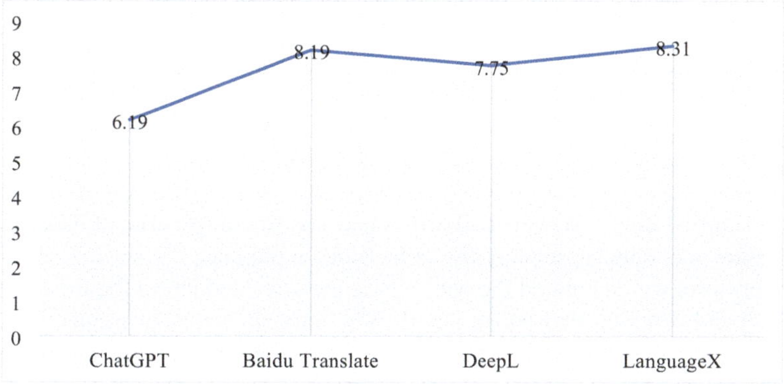

Fig. 3 Perceived difficulty level of the text per tool

respectively. Furthermore, based on the tool type, the text translated using ChatGPT was perceived as easier to PE, as outlined in Fig. 3.

Furthermore, we computed the data into SPSS and performed a one-way ANOVA to determine the statistical and practical differences among the variables. Overall, there was a high f-value (7.97), and the p-value was.003, hence statistically significant. The effect size was equally large (Eta-sq = .67), indicating that, practically, there was a significant difference in the data of the difficulty levels obtained. In contrast, tool-based multiple comparisons showed that only ChatGPT had a significant statistical difference from traditional MT tools (.005,.03,.005, for Baidu Translate, DeepL, and LanguageX, respectively). The difference in the difficulty level of the three MT systems was not statistically different.

4.2 RQ2: Do GenAI-Translated Technical Texts Need Less Effort and Time to Post-Edit Than Traditional Machine-Translated Technical Texts?

We determined effort by computing the total time spent on the task and the time spent on terminological research. We also analyzed the pause length and the number of prompts/requests during the MTPE task. In this section, we present the MTPE time and effort.

4.3 Trainees Spent the Same Time on the PE Task

Our video analysis indicated that all the trainees, irrespective of the tool they used, spent an average of 40 m 51 s post-editing the text, with trainees using the Baidu MT system using slightly less time, as indicated in Table 8.

We performed a one-way ANOVA to determine the statistical difference among the various tools' data. No statistical difference was found (p-value of.33), meaning all tool users spent approximately the same time on the task.

Furthermore, we calculated the actual PE time after deducting the time spent on terminological research and pause length. The data showed that trainees spent an average of 26 m 47 s post-editing the text. As indicated in Fig. 4, the most time used was 29 m 12 s, and the least time was 23 m 19 s.

Pair-wise, their pair working with the LanguageX MT system spent the least time (25 m 49 s) post-editing, followed by the Baidu MT system (26 m 01 s), ChatGPT (27 m), and DeepL MT system (28 m 17 s). Furthermore, we performed a one-way

Table 8 Average time spent on the MPTE task per tool used

Tool	Trainee	Individual completion time	Average MTPE completion time per tool
ChatGPT	CGPT1	40 m 52 s	40 m 38 s
	CGPT2	40 m 23 s	
Baidu Translate	BDUT1	39 m 37 s	39 m 36 s
	BDUT2	39 m 34 s	
DeepL	DPL1	41 m 10 s	41 m 05 s
	DPL2	40 m 51 s	
LanguageX	LANX1	44 m	42 m 10 s
	LANX2	40 m 20 s	

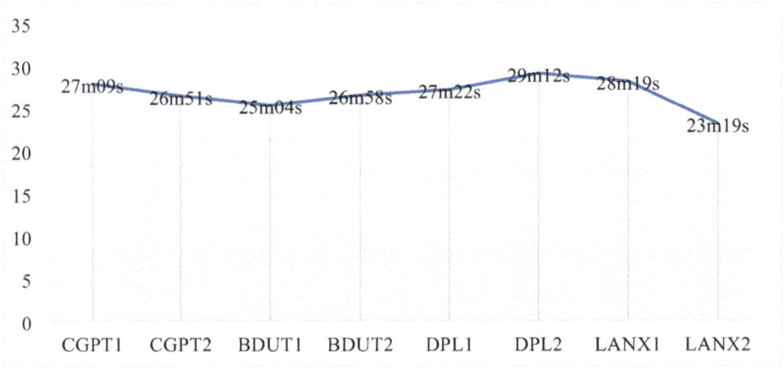

Fig. 4 Actual PE time

ANOVA to determine the statistical differences in PE time among the pairs. The *F*-value (.64) was significantly low, and the *p*-value was $p = .63$, therefore insignificant. The data meant the pairs spent the same time on the actual PE task.

Trainees using ChatGPT Exerted more PE Effort

We measured PE effort by analyzing the time spent on terminological research, pause length, the number of requests and prompts, and the perceived difficulty level of the text (Jakobsen, 2019; Kaponen, 2012). We measured the length of pauses by coding trainees' screen recordings, and we performed a physical count to determine the number of requests for information and ChatGPT prompts. Meanwhile, the trainees and the three evaluators determined the task's difficulty level.

Terminological Research Time

We analyzed the time spent on terminological research and pause length to predict PE effort. Our analysis showed that in total, trainees used 7 m 25 s conducting terminology, i.e., 18.16% of the total time spent on the MTPE activity. However, we found that trainees who post-edited the text using ChatGPT as their OR spent more time on terminological research, as indicated in Fig. 5.

According to Fig. 4, the two trainees who used ChatGPT to post-edit the text spent considerable time on terminological research. In particular, CGPT1 and CGPT2 spent 24.14% and 26.29%, respectively, of their total MTPE on terminological research. Other pairs spent an average of 5 m 02 s (Baidu Translate), 7 m 07 s (DeepL), and 7 m 17 s (LanguageX). Trainees who post-edited the text translated using Baidu Translate spent the least time on terminological research because they consulted the fewest OR.

We performed a one-way ANOVA to determine the statistical differences among the data of various pairs. The *F*-value was high, at 34.34, and there was a statistically

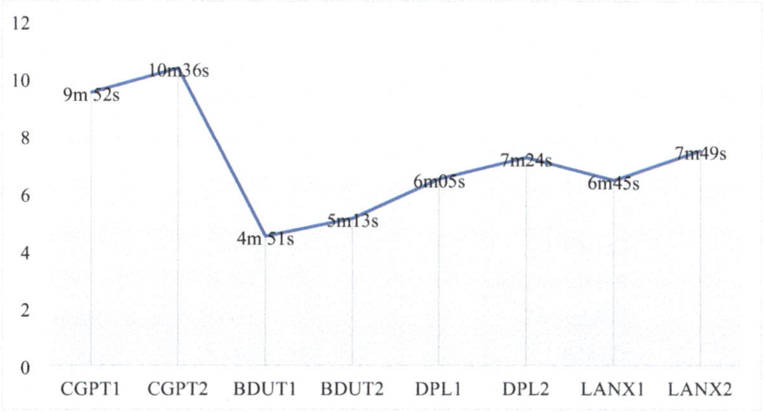

Fig. 5 Time spent on terminology research

significant difference among various pairs. In particular, there were significant statistical differences (at the 0.05 level) between ChatGPT tool users and between Baidu Translate users and all other tool users. In contrast, no statistical differences were found in terminological research time between DeepL and LanguageX tool users, as outlined in Table 9.

In terms of effort, the data indicated that trainees using ChatGPT exerted more effort in terminological research than trainees who used traditional MT systems. The screen recording showed that trainees consistently interacted with ChatGPT, mainly asking about word choice, semantic equivalents, and collocations.

Pause Length

Our data analysis indicated that trainees who post-edited the text using ChatGPT had shorter pauses overall than trainees using other MT systems. In particular, the two trainees who used ChatGPT paused for 3 m 51 s and 2 m 56 s, respectively, during the entire activity. That means, on average, they paused for 3 m 24 m. In contrast, other pairs had much longer pauses, as indicated in Fig. 6.

We performed a one-way ANOVA on SPSS to determine the statistical differences between the pause lengths of various trainee pairs. The F-value was 8.24 (high), and there was a statistical difference between ChatGPT data and Baidu Translate ($p =$ .005) and LanguageX ($p =$ .04). No other statistical differences were found. The data confirms the screen recording of ChatGPT tool users showing constant activity as trainees continuously interact with the tool.

Based on previous research regarding pause-based PE effort (Alves et al., 2016; O'Brien, 2006), we determined that trainees who used ChatGPT as a post-editing tool had a lower cognitive effort than those with traditional MT systems. In other words, they tended to interact with and depend more on ChatGPT than their cognitive

Table 9 Statistical differences in the terminological research time of various pairs

Pairs/Tools	Relationship with other pairs/tools	*P*-value
ChatGPT	Baidu Translate	.002
	DeepL	.01
	LanguageX	.01
Baidu Translate	ChatGPT	.002
	DeepL	.05
	LanguageX	.04
DeepL	ChatGPT	.01
	Baidu Translate	.05
	LanguageX	.99 (No statistical difference)
LanguageX	ChatGPT	.01
	Baidu Translate	.04
	DeepL	.99 (No statistical difference)

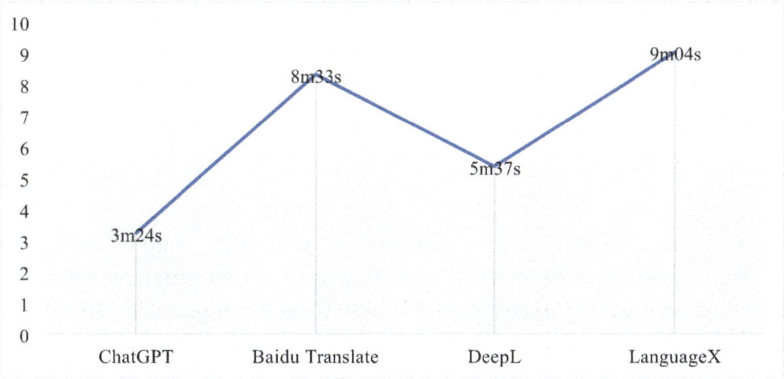

Fig. 6 Average pause length per trainee pair per tool

abilities. In contrast, LanguageX had the longest pauses, hence the most cognitive effort.

Requests and Prompts

We tallied trainees' requests for information and prompts (for ChatGPT users) to understand how much trainees depended on different information sources while post-editing. The literature on post-editing efforts indicates that the percentage of time spent on online resources (OR) correlates with PE effort (Witczak, 2021). In addition, numerical indicators have also been used to measure the technical effort made during PE (Zaretskaya et al., 2016).

Based on our analysis, ChatGPT tool users requested more information than traditional MT system users. The pair made 13 and 15 prompts, respectively, i.e., an average of 14 prompts/requests. This was significantly higher than the request made by trainees using traditional MT systems, as indicated in Fig. 7.

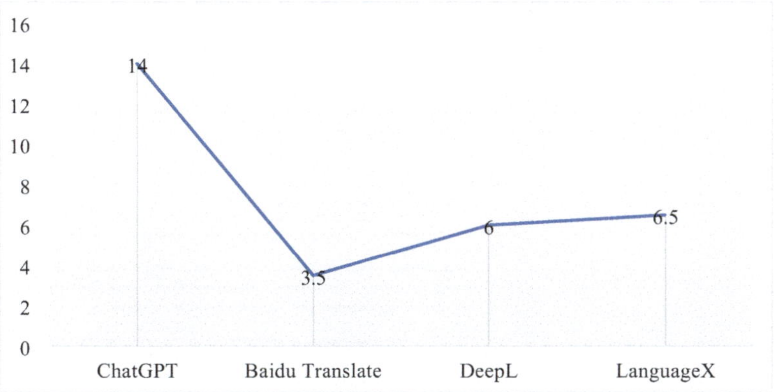

Fig. 7 Average number of prompts/requests by trainee pairs per MTPE tool used

The data showed that trainees who used Baidu Translate made the least requests for information. The actual screen-recorded video shows that this pair mostly used the Baidu search engine for terminology. We determined the statistical significance of the data of the four pairs via one-way ANOVA. The F-value was 35.09 (high), and the p-value between the groups was.002, therefore, significant. The data further confirmed statistical differences between ChatGPT and all traditional MT systems (Baidu Translate: $p = < .002$; DeepL: $p = < .005$; LanguageX: $p = < .005$). In contrast, there were no statistical differences among the data of traditional MT systems. There was also a high effect size (Eta-sq = .96) or practical significance in the data. The data means trainees using ChatGPT made a higher PE effort than those who post-edited text translated using traditional MT systems.

4.4 RQ3: Do Some Trainees' PE Practices Deserve Particular Attention?

Generative AI Prompts

We found that trainees who used ChatGPT did not always use accurate prompts. We documented five such instances, including two that suggested a lack of understanding of how AI chatbots function. For instance, trainee CGPT2 began by asking ChatGPT, "Can you help translate a Chinese manual to English?" ChatGPT responded, as outlined in Fig. 8.

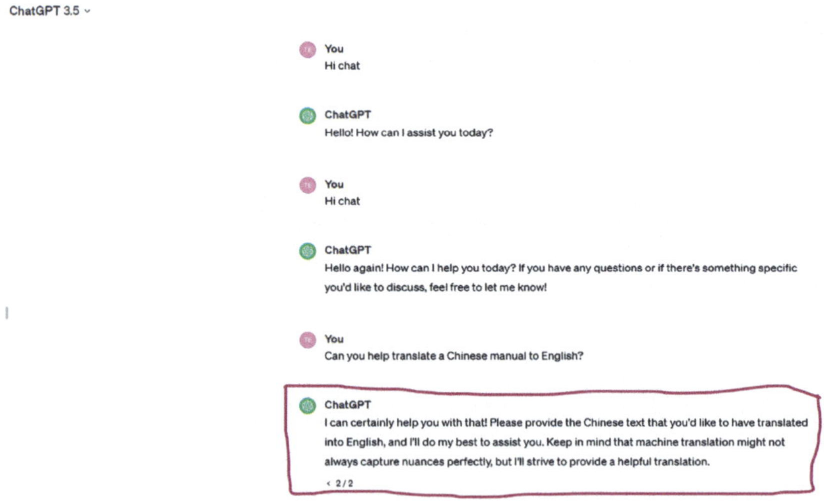

Fig. 8 Initial conversation between Trainee CGPT2 and ChatGPT

Table 10 ChatGPT edited text showing a heightened language register

Original version	Post-edited version
Follow these 5 steps to install, ensuring the finished product matches the operation of the experienced technician perfectly	Follow these 5 steps for a **flawless installation, replicating the perfection** achieved by the experienced technician
The final step is to fix the eccentric wheels by placing them in the holes. The eccentric wheel should be correctly placed in the hole, not higher or lower than the board	The final step involves **securing** the eccentric wheels by placing them into the designated holes. Ensure that the eccentric wheels sit correctly within the holes, **neither protruding above nor sinking below the board surface**

Then, trainee CGPT2 provided the manual, which ChatGPT translated. Following the translation, Trainee CGPT2 prompted, "Can you post-edit it for me to make it more readable?" ChatGPT thought it was being asked to improve the manual's readability. Consequently, it made several changes, remarkably increasing the language register, arguably making it harder to understand, as outlined in the example in Table 10.

In this example, we believe that words and expressions like "flawless installation, replicating the perfection, protruding above or sinking below" could be challenging for non-native English speakers. We also presume that trainee CGPT2 lacked basic knowledge of how ChatGPT works when they asked the chatbot to post-edit a text it had just translated.

Source and Target Text Alignment

We found that trainees (both using GenAI and MT systems) wasted considerable time struggling to align the source text and the machine-translated version that was being post-edited. We found several text alignments, including those in Fig. 9.

Because they struggled to align the source and target texts, some trainees spent significant time adjusting the text rather than focusing on the post-editing task. For trainees who placed the target text below the source text (Image 2), significant time was wasted scrolling up and down the computer monitor during PE. We coded the time Trainees BDUT1 and LANX1 spent aligning and re-aligning their text and found that they used 1 m 56 s (7.2%) and 2 m 21 s (11.8%) of their total PE time, respectively.

5 Discussion

This study investigated the performance of ChatGPT, a generative AI chatbot, in comparison to traditional neural machine translation (NMT) systems (Baidu Translate, DeepL, and LanguageX) for translating a technical furniture assembly manual,

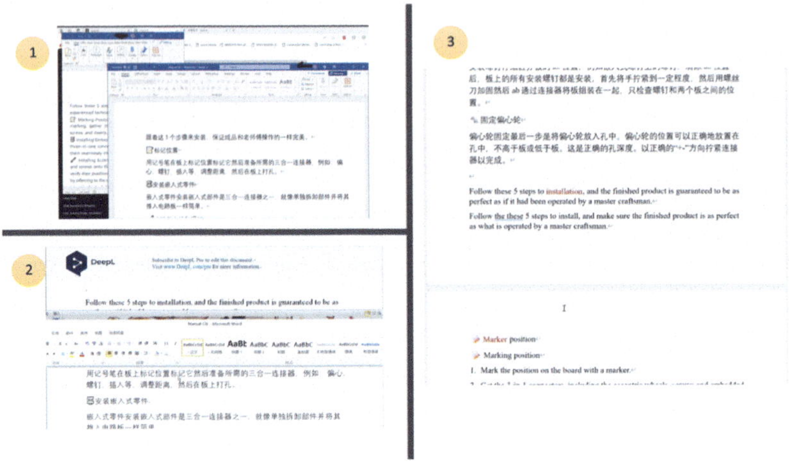

Fig. 9 Examples of how trainees aligned the source text and target texts. *Note* Image 1 = side-by-side alignment; Image 2 = sequential alignment using split screen; Image 3 = sequential alignment on different pages

with a focus on error rates and post-editing (PE) effort. The findings revealed nuanced dynamics in human-AI interaction, and they offer significant implications for translator training and industry practice.

The study found that ChatGPT-translated technical texts contained fewer fluency and adequacy errors compared to texts translated by traditional NMT systems, aligning with trainees' and evaluators' perceptions that these texts were easier to post-edit. However, trainees using ChatGPT as a PE tool exerted greater effort, spent more time on terminological research (24.14–26.29% of total PE time), and generated more prompts/requests (average of 14 per trainee pair) compared to those using NMT systems. Conversely, trainees using NMT systems exhibited longer pause lengths, suggesting higher cognitive effort. No significant differences were observed in total PE time across tools (average: 40 min 51 s). Additionally, trainees faced challenges with prompt accuracy and aligning source and target texts, which impacted PE efficiency. These findings highlight a tension between perceived ease and actual effort in GenAI-assisted PE, underscoring the need for targeted training.

The findings align with prior research on the translation capabilities of generative AI. The lower fluency and adequacy errors in ChatGPT-translated texts corroborate studies by Hendy et al. (2023), Jiang and Zhang (2024), Manakhimova et al. (2023), and Sanz-Valdivieso and López-Arroyo (2023), which demonstrate ChatGPT's high-quality output, often rivaling or surpassing NMT systems in general and specialized texts. However, the study's observation that ChatGPT struggles with domain-specific terminology and produces errors comparable to those of DeepL in the wrong term category supports the findings of Cady et al. (2023) and Khoshafah (2023), who note GenAI's limitations in technical vocabulary. Additionally, the importance of prompt accuracy in achieving high-quality outputs aligns with Korzynski et al.

(2023), who emphasize that effective prompt engineering is crucial for optimizing GenAI performance in translation tasks.

The increased terminological research time by ChatGPT users, despite the tool's integrated knowledge base, suggests a lack of trust in its terminology choices or a need for verification, particularly for domain-specific terms like "偏心轮" (eccentric wheel). This aligns with Khoshafah's (2023) concept of AI reliance, where users cross-check GenAI outputs due to occasional inaccuracies in specialized domains. The interactive nature of ChatGPT may also encourage iterative querying, as trainees explore multiple semantic equivalents or collocations, contributing to prolonged research time. This behavior may reflect trainees' awareness of ChatGPT's limitations, as noted by Cady et al. (2023), or their inexperience in crafting precise prompts to elicit accurate responses.

The discrepancy between perceived ease (ChatGPT texts rated as less challenging, with mean difficulty scores of 6.87–8.19) and actual effort (requiring more prompts and research time) suggests a potential "cognitive illusion." ChatGPT's engaging interface may create an impression of simplicity, masking the cognitive and technical demands of crafting prompts and validating responses. As Korzynski et al. (2023) argue, effective GenAI use requires digital literacy skills, which the trainees in this study lacked, as evidenced by vague prompts such as "Can you post-edit it for me to make it more readable?" leading to inappropriate outputs (e.g., heightened language registers). This tension underscores the need for training to align perceived and actual effort in GenAI-assisted PE.

To address these findings, translator training programs should integrate GenAI tools, such as ChatGPT, into their curricula with actionable strategies to enhance proficiency and efficiency.

1. *Prompt engineering exercises*: Trainers should design task-based learning (TBL) activities to teach specific, domain-relevant prompts. For example, trainees could translate a furniture manual excerpt using prompts like: "Translate this Chinese furniture assembly manual into English using concise active voice, adhering to technical writing conventions (e.g., short sentences, precise terminology." Another task could involve revising translations with prompts such as: "Revise this translation to ensure all technical terms align with standard English furniture assembly terminology, avoiding synonyms like 'biased gear' for 'eccentric wheel.'" These exercises, supported by iterative feedback and BLEU/METEOR score evaluations (Ajai Krishna et al., 2024), foster critical thinking and digital competence (Korzynski et al., 2023).
2. *Text alignment strategies*: To reduce time wasted on aligning source and target texts, trainers should teach screen-splitting techniques using CAT tools like Trados or SmartCat, which offer side-by-side editors. For personal devices, free tools like Windows Snap Assist or macOS SplitView can align texts efficiently. A classroom activity could include: (1) opening source and target texts in separate windows, (2) using Snap Assist to align them side-by-side, and (3) practicing PE with numbered or color-coded segments to track correspondence. This addresses

inefficiencies observed in trainees BDUT1 and LANX1, who spent 7.2–11.8% of PE time on alignment.

3. *Adapting to resource constraints:* In low-resource settings without dual monitors or unlimited GenAI access, trainers can recommend free split-screen tools or offline terminology databases like IATE or TermBank to verify terms like "eccentric wheel" offline. Mock prompt-response exercises using paper or basic text editors can simulate GenAI interactions, building digital literacy without constant AI access. Workshops on open-source CAT tools like OmegaT can further support PE training, ensuring accessibility and industry relevance.

The findings suggest that translation institutions must adapt to the growing role of GenAI in PE. Institutions should invest in training sessions or workshops to equip trainers with the knowledge of GenAI chatbots to enhance seamless integration into curricula. Providing access to GenAI tools, ideally on computers with dual monitors or split-screen capabilities, can enhance PE efficiency, as supported by Owens et al. (2012). In resource-constrained environments, institutions can leverage open-source tools and offline resources to ensure equitable access. Additionally, policies should emphasize the development of digital competence frameworks that incorporate prompt engineering and text alignment as core skills. Through fostering an enabling environment for GenAI integration, institutions can prepare trainees for industry demands that align with the evolving landscape of AI-driven translation.

6 Conclusion

This study investigated the efficacy of ChatGPT, a generative AI (GenAI) chatbot, as both a translation and post-editing (PE) tool compared to traditional neural machine translation (NMT) systems, including Baidu Translate, DeepL, and LanguageX, using a technical furniture assembly manual. By addressing three research questions, it provides valuable insights into error rates, PE effort, and trainee practices, contributing to the evolving discourse on GenAI's role in machine translation post-editing (MTPE). ChatGPT-translated texts exhibited fewer fluency and adequacy errors and were perceived as easier to post-edit than those translated by traditional NMT systems. However, trainees using ChatGPT exerted greater PE effort, spending more time on terminological research and generating more prompts, though they had shorter pause lengths, suggesting lower cognitive effort. In contrast, NMT system users displayed longer pauses, indicating higher cognitive demands. Challenges with crafting accurate prompts and aligning source and target texts hindered PE efficiency, highlighting the need for targeted training to optimize GenAI use.

These findings align with prior research demonstrating ChatGPT's superior translation quality in general and specialized texts, as noted by Hendy et al. (2023), Jiang and Zhang (2024), Manakhimova et al. (2023), and Sanz-Valdivieso and López-Arroyo (2023). However, the study confirms ChatGPT's limitations in domain-specific terminology, producing errors comparable to DeepL, as observed by Cady et al. (2023) and Khoshafah (2023). The critical role of precise prompt engineering in optimizing GenAI outputs further corroborates Korzynski et al.'s (2023) emphasis on digital literacy as a key competency for effective AI utilization.

The increased PE effort among ChatGPT users, despite perceptions of ease, suggests a "cognitive illusion" driven by the chatbot's interactive interface, which may mask the demands of prompt crafting and response verification. This aligns with Khoshafah's (2023) observations on AI reliance, where users frequently verify GenAI outputs due to occasional inaccuracies in specialized domains. Trainees' prolonged terminological research reflects either a lack of trust in ChatGPT's domain-specific outputs or inexperience with effective prompt strategies, underscoring the need for training to bridge the gap between perceived and actual effort in GenAI-assisted PE.

To leverage GenAI effectively, translator training programs must prioritize prompt engineering through task-based learning activities, teaching trainees to craft domain-specific prompts, such as "Translate this Chinese furniture assembly manual into English using concise active voice, adhering to technical writing conventions." Trainers should also introduce screen-splitting techniques using tools like Trados or free alternatives like Windows Snap Assist to improve text alignment efficiency. In low-resource settings, offline terminology databases like IATE or TermBank and mock prompt exercises can ensure accessibility, fostering digital competence and industry readiness. Translation institutions should integrate GenAI into curricula by providing training workshops for educators and ensuring access to tools like ChatGPT, ideally with dual-monitor setups to enhance efficiency (Owens et al., 2012). In resource-constrained environments, policies should support open-source CAT tools and offline resources to democratize access. By embedding digital literacy and prompt engineering as core competencies, institutions can prepare trainees for an AI-driven translation landscape, aligning pedagogical practices with industry trends.

7 Limitations and Further Research Avenues

This study on ChatGPT as a translation and post-editing (PE) tool compared to traditional neural machine translation (NMT) systems has limitations that affect its generalizability. The small sample size of eight graduate trainees limits statistical power, potentially missing subtle differences in PE effort due to variability in performance. Focusing solely on ChatGPT restricts its applicability to other GenAI models, which may vary in terms of translation and PE performance. The lack of formal pre-assessment training for evaluators may introduce bias in subjective scoring (e.g., style, naturalness), despite high inter-rater reliability. Relying only on screen recordings limits insights into trainees' cognitive processes, such as prompt-crafting decisions.

Future research should compare ChatGPT with newer models, such as GPT-4 or Claude, to assess improvements in terminological accuracy and reduced PE effort. Domain-specific fine-tuning on technical corpora, such as furniture manuals, could enhance GenAI performance. Mixed-methods approaches, combining screen recordings with think-aloud protocols (O'Brien, 2005) and semi-structured interviews, could reveal why trainees' prompts fail or succeed, addressing the observed "cognitive illusion" of perceived ease. Expanding participant pools to include professionals, testing diverse text types (e.g., medical, legal), and exploring other language pairs would improve generalizability. These studies will advance the integration of GenAI in translation training, fostering effective human-AI collaboration.

Funding *No funding was obtained for this study*

Data Availability *Data will be made available upon reasonable request*

Disclosure Statement
The authors report that there are no competing interests to declare.

Appendix

Criteria for assessing MT errors.

MTPE Tool_________________.

Fluency	**Item**	**Description**	**Number of errors**	**Weight/Score**
	Naturalness 10pts	How natural and smooth the translated text sounds. This includes aspects of sentence structure and readability		Subjective score on a total of 10
	Language 20pts	Grammar Tenses Collocations Prepositions Noun use Miscellaneous	Number of errors	-.5pt for each error
	Style 10pts	It examines whether the translation is consistent with manuals in English	Number of errors	Subjective rating on 10pts
	Punctuation and Formatting 10pts	Correct use of punctuation marks and formatting conventions, such as proper spacing, indentation, and paragraph breaks	Number of errors	-.5pts for each error

(continued)

(continued)

Adequacy	**Mistranslation** 10pts	A different meaning or interpretation than the original is conveyed	Number of errors	-1 pt per error
	Under-translation 10pts	Not all the meaning or nuances of the source text are conveyed	Number of errors	-1 pt per error
	Wrong term 10pts	Wrong terminology	Number of errors	-1 pt per error
	Omission 5pts	Part of the source text's meaning is omitted	Number of errors	-1 pt per error
	Semantically inaccurate 10pts	The meaning of the translation is incorrect	Number of errors	-1 pt per error
	Addition 5pts	The target text contains more semantic elements than the source text	Number of errors	-1 pt per error

References

Abdous, M. H. (2011). A process-oriented framework for acquiring online teaching competencies. *Journal of Computing in Higher Education, 23*(1), 60–77.

Ajai Krishna, T. S., Akshaya, R., Bomb, A., Balamurugan, K., Angel Arul Jothi, J., & Mary Anita Rajam, V. (2024, February). Evaluating the language translation accuracy of GPT-3.5 using prompt engineering. In *International Conference on Computational Intelligence in Data Science* (pp. 54–67). Cham: Springer Nature Switzerland.

Alves, F., Koglin, A., Mesa-Lao, B., Martínez, M. G., de Lima Fonseca, N. B., de Melo Sá, A., Gonçalves, J. L., Sarto Szpak, K., Sekino, K., & Aquino, M. (2016). Analysing the impact of interactive machine translation on post-editing effort. *New directions in empirical translation process research: exploring the CRITT TPR-DB*, 77–94.

Bojar, O. (2011). Analyzing error types in English-Czech machine translation. *The Prague Bulletin of Mathematical Linguistics, 95*, 63–76.

Bolhuis, S. (2003). Towards process-oriented teaching for self-directed lifelong learning: A multidimensional perspective. *Learning and Instruction, 13*(3), 327–347.

Cady, L., Tsou, B. K., & Lee, J. S. (2023, September). Comparing Chinese-English MT performance involving ChatGPT and MT providers and the efficacy of AI mediated post-editing. In *Proceedings of Machine Translation Summit XIX, Vol. 2: Users Track* (pp. 205–216). https://aclanthology.org/2023.mtsummit-users.20

Carl, M., Dragsted, B., Elming, J., Hardt, D., & Jakobsen, A. L. (2011). The process of post-editing: A pilot study. In Sharp B., Zock, M., Carl, M., & Jakobsen, A. L. (eds.), *Human-Machine*

Interaction in Translation: Proceedings of the 8th International NLPSCS Workshop, 131–142, Copenhagen 20–21 Aug. Copenhagen Studies in Language, 41.

Daems, J., Vandepitte, S., Hartsuiker, R. J., & Macken, L. (2017). Identifying the machine translation error types with the greatest impact on post-editing effort. *Frontiers in Psychology, 8,* 1282. https://doi.org/10.3389/fpsyg.2017.01282

Farrell, M. (2023, July). Preliminary evaluation of ChatGPT as a machine translation engine and as an automatic post-editor of raw machine translation output from other machine translation engines. In *Proceedings of the International Conference HiT-IT 2023* (pp. 108–113). Incoma Ltd.

Foucrier, T., & Wiek, A. (2019). A process-oriented framework of competencies for sustainability entrepreneurship. *Sustainability, 11*(24), 7250. https://doi.org/10.3390/su11247250

Gijbels, D., Donche, V., Richardson, J. T., & Vermunt, J. D. (2014). *Learning patterns in higher education. Dimensions and research perspectives.* Routledge.

Grandbastien, M., Oubahssi, L., & Claes, G. (2003). A process oriented approach for modelling on line Learning Environments. In *AIED2003* (pp. 140–152).

Guerberof-Arenas, A., Valdez, S., & Dorst, A. G. (2024). Does training in post-editing affect creativity? Journal of Specialized Translation, 41, 74–97. https://doi.org/10.26034/cm.jostrans.2024.4712

Haque, R., Hasanuzzaman, M., & Way, A. (2020). Analysing terminology translation errors in statistical and neural machine translation. *Machine Translation, 34,* 149–195. https://doi.org/10.1007/s10590-020-09251-z

Hendy, A., Abdelrehim, M., Sharaf, A., Raunak, V., Gabr, M., Matsushita, H., Jin Kim, Y., Afify, M., & Awadalla, H. H. (2023). How good are GPT models at machine translation? A comprehensive evaluation. https://doi.org/10.48550/arXiv.2302.09210

Heston, T. F., & Khun, C. (2023). Prompt engineering in medical education. *International Medical Education, 2*(3), 198–205. https://doi.org/10.3390/ime2030019

Jakobsen, A. L. (2019). Segmentation in translation: A look at expert behaviour. In D. Li, V. L. Cheng Lei, & Y. He (Eds.), *Researching cognitive processes of translation,* 71–108, Singapore: Springer.

Jia, Y., Carl, M., & Wang, X. (2019). Post-editing neural machine translation versus phrase-based machine translation for English-Chinese. *Machine Translation, 33*(1), 9–29. https://doi.org/10.1007/s10590-019-09229-6

Jiang, Z., & Zhang, Z. (2024). Can ChatGPT Rival Neural Machine translation? A comparative study. https://doi.org/10.48550/arXiv.2401.05176

Khoshafah, F. (2023). ChatGPT for Arabic-English translation: Evaluating the accuracy. *Research Square, Preprint.* https://doi.org/10.21203/rs.3.rs-2814154/v2

Končar, J. (2020). *Translation of user manuals from Croatian into English* (Doctoral dissertation, University of Zagreb. University of Zagreb, Faculty of Humanities and Social Sciences. Department of English language and literature).

Koponen, M. (2012, June). Comparing human perceptions of post-editing effort with post-editing operations. In *Proceedings of the seventh workshop on statistical machine translation* (pp. 181–190).

Korzynski, P., Mazurek, G., Krzypkowska, P., & Kurasinski, A. (2023). Artificial intelligence prompt engineering as a new digital competence: Analysis of generative AI technologies such as ChatGPT. *Entrepreneurial Business and Economics Review, 11*(3), 25–37.

Lee, T. K. (2023). Artificial intelligence and posthumanist translation: ChatGPT versus the translator. *Applied Linguistics Review,* (0). https://doi.org/10.1515/applirev-2023-0122

Lee-Jahnke, H. (2005). New cognitive approaches in process-oriented translation training. *Meta, 50*(2), 359–377. https://doi.org/10.7202/010942ar

Liu, Y., Ju, S., & Wang, J. (2024). Exploring the potential of ChatGPT in medical dialogue summarization: A study on consistency with human preferences. *BMC Medical Informatics and Decision Making, 24*(1), 75. https://doi.org/10.1186/s12911-024-02481-8

Lommel, A. (2018). Metrics for translation quality assessment: a case for standardising error typologies. *Translation quality assessment: From principles to practice*, 109–127.

Lörscher, W. (1992). Process-oriented research into translation and implications for translation teaching. *Traduction, Terminologie, Rédaction*, *5*(1), 145–161. http://id.erudit.org/iderudit/037110ar

Malta, G., Fontes, C. S., & Silva, I. A. L. D. (2019). Translation from a process-oriented Approach. *Cadernos De Tradução, 39*(1), 191–215. https://doi.org/10.5007/2175-7968.2019v39n

Manakhimova, S., Avramidis, E., Macketanz, V., Lapshinova-Koltunski, E., Bagdasarov, S., & Möller, S. (2023, December). Linguistically motivated evaluation of the 2023 state-of-the-art machine translation: Can ChatGPT outperform NMT?. In *Proceedings of the Eighth Conference on Machine Translation* (pp. 224–245). December 6–7. https://aclanthology.org/2023.wmt-1.23.pdf

Moorkens, J., Castilho, S., Gaspari, F., Toral, A., & Popović, M. (2024). Roundtable: Translation automation and sustainability. *The Journal of Specialised Translation*, (41). https://doi.org/10.26034/cm.jostrans.2024.4737

Moslem, Y., Romani, G., Molaei, M., Kelleher, J., Haque, R., & Way, A. (2023, December). Domain terminology integration into machine translation: Leveraging large language models. In *Proceedings of the Eighth Conference on Machine Translation* (pp. 902–911). https://aclanthology.org/2023.wmt-1.82.pdf

O' Brien, S. (2006). Pauses as indicators of cognitive effort in post-editing machine translation output. *Across languages and cultures*, *7*(1), 1–21. https://doi.org/10.1556/Acr.7.2006.1.1

O'Brien, S. (2005). Methodologies for measuring the correlations between post-editing effort and machine translatability. *Machine Translation, 19*, 37–58. https://doi.org/10.1007/s10590-005-2467-1

O'Brien, S. (2022). How to deal with errors in machine translation: Post-editing. In D. Kenny (Ed.), *Machine translation for everyone: Empowering users in the age of artificial intelligence* (pp. 105–120). Language Science Press.

Omazić, M., & Šoštarić, B. (2023). New resources and methods in translating legal texts: machine translation and post-editing of machine-translated legal texts. *Language (s) and Law*, 71.

Owens, J. W., Teves, J., Nguyen, B., Smith, A., Phelps, M. C., & Chaparro, B. S. (2012). Examination of dual vs. Single monitor use during common office tasks. *Proceedings of the Human Factors and Ergonomics Society Annual Meeting*, *56*(1), 1506–1510. https://doi.org/10.1177/1071181312561299

Peng, K., Ding, L., Zhong, Q., Shen, L., Liu, X., Zhang, M., Ouyang, Y., & Tao, D. (2023). Towards making the most of ChatGPT for machine translation. https://doi.org/10.48550/arXiv.2303.13780

Qian, M. (2023, September). Performance evaluation on human-machine teaming augmented machine translation enabled by GPT-4. In *Proceedings of the First Workshop on NLP Tools and Resources for Translation and Interpreting Applications* (pp. 20–31). https://aclanthology.org/2023.nlp4tia-1.4.pdf

Sanz-Valdivieso, L., & López-Arroyo, B. (2023). Google Translate vs. ChatGPT: Can non-language professionals trust them for specialized translation? In *International Conference Human-informed Translation and Interpreting Technology (HiT-IT 2023)* (pp. 97–107).

Specia, L., & Farzindar, A. (2010). Estimating machine translation post-editing effort with HTER. In *Proceedings of the Second Joint EM+/CNGL Workshop: Bringing MT to the User: Research on Integrating MT in the Translation Industry* (pp. 33–43). https://aclanthology.org/2010.jec-1.5.pdf

Stasimioti, M., Sosoni, V., Kermanidis, K. L., & Mouratidis, D. (2020, November). Machine translation quality: A comparative evaluation of SMT, NMT and tailored-NMT outputs. In *Proceedings of the 22nd annual conference of the European Association for Machine Translation*, pages 441–450, Lisboa, Portugal. European Association for Machine Translation. https://aclanthology.org/2020.eamt-1.47.pdf.

Tekwa, K. (2024). Process-oriented collaborative translation within the training environment: Comparing team and individual trainee performances using a video-ethnography approach. *Education and Information Technologies, 29*(5), 6443–6469. https://doi.org/10.1007/s10639-023-12046-3

Toral, A., Wieling, M., & Way, A. (2018). Post-editing effort of a novel with statistical and neural machine translation. *Frontiers in Digital Humanities, 5*, 1–11. https://doi.org/10.3389/fdigh.2018.00009

Vermunt, J. D., & Vermetten, Y. J. (2004). Patterns in student learning: Relationships between learning strategies, conceptions of learning, and learning orientations. *Educational Psychology Review, 16*(4), 359–384. https://doi.org/10.1007/s10648-004-0005-y

Vermunt, J., & Verschaffel, L. (2000). Process-oriented teaching. In R-J. Simons, J. Linden, & T. Duffy (Eds.), *New learning* (pp. 209–225). Dordrecht: Springer Netherlands.

Vermunt, J., & Verschaffel, L. (2000b). Process-oriented teaching. *New learning* (pp. 209–225). Springer, Netherlands.

Vrieling, E. M., Bastiaens, T. J., & Stijnen, S. (2010). Process-oriented design principles for promoting self-regulated learning in primary teacher education. *International Journal of Educational Research, 49*(4–5), 141–150.

Wang, J. (2023). A ChatGPT-driven study of translating and post-editing Chinese enterprise publicity materials. *Modern Languages, Literatures, and Linguistics, 2*(02).

Wang, Q., Ding, L., Cao, Y., Tian, Z., Wang, S., Tao, D., & Guo, L. (2023). Recursively summarizing enables long-term dialogue memory in large language models. https://doi.org/10.48550/arXiv.2308.15022

White, J., Fu, Q., Hays, S., Sandborn, M., Olea, C., Gilbert, H., Elnashar, A., Spencer-Smith, J., Schmidt, D. C. (2023). A prompt pattern catalog to enhance prompt engineering with chatgpt. *Preprint: 2302.11382*. https://doi.org/10.1007/s10439-023-03272-4

Witczak, O. (2021). Information searching in the post-editing and translation process. Doctorat Thesis, Adam Mickiewicz University, Poznań.

Zaretskaya, A., Vela, M., Corpas Pastor, G., & Seghiri, M. (2016). Measuring post-editing time and effort for different types of machine translation errors. *New Voices in Translation Studies, 15*, 63–92.

Zhang, M. (2019). Problems and developments in translation history research—An interview with Prof. Anthony Pym. *Journal of Beijing International Studies University, 41*(5), 81. https://doi.org/10.12002/j.bisu.228

Zhong, Q., Ding, L., Liu, J., Du, B., & Tao, D. (2023). Can chatgpt understand too? a comparative study on chatgpt and fine-tuned bert. https://doi.org/10.48550/arXiv.2302.10198

LLM-Based Machine Interpreting Evaluation: Implications for Interpreter Education in the Age of AI

Zixuan Wang, Hui Jiao, and Xiaojun Zhang

Abstract This study investigates the potential of Large Language Model (LLM)-based approaches for evaluating machine interpreting (MI) output, with a focus on implications for interpreter education. First, two experiments using GPT-4o were conducted to assess the quality of Automatic Speech Recognition (ASR) and Machine Translation (MT) outputs. The first experiment applied an adapted GEMBA-SQM (Scalar Quality Metric) prompting strategy to generate overall scores across three interpreting modes: ASR-MT, ST-ASR-MT, and ST-ASR-MT-RT. Although the ST-ASR-MT mode showed relatively better alignment with human judgments, the overall performance was limited. The GEMBA approach produced rough scores without pinpointing specific errors or their severity. To address these limitations, a more structured prompting method—MIEval—was developed. This framework incorporates Word Error Rate (WER) for evaluating ASR and the Multidimensional Quality Metric (MQM) for assessing MT. Applied to the ST-ASR-MT and ST-ASR-MT-RT modes, MIEval significantly improved alignment with human evaluations, particularly in the ST-ASR-MT-RT mode, where reference texts supported more accurate error identification and severity analysis. The findings highlight that prompts with detailed evaluation criteria yield more reliable and informative results. Beyond evaluating technical performance, this study also demonstrates how educators can adapt the experimental approach for pedagogical purposes, offering strategies to train the next generation of interpreters in the age of AI.

Keywords Large language model (LLM) · Machine interpreting (MI) · Multidimensional quality metric (MQM) · MIEval

Z. Wang · H. Jiao · X. Zhang (✉)
Xi'an Jiaotong-Liverpool University, Suzhou, China
e-mail: Xiaojun.Zhang01@xjtlu.edu.cn

X. Zhang
Anhui Provincial Key Laboratory of Multimodal Cognitive Computation, Anhui University, Hefei, China

T. Yin et al. (eds.), *AI Through LLMs*, New Frontiers in Translation Studies,
https://doi.org/10.1007/978-981-95-4798-2_6

1 Introduction

Recent advances in artificial intelligence have transformed how language is processed, understood, and generated. Among the most influential of these technologies are Large Language Models (LLMs), which are AI systems trained on massive datasets capable of performing a wide range of natural language processing (NLP) tasks, such as machine translation (MT), automatic speech recognition (ASR), summarization, and dialogue generation (El Amri, 2024). Examples of prominent LLMs include OpenAI's GPT series (Radford et al., 2018), Google's LaMDA (Thoppilan et al., 2022), and Anthropic's Claude (Bai et al., 2022) and DeepSeek (Guo et al., 2025).

As LLMs become increasingly influential in language tasks, understanding how they operate is no longer optional for interpreter educators—it is essential. To harness the potential of these models in both practice and pedagogy, trainers must first grasp the core mechanism that drives them: prompting, which can be any form of text, question, information, or even code (Phoenix & Taylor, 2024). The content of the prompt will directly influence the probability of each subsequent word generated by the models, meaning that the structure and the wording of the prompt significantly affect the quality and relevance of the output. Therefore, a well-structured prompt—one that provides context, clearly defined tasks, examples, constraints, and desired tone—can significantly affect the accuracy and relevance of the model's output (Mizrahi & Serfaty, 2024). Although there is no universal template for effective prompting, customizing prompts for specific tasks is essential for leveraging LLM capabilities effectively.

Since LLMs are pretrained on large-scale language data, they are particularly effective for tasks such as machine translation—especially when guided by clear and well-structured prompts (Hendy et al., 2023; Jiao et al., 2023; Jiao et al., 2024). More recently, however, researchers have turned their attention to LLMs' potential not just to generate translations, but to evaluate them automatically (Fernandes et al., 2023; Kocmi & Federmann, 2023a; Lu et al., 2023). Traditionally, researchers relied on metrics such as BLEU (Papineni et al., 2002), TER (Snover et al., 2006), and METEOR (Banerjee & Lavie, 2005) to evaluate machine translation. For example, the BLUE compares the n-gram (contiguous sequences of n words) of machine outputs with that of the reference translations. The more matches, the score is better. However, recent research has criticized BLEU for its poor correlation with human evaluations, calling for its discontinuation (Freitag et al., 2022). It is true that this metric has its limitation: it only evaluates the machine outputs at words or phrase level without considering the overall context. Therefore, a merely automated metrics evaluation is not enough to decide whether the translation is "good quality" or not. Because of that, various methods using LLMs for translation evaluation have emerged. Notably, GEMBA (Kocmi & Federmann, 2023a) demonstrated that GPT-4 achieves a higher correlation with human at the system level in translation assessment. Additionally, AUTOMQM (Fernandes et al., 2023) showcased improved performance with PaLM-2 (Chowdhery et al., 2023) models, signaling further advancements in machine translation evaluation.

In this chapter, we present a study that explores how LLMs can be used to evaluate machine interpreting (MI) rather than machine translation. Our goal is not only to assess the technical performance of LLM-based evaluation methods but also to explore how they can be meaningfully integrated into interpreter education and training in the era of AI. We examine two approaches:

1. A rough scoring approach using a general-purpose prompt adapted from the GEMBA framework; and.
2. An optimized approach we proposed which combines structured scoring elements from the Multidimensional Quality Metrics (MQM) and Word Error Rate (WER).

Section 2 reviews literature on MI evaluation. Section 3 presents the rough scoring experiment, and Sect. 4 introduces the optimized approach. Section 5 focuses on pedagogical implications. Finally, Section 6 presents the conclusions of this study along with a discussion of its limitations.

2 Related Work

2.1 Notions of Machine Interpreting Quality and its Assessment

Machine interpreting is defined as "the technology that allows the translation of spoken texts from one language to another by means of a computer program (Fantinuoli, 2018, p.5)." There are primarily two approaches to machine interpreting, one is the cascading approach, and the other is the end-to-end approach (Fantinuoli, 2021). For machine interpreting with cascading, it involves three key components: automatic speech recognition, machine translation, and speech-to-text (STT) synthesis. In cascading approach, the output of ASR will be the input of MT. In the similar way, the output of MT and ASR would be the input of STT. The advantage of this approach lies in the clarity and transparency of each stage. If any issues arise, they can be precisely traced back to their origin in each respective stage. However, the disadvantage is when problems occur in one stage, it will influence the following stage.

Machine interpreting with an end-to-end approach seeks to enable direct speech-to-speech translation without segmenting the process into distinct stages. While this approach holds significant promise, it is still in its early stages of development (Fantinuoli, 2021). Researchers have been actively working to enhance the performance of end-to-end speech translation systems by introducing innovative model architectures (Karita et al., 2019; Zhang et al., 2020) and integrating ASR and MT tasks within a unified model framework (Anastasopoulos et al., 2022; Indurthi et al.,

2021; Zheng et al., 2021). However, a notable limitation of this approach is the difficulty in diagnosing issues when errors occur, as the tightly coupled nature of the system makes it challenging to pinpoint the root cause of the problem.

Earlier evaluations of machine interpreting primarily relied on human evaluators, a practice that dates back to the 1990s. During this period, the MI systems were assessed through human ratings using four categories: Good, Rough, Understandable, and Not Intelligible (Amtrup, 1999). Another approach to evaluating the performance of machine interpreting systems draws inspiration from the Test of English for International Communication (TOEIC), which measures English communication skills in language learners. This method, known as Translation-Paired Comparison (Sugaya & Yasuda, 2019), involves comparing two translations—one generated by the machine and the other by a TOEIC test taker. These translations are then evaluated sentence by sentence by bilingual speakers proficient in both languages. The aim is to express the machine's performance in TOEIC score, by comparing the machine's output with the performance of test takers across different score levels. However, this method requires a certain budget, as it involves finding test takers and conducting evaluations of the translated sentences (Sugaya & Yasuda, 2019). To reduce the cost, this method was partly automated by substituting human evaluation of sentences by BLEU and TER.

A more recent approach involves bilingual annotators rating the similarity between the input and output. Unlike text-based evaluations, this method focuses on the machine's voice output. The annotators primarily assess four key aspects: emphasis, intonation, rhythm, and perceived emotion, along with two auxiliary aspects: manner and meaning (Huang et al., 2023). These studies, however, still require considerable human labor. At the same time, Wang and Yuan (2023) propose build supervised machine learning model to predict the quality of interpreting which shows great potential of automatic scoring with little human evaluation. Although Wang and Yuan were pioneers in this area, their work specifically focused on the automatic assessment of communicative effectiveness.

2.2 Evaluation Using LLMs

The use of LLMs for translation evaluation was pioneered by GEMBA (Kocmi & Federmann, 2023a), a zero-shot prompting technique that marked a significant step in leveraging LLMs for automated quality assessment. It was tested on nine versions of GPT models and found success in generating a quality score for system-level evaluation by directly prompting GPT. Following GEMBA, EAPrompt (Lu et al., 2023), a novel prompting method that combines Chain of Thought (Wei et al., 2022) reasoning with error analysis, has shown promise in producing explainable and reliable machine translation evaluations at both the system and segment levels using GPT models. AutoMQM (Fernandes et al., 2023), another prompting technique, leverages LLMs' reasoning and in-context learning capabilities to identify and categorize translation errors, proving effective with PaLM-2 models. Building on these efforts,

GEMBA-MQM employs a fixed three-shot prompting method with GPT-4 to mark error spans, enhancing the original GEMBA results by improving the evaluation of translation quality (Kocmi & Federmann, 2023b). Following this, Huang et al. (2024) adopted GEMBA-SQM to evaluate performance across four modes: Translation-only (T), Source-Translation (S-T), Reference-Translation (R-T), and Source-Reference-Translation (SRT). The results indicate that while source information can sometimes be counterproductive, reference information consistently enhances evaluation accuracy. The most recent research (Jiao et al., 2025) shows LLMs can provide useful feedback for translation assessment. However, the use of LLMs for MI evaluation has not yet been thoroughly researched.

2.3 Quality Metric

2.3.1 ASR Quality Evaluation Metric

The evaluation of ASR quality has traditionally relied on the Word Error Rate (WER), a metric that calculates the number of word-level errors between the ASR output and a reference transcription. Specifically, WER is based on the Levenshtein Distance (Levenshtein, 1966), which measures the minimum number of substitutions, insertions, and deletions required to transform one sequence into another. Though not originally developed for ASR, this method was adapted to quantify transcription accuracy in speech processing. While WER has been the standard for evaluating the accuracy of word recognition in ASR systems, recent studies have pointed out its limitations. Most notably, it evaluates transcription purely at the surface word level, without accounting for contextual meaning, syntax, or the communicative intent behind utterances (He et al., 2011; Sasindran et al., 2023). For example, a transcription with low WER might still distort the speaker's message if critical function words are missed or homophones are misrecognized.

2.3.2 MT Quality Evaluation Metric

The concept of translation quality has always been a controversial topic within translation studies, primarily because of the subjective nature of what constitutes "quality" in translation. Different individuals hold diverse views on this matter, leading to a lack of universal standards for evaluating translation quality. Until 1990s, however, the advent of software localization, with its business consideration, led to the development of objective quality measures, prompting the emergence of various company-specific metrics (Lommel et al., 2014). Among these, the LISA QA Model (LISA, 2006) and SAE J2450 (Society of Automotive Engineers, 2016) have gained wide recognition.

The LISA QA Model classifies errors according to three levels of severity: Minor, Major, and Critical. It specifically addresses content-related errors under the "Doc

Lan-gauge" category, covering a range of issues from mistranslations and inaccuracies to problems to terminology, language, style, cultural relevance, and consistency. Errors related to the formatting of documents and software are categorized separately. On the other hand, the SAE J2450 standard identifies seven primary error types, including wrong term usage, syntactic errors, omissions, word structure or agreement errors, misspellings, punctuation mistakes, and miscellaneous errors. It further categorizes these errors into two levels of severities: Serious and Minor.

Despite their widespread use, both the LISA QA Model and SAE J2450 have been criticized for their one-size-fits-all approach to translation evaluation. These models apply uniform standards across a wide range of translation tasks, without accounting for the specific purpose, audience, or domain of the translation. Moreover, they tend to evaluate translation quality in binary terms, labeling segments as either correct or incorrect. This binary model—referred to as a measure of absolute translation quality—fails to reflect the nuanced, multifaceted nature of real-world translation, where acceptability can depend on function, context, and intent (Lommel et al., 2014).

In response to these limitations, the Multidimensional Quality Metrics (MQM) framework was developed as part of the EU-funded QTLaunchPad project (Lommel et al., 2014). Based on a comprehensive review of over 20 existing translation quality models, MQM offers a flexible and hierarchical taxonomy of error categories that can be tailored to specific translation contexts, including machine translation. MQM errors are organized into multiple dimensions, such as accuracy (e.g., omissions, additions, mistranslations), fluency (e.g., grammar, spelling, punctuation), and design (e.g., formatting or layout). Each error is not only labeled but can also be weighted based on its severity (e.g., minor, major, critical), allowing for graded evaluation rather than a binary pass/fail outcome. Rather than relying on a fixed error set, MQM allows evaluators to customize quality profiles that prioritize different aspects of translation depending on task requirements.

3 Rough Score Evaluation

Previous research on utilizing LLMs for evaluation has primarily focused on machine translation, with little attention given to machine interpreting. In this section, we extend prior work by adapting the GEMBA-SQM prompt to evaluate machine interpreting across three distinct modes: ASR-Machine Translation (ASR-MT), Source-ASR-Machine Translation (ST-ASR-MT), and Source-ASR-Machine Translation-Reference Translation (ST-ASR-MT-RT) at sentence level. The prompt for each mode can be found in Appendix A. Our objective is to examine the correlation and consistency between the scores generated by each of the three evaluation modes and their alignment with human evaluation.

3.1 Experimental Setup

3.1.1 Data

For this study, we selected a TED Talk as the primary source material, accompanied by its official English transcript and a human-translated Chinese version, which served as the source text and reference translation, respectively. The chosen talk comprises 102 sentences, providing a well-balanced corpus for educational purposes—substantial enough to uncover meaningful patterns, yet compact enough for in-class exploration. The interpreting system evaluated was iFLYREC's Multilingual Simultaneous Interpreting System, which uses a cascading architecture. This structure evaluates the two components independently, helping trainees grasp how specific errors, whether in transcription or translation, accumulate across the interpreting pipeline. The speech materials can be substituted based on thematic focus, difficulty level, or domain-specific content (e.g., medical, legal, or technical) for classroom use. Alternatively, trainees can be encouraged to select their own materials to promote active engagement and develop their ability to choose the data for evaluation tasks.

3.1.2 Machine Evaluation

For this study, we used GPT-4o, the latest model in the GPT series, which supports an expanded output length of up to 16,384 tokens. We applied an adapted GEMBA-SQM prompting strategy to assess machine interpreting quality at the sentence level across three different modes: ASR-MT, ST-ASR-MT, and ST-ASR-MT-RT. This prompt is designed to generate scores that reflect how well the meaning is preserved in both the ASR and MT stages. After obtaining scores for the ASR and MT stages separately, we combined them into an overall MI score for each sentence using the Weighted Linear Combination (WLC) method—also known as Simple Additive Weighting (SAW)—a straightforward and widely accepted approach for evaluating multiple criteria simultaneously (Hwang & Yoon, 1981).

While GPT-4o offers powerful capabilities, it may not be accessible for all educators due to resource constraints or licensing. Alternative large language models such as Deepseek, Claude, or others could be explored as substitutes. Since this study only explored GPT model, it is important that educators test and validate the effectiveness of these alternatives within their specific training environments to ensure reliable and meaningful evaluation results.

$$A_i^{WLC-score} = \sum_{j=1}^{n} w_j a_{ij}, for\ i = 1, 2, 3, \ldots, m \tag{1}$$

$$\begin{aligned} MI\ Score &= w1 \cdot asrScore + w2 \cdot mtScore \\ &* \text{where w1 + w2 = 1} \end{aligned} \tag{2}$$

3.1.3 Human Evaluation

The evaluation of ASR performance primarily relies on the WER metric which measures the number of errors in the ASR transcript by counting three types of mistakes: substitutions (incorrect words replacing correct ones), insertions (extra words added), and deletions (missing words). These errors are compared against the original source transcript to calculate the WER, which is expressed as a percentage representing the proportion of errors in the ASR output. To make this score more intuitive, we convert WER into the Word Accuracy Rate (WAR). The WAR is simply the complement of WER, showing the percentage of words the ASR system correctly recognized. For example, if the WER is 25%, this means 25% of the words were incorrect, so the WAR would be 75%, indicating the ASR correctly transcribed 75% of the words. This WAR value is then used to assign the final ASR score. In this example, the ASR score would be 75 out of 100. Since this study focuses on sentence-level evaluation, the ASR score is calculated individually for each sentence.

$$WER = \frac{100 * (\ sub + ins + del\ )}{total\ number\ of\ words\ in\ reference\ transcript} \tag{3}$$

$$WAR = 100\% - \mathrm{WER} \tag{4}$$

The evaluation of MT performance follows the MQM framework, which categorizes errors, assigns a severity level, and applies penalty points and weights for each error type. In this experiment, penalty points for error severities are set as follows: minor errors incur a 1-point penalty, major errors a 5-point penalty, and critical errors a 25-point penalty (recommend by MQM). The weight assigned to each error type is uniformly set to 1, indicating equal importance across error categories. This consistent weighting implies that each error contributes proportionally to the overall MT score based solely on its severity level, without additional adjustments for specific error types. The calculation formula for the MT score can be found on the MQM website. The final MT score for each sentence is computed using this formula. Once the ASR and MT scores are calculated for each sentence, an overall score is derived using the WLC method.

For educators, human evaluation can be transformed into a practical classroom activity, where trainers take on the role of annotators. Appendix D provides a ready-to-use evaluation sheet designed specifically for interpreting trainees to assess ASR and MT output using the WER and MQM frameworks. This resource can be easily adapted for in-class exercises, group projects, or homework assignments. The sheet includes clear instructions and sample templates to guide students step by step through each metric.

3.1.4 Evaluation Metric

To examine whether machine-assigned scores align with human evaluations, we used two statistical methods: Pearson Correlation Coefficient (Pearson, 1896) and Kendall's Tau (Kendall, 1938).

Pearson Correlation Coefficient (often written as r) measures how closely two sets of numerical scores are related. It gives a value between −1 and +1:

- A score close to +1 means that when one set of scores goes up, the other tends to go up as well—this is a strong positive correlation.
- A score close to −1 means that when one set goes up, the other tends to go down—this is a strong negative correlation.
- A score near 0 suggests little or no relationship between the two sets of scores.

Pearson is useful for trainers who want to show students how consistent (or inconsistent) AI evaluations are when compared with human judgment, helping them better understand the reliability of machine scoring in interpreting tasks. However, Pearson is known to be sensitive to outliers—that is, unusually high or low scores—which can skew the results and give a misleading impression of how strong the overall relationship is (Deutsch et al., 2023). To address this, we also used Kendall's Tau (τ), a different method that compares the ranking of scores rather than the actual numbers. For example, if both humans and machines rank one sentence as better than another, Kendall's Tau counts that as agreement, regardless of the exact scores. Like Pearson, it produces a score between −1 and +1, with the same interpretation:

- A score close to +1 means perfect agreement in ranking,
- A score close to −1 means perfect disagreement,
- A score near 0 means no clear pattern.

Besides, we calculated the Absolute Score Difference between machine and human scores to quantify the disparity between the two. This was then visualized using a boxplot.

$$AbsoluteScoreDifference = |S_h - S_m| \tag{5}$$

where $S_h = Human\ Score$; $S_m = Machine\ Score$

3.2 Results

Table 1 presents a summary of the Pearson and Kendall correlation values for all three modes: ASR-MT, ST-ASR-MT, and ST-ASR-MT-RT. Overall, both the ST-ASR-MT and ST-ASR-MT-RT modes show higher alignment with human evaluations, producing scores that are more similar to human judgments across both the ASR and MT stages. As a result, these modes exhibit even better correlations with human scores in the overall evaluation. In contrast, the ASR-MT mode underperforms.

Table 1 Correlation results across three modes

Modes	Overall	ASR	MT
ASR-MT	r = 0.64	r = 0.58	r = 0.54
	τ = 0.51	τ = 0.51	τ = 0.51
ST-ASR-MT	r = 0.85	r = 0.73	r = 0.79
	τ = 0.66	τ = 0.62	τ = 0.61
ST-ASR-MT-RT	r = 0.80	r = 0.70	r = 0.68
	τ = 0.62	τ = 0.59	τ = 0.56

* Computed by Origin

3.2.1 ASR Score Analysis

We can see that both the ST-ASR-MT mode and the ST-ASR-MT-RT mode exhibit a strong positive correlation and consistency with human evaluation metrics. Specifically, the ST-ASR-MT mode achieves Pearson and Kendall coefficients of 0.73 and 0.62, respectively, while the ST-ASR-MT-RT mode achieves slightly lower Pearson and Kendall coefficients of 0.70 and 0.59, respectively. In contrast, the ASR-MT mode shows only a moderate positive correlation and consistency, with a Pearson correlation coefficient of 0.58 and Kendall coefficients of 0.51 (Fig. 1 shows the individual ASR scores assigned by human and machine with regression lines).

Since it is difficult to directly see the distance between human and machine scores, we also calculate the absolute score difference for each sentence and present the results in a boxplot (Fig. 2). Interestingly, although the ASR-MT mode is less aligned with human evaluations, it exhibits a smaller maximum score difference (25) compared to the larger maximum score differences of 30 and 50 observed in the ST-ASR-MT and ST-ASR-MT-RT modes, respectively. However, all modes show a minimum score difference of zero. Although the ASR-MT mode shows smaller interquartile range than the other two, it exhibits a positive skew. Additionally, ASR-MT mode contains more outliers (5), while ST-ASR-MT and ST-ASR-MT-RT modes have only 2 and 3 outliers, respectively.

To investigate the reasons for the unusually large score differences (outliers), we present examples of these outliers in Table 5. We found that in the ASR-MT mode, where the source transcript is not provided, the model may focus more on the overall coherence and perceived meaning of the output, potentially overlooking errors that would normally be considered significant by human evaluators. For example, consider the source text: "A depletable energy? Fossil fuel?" which is transcribed as "a depletable energy for so few." In this case, the human ASR score is 40, while the machine assigns a significantly higher score of 80. This discrepancy arises because the model interprets the transcribed sentence as making logical sense, even though it deviates from the intended meaning of the original text. Nonetheless, the absolute score difference of 40 makes this an outlier.

In contrast, the ST-ASR-MT and ST-ASR-MT-RT modes, which include the source transcript, allow the model to evaluate with a clearer reference, leading to

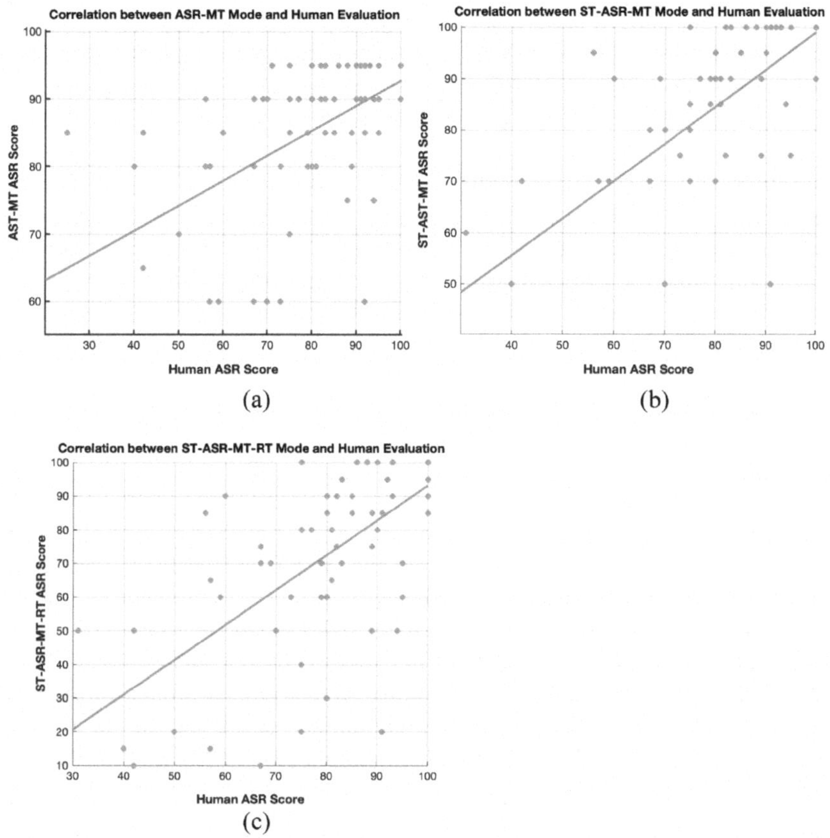

Fig. 1 The figure shows Human and machine ASR score in different modes. (**a**) ASR-MT mode; (**b**) ST-ASR-MT mode; (**c**) ST-ASR-MT-RT mode

Fig. 2 Boxplot for ASR score difference between human and machine

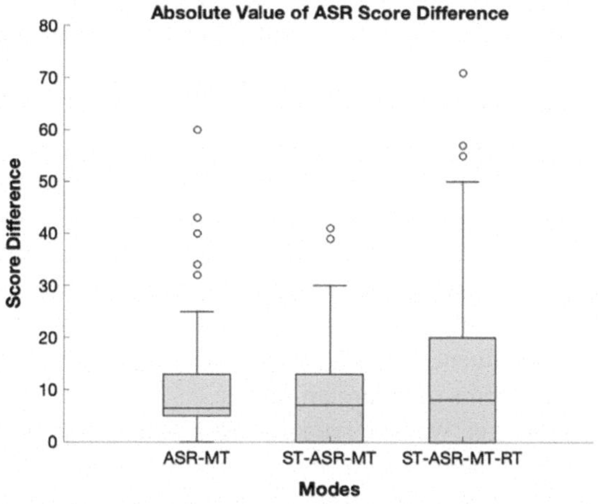

a more consistent and accurate assessment of how well the meaning is preserved in relation to the original speech. For example, consider the sentence: "That is how you all happen to use and enjoy water." In this case, the ASR incorrectly transcribes "water" as "AutoML." The model assigns scores of 50 and 20 in the ST-ASR-MT and ST-ASR-MT-RT modes, respectively, due to a shift in meaning caused by incorrect transcription. This example is an outlier because the human score for this sentence is 91. According to the WER metric, only one word differs from the source transcript, leading to a much higher human score compared to the machine score. However, even with the same ST and ASR texts, the model generates significantly different scores for the same sentence across modes if a standard scoring method is not used.

After analyzing the ASR scores, we found that a source transcript is essential for the model to accurately evaluate ASR scores. And a clear and consistent evaluation framework is needed to ensure machine evaluation is internally consistent.

3.2.2 MT Score Analysis

We can see that both the ST-ASR-MT mode and the ST-ASR-MT-RT mode exhibit a strong positive correlation and consistency with human evaluation metrics. Specifically, the ST-ASR-MT mode achieves Pearson and Kendall coefficients of 0.79 and 0.61, respectively, while the ST-ASR-MT-RT mode achieves slightly lower Pearson and Kendall coefficients of 0.68 and 0.56, respectively. In contrast, the ASR-MT mode shows only a moderate positive correlation and consistency, with a Pearson correlation coefficient of 0.54 and Kendall coefficients of 0.51 (Fig. 3 shows the individual MT scores assigned by human and machine with regression lines).

Figure 4 shows the absolute score difference in MT stage. We can see that all modes show a minimum score difference of 0. However, the ASR-MT and ST-ASR-MT modes have the largest maximum score differences of 70 and 65, while the ST-ASR-MT-RT mode on has maximum score differences of 40. Both the ASR-MT and ST-ASR-MT modes show large interquartile ranges, but the ASR-MT mode is more positively skewed. While the ST-ASR-MT-RT mode has a smaller interquartile range, it contains more outliers (14), compared to 12 in the ASR-MT mode and only 6 in the ST-ASR-MT mode.

To investigate the reasons for the large number of outliers, we present examples in Table 6. We observe that most examples receive a human score of 0, while the machine assigns them much higher scores. This discrepancy occurs because, for human evaluator using MQM metric, a single critical error can invalidate the entire sentence. And it is understandable that without access to the source transcript, the ASR-MT mode appears to assume that the ASR output is the actual source text, which influences its evaluation of the MT segment. In the end, the machine gave higher scores than human scores.

However, we observed a similar situation in both the ST-ASR-MT and ST-ASR-MT-RT modes, which seems confused because these two modes have a source text to refer to. We found that both modes displayed a tendency to assign overly generous scores to instances that human had classified as containing critical or major errors.

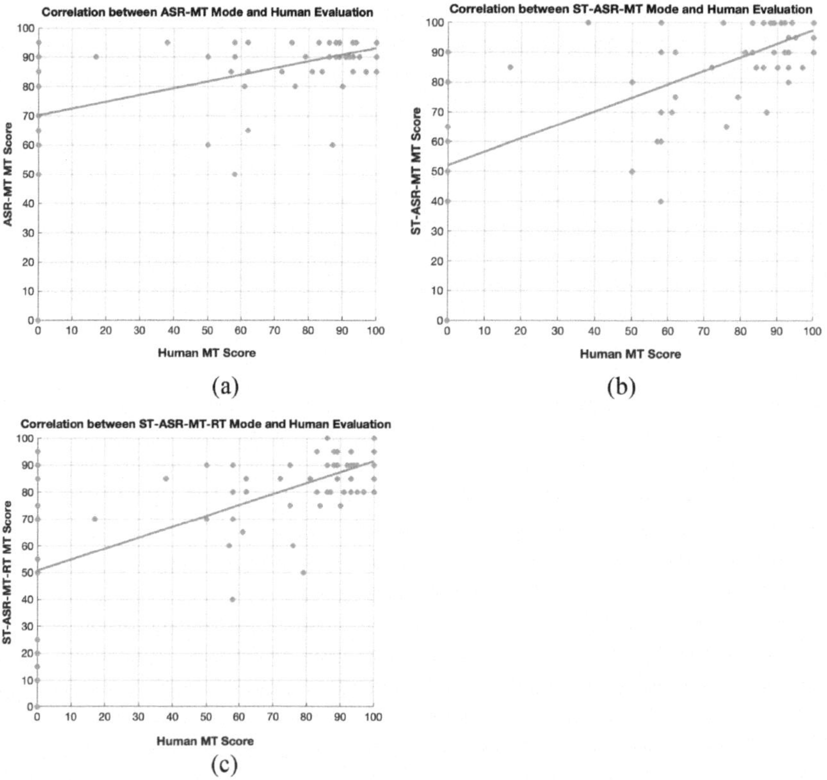

Fig. 3 The figure shows human and machine MT score in different modes. (**a**) ASR-MT mode; (**b**) ST-ASR-MT mode; (**c**) ST-ASR-MT-RT mode

Fig. 4 Boxplot for MT score difference between human and machine

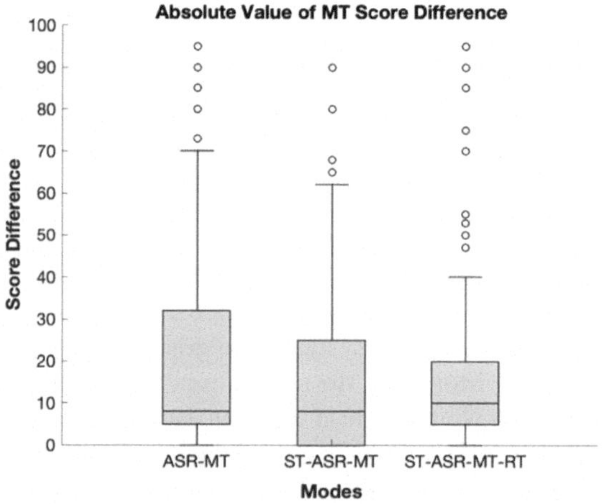

We wanted to find the rationale of giving such scores but found that the comments given by the model in ST-ASR-MT mode lacked specificity, so it is difficult to see the reasons. But the comments in ST-ASR-MT-RT mode are more detailed. From which we found an unusual case. For instance, the model provided feedback "种耗竭性能源?化石燃料? is accurate and well-aligned with the original intent," and assigned a score of 90 while human assigned a score of 0. The reason the model assigns such high scores is that it mistakenly treats the reference translation as the machine translation. Interestingly, even when the model was evaluating the reference translation, which theoretically should result in a perfect match and a score of 100, it did not assign a full score.

On the other hand, aside from assigning overly generous scores to sentences with major and critical errors, we also found that when errors were classified as minor or deemed "no error" by human evaluators, the model tended to provide more rigid scores (not within the outliner examples). This pattern was particularly evident in the ST-ASR-MT-RT mode. This rigidity is likely due to the influence of the reference translation: when a reference is provided, GPT's evaluation seems constrained by the phrasing of the reference, leading to a more fixed and less flexible scoring approach. For example, the omission of "so" or small wording differences resulted in a 10-point deduction, and the absence of "of course" even led to a 25-point penalty.

After analyzing the MT scores, we found that the ST-ASR-MT mode performs better than ST-ASR-MT-RT in general, because the reference text may overly influence the model. However, without clear guidelines, the model tends to assign scores inconsistently across all modes, sometimes too high and other times too low. Occasionally, the model becomes confused and deviates from the intended evaluation criteria.

3.2.3 Summary

Among the three tested modes, the ST-ASR-MT mode (which includes both the source transcript and machine outputs) demonstrated the strongest performance, while the ASR-MT mode (which excludes the source) performed the weakest across both ASR and MT stages. This suggests that accessing to source texts can significantly enhance the evaluation of meaning preservation. Interestingly, the ST-ASR-MT-RT mode, which includes both the source and reference translation, resulted in a decline in performance during the MT stage. This suggests that reference texts may inadvertently narrow the scoring focus, prompting the language model to evaluate translations too rigidly against a "gold standard," rather than appreciating acceptable variation. Moreover, the study found that using LLMs without a structured evaluation framework can lead to inconsistent results. In some cases, the model provided detailed rationales for score deductions, while in others, feedback was vague or contradictory. This highlights the importance of using clear, structured prompts and evaluation guidelines.

Nonetheless, this approach can serve as a valuable teaching resource. Educators can use it to demonstrate how LLMs evaluate meaning preservation and highlight the limitations of rough score prompting. Trainees can be encouraged to critically reflect on the capabilities and shortcomings of LLMs in interpreting tasks, and to design improved prompting strategies that enhance evaluation accuracy and reliability.

4 Optimized Score Evaluation

In this section, we propose an integrated prompt, called MIEval, for evaluating machine interpreting across two modes: ST-ASR-MT and ST-ASR-MT-RT. We provide specific and separate guidelines for both the ASR and MT stages. Since the ASR stage requires a source transcript, we exclude the ASR-MT mode from our evaluation. The prompts for each mode can be found in Appendix C. Our objective is to assess whether a structured evaluation framework improves the correlation and consistency between machine-generated scores and human assessments.

4.1 Experimental Setup

4.1.1 Data

Since the goal of our experiment is to compare the performance of GEMBA and MIEval, we use the same 102 sentences and iFlYREC from Sect. 3.

4.1.2 Machine Evaluation

In this evaluation, we utilized the same GPT-4o model as in our previous experiments. For the ASR stage, our prompt was based on WAR but excluded punctuation, capitalization, numerals, contractions, extra spaces, and hyphens from being counted as errors. This adjustment was made after observing that conventional WER calculation tools treated every minor variation as an error, even when these did not impact the meaning of the text. Our refined approach aims to capture more meaningful accuracy metrics by focusing on content rather than formatting. Then, the WAR is calculated for each sentence. For the MT stage, we adapted the GEMBA-MQM prompting method (Kocmi & Federmann, 2023b), but extended it by prompting the LLM to perform the actual score calculation. Each sentence is evaluated individually, and the MT score is automatically generated based on the identified errors and their severity. After obtaining the ASR and MT scores, the WLC is still used for the overall MI score calculation. However, during pilot testing, we observed a consistent issue: the language model struggled with accurate word counting, which impacted score reliability. To mitigate this, we manually inserted word counts following each source sentence in the prompt. This ensured that the model's scoring process remained accurate and unaffected by its internal counting limitations.

Educators can replicate this refined setup in the classroom to help trainees understand how specific technical decisions, such as excluding punctuation or adding word counts, can lead to more meaningful and accurate evaluations. This hands-on exploration fosters critical thinking about how assessment parameters influence outcomes.

4.1.3 Human Evaluation

The same human evaluation method used in the previous experiment is retained in this stage.

4.1.4 Evaluation Metric

We used the Pearson and Kendall correlation coefficient and Absolute Score Difference, as described previously, to evaluate the alignment between human and machine evaluation scores. Furthermore, to evaluate the performance of error identification of the machine, we calculate Precision, Recall, and finally F1-Score. Precision measures how many errors identified by the machine are also identified by humans, while Recall calculates how many errors identified by humans are also recognized by the machine. To evaluate overall performance, we compute the F1-Score, which is the harmonic mean of Precision and Recall, balancing both metrics into a single score. To calculate the F1-Score, we need to know True Positives (TP), False Positives (FP), and False Negatives (FN). TP refers to errors correctly identified by both machine and human. FP refers to errors identified by the machine but not by the human. FN refers to errors identified by the human but missed by the machine. However, we consider only the actual errors identified by both humans and machines, without accounting for the severity levels assigned. Therefore, even if humans and machines assign different severity levels to the same error, it is still counted as an error identified by both.

$$Precision = \left(\frac{True\ Positives(TP)}{True\ Positives(TP) + False\ Positives(FP)} \right) * 100 \tag{6}$$

$$Recall = \left(\frac{True\ Positives(TP)}{True\ Positives(TP) + False\ Nositives(FP)} \right) * 100 \tag{7}$$

$$F1\ Score = \left(2 * \left(\frac{Precision * Recall}{Precision + Recall} \right) \right) * 100 \tag{8}$$

4.2 Results

Table 2 presents a summary of the Pearson and Kendall correlation values for both modes: ST-ASR-MT and ST-ASR-MT-RT. In general, both the ST-ASR-MT and ST-ASR-MT-RT modes show higher alignment with human evaluations, producing scores that are more similar to human judgments across both the ASR and MT stages. As a result, these modes exhibit even better correlations with human scores in the overall evaluation. Notably, the performance is greatly improved when compared to Rough Score Evaluation. And the ASR scores across two modes are more internally consistent.

4.2.1 ASR Score Analysis

We can see that both the ST-ASR-MT mode and the ST-ASR-MT-RT mode exhibit a strong positive correlation and consistency with human evaluation metrics. Specifically, the ST-ASR-MT-RT mode achieves Pearson and Kendall coefficients of 0.91 and 0.81, respectively, while the ST-ASR-MT mode achieves slightly lower Pearson and Kendall coefficients of 0.90 and 0.79, respectively (Fig. 5 shows the individual ASR scores assigned by human and machine and regression lines). Even though the results of the two modes are close, there is still a tiny difference. This is because when evaluating both modes, the model recalculates ASR scores independently each time. This approach occasionally results in scoring inconsistently for identical sentences, even when clear guidelines are provided—a challenge also observed in the previously adopted GEMBA prompting method.

Figure 6 illustrates the absolute ASR score differences between human and machine evaluations. Interestingly, the two modes exhibit similar maximum score differences of 17 and minimum score differences of 0. They also have comparable numbers of outliers: 5 in the ST-ASR-MT mode and 4 in the ST-ASR-MT-RT mode. Both modes display a significant positive skew; however, the interquartile range is larger in the ST-ASR-MT mode.

Upon examining the outlier examples (Table 7), we found that the large score differences are due to occasional failures to recognize errors. For instance, in the following example, the ST-ASR-MT mode only identifies the error "erage" but ignores the deletion error "for the" resulting in a high score of 93.

Table 2 Correlation results across three modes

Modes	Overall	ASR	MT
ST-ASR-MT	$r = 0.86$	$r = 0.90$	$r = 0.80$
	$\tau = 0.70$	$\tau = 0.79$	$\tau = 0.64$
ST-ASR-MT-RT	$r = 0.93$	$r = 0.91$	$r = 0.91$
	$\tau = 0.79$	$\tau = 0.81$	$\tau = 0.66$

* Computed by Origin

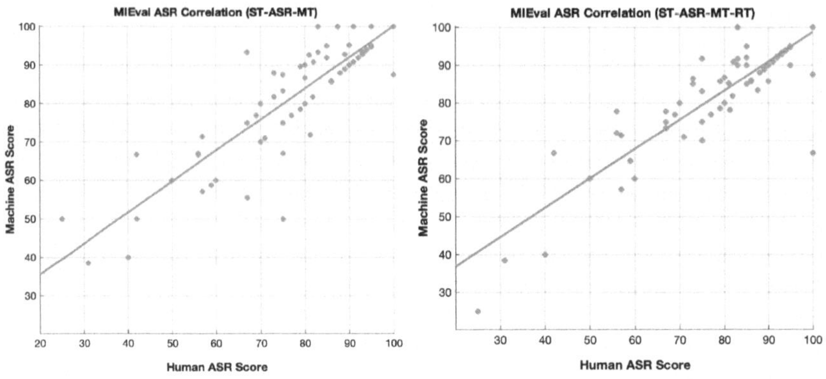

(a) (b)

Fig. 5 The figure shows MIEval human and machine ASR score in different modes. **(a)** ST-ASR-MT mode; **(b)** ST-ASR-MT-RT mode

Fig. 6 Boxplot for MIEval ASR score difference

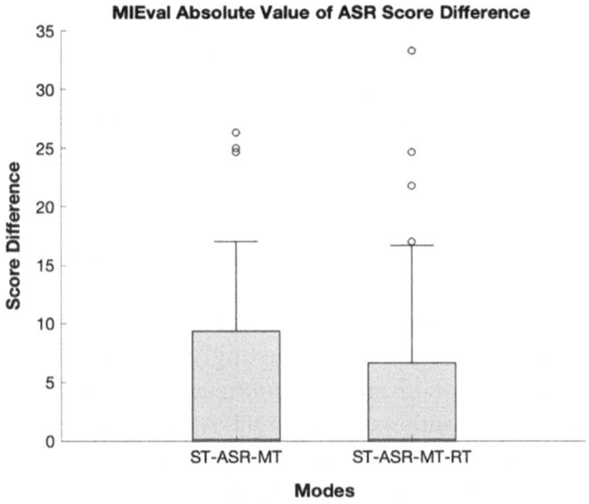

ST:	The average growth of our economy is about 15 percent for the past 5 years.
ASR:	The erage growth of our economy is about 15%. Past 5 years,

Another issue is that even when we instructed the model to calculate the number of erroneous words, it failed to do so and instead only counted the total number of errors. For example, in the following case, the ST-ASR-MT-RT mode correctly identified substitution error (e.g., "1782" being substituted with "1,700 and 82"), but it counted this as 1 error rather than 3 erroneous words in the numerator of the calculation, resulting in a high score of 92.

ST:	So Brazil has 1782 millimeters per year of precipitation of rain.
ASR:	So Brazil has 1700 and 82 millimeters per year of precipitation of rain.

Additionally, in the following example, the model interprets "worry" as being deleted and "very" as being added, whereas humans consider "worry" to be substituted with "very." Although both interpretations are reasonable, they will result in differences in scoring. In other words, the model may occasionally make judgments that are unexpected by humans.

ST:	Do you worry much?
ASR:	Do you very much?

After analyzing the ASR scores, we found that while the overall performance of the ASR stage has significantly improved, small mistakes and unexpected situations still occur even when clear instructions are provided.

4.2.2 MT Score Analysis

We can see that both the ST-ASR-MT mode and the ST-ASR-MT-RT mode exhibit a strong positive correlation and consistency with human evaluation metrics. Specifically, the ST-ASR-MT mode achieves Pearson and Kendall coefficients of 0.80 and 0.64, respectively, while the ST-ASR-MT-RT mode achieves slightly higher Pearson and Kendall coefficients of 0.91 and 0.66, respectively (Fig. 7 shows the individual MT scores assigned by human and machine and regression lines). The performance of MIEval in MT stage is largely improved compared to GEMBA prompting.

Figure 8 shows the absolute score differences between human and machine evaluations. Interestingly, the two modes show similar maximum score difference (34 and 31 respectively) and minimum score difference of 0. And both modes exhibit a similar short interquartile range and a positive skew. However, the ST-ASR-MT-RT mode exhibits fewer outliers (7) compared to the ST-ASR-MT mode, which has 12 outliers.

To investigate the reasons for the unusual values, we look at the outlier examples (Table 8). In the ST-ASR-MT mode, we observed that when human evaluators assign higher scores, the model tends to give lower scores, and when human evaluators assign lower scores, the model assigns higher scores. However, the situation improves in the ST-ASR-MT-RT mode when a reference translation is provided. The reference text may provide a specific baseline that allows the model to judge severity more accurately. With a reference as context, the model can more effectively determine whether an error is minor or critical, leading to higher alignment with human evaluations in the ST-ASR-MT-RT mode.

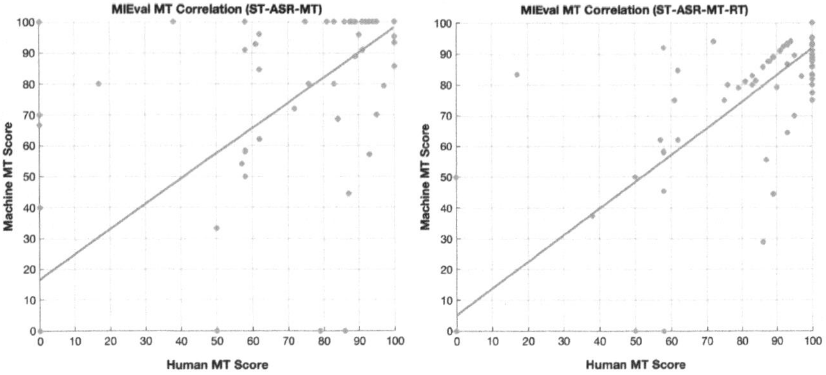

(a) (b)

Fig. 7 The figure shows MIEval correlation between human and machine MT score in different modes. **(a)** Correlation in ST-ASR-MT mode; **(b)** Correlation in ST-ASR-MT-RT mode

Fig. 8 Boxplot for MIEval MT absolute score difference

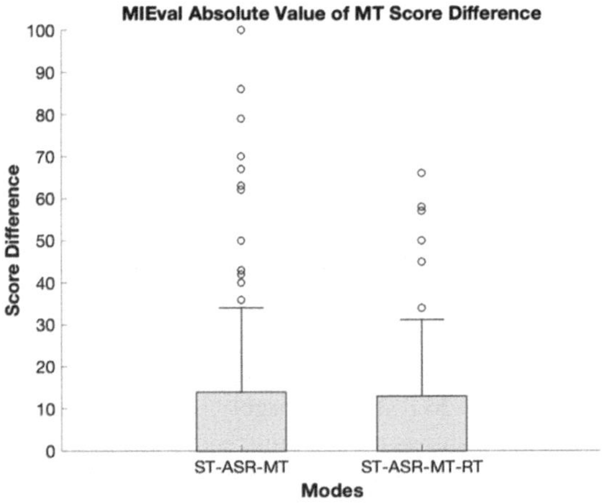

Despite this improvement, the model in the ST-ASR-MT-RT mode sometimes seems to over-rely on the reference text, sometimes penalizing the machine translation more harshly when there are differences in logical connections between the machine-translated sentence and the reference text. For instance, consider the example:

ST:	Resources weren't there to develop.
ASR:	Resources weren't there to develop them.
MT:	没有资源可以开发 (No resources to develop)

RT: 而是匮乏的资源不允许城市的发展 (But it's the lack of resources that doesn't allow cities to develop)

While the human evaluator considered the machine translation to be relatively close to the source text (ST) and assigned a score of 86, the model in the ST-ASR-MT-RT mode perceived the machine translation to be significantly further from the reference text and thus assigned a much lower score of 29. This discrepancy occurs because the reference translation introduces a logical connection that is not explicitly present in the machine-translated sentence, but the model is heavily reliant on the reference text and penalizes the machine translation for not aligning with it.

Another issue that arises with the reference text is the treatment of cultural or idiomatic expressions. For example, "reaction to lack of water" is simple but challenging to translate into Chinese. The reference translation uses the idiomatic expression "物极必反" ("extreme things will reverse"), which is an idiomatic expression that doesn't directly correspond to the original meaning of the sentence. In cases like this, the model struggles with how to evaluate the error because the reference translation introduces cultural or idiomatic nuances that don't directly align with the machine translation. This is a similar issue that was observed with the GEMBA prompting approach, where the model also struggled with idiomatic expressions and culture-specific references, leading to inconsistencies in scoring.

Interestingly, while rough score evaluations without reference text produced results more aligned with human assessments, the optimized MIEval approach benefits significantly from the inclusion of a reference text. To investigate this, we further look at the errors identified by human and machine.

Table 3 shows the sum of True Positive, False Positive, and False Negative in both modes. We can see that ST-ASR-MT-RT mode has more errors (65) identified by both machine and human, while ST-ASR-MT mode has less (43). On the one hand, ST-ASR-MT-RT mode also identified overly too many errors (43) that are not flagged by human than in the ST-ASR-MT mode. On the other hand, ST-ASR-MT mode has much more errors identified by the human but missed by the machine (25) than ST-ASR-MT-RT mode (5).

It is difficult to tell which one performs better by merely looking at the error numbers. Therefore, we calculate the error matches rate between human and machine translation. In the ST-ASR-MT mode, 69.35% errors identified by the machine are actually correct and 63.23% human-identified errors were correctly identified by the machine. The balanced match rate for this mode is 66.13. In the ST-ASR-MT-RT mode, 60.18% errors identified by the machine are actually correct, lower than in the

Table 3 Sum of true positive, false positive, and false negative

Modes	True Positive	False Positive	False Negative
ST-ASR-MT	43	19	25
ST-ASR-MT-RT	65	43	5

Table 4 Results of precision, recall, and F1-score

Modes	Precision (%)	Recall (%)	F1-Score (%)
ST-ASR-MT	69.35	63.23	66.13
ST-ASR-MT-RT	60.18	92.85	73.01

ST-ASR-MT mode, but 92.85% human-identified errors were correctly identified by the machine, much higher than in the ST-ASR-MT mode. The balanced match rate is also higher for this mode, which is 73.01. The results show that error identification improves significantly when reference texts are provided, particularly with errors identified by humans being way more frequently recognized by the machine in the ST-ASR-MT-RT mode (Table 4).

After analyzing the MT scores and errors, we found that the ST-ASR-MT-RT mode performs better than ST-ASR-MT in general. Despite instructions to evaluate the severity of errors, the model sometimes struggles to correctly identify the severity level when no reference text is available. With the reference text, the model appears to have better guidance, leading to more accurate identification of the errors.

4.2.3 Summary

By using the MIEval prompting method, we observe considerable improvements in both the ASR and MT scores. The ASR scores show more stable correlation across both modes, suggesting that the MIEval prompt—by providing structured calculation rules and clear evaluation criteria—enhances the consistency and reliability of machine-based evaluation. In the MT stage, there is a noticeable difference between the ST-ASR-MT and ST-ASR-MT-RT modes. The ST-ASR-MT-RT mode performs significantly better, as the inclusion of a reference translation provides a concrete baseline for the model to assess the severity of errors more effectively and consistently. Without this reference, the model tends to struggle in identifying and weighing errors appropriately, leading to less reliable MT scores. In summary, while both modes benefit from the structured nature of the MIEval prompt, the ST-ASR-MT-RT mode demonstrates the strongest alignment with human evaluation. Overall, MIEval outperforms the more loosely structured GEMBA-adopted prompts.

From a pedagogical perspective, educators can use the contrast between MIEval and GEMBA to teach trainers how prompt structure influences evaluation outcomes. Through guided classroom activities, students can analyze how MIEval's scoring and predefined severity scales lead to more consistent results compared to the more open-ended GEMBA approach. More importantly, educators can engage trainees in refining the MIEval prompt itself—adapting it to different interpreting domains (e.g., legal or medical), modifying how errors are weighted, or testing how various reference materials impact scoring accuracy. These exercises not only build students' awareness of evaluation mechanics but also cultivate skills in prompt engineering, critical analysis, and human–machine collaboration, making evaluation literacy an integral part of interpreter education.

5 Implications for Interpreter Education

The findings of this study have significant implications for interpreter education, particularly in the integration of AI-assisted evaluation into classroom practice. The key implication is the role of structured prompting as a trainable skill in interpreter education. The results of this study show that MIEval's structured integration of WER and MQM leads to more reliable assessments than vague, open-ended prompts. Educators can leverage this insight by incorporating prompt design assignments into the curriculum. For example, trainees could be tasked with modifying MIEval prompts to prioritize fluency over accuracy in conversational settings or to emphasize technical terminology in medical interpreting. This builds a foundation in prompt engineering, now an essential competency in human–AI interaction.

To further support pedagogical implementation, we suggest several modules for LLM-based interpreter education, grounded in the practical findings of this study:

Module 1: Introduction to Evaluation Metrics.

This foundational module introduces trainees to key metrics used in machine interpreting and translation evaluation. It covers traditional automatic evaluation scores such as BLEU, TER, and METEOR, explaining how these metrics compare machine-generated outputs with reference translations based on word or phrase matching. Trainees will learn why these metrics, despite their widespread use, often show poor correlation with human judgments due to their inability to fully capture meaning preservation, contextual nuances, or error severity. Building on this foundation, the module then introduces advanced metrics like MQM, which are central to the MIEval framework tested in this study. Understanding these metrics enables trainees to critically assess the strengths and weaknesses of different evaluation approaches and better appreciate how LLM-based evaluation methods can offer more nuanced and reliable assessments.

Module 2: Prompt Engineering.

This module equips students with practical skills to design, test, and refine prompts for LLM-based interpreting evaluation, emphasizing the importance of clear, structured instructions. Drawing on the study's findings that MIEval's integration of WER and MQM with detailed prompting significantly improves evaluation accuracy, trainees will experiment with customizing prompts to highlight different evaluation priorities—such as fluency versus accuracy depending on the interpreting context. Assignments may include modifying existing prompts to address specific error types, enabling trainees to understand how prompt wording and structure directly influence the LLM's assessment outcomes. Through hands-on exercises, students develop the ability to engineer prompts that optimize AI evaluation performance and better align with human judgment.

Module 3: Human–Machine Collaboration in Error Analysis.

This module focuses on developing students' critical skills in assessing and refining AI-generated evaluation outputs. Based on the study's observation that LLMs can sometimes misclassify errors or over-rely on reference texts, trainees will learn how to compare machine-generated evaluation with human assessments to identify discrepancies and biases. Trainees collaboratively debug LLM evaluation results by cross-referencing source texts, reference translations, and output scores. This module cultivates a nuanced understanding of the strengths and limitations of LLM evaluation, encouraging future interpreters to use AI tools as supportive aids rather than infallible authorities.

Module 4: Corpora Development.

This module emphasizes the importance of building and curating diverse, high-quality corpora to support reliable LLM-based evaluation. Reflecting on the limitations identified in this study—particularly the small and domain-specific dataset used— trainees will explore methods for collecting, annotating, and managing data across different languages, domains, and interpreting modes. If available, trainees can also be introduced to how corpora may be used to fine-tune LLMs for more domain-specific evaluation.

Module 5: Capstone Project.

A capstone project can extend this curriculum by asking trainees to develop domain-specific adaptations of MIEval, such as for legal, healthcare, or diplomatic interpreting, requiring them to synthesize prompt design, evaluation metrics, and context-aware reasoning.

The educational value of LLM-based evaluation lies in transforming how trainees learn to assess, refine, and collaborate with AI. MIEval is not merely a model for automatic evaluation; it is a pedagogical tool that can support the development of interpreters who are reflective, adaptive, and prepared for an increasingly AI-mediated professional landscape.

6 Conclusion

This study explored the potential of large language models to evaluate machine interpreting, comparing a rough score evaluation adapted from the GEMBA-SQM prompt with an optimized approach, MIEval. The rough evaluation revealed that the inclusion of source texts improves scoring consistency across the ASR and MT stages, particularly in the ST-ASR-MT and ST-ASR-MT-RT modes. However, reliance on reference texts in the MT stage led to overly rigid evaluations, as models tended to focus on literal similarity rather than contextual accuracy. To address these issues, the MIEval framework was proposed and tested. By integrating WER and MQM, MIEval significantly enhanced alignment with human judgment across both ASR and MT stages. The framework produced more stable and interpretable results, particularly in scenarios that provided source and reference texts in a balanced way.

Beyond its technical performance, this study also highlights how LLM-based evaluation approaches can be meaningfully integrated into interpreter training. By engaging with these methods, trainees can gain a clearer understanding of both the potential and the limitations of LLMs, fostering critical thinking about how to collaborate with AI tools in their future professional practice.

Nonetheless, the study has several limitations. First, the evaluation was conducted solely at the sentence level, which may not fully capture the complexity and context of longer texts or discourse-level nuances in translation quality. Second, the relatively small and homogeneous data sample limits the generalizability of the findings; larger and more diverse datasets are recommended to better understand performance across different languages, domains, and interpreting scenarios. Third, both experiments utilized the same dataset, potentially introducing bias or constraining the findings. Finally, the study relied exclusively on the GPT-4o model, which may not represent the best-performing model for machine interpreting evaluation; exploring alternative or newer models could yield further improvements. To address these limitations, educators can adapt this research by designing tasks that guide trainees in refining and retesting the MIEval approach at the text level, using larger datasets and experimenting with different LLM models.

In conclusion, this study demonstrated that structured, prompt-based LLM evaluation—embodied in the MIEval framework—not only enhances scoring accuracy for machine interpreting but can also open new avenues for interpreter education. As LLMs continue to evolve, their thoughtful integration into training contexts will be vital for preparing the next generation of interpreters to work alongside AI as informed, critical, and adaptive professionals.

Acknowledgements The research presented in this study has been carried out in the framework of XJTLU Research Development Fund (ref no. RDF-22-01-053), the Open Project of Anhui Provincial Key Laboratory of Multimodal Cognitive Computation, Anhui University (ref no. MMC202414), National Science and Technology Terminology Committee Fund (ref no. YB2023009), and research project VIP II (ref no. PID2020-112818GB I00/AEI/10.13039/501100011033).

Appendix A

GEMBA Prompt Adoption

ASR-MT

Score the following speech-to-text transcription and translation from {src_lang} to {tgt_lang} with respect to the ASR transcript and machine translation on a continuous scale from 0 to 100 that starts on "No meaning preserved," goes through "Some meaning preserved," then "Most meaning preserved and few grammar mistakes," up to "Perfect meaning and grammar."

{src_lang} ASR transcript: "{ASR}".
{tgt_lang} translation: "{translation}".
ASR Score (0–100):
MT Score (0–100):

ST-ASR-MT

Score the following speech-to-text transcription and translation from {src_lang} to {tgt_lang} with respect to the Source transcript, ASR transcript, and machine translation on a continuous scale from 0 to 100 that starts on "No meaning preserved," goes through "Some meaning preserved," then "Most meaning preserved and few grammar mistakes," up to "Perfect meaning and grammar."
{src_lang} transcript: "{source}".
{src_lang} ASR transcript: "{ASR}".
{tgt_lang} translation: "{translation}".
ASR Score (0–100):
MT Score (0–100):

ST-ASR-MT-RT

Score the following speech-to-text transcription and translation from {src_lang} to {tgt_lang} with respect to the Source transcript, ASR transcript, machine translation, and human reference on a continuous scale from 0 to 100 that starts on "No meaning preserved," goes through "Some meaning preserved," then "Most meaning preserved and few grammar mistakes," up to "Perfect meaning and grammar."
{src_lang} transcript: "{source}".
{src_lang} ASR transcript: "{ASR}".
{tgt_lang} human reference: "{reference}".
{tgt_lang} translation: "{translation}".
ASR Score (0–100):
MT Score (0–100):

Appendix B

See Tables 5, 6, 7, 8.

Table 5 ASR examples of outliers with scores

Examples from ASR-MT Mode	Human Score	Machine Score
ST: The question is how. **ASR:** This is	25	85
ST: These risks directly affect the sustainability of this nation and its continuity. **ASR:** These risks direct effect, the sustainability of this nation. And let's continue with you.	42	85
ST: A depletable energy? Fossil fuel? **ASR:** a depletable energy for so few	40	80
ST: But what gels all of it, what enables it, is legislation, policies, regulations. **ASR:** but with gels all of it what enables it is legislation, policies, regulations.	92	60
ST: So that's what we are planning to do. **ASR:** So that's what we planning to do within 2 years.	56	90
Examples from ST-ASR-MT Mode	**Human Score**	**Machine Score**
ST: That is how you all happen to use and enjoy water. **ASR:** That is how you all happen to use and enjoy AutoML.	91	50
ST: So that's what we are planning to do. **ASR:** So that's what we planning to do within 2 years.	56	95
Examples from ST-ASR-MT-RT Mode	**Human Score**	**Machine Score**
ST: That is how you all happen to use and enjoy water. **ASR:** That is how you all happen to use and enjoy AutoML	91	20
ST: This is the situation in Qatar, for those who don't know. **ASR:** This is a situation another for those who don't know	75	20
ST: Do we have the comparative advantage to use another sort of energy? **ASR:** Do we have the comparative advantage to use the other filterbank?	67	10

Table 6 MT examples of outliers with scores

Examples from ASR-MT Mode	Human Score	Machine Score
ASR: We realize that there are some differences in access. **MT:** 我们意识到。在获取方面有一些差异。	0	85
ASR: I don't know if this was a reaction or lack of water. **MT:** 我不知道这是一种反应还是缺水。	0	90
ASR: not only cities that we're building, but cities with dreams and people who are wishing to be scientists, doctors live **MT:** 仅是我们正在建设的城市而且是有梦想的城市和希望成为科学家的人。医生活着	0	85
ASR: Other has 74, and we have that growth rate. **MT:** 其他国家有74毫米，我们有这样的增长率。	0	85
ASR: That is our link if you can see it. **MT:** 如果你能看到它，那就是我们的链接。	0	90
ASR: That is how you all happen to use and enjoy AutoML. **MT:** 这就是你们所有人使用和享受AutoMer的方式。	0	80
ASR: The limited number of farmers that we have been pushed out of the farming practices as a result of open market policy and bringing the biggest competitions, et cetera. **MT:** 由于开放的市场政策，以及带来最大的竞争等等，我们已经被赶出了农业实践的农民数量有限。	17	90
ASR: Indeed, there is. **MT:** 事实上，	0	95
ASR: So if we're gonna need energy, what sort of energy **MT:** 所以如果我们需要能源，	0	90
ASR: a depletable energy for so few **MT:** 那么对于这么少的人来说，什么样的能源是可消耗的能源?	0	85
ASR: Do we have the comparative advantage to use the other filterbank? **MT:** 我们有使用其他滤波器组的比较优势吗?	0	90
ASR: Our objective is to be a millennium city, just like many millennium cities around this llama grow. Llama, Paris, MOSS, Cairo. **MT:** 我们的目标是成为一座千年之城，就像这座美洲驼周围的许多千年之城一样。美洲驼，巴黎，莫斯，开罗。	0	85
Examples from ST-ASR-MT Mode	**Human Score**	**Machine Score**
ST: And when the resources came, be it oil, we started building these fancy technologies and bringing people together because we needed the concentration. **ASR:** And when the resources came, Pete oil, you started building these fancy technologies and bringing people together because we need the concentration. **MT:** 当资源来的时候，皮特石油公司，你开始建立这些奇特的技术，把人们聚集在一起，因为我们需要集	0	65

(continued)

Table 6 (continued)

Examples from ASR-MT Mode	Human Score	Machine Score
ST: I don't know if this was a reaction to lack of water. **ASR:** I don't know if this was a reaction or lack of water. **MT:** 我不知道这是一种反应还是缺水。	0	90
ST: Not only cities that we're building, but cities with dreams and people who are wishing to be scientists, doctors. **ASR:** not only cities that we're building, but cities with dreams and people who are wishing to be scientists, doctors live **MT:** 仅是我们正在建设的城市而且是有梦想的城市和希望成为科学家的人。医生活着	0	65
ST: The limited number of farmers that we have, have been pushed out of their farming practices as a result of open market policy and bringing the big competitions, etc., etc. **ASR:** The limited number of farmers that we have been pushed out of the farming practices as a result of open market policy and bringing the biggest competitions, et cetera. **MT:** 由于开放的市场政策，以及带来最大的竞争等等，我们已经被赶出了农业实践的农民数量有限。	0	85
ST: Indeed there is. **ASR:** Indeed, there is. **MT:** 事实上，	0	90
ST: So if we're going to need energy, what sort of energy? **ASR:** So if we're gonna need energy, what sort of energy **MT:** 所以如果我们需要能源，	0	80
Examples from ST-ASR-MT-RT Mode	**Human Score**	**Machine Score**
ST: No cities like you see today in Doha or Dubai or Abu Dhabi or Kuwait or Riyadh. **ASR:** No cities like you see today and know how to buy Abu Dhabi or Kuwait rerank. **MT:** 没有你今天看到的城市，知道如何购买阿布扎比或科威特重新排名。 **RT:** 那时也没有像多哈、迪拜、阿布扎比、科威特或利雅得这样的城市。	0	50
ST: There are about five or six accents in this country as I speak. **ASR:** There are about five. **MT:** 大约有五个人。 **RT:** 这个国家有大概五六种不同的口音——这些口音我都会讲。	0	50

(continued)

Table 6 (continued)

Examples from ASR-MT Mode	Human Score	Machine Score
ST: And when the resources came, be it oil, we started building these fancy technologies and bringing people together because we needed the concentration. **ASR:** And when the resources came, Pete oil, you started building these fancy technologies and bringing people together because we need the concentration. **MT:** 当资源来的时候，皮特石油公司, 你开始建立这些奇特的技术, 把人们聚集在一起，因为我们需要集 **RT:** 而有了石油资源以后， 我们开始发展先进科技, 将人们集中起来，因为我们需要集中。	0	70
ST: And we realized that there are some differences in accents. **ASR:** We realize that there are some differences in access. **MT:** 我们意识到。在获取方面有一些差异。 **RT:** 于是我们发现，原来大家的口音都不一样。	0	55
ST: I don't know if this was a reaction to lack of water. **ASR:** I don't know if this was a reaction or lack of water. **MT:** 我不知道这是一种反应还是缺水。 **RT:** 我不知道是不是"物极必反"的原因在作怪。	0	85
ST: This is history being made in this region. **ASR:** This is history being made in this region. **MT:** 这是这个地区正在创造的历史 **RT:** 这是这一地域从前的历史。	38	85
ST: Not only cities that we're building, but cities with dreams and people who are wishing to be scientists, doctors. **ASR:** not only cities that we're building, but cities with dreams and people who are wishing to be scientists, doctors live **MT:** 仅是我们正在建设的城市而且是有梦想的城市和希望成为科学家的人。医生活着 **RT:** 与其说我们的前辈曾在建造城市， 倒不如说他们曾在编织梦想。他们不仅梦想着建造城市也梦想着成为科学家和医生。	0	70
ST: Qatar has 74, and we have that growth rate. **ASR:** Other has 74, and we have that growth rate. **MT:** 其他国家有74毫米，我们有这样的增长率。 **RT:** 卡塔尔却仅有 74 毫米，但我们的城市发展速度飞快。	0	85
ST: The limited number of farmers that we have, have been pushed out of their farming practices as a result of open market policy and bringing the big competitions, etc., etc. **ASR:** The limited number of farmers that we have been pushed out of the farming practices as a result of open market policy and bringing the biggest competitions, et cetera. **MT:** 由于开放的市场政策，以及带来最大的竞争等等，我们已经被赶出了农业实践的农民数量有限。 **RT:** 我们人数有限的农民都被迫抛弃他们的农作,由于开放的市场政策和强大的竞争等等原因。	17	70

(continued)

Table 6 (continued)

Examples from ASR-MT Mode	Human Score	Machine Score
ST: Indeed there is. **ASR:** Indeed, there is. **MT:** 事实上， **RT:** 其实是有的。	0	95
ST: So if we're going to need energy, what sort of energy? **ASR:** So if we're gonna need energy, what sort of energy **MT:** 所以如果我们需要能源， **RT:** 那么我们到底需要哪种能源呢?	0	95
ST: A depletable energy? Fossil fuel? **ASR:** a depletable energy for so few **MT:** 那么对于这么少的人来说，什么样的能源是可消耗的能源? **RT:** 一种耗竭性能源?化石燃料?	0	95
ST: Do we have the comparative advantage to use another sort of energy? **ASR:** Do we have the comparative advantage to use the other filterbank? **MT:** 我们有使用其他滤波器组的比较优势吗? **RT:** 我们有没有相对优势去用另一种能源?	0	75
ST: Our objective is to be a millennium city, just like many millennium cities around: Istanbul, Rome, London, Paris, Damascus, Cairo. **ASR:** Our objective is to be a millennium city, just like many millennium cities around this llama grow. Llama, Paris, MOSS, Cairo. **MT:** 我们的目标是成为一座千年之城，就像这座美洲驼周围的许多千年之城一样。美洲驼，巴黎，莫斯，开罗。 **RT:** 我们的目标是建立一个千年之城，就像我们周围许多的千年之城: 伊斯坦布尔、罗马、伦敦、巴黎、大马士革、开罗。	0	70

Table 7 ASR examples of outliers with scores (MIEval)

Examples from ST-ASR-MT Mode	Human Score	Machine Score
ST: The average growth of our economy is about 15 percent for the past 5 years. **ASR:** The erage growth of our economy is about 15%. Past 5 years,	67	93
ST: The question is how. **ASR:** This is.	25	50
ST: Do you worry much? **ASR:** Do you very much?	75	50
ST: And there's predictions that we'll be 9 billion by 2050. **ASR:** and there's predictions that will be non believed in 1050.	42	67
Examples from ST-ASR-MT-RT Mode	**Human Score**	**Machine Score**
ST: And there's predictions that we'll be 9 billion by 2050. **ASR:** and there's predictions that will be non believed in 1050.	42	67
ST: So Brazil has 1782 millimeters per year of precipitation of rain. **ASR:** So Brazil has 1700 and 82 millimeters per year of precipitation of rain.	75	92
ST: These risks directly affect the sustainability of this nation and its continuity. **ASR:** These risks direct effect, the sustainability of this nation. And let's continue with you.	42	67
ST: Indeed there is. **ASR:** Indeed, there is	100	67
ST: So that's what we are planning to do. **ASR:** So that's what we planning to do within 2 years.	56	78

Table 8 MT examples of outliers with scores (MIEval)

Examples from MIEval ST-ASR-MT Mode	Human Score	Machine Score
ST: So that is the chapter two: the oil era. **ASR:** That is the chapter two, the all there. **MT:** 这就是第二章,	87	44
ST: And this is amongst the highest worldwide. **ASR:** and this is amongst the highest worldwide. **MT:** 这是世界上用水量最高的国家之一	86	0
ST: I don't know if this was a reaction to lack of water. **ASR:** I don't know if this was a reaction or lack of water. **MT:** 我不知道这是一种反应还是缺水。	0	100
ST: This is history being made in this region. **ASR:** This is history being made in this region. **MT:** 这是这个地区正在创造的历史	38	100
ST: Not only cities that we're building, but cities with dreams and people who are wishing to be scientists, doctors. **ASR:** not only cities that we're building, but cities with dreams and people who are wishing to be scientists, doctors live **MT:** 仅是我们正在建设的城市而且是有梦想的城市和希望成为科学家的人。医生活着	0	70
ST: Build a nice home, bring the architect, design my house. **ASR:** build an Python, bring the architect, design my house. **MT:** 建造一条巨蟒，带来建筑师，设计我的房子。	50	0
ST: It is that thing that we pump out of the ground, we burn tons of, probably most of you used it coming to Doha. **ASR:** It is that thing that we pump out of the ground. We burned tons of probably most of you used it coming to datahub. **MT:** 它是我们从地下抽出的东西。我们烧掉了成吨的东西，可能你们中的大多数人在来到DataHub时都用过它。	79	0
ST: This is the best technology that this region could ever have: desalination. **ASR:** This is the best technology that this region could ever have desalination. **MT:** 这是这个地区有史以来最好的海水淡化技术。	58	100
ST: We've turned seven billion only a few months ago. **ASR:** 27 billion on a few months ago. **MT:** 几个月前是270亿	0	40
ST: The limited number of farmers that we have, have been pushed out of their farming practices as a result of open market policy and bringing the big competitions, etc., etc. **ASR:** The limited number of farmers that we have been pushed out of the farming practices as a result of open market policy and bringing the biggest competitions, et cetera. **MT:** 由于开放的市场政策，以及带来最大的竞争等等，我们已经被赶出了农业实践的农民数量有限。	17	80

(continued)

Table 8 (continued)

Examples from MIEval ST-ASR-MT Mode	Human Score	Machine Score
ST: Indeed there is. **ASR:** Indeed, there is. **MT:** 事实上,	0	67
ST: So we know very well — I showed you earlier — that we need this energy. **ASR:** So we know very well that showed earlier that we need these energy. **MT:** 所以我们很清楚，这表明我们需要这些能源,	93	57
Examples from MIEval ST-ASR-MT-RT Mode	**Human Score**	**Machine Score**
ST: Resources weren't there to develop them. **ASR:** Resources weren't there to develop. **MT:** 没有资源可以开发, **RT:** 而是匮乏的资源不允许城市的发展。	86	29
ST: I don't know if this was a reaction to lack of water. **ASR:** I don't know if this was a reaction or lack of water. **MT:** 我不知道这是一种反应还是缺水。 **RT:** 我不知道是不是"物极必反"的原因在作怪。	0	50
ST: Build a nice home, bring the architect, design my house. **ASR:** build an Python, bring the architect, design my house. **MT:** 建造一条巨蟒，带来建筑师，设计我的房子。 **RT:** 建造美丽的家园，找来设计师设计自己的房子。	50	0
ST: This is the best technology that this region could ever have: desalination. **ASR:** This is the best technology that this region could ever have desalination. **MT:** 这是这个地区有史以来最好的海水淡化技术。 **RT:** 这是这一地区有史以来最伟大的科技:海水淡化技术。	58	92
ST: This is the situation in Qatar, for those who don't know. **ASR:** This is a situation another for those who don't know **MT:** 对于那些不知道的人来说，这是另一种情况。 **RT:** 卡塔尔不为人知的情况是,	58	0
ST: The limited number of farmers that we have, have been pushed out of their farming practices as a result of open market policy and bringing the big competitions, etc., etc. **ASR:** The limited number of farmers that we have been pushed out of the farming practices as a result of open market policy and bringing the biggest competitions, et cetera. **MT:** 由于开放的市场政策，以及带来最大的竞争等等，我们已经被赶出了农业实践的农民数量有限。 **RT:** 我们人数有限的农民都被迫抛弃他们的农作,由于开放的市场政策和强大的竞争等等原因。	17	83
ST: So that's what we are planning to do. **ASR:** So that's what we planning to do within 2 years. **MT:** 所以这就是我们计划在两年内要做的。 **RT:** 这就是我们规划要做的事。	89	44

Appendix C

Prompt with Score Calculation

You are a professional machine interpreted text evaluator. Your evaluation is separated into ASR and MT stages.

ASR Evaluation

Based on the source and ASR transcripts given, calculate the WER and WAR for each sentence. The error types such as deletion, insertion, and substitution should be listed. The WER = (100*(deleted words + inserted words + substituted words))/ total word of source transcript. The WAR (the ASR Score) = (1-WER) *100. The text has to be normalized where punctuation, capitalizations, numerals, contractions, extra space, and hyphens will not be considered as mistakes. Substitution (a wrong word replaces the correct word), insertion (addition of a word that was never said), and deletion (a right word was omitted).

ASR errors:
ASR Score:

MT Evaluation

Based on the source transcript, machine translation, and reference translation given, calculate the score of machine translation based on MQM framework for each sentence. The error types to be identified are accuracy (addition, mistranslation, omission, untranslated text), fluency (character encoding, grammar, inconsistency, punctuation, register, spelling). Each error has Error Severity Levels of critical, major, and minor based on the comprehension of the text.

The MQM calculations are:

1. Evaluation Word Count (EWC) = source text word count.
2. Error Type Weights (ETW) = 1 for all errors.
3. Error Severity Levels.
4. Severity Penalty Multipliers: Minor (1), Major (5), Critical (25).
5. Absolute Penalty Total (APT) = total penalty points.
6. Per-Word Penalty Total (PWPT) = APT/EWC.
7. Raw Quality Score = 100-(PWPT*100).

MT errors:
MT Score:

Appendix D

Interpreter Training Activity Sheet

Part 1: ASR Evaluation Using Word Error Rate

Instructions:

1. Compare the ASR output with the source transcript.
2. Identify Substitutions (S), Insertions (I), and Deletions (D).
3. Count the total number of words in the reference transcript (N).
4. Calculate:
5. WER = (S + I + D) / N × 100%.
6. WAR = 100% - WER.

WER Calculation Table.

Source	Reference	S	I	D	WER (%)	WAR (%)
–	–	–	–	–	–	–
–	–	–	–	–	–	–

Part 2: MT Evaluation Using MQM

Instructions:

1. Compare the machine translation (MT) with the reference translation.
2. Use the MQM error taxonomy to identify errors.
3. Assign a severity level:
   (a) Minor = 1 point.
   (b) Major = 5 points.
   (c) Critical = 25 points.
4. Decide weight for each error category.
5. Calculate the MQM penalty total and subtract from 100 to get the MT Score.

MQM Error Log Sheet.

Source	Reference	Error Type	Severity (Minor = 1/Major = 5/Critical = 25)	Penalty
–	–	–	–	–
–	–	–	–	–
Total Penalty:		–	–	–
Final MT Score:		–	–	–

Sample Discussion for Classroom Use

1. **Do you agree with the severity levels your team assigned to each error (e.g., minor, major, critical)? Why or why not?**

Reflect on whether the severity of each error truly reflects its impact on the overall meaning and usability of the translation or transcription. Provide examples where you might assign a different level and explain your reasoning.

2. **How did your team determine the weight for each error category?**

Discuss the rationale behind your weighting decisions. Did certain types of errors (e.g., mistranslations, omissions, terminology misuse) seem more impactful than others? How did your team reach a consensus?

3. **Can you identify examples where the WER (Word Error Rate) suggests high accuracy, but the meaning is still unclear or compromised?**

Consider whether a low number of word errors always means good quality. Are there cases where correct words are used, but the message is distorted or misunderstood? Why does this happen, and what does it say about WER as an evaluation metric?

References

Amtrup, J. W. (1999). *Incremental speech translation*. Springer.

Anastasopoulos, A., Barrault, L., Bentivogli, L., Bojar, O., Cattoni, R., Currey, A., … & Watanabe, S. (2022). Findings of the IWSLT 2022 Evaluation Campaign. In *Proceedings of the 19th international conference on spoken language translation* (IWSLT 2022) (pp. 98–157). Association for Computational Linguistics.

Bai, Y., Kadavath, S., Kundu, S., Askell, A., Kernion, J., Jones, A., … & Kaplan, J. (2022). Constitutional ai: Harmlessness from ai feedback. arXiv preprint arXiv:2212.08073.

Banerjee, S., & Lavie, A. (2005, June). METEOR: An automatic metric for MT evaluation with improved correlation with human judgments. In *Proceedings of the acl workshop on intrinsic and extrinsic evaluation measures for machine translation and/or summarization* (pp. 65–72).

Chowdhery, A., Narang, S., Devlin, J., Bosma, M., Mishra, G., Roberts, A., et al. (2023). Palm: Scaling language modeling with pathways. *Journal of Machine Learning Research, 24*(240), 1–113.

Deutsch, D., Foster, G., & Freitag, M. (2023). Ties matter: Meta-evaluating modern metrics with pairwise accuracy and tie calibration. arXiv preprint arXiv:2305.14324.

El Amri, A. (2024). *LLM Prompt Engineering for Developers: The Art and Science of Unlocking LLMs' True Potential*. Aymen El Amri. Packt Publishing, Limited.

Fantinuoli, C. (2018). Interpreting and technology: The upcoming technological turn. *Interpreting and technology*, 1–12.

Fantinuoli, C. (2021, November). Conference interpreting and new technologies. In *The Routledge handbook of conference interpreting* (pp. 508–522). Routledge.

Fernandes, P., Deutsch, D., Finkelstein, M., Riley, P., Martins, A. F., Neubig, G., ... & Firat, O. (2023). The devil is in the errors: Leveraging large language models for fine-grained machine translation evaluation. arXiv preprint arXiv:2308.07286.

Freitag, M., Rei, R., Mathur, N., Lo, C. K., Stewart, C., Avramidis, E., ... & Martins, A. F. (2022, December). Results of WMT22 metrics shared task: Stop using BLEU–neural metrics are better and more robust. In *Proceedings of the Seventh Conference on Machine Translation* (WMT) (pp. 46–68).

Guo, D., Yang, D., Zhang, H., Song, J., Zhang, R., Xu, R., ... & He, Y. (2025). Deepseek-r1: Incentivizing reasoning capability in llms via reinforcement learning. arXiv preprint arXiv:2501.12948.

He, X., Deng, L., & Acero, A. (2011, May). Why word error rate is not a good metric for speech recognizer training for the speech translation task?. *In Proceedings of 2011 IEEE International Conference on Acoustics, Speech and Signal Processing* (ICASSP) (pp. 5632–5635). IEEE..

Hendy, A., Abdelrehim, M., Sharaf, A., Raunak, V., Gabr, M., Matsushita, H., ... & Awadalla, H. H. (2023). How good are gpt models at machine translation? a comprehensive evaluation. arXiv preprint arXiv:2302.09210..

Huang, W. C., Peloquin, B., Kao, J., Wang, C., Gong, H., Salesky, E., ... & Chen, P. J. (2023, June). A holistic cascade system, benchmark, and human evaluation protocol for expressive speech-to-speech translation. In *Proceedings of ICASSP 2023–2023 IEEE International Conference on Acoustics, Speech and Signal Processing* (ICASSP) (pp. 1–5). IEEE.

Huang, X., Zhang, Z., Geng, X., Du, Y., Chen, J., & Huang, S. (2024). Lost in the source language: How large language models evaluate the quality of machine translation. arXiv preprint arXiv:2401.06568.

Hwang, C.-L., & Yoon, K. (1981). *Multiple attribute decision making: Methods and applications—A state-of-the-art survey*. Springer. https://link.springer.com/book/10.1007/978-3-642-48318-9

Indurthi, S., Zaidi, M. A., Lakumarapu, N. K., Lee, B., Han, H., Ahn, S., ... & Hwang, I. (2021, June). Task aware multi-task learning for speech to text tasks. In *Proceedings of ICASSP 2021–2021 IEEE International Conference on Acoustics, Speech and Signal Processing* (ICASSP) (pp. 7723–7727). IEEE..

Jiao, H., Hu, W., & Zhang, X. (2025). To eat or to feed: can large language models provide useful feedback in translation education? *The Interpreter and Translator Trainer*. https://doi.org/10.1080/1750399X.2025.2533074.

Jiao, H., Peng, B., Zong, L., Zhang, X., & Li, X. (2024). Gradable ChatGPT translation evaluation. arXiv preprint arXiv:2401.09984.

Jiao, W., Wang, W., Huang, J. T., Wang, X., Shi, S., & Tu, Z. (2023). Is ChatGPT a good translator? Yes with GPT-4 as the engine. arXiv preprint arXiv:2301.08745..

Karita, S., Chen, N., Hayashi, T., Hori, T., Inaguma, H., Jiang, Z., ... & Zhang, W. (2019, December). A comparative study on transformer vs rnn in speech applications. In *Proceedings of 2019 IEEE automatic speech recognition and understanding workshop* (ASRU) (pp. 449–456). IEEE.

Kendall, M. G. (1938). A new measure of rank correlation. *Biometrika, 30*(1–2), 81–93.

Kocmi, T., & Federmann, C. (2023a). Large language models are state-of-the-art evaluators of translation quality. arXiv preprint arXiv:2302.14520.

Kocmi, T., & Federmann, C. (2023b). GEMBA-MQM: Detecting translation quality error spans with GPT-4. arXiv preprint arXiv:2310.13988.

Lcvenshtcin, V. I. (1966). Binary coors capable or 'correcting deletions, insertions, and reversals. *Soviet physics-doklady, 10*(8).

LISA. (2006). LISA QA Model 3.1: Assisting the localization development, production and quality control processes for global product distribution [Press release].

Lommel, A., Uszkoreit, H., & Burchardt, A. (2014). Multidimensional quality metrics (MQM): A framework for declaring and describing translation quality metrics. *Tradumàtica, 12*, 0455–0463.

Lu, Q., Qiu, B., Ding, L., Xie, L., & Tao, D. (2023). Error analysis prompting enables human-like translation evaluation in large language models: A case study on chatgpt.

Mizrahi, G., & Serfaty, D. (2024). *Unlocking the secrets of prompt engineering*. Packt Publising.

Papineni, K., Roukos, S., Ward, T., & Zhu, W. J. (2002, July). Bleu: a method for automatic evaluation of machine translation. In *Proceedings of the 40th annual meeting of the Association for Computational Linguistics* (pp. 311–318).
Pearson, K. (1896). VII. Mathematical contributions to the theory of evolution.—III. Regression, heredity, and panmixia. *Philosophical Transactions of the Royal Society of London (Series A), 187*, 253–318.
Phoenix, J., & Taylor, M. (2024). *Prompt engineering for generative AI: future-proof inputs for reliable AI outputs at scale*. O'Reilly.
Radford, A., Narasimhan, K., Salimans, T., & Sutskever, I. (2018). *Improving language understanding by generative pre-training*. OpenAI. https://cdn.openai.com/research-covers/language-unsupervised/language_understanding_paper.pdf
Sasindran, Z., Yelchuri, H., Prabhakar, T. V., & Rao, S. (2023, December). H eval: A new hybrid evaluation metric for automatic speech recognition tasks. In *Proceedings of 2023 IEEE Automatic Speech Recognition and Understanding Workshop* (ASRU) (pp. 1–7). IEEE.
Snover, M., Dorr, B., Schwartz, R., Micciulla, L., & Makhoul, J. (2006). A study of translation edit rate with targeted human annotation. In *Proceedings of the 7th Conference of the Association for Machine Translation in the Americas: Technical Papers* (pp. 223–231).
Society of Automotive Engineers. (2016). *SAE J2450: Translation quality metric*. https://www.sae.org/standards/content/j2450_201608/.
Sugaya, F., & Yasuda, K. (2019). Measuring the Capability of a Speech Translation System. In *Speech-to-Speech Translation* (pp. 77–85). Springer Singapore.
Thoppilan, R., De Freitas, D., Hall, J., Shazeer, N., Kulshreshtha, A., Cheng, H. T., ... & Le, Q. (2022). Lamda: Language models for dialog applications. arXiv preprint arXiv:2201.08239.
Wang, X., & Yuan, L. (2023). Machine-learning based automatic assessment of communication in interpreting. *Frontiers in Communication, 8*, 1047753.
Wei, J., Wang, X., Schuurmans, D., Bosma, M., Xia, F., Chi, E., et al. (2022). Chain-of-thought prompting elicits reasoning in large language models. *Advances in Neural Information Processing Systems, 35*, 24824–24837.
Zhang, B., Titov, I., Haddow, B., & Sennrich, R. (2020). Adaptive feature selection for end-to-end speech translation. arXiv preprint arXiv:2010.08518.
Zheng, R., Chen, J., Ma, M., & Huang, L. (2021). Fused acoustic and text encoding for multimodal bilingual pretraining and speech translation. In *International Conference on Machine Learning* (pp. 12736–12746). PMLR.

Zixuan Wang is a PhD student at the University of Liverpool. Her research focuses on the application of large language models (LLMs) in translation studies, with particular attention to how these technologies can be used to serve as translators, evaluators, and post-editors. She is the recipient of the 2024 Award for Outstanding Paper at the Fudan University Symposium in Translation Studies.

Hui Jiao is a fully funded PhD student at the University of Liverpool. Her research focuses on large language model (LLM) translation and hallucination phenomena. She has published relevant papers in *The Interpreter and Translator Trainer*, *Procesamiento del Lenguaje Natural*, and the *Advances in Brain Inspired Cognitive System* (Springer). Current work focuses on enhancing the translation quality of LLMs through prompt engineering; investigating, detecting and mitigating LLM hallucination in specific translation tasks; alongside establishing open, reproducible resources—datasets, error taxonomies, and benchmarks—for translation quality assessment. She welcomes collaboration with academics and industry on faithful LLM translation generation, evaluation and error-annotation standards.

Xiaojun Zhang is an associate professor in translation technology at Xi'an Jiaotong-Liverpool University, China. He is the adjunct professor of The Open University of Cyprus and Northwestern Polytechnical University. He plays the roles of Director at International Association of Translation and Interpreting Cognition (IATIC) and World Interpreter and Translator Trainer Association (WITTA), and Professional Conduct Committee member of Association for Computational Linguistics (ACL) as well.

An Empirical Study on AI-Driven Evaluation of Student Translations Using Large Language Models

Sirui Peng and Jing Zhang

Abstract This study explores the applicability of Large Language Models (LLMs) in the assessment of student translations, focusing on their stability, reliability, and adaptability to evaluation criteria. Based on the Human Translation Quality Evaluation (HTQE) criteria, the study selects culturally themed expository texts from English-Chinese bidirectional translation corpora to assess the consistency and bias of LLM-generated scores using Intraclass Correlation Coefficients (ICC) and Pearson correlation analysis. Results indicate that LLMs exhibit stability and alignment with human scoring in structured dimensions such as grammatical accuracy and terminology consistency. However, reliability fluctuates significantly in higher-order semantic dimensions, such as intent reproduction and cultural adaptation. Furthermore, LLM-generated scores for English-to-Chinese translation show higher consistency than those for Chinese-to-English translation, reflecting the influence of training data distribution. Current LLMs remain constrained by the transparency of their evaluation mechanisms and their ability to comprehend context, making it challenging to replicate the holistic judgment of human evaluators. To enhance the applicability of LLMs in translation pedagogy, this study proposes optimizing human–machine collaborative evaluation, refining translation evaluation criteria, and fostering students' translation evaluation skills. By expanding the application of LLMs in translation quality evaluation, this study provides empirical support for the enhancement of intelligent evaluation systems.

Keywords Large language models · AI-driven evaluation · Translation quality evaluation · Automated scoring · Translation teaching

S. Peng
Chengdu Sport University, Chengdu, China

J. Zhang (✉)
Sichuan Normal University, Chengdu, China
e-mail: jingzhang@sicnu.edu.cn

T. Yin et al. (eds.), *AI Through LLMs*, New Frontiers in Translation Studies,
https://doi.org/10.1007/978-981-95-4798-2_7

1 Introduction

Under the strategic initiative to "enhance the global communication power of Chinese civilization and strengthen international communication capacity," translation education is tasked with the critical mission of cultivating interdisciplinary talents who possess both linguistic competence and cultural communication literacy. As the scale of translation instruction continues to expand, traditional quality evaluation systems face two pressing challenges: first, manual evaluation methods that rely on teachers' subjective judgment suffer from inefficiency and inconsistency, which undermines the objectivity of evaluation outcomes (Yang, 2019); second, current evaluation standards tend to overemphasize surface-level linguistic features while failing to incorporate cultural transfer competence, thereby limiting the pedagogical value of evaluation feedback.

In light of these challenges, AI-driven evaluation models have emerged as a promising solution. With their efficiency, objectivity, and quantifiability, AI-driven evaluation tools can provide students with immediate feedback, helping them identify translation problems and refine their strategies to enhance learning outcomes. Moreover, AI systems grounded in multi-dimensional evaluation frameworks can simultaneously assess linguistic accuracy and cultural appropriateness, offering teachers comprehensive data that reflect both language ability and cultural literacy. However, differences in students' translation proficiency lead to diverse translation styles and error types, which remains a major technical barrier to the validity of AI-driven evaluation. Large Language Models (LLMs), equipped with powerful semantic understanding and vast training data, show great potential in overcoming the limitations of traditional evaluation. They can efficiently and objectively identify translation errors with precision and offer personalized suggestions for improvement. This not only reduces teachers' workload but also supports the development of a dynamic, context-rich evaluation ecosystem (Chen et al., 2024; Liu, 2024). While existing research shows that ChatGPT has achieved a high level of consistency with expert ratings in writing assessment (Huang & Guo, 2024), the applicability of LLMs in Human Translation Quality Evaluation (HTQE) still requires systematic investigation—particularly regarding their performance across different evaluation dimensions, alignment with human ratings, and compatibility with existing evaluation standards.

This study responds to the practical needs of translation education in China by focusing on the application of LLMs in the evaluation of student translations. Using bilingual corpora of cultural-themed expository texts, we construct an evaluation metric system tailored to educational contexts and systematically examine LLMs' scoring stability in English to Chinese and Chinese to English translation tasks, their consistency with human evaluation, and their adaptability to HTQE standards. The core objectives of this study are twofold. First, it aims to evaluate the feasibility of applying LLMs to student translation evaluation and to examine their performance across various evaluation dimensions. Second, it seeks to analyze the pedagogical washback of AI-driven evaluation and to explore how LLMs can be effectively integrated to enhance the quality and operability of translation evaluation systems, ultimately contributing to the intelligent development of translation education.

2 Literature Review

2.1 Automated Evaluation of Student Translation Quality

Over the past fifteen years, Chinese academia has made notable progress in the field of computer-assisted translation evaluation, with several landmark technological breakthroughs. The automatic scoring system for Chinese–English translation developed by Wang (2008) and the English–Chinese counterpart built by Jiang and Wen (2012) mark a significant shift from theoretical exploration to practical engineering in this area. However, it is important to note that these pioneering achievements remain largely confined to the laboratory and have not yet been transformed into broadly applicable instructional solutions. Their potential for educational implementation has yet to be fully realized.

The technological evolution of automated evaluation of translation quality in China can be divided into two interrelated stages.

The first stage centered on rule-driven approaches and feature engineering, with a focus on building foundational frameworks for computer-assisted evaluation. Wang (2008) pioneered the development of a Chinese–English automatic scoring system. This system introduced a dual-dimensional evaluation framework based on linguistic form (e.g., lexical density, syntactic complexity) and semantic content (e.g., semantic coverage), establishing a basic paradigm for the quantitative evaluation of translation quality. Its innovation lay in combining rule-based matching with feature extraction techniques, offering a methodological reference for subsequent studies. Building on this, Jiang (2013) incorporated a multiple linear regression model, integrating over twenty linguistic features to significantly enhance the explanatory power of the scoring model.

It is worth noting that this stage also saw diverse explorations of alternative technical pathways. For instance, Wang and Chang (2009) developed a test-point matching model based on manually constructed dictionaries and machine translation word-alignment techniques. While this approach achieved semi-automated scoring, its reliance on manually annotated data limited the system's transferability (Yuan, 2016). Overall, while evaluation systems during this period made breakthroughs in analyzing surface-level linguistic features, they remained notably limited in assessing macro-level dimensions such as textual coherence and translation creativity.

With the growing influence of machine learning technologies, research in the second stage shifted toward data-driven intelligent evaluation paradigms. Yuan (2016) developed a feature set for human translation quality and a corresponding machine learning-based evaluation system. This marked the first instance of quality prediction across two dimensions: content adequacy and linguistic fluency, signaling a shift from rule-based to algorithm-driven evaluation. Han and Lu (2021) extended the scope of evaluation to interpreting tasks, validating the sentence-level effectiveness of statistical metrics such as BLEU and NIST, thereby providing empirical support for cross-modal technology transfer. More recent studies demonstrate the potential of deep learning applications. Cui and Liang (2024), along with Gong (2024), trained neural network models on large corpora of student translations and confirmed a high correlation between algorithm-generated evaluations and human judgments. Wang et al. (2022) further introduced artificial intelligence technologies to develop an automatic scoring system for interpreting, based on China's Standards of English Language Ability (CSE) interpreting scale. Data showed that the system scores closely approximated those of human raters within homogeneous student groups.

Nevertheless, existing systems continue to face technical limitations in assessing deeper competencies such as cultural adaptability and contextual sensitivity—challenges that open up space for the integration of emerging technologies like Large Language Models (LLMs).

Despite advancements of neural network models in automatic evaluation, their scope of application remains significantly imbalanced. According to recent statistics, approximately 63% of current automatic evaluation research focuses on machine translation quality evaluation, while studies targeting human translation account for only 0.9% (Han, 2024). This reveals a pressing need to expand the applicability of existing methods for evaluating human translations, especially in translation teaching contexts where the effectiveness of current technologies is constrained by multiple factors.

First, neural networks require large-scale pretrained data and high-performance computing resources, leading to high deployment costs that limit their practical use in educational settings. Second, pretrained neural models often exhibit weak domain adaptability, and for subject areas with limited training data, the accuracy of evaluation results remains to be verified (Chatzikoumi, 2020; Gong, 2024). Third, while current systems can produce objective quantitative scores, they generally lack qualitative insights such as error categorization and improvement strategies, making it difficult for students to translate feedback into targeted skill development (Zhou et al., 2008). Fourth, the reliability of automated evaluation models in detecting subtle linguistic nuances and conducting fragment-level translation quality analysis is limited—especially when dealing with linguistic and cultural specificity, where evaluation accuracy becomes harder to guarantee (Gong, 2024; Lavie, 2010).

These limitations are particularly pronounced in tasks involving cultural adaptation and contextual interpretation. For example, when evaluating translations of culturally embedded Chinese expressions, existing systems often fail to recognize the integrity of cultural imagery transfer or assess audience acceptability, still requiring expert judgment from teachers. This reveals a crucial fact: current automated evaluation systems primarily serve as auxiliary tools, and the mechanism for effective collaboration with human evaluation remains underdeveloped.

Against this backdrop, the development of intelligent evaluation tools that offer both operational feasibility and rich feedback has become an urgent need. The technical characteristics of LLMs provide a potential breakthrough: their high efficiency, low cost, and responsiveness allow them to deliver personalized, qualitative feedback, fostering learner autonomy and helping mitigate disparities in educational resources (Yang & Li, 2024; Zhou, 2020). With deep semantic understanding derived from extensive multimodal pretraining, LLMs are capable of both fine-grained error diagnosis and generating pedagogically meaningful revision suggestions. This dual function—quantitative evaluation combined with qualitative diagnosis—lays the technical foundation for constructing a new paradigm of human–machine collaborative evaluation.

2.2 LLMs in Translation Quality Evaluation

Compared with the relatively underdeveloped field of human translation quality evaluation (HTQE), the use of Large Language Models (LLMs) in machine translation quality evaluation (MTQE) has evolved into a more mature application paradigm. Existing studies have shown that LLMs offer distinct advantages in areas such as zero-shot evaluation, multilingual adaptability, and fine-grained analysis (Fernandes et al., 2023; Huang et al., 2024; Qian et al., 2024). These advantages have given rise to five primary technical approaches: direct prediction based on generated content, probability-based scoring, pseudo-data generation for training, model architecture adaptation, and retrieval-augmented evaluation (Zhao et al., 2024). Among these, direct prediction based on generated content is the most feasible for classroom implementation due to its relatively low technical threshold.

The GEMBA framework (GPT Estimation Metric Based Assessment) proposed by Kocmi and Federmann (2023) demonstrates that GPT-3.5 and newer models can conduct system-level evaluation through zero-shot prompting. However, their performance at the discourse level remains limited. To address this, Lu et al. (2023) integrated Chain-of-Thought (CoT) reasoning and error analysis (EA) to develop the EAPrompt method, which significantly outperforms traditional metrics across multiple evaluation dimensions. Similarly, the Knowledge-Prompted Estimator (KPE) constructed by Yang et al. (2023) employs a multi-step prompting strategy, substantially reducing misclassification rates in paragraph-level evaluations. Qian et al. (2024) compared three prompting strategies across LLMs of varying sizes and found that CoT performed especially well in larger models. They also highlighted the critical role of source texts and reference translations in ensuring evaluation accuracy, and noted that LLM performance varies across high- and low-resource languages.

Despite these breakthroughs in MTQE, transferring such technological pathways to HTQE contexts encounters three fundamental challenges.

First, the evaluation subject differs substantially. Student translations often exhibit highly individualized features, including both systematic linguistic errors (e.g.,

Chinglish structures) and strategic choices (e.g., handling of culturally loaded terms). These errors are more random and dispersed. In contrast, machine translations tend to produce more predictable errors such as lexical mismatches and syntactic deviations, which are easier to address through pattern recognition. Furthermore, most MTQE datasets derive from shared tasks in machine translation or natural language processing workshops, typically comprising isolated sentences, and therefore fail to test the discourse-level evaluation capabilities of LLMs.

Second, the evaluation goal diverges. HTQE aims to support a full "evaluation–diagnosis–improvement" cycle. It requires systems not only to produce quantitative scores but also to offer pedagogical feedback, such as guidance on cultural transfer strategies. By contrast, MTQE primarily focuses on system optimization, and its feedback mechanisms are geared toward algorithmic tuning rather than learner development.

Third, HTQE requires dynamic and adaptive evaluation standards. In instructional contexts, evaluation criteria must evolve in line with learners' proficiency levels. Students at different stages differ in linguistic ability and cultural knowledge, so evaluation standards must exhibit flexibility and adaptability to meet diverse learning needs. This stands in stark contrast to MTQE's relatively static evaluation metrics.

Given these technological gaps, this study focuses on verifying the applicability of LLMs within HTQE contexts by addressing three core research questions:

- RQ1 (Scoring Stability): Do LLM-generated scores for student translations exhibit consistency?
- RQ2 (Human–Model Consistency): To what extent do LLM-generated scores correlate with human teacher evaluations?
- RQ3 (Standard Alignment): Can LLMs accurately interpret HTQE evaluation criteria to provide automated scoring of student translations?

3 Research Design and Methods

3.1 Translation Quality Evaluation Criteria

Translation quality evaluation has undergone over half a century of theoretical evolution, forming two major methodological systems: qualitative and quantitative. Qualitative methods, represented by Nida's (1964) reader-response theory, Reiss's (1971) text typology, House's (1997, 2015) systemic functional model, and Williams's (2004) argumentation-centered approach, emphasize descriptive and qualitative evaluation. Quantitative methods, on the other hand, have developed quantifiable operational models, such as error deduction, criterion-referenced scoring, and holistic scoring frameworks (Yang, 2019).

Given the dual demands of instructional contexts for both efficiency and diagnostic utility, this study integrates Colina's (2008, 2009) functionalist theory and

Williams's (2004) argumentation-centered model to construct a dynamic weight–multi-dimensional evaluation framework. Colina's emphasis on aligning assessment criteria with the communicative function of the source text underpins the flexible weighting mechanism in this framework, allowing evaluators to prioritize different dimensions based on text type and instructional objectives. Williams's model further informs this approach by emphasizing evaluative dimensions and the coherence of argumentation over isolated error counting. This supports a holistic assessment of translation quality that moves beyond micro-textual analysis to consider the rationale behind scoring decisions. Together, these perspectives help address the limitations of earlier rule-driven models by promoting context-sensitive, explainable, and pedagogically actionable evaluation.

The evaluation criteria comprise four core parameters: target language expression, text function, source content (general), and domain-specific content. Each parameter includes specific evaluation dimensions. To ensure ease of implementation, each dimension is scored on a scale of 0 to 10, with two-point intervals defining five grading levels. The evaluation criteria were developed through a rigorous process. First, three translation instructors and two industry experts jointly revised each source text to produce a reference translation and curated lists of culturally loaded and domain-specific terms, the latter having only one accepted translation. Then, three instructors each independently trial-scored three translations per text. Through group discussion, they refined the scoring dimensions. In a final round, another random sample of three translations per text was scored using the draft criteria. Based on this round, the criteria were revised and finalized into a four-parameter, five-dimension system (see Table 1).

To support a more precise interpretation of the evaluation criteria, a few key terms used in the table are defined below, as they represent higher-order pragmatic and semantic dimensions of translation quality that may not be immediately self-evident. *Reproduction of communicative intent* refers to the extent to which the translation preserves the speaker's original purpose, tone, and pragmatic function. *Cultural contextual appropriateness* denotes how well the translation aligns with the sociocultural norms, expectations, and background knowledge of the target audience. *Effectiveness of cultural imagery transfer* assesses the translator's ability to render culturally specific metaphors, symbols, and references in a way that retains their intended meaning and emotional impact in the target language.

3.2 *Experimental Dataset*

Following the principle of ecological validity, this study constructed a bilingual parallel corpus tailored for translation teaching evaluation. Materials were drawn from authentic course content, comprising eight expository texts on topics including philosophy, clothing culture, music culture, festival culture, and architecture (four texts each in Chinese and English).

Table 1 Human translation quality evaluation criteria

Parameters	Dimensions	Weight	Descriptions
Target language expression	1. Naturalness and clarity	20%	• Linguistic naturalness (pragmatic level) • Discourse coherence (discourse level) • Information acceptability (pragmatic level)
	2. Grammar and vocabulary	10%	• Syntactic conformity (grammatical level) • Lexical appropriateness (semantic level) • Form accuracy (grammatical level)
Text function	3. Intent and context	25%	• Reproduction of communicative intent (pragmatic level) • Cultural contextual appropriateness (pragmatic level)
Source content (general)	4. Content and information	25%	• Integrity of information (semantic level) • Logical consistency (semantic level)
Domain-specific content	5. Cultural and terminology accuracy	20%	• Effectiveness of cultural imagery transfer (semantic/pragmatic level) • Terminological conformity (semantic level)

A three-dimensional design framework was used: topic diversity ensured rich cultural representation; linguistic difficulty (based on Flesch Reading Ease for English and the Chinese Proficiency Standards) ensured appropriate challenge; and cultural density (1.42%–2.72%) balanced feasibility and validity. English texts were classified into high (Flesch 12.23–14.36) and low (9.37–10.14) difficulty groups. Chinese texts were similarly divided (11.75–12.00 and 9.18–9.67). Word/character counts were tightly controlled between 249 and 353 to limit extraneous variance.

Participants were 17 final-year undergraduates from a top-tier English program in China, all of whom had completed six semesters of translation coursework and demonstrated strong interest in translation practice. Each participant completed both C–E and E–C translations for all eight texts. The final dataset included 136 valid translations (68 in each direction), representing authentic translation behavior under classroom conditions.

Statistical analysis confirmed desirable distribution characteristics. C–E translation scores followed a normal distribution ($M = 7.71$, SD $= 0.61$, $W = 0.97$, $p =$

0.15); E–C scores also met normality assumptions ($M = 7.23$, SD = 0.37, $W = 0.96$, $p = 0.21$). Score variability (CV = 8.2%–9.7%) and score range confirmed sufficient dispersion for evaluating model validity while retaining authenticity of classroom practice.

3.3 Evaluation Methods

This study adopts a dual-track evaluation paradigm, combining human and automated evaluation, with multi-dimensional triangulation to ensure result validity.

The human evaluation team comprised three experienced university instructors with over five years of translation teaching experience. Prior to formal evaluation, the team underwent rubric calibration: a workshop was held to interpret the HTQE scale, followed by trial scoring of 20 randomly selected translations. Intra-group consistency was confirmed (ICC = 0.89, $p = 0.01$), establishing a shared scoring baseline. During formal evaluation, all 136 translations were scored independently by the three raters under double-blind conditions.

For the automated evaluation system, GPT-4, Claude 3.5, and Gemini Pro were selected based on technical maturity and academic credibility. The method draws on Kocmi and Federmann's (2023) system-level architecture and Lu et al.'s (2023) prompt engineering framework to develop a Structured Quality Assessment Framework (SQAF). This framework includes four progressive modules: (1) Role Definition—establishing the model's role as a professional evaluator; (2) Task Decomposition—breaking down scoring into multi-dimensional components; (3) Constraint Conditions—aligning outputs with both the rubric and reference translations; (4) Reasoning Support—employing Chain-of-Thought (CoT) to increase transparency.

Technically, a zero-shot prompt template with a four-part structure was created (see Table 2). It defines evaluator role, task goals, dimension-specific skills, and constraints (e.g., no creative interpretation). EAPrompt's error analysis logic was also integrated, breaking down each evaluation dimension into sub-tasks—for example, in assessing "cultural term accuracy," the model must identify culture-specific terms, analyze transfer strategies, and reason about audience acceptability. To ensure integrity of evaluative context, each task included the source text, reference translation, term list, and cultural annotations.

The evaluation process was implemented in strict accordance with experimental methodological standards. In the pre-experimental phase, three translations on the themes of philosophy, clothing, and music were selected to test model adaptability. Results indicated consistency among the three models in their interpretation of dimension weights.

During the formal evaluation, a triple assurance mechanism was employed: each translation was independently evaluated three times by three different models, generating a total of 1224 data points (136 translations $\times$ 3 models $\times$ 3 rounds). A buffer

Table 2 Four-part zero-shot prompt template

Modules	Components	Specific content examples
Role	Role definition	As a professional translation quality evaluation system, you are expected to possess a dual disciplinary background in linguistics and translation studies, and to conduct multi-dimensional quality evaluation strictly in accordance with established standards
Task goals	Evaluation dimensions	Naturalness and clarity, accuracy of cultural terms, grammatical conformity, fidelity to communicative intent, and completeness of content (Upload detailed descriptors for each dimension)
	Scoring	Each dimension is scored on a 10-point scale (0–10), with every 2-point difference representing a significant performance gap. The total score is calculated as a weighted sum
	Operational procedures	1. Cultural term identification → Glossary identification → Error counting
		2. Grammar checking → Error classification and weighted scoring
		3. Intent analysis → Semantic similarity calculation
		4. Information completeness → Bidirectional alignment verification
		(Upload glossary and reference translation)
Dimension-specific skills	Core skills	• Cross-cultural communication competence
		• Grammar error pattern recognition
		• Terminology database retrieval
	Computational tools	• Pretrained language model (for fluency analysis)
		• Syntactic parser (for complexity detection)
		• Word embedding model (for lexical appropriateness)
		• Named entity recognition (for factual accuracy)
Operational limitations	Constraints	• No repeated deduction for the same error
		• Cultural and terminology term evaluation must be based on the provided glossary
		• Must provide reason for point deduction and suggestions for improvement
		• Any form of creative interpretation is prohibited

period of at least 24 hours was set between scoring sessions to control for model state fluctuations, and all evaluation session records were fully preserved to enable process traceability.

4 Data Analysis and Discussion

This study constructed an evaluation database comprising two independent datasets: the human evaluation group (3 instructors × 136 translations × 5 dimensions) and the intelligent evaluation group (3 models × 136 translations × 5 dimensions × 3 evaluations). Weighted composite scores were calculated for each translation based on the dimension weights defined in the HTQE evaluation criteria. All data were processed using SPSS 26, and two-tailed tests ($\alpha = 0.05$) were used for statistical analysis.

4.1 Analysis of LLMs' Scoring Stability

This study employed the Intraclass Correlation Coefficient (ICC) to assess scoring stability, using a one-way random effects model. ICC(1,1) is suitable for evaluating repeated ratings of the same translation by a single rater. Typically, ICC > 0.75 indicates excellent consistency, 0.40–0.75 is acceptable, and < 0.40 is considered unreliable (Cicchetti, 1994; Koo & Li, 2016). In addition, the mean standard deviation (SD) across three rating rounds was calculated to measure scoring fluctuation. Distribution characteristics were further examined using the Shapiro–Wilk normality test, skewness, and kurtosis. Levene's test for homogeneity of variances was used to assess consistency across rating rounds, with p-values < 0.05 indicating significant variance differences. Data analysis (see Table 3) revealed notable differences among LLMs across tasks and evaluation dimensions. Stability characteristics can be summarized as follows.

For English to Chinese translation tasks, Claude demonstrated excellent scoring stability, with an overall ICC of 0.89 (mean SD = 0.26), and a particularly high ICC of 0.91 in Dimension 2. Its mean SD (0.26) was significantly lower than that of ChatGPT (0.55) and Gemini (0.41). Except for Dimension 2 ($p = 0.08$), Levene's test returned p-values > 0.05 across dimensions, indicating manageable score dispersion across rating rounds. Notably, Claude maintained high consistency in Dimension 3 (ICC = 0.79), which relates to culturally loaded terms, confirming its competence in specialized terminology evaluation. ChatGPT displayed task sensitivity, with pronounced variability across dimensions ($\Delta = 0.22$). Dimension 4 (ICC = 0.45) and Dimension 5 (Levene $p = 0.04$) indicated systematic fluctuation in the evaluation of syntactic complexity and cultural transfer, possibly reflecting model biases in language structure preferences. Gemini's score distribution showed a bimodal pattern (Dimension 2: skewness = − 1.41, kurtosis = 2.24), while its ICC for Dimension 5 (0.36)

Table 3 Results of LLM scoring stability analysis

Model	Translation direction	Dimensions	ICC	Mean SD	Mean	Skewness	Kurtosis	Shapiro–Wilk Statistic	*p*-value	Levene statistic	Levene *p*-value
ChatGPT	English to Chinese	Dimension 1	0.670c	0.46	7.21	−0.16	−0.12	0.88	0	0.81	0.44
		Dimension 2	0.650c	0.85	8.08	−0.49	−0.54	0.91	0	2.77	0.07
		Dimension 3	0.610c	0.56	7.13	0.04	−0.04	0.91	0	1.34	0.26
		Dimension 4	0.450c	0.83	7.79	−0.25	−0.75	0.91	0	0.04	0.96
		Dimension 5	0.670c	0.84	7.89	−0.34	−0.37	0.93	0	3.27	0.04
		Total	0.680c	0.55	7.59	−0.29	−0.79	0.97	0	0.97	0.38
	Chinese to English	Dimension 1	0.580c	0.45	6.32	−0.37	0.38	0.87	0	0.52	0.6
		Dimension 2	0.670c	0.68	6.16	−0.04	−0.45	0.93	0	1.69	0.19
		Dimension 3	0.530c	0.52	5.77	0.01	−0.47	0.9	0	0.16	0.85
		Dimension 4	0.370c	0.66	6.93	0.11	0.29	0.89	0	1.59	0.21
		Dimension 5	0.600c	0.59	6.64	−0.66	0.66	0.87	0	1.8	0.17
		Total	0.670c	0.44	6.47	−0.37	0.69	0.97	0	2.44	0.09
Claude	English to Chinese	Dimension 1	0.820c	0.28	8.57	−0.31	−0.5	0.86	0	0.66	0.52
		Dimension 2	0.910c	0.28	8.67	−0.33	−0.89	0.88	0	2.54	0.08
		Dimension 3	0.790c	0.23	9.05	−0.26	−0.16	0.81	0	0.35	0.71
		Dimension 4	0.750c	0.43	8.8	−0.4	−0.46	0.86	0	0.94	0.39
		Dimension 5	0.800c	0.32	8.78	−0.4	−0.05	0.86	0	1.63	0.2
		Total	0.890c	0.26	8.75	−0.32	−0.42	0.97	0	1.83	0.16
	Chinese to English	Dimension 1	0.770c	0.31	8.03	−0.18	−0.79	0.85	0	1.83	0.16
		Dimension 2	0.690c	0.53	8.12	−0.37	−0.52	0.9	0	0.66	0.52
		Dimension 3	0.790c	0.33	7.96	−0.18	−0.94	0.84	0	0.02	0.98

(continued)

Table 3 (continued)

Model	Translation direction	Dimensions	ICC	Mean SD	Mean	Skewness	Kurtosis	Shapiro–Wilk Statistic	*p*-value	Levene statistic	Levene *p*-value
		Dimension 4	0.640c	0.41	8.98	−0.19	−0.52	0.83	0	3.11	0.05
		Dimension 5	0.430c	0.58	8.68	−0.49	0.19	0.86	0	1.14	0.32
		Total	0.730c	0.38	8.44	−0.28	−0.37	0.98	0.01	4.52	0.01
Gemini	English to Chinese	Dimension 1	0.540c	0.5	9.04	−0.88	0.33	0.82	0	3.88	0.02
		Dimension 2	0.430c	0.76	8.87	−1.41	2.24	0.8	0	8.09	0
		Dimension 3	0.620c	0.46	9.23	−1.05	0.55	0.78	0	0.16	0.85
		Dimension 4	0.510c	0.68	9.01	−0.79	−0.33	0.82	0	1.7	0.19
		Dimension 5	0.360c	0.54	9.41	−1.58	1.89	0.68	0	0.85	0.43
		Total	0.490c	0.41	9.16	−1.36	1.76	0.85	0	1.75	0.18
	Chinese to English	Dimension 1	0.520c	0.72	7.67	−0.07	−0.64	0.9	0	1.39	0.25
		Dimension 2	0.280c	1.36	7.81	−0.36	−0.56	0.92	0	1.87	0.16
		Dimension 3	0.610c	0.83	7.56	−0.22	−0.22	0.94	0	0.39	0.68
		Dimension 4	0.590c	0.63	8.78	−0.38	− 0.81	0.87	0	13.48	0
		Dimension 5	0.340c	1	8.7	−1.59	2.66	0.78	0	17.68	0
		Total	0.540c	0.67	8.22	−0.35	−0.81	0.97	0	6.35	0

and Levene's result ($p = 0.43$) jointly suggested instability in assessing cultural appropriateness.

In the Chinese to English translation tasks, Claude again showed high scoring stability, with an ICC as high as 0.79 and relatively small, balanced variance. ChatGPT's scoring consistency was slightly lower compared to the E–C tasks, with ICC values ranging from 0.37 to 0.67. Although its score distribution did not meet normality assumptions, variance homogeneity was acceptable. Gemini had the lowest stability, with ICC values as low as 0.28. Some dimensions showed high score dispersion and low inter-round consistency.

Cross-task analysis showed that Claude exhibited strong systemic robustness (mean ICC difference between tasks $\Delta = 0.15$). Its overall score skewness (close to -0.3) suggested a strict threshold effect, indicating the potential need for a dynamic calibration mechanism. ChatGPT demonstrated directional sensitivity, with its mean ICC dropping by 9.8% in the C–E tasks. Its "strict-but-stable" characteristics were particularly evident in Dimension 2 (grammar and vocabulary), making it a viable filtering aid for human evaluation. Gemini's structural deficiencies became more pronounced in the C–E task. Dimension 5 exhibited variance heterogeneity as high as 17.68 ($p = 0.00$), and negative skewness (-1.59), suggesting overfitting risks in evaluating culturally loaded items. Under its current architecture, the model does not yet support reliable evaluation.

4.2 Consistency Between LLMs and Human Ratings

To assess the consistency between human and LLM-based evaluations, a dual-metric validation approach was adopted. First, a two-way mixed-effects model ICC(3,1) was used to test absolute agreement, treating human raters and LLMs as fixed effects and student translations as random effects. Second, Pearson correlation coefficients were calculated to measure the linear association in rating trends. This combined method accounts for both agreement in score levels (ICC) and similarity in scoring patterns (Pearson r), ensuring that findings reflect inherent system properties.

Table 4 summarizes model-specific human–machine absolute agreement patterns. ChatGPT displayed the strongest overall consistency with human raters, particularly in E–C translations, where it achieved an ICC of 0.811 and performed best in Dimension 5 (terminology and cultural accuracy, ICC = 0.802), confirming its reliability in domain-specific interpretation. Claude showed moderate alignment in Dimension 2 (grammar and vocabulary, ICC = 0.567) in E–C tasks, but its overall performance was hindered by low total ICC values and wide confidence intervals, indicating inconsistency in applying human-like judgment across dimensions and translation directions. Gemini revealed the lowest agreement overall, especially in Dimension 4 (content and information, ICC = 0.031) in C–E tasks, suggesting substantial difficulty in capturing and evaluating accurate information transfer and content fidelity.

Building on the model-level trends, a closer look at the E–C translation tasks reveals that ChatGPT demonstrated a systematic advantage, achieving an overall

Table 4 Human–machine scoring absolute agreement test (ICC)

Model	Translation direction	Dimensions	ICC	CI Lower	CI Upper	F value	Significance
ChatGPT	English to Chinese	Dimension 1	0.695c	0.44	0.83	3.82	0
		Dimension 2	0.537c	0.25	0.71	2.14	0
		Dimension 3	0.255c	−0.18	0.56	2.03	0
		Dimension 4	0.632c	0.4	0.77	2.9	0
		Dimension 5	0.802c	0.67	0.88	5.46	0
		Total	0.811c	0.69	0.88	5.22	0
	Chinese to English	Dimension 1	0.224c	−0.17	0.52	1.93	0
		Dimension 2	0.204c	−0.16	0.47	1.37	0.1
		Dimension 3	−0.019c	−0.12	0.11	0.92	0.63
		Dimension 4	0.323c	−0.16	0.61	2.05	0
		Dimension 5	0.598c	0.35	0.75	2.53	0
		Total	0.257c	−0.16	0.54	1.77	0.01
Claude	English to Chinese	Dimension 1	0.521c	−0.22	0.8	4.53	0
		Dimension 2	0.567c	0.13	0.77	2.97	0
		Dimension 3	0.240c	−0.18	0.55	1.99	0
		Dimension 4	0.344c	−0.2	0.68	3.14	0
		Dimension 5	0.503c	−0.22	0.79	3.89	0
		Total	0.527c	−0.15	0.83	8.44	0
	Chinese to English	Dimension 1	0.415c	−0.06	0.67	2.22	0
		Dimension 2	0.137c	−0.14	0.39	1.47	0.06
		Dimension 3	0.446c	0.02	0.68	2.22	0
		Dimension 4	−0.131c	−0.41	0.18	0.67	0.95
		Dimension 5	0.099c	−0.1	0.32	1.58	0.03
		Total	0.123c	−0.12	0.37	1.67	0.02
Gemini	English to Chinese	Dimension 1	0.300c	−0.17	0.64	3.05	0
		Dimension 2	0.458c	−0.09	0.71	2.59	0
		Dimension 3	0.262c	−0.18	0.58	2.19	0
		Dimension 4	0.307c	−0.17	0.65	3.16	0
		Dimension 5	0.278c	−0.17	0.61	2.75	0
		Total	0.358c	−0.11	0.72	6.15	0
	Chinese to English	Dimension 1	0.638c	0.41	0.78	2.92	0
		Dimension 2	0.132c	−0.19	0.4	1.25	0.18
		Dimension 3	0.174c	−0.35	0.49	1.21	0.22
		Dimension 4	0.031c	−0.2	0.26	1.07	0.4

(continued)

Table 4 (continued)

Model	Translation direction	Dimensions	ICC	CI Lower	CI Upper	F value	Significance
		Dimension 5	0.304c	−0.17	0.65	3.29	0
		Total	0.236c	−0.17	0.53	1.89	0.01

ICC of 0.811 (95% CI [0.69, 0.88]). It performed best in Dimension 5 (cultural and terminology accuracy) with an ICC of 0.802 (CI [0.67, 0.88]), indicating a high degree of alignment with human evaluation standards. Claude showed localized strength in Dimension 2 (grammar and vocabulary) with an ICC of 0.567 (CI [0.13, 0.77]), but its overall ICC was relatively low at 0.527 (CI [−0.15, 0.83]), suggesting systemic bias between its strict grammatical norms and the more flexible human scoring practices. Gemini exhibited poor overall agreement (ICC = 0.358), with Dimension 3 (intent and context) showing confidence intervals crossing zero (CI [−0.18, 0.58]), reflecting unreliable performance in interpreting textual intent.

For the C–E translation tasks, increased task complexity exacerbated human–model discrepancies, with all three models showing overall ICC values below 0.26. Gemini performed relatively well in Dimension 1 (naturalness and clarity) with an ICC of 0.638 (CI [0.41, 0.78]), but showed near-zero agreement in Dimension 4 (content and information) with an ICC of 0.031 (CI [−0.20, 0.26]), indicating structural deficiencies in evaluating content completeness. Claude maintained moderate consistency in Dimension 3 (intent and context) with an ICC of 0.446 (CI [0.02, 0.68]), but had negative agreement in Dimension 4 (ICC = − 0.131, CI [−0.41, 0.18]), suggesting fundamental misalignment with human criteria. ChatGPT remained relatively consistent in Dimension 5 (ICC = 0.598, CI [0.35, 0.75]), but showed a breakdown in consistency for Dimension 3 (ICC = − 0.019, CI [−0.12, 0.11]), highlighting limitations in evaluating cross-linguistic intent transfer.

Following the ICC-based agreement results in Table 4, Table 5 presents scoring trend alignment using Pearson correlation coefficients. Among the three models, Claude demonstrates the strongest performance in English-to-Chinese tasks ($r = 0.800$), but shows notably lower correlations in Chinese-to-English tasks ($r = 0.281$), indicating higher sensitivity to translation direction. ChatGPT shows a more balanced performance across both directions ($r = 0.733$ in English-to-Chinese; $r = 0.339$ in Chinese-to-English), and consistently achieves the highest correlations in Dimension 5 (cultural and terminology accuracy) regardless of direction. Gemini performs comparably to ChatGPT ($r = 0.726$ and $r = 0.394$, respectively), with its strongest performance also found in Dimension 5.

In terms of direction-specific performance, Pearson correlation results for the E–C translation tasks showed strong human–machine alignment. Claude showed the strongest overall correlation ($r = 0.800$, $p < 0.001$), with a particularly high correlation in Dimension 2 (grammar and vocabulary) at 0.611 ($p < 0.001$). ChatGPT demonstrated the best disciplinary alignment in Dimension 5 (cultural and terminology accuracy), with a correlation of 0.692 ($p < 0.001$). Although Gemini also

Table 5 Trend correlation analysis between human and machine scoring (Pearson r)

Model	Translation direction	Dimensions	Statistic type	Value
ChatGPT	English to Chinese	Total	Pearson correlation	0.733**
			Sig. (2-tailed)	0
		Dimension 1	Pearson correlation	0.590**
			Sig. (2-tailed)	0
		Dimension 2	Pearson correlation	0.512**
			Sig. (2-tailed)	0
		Dimension 3	Pearson correlation	0.399**
			Sig. (2-tailed)	0.001
		Dimension 4	Pearson correlation	0.498**
			Sig. (2-tailed)	0
		Dimension 5	Pearson correlation	0.692**
			Sig. (2-tailed)	0
	Chinese to English	Total	Pearson correlation	0.339**
			Sig. (2-tailed)	0.005
		Dimension 1	Pearson correlation	0.341**
			Sig. (2-tailed)	0.005
		Dimension 2	Pearson correlation	0.199
			Sig. (2-tailed)	0.106
		Dimension 3	Pearson correlation	− 0.046
			Sig. (2-tailed)	0.713
		Dimension 4	Pearson correlation	0.348**
			Sig. (2-tailed)	0.004
		Dimension 5	Pearson correlation	0.434**
			Sig. (2-tailed)	0
Claude	English to Chinese	Total	Pearson correlation	0.800**
			Sig. (2-tailed)	0
		Dimension 1	Pearson correlation	0.639**
			Sig. (2-tailed)	0
		Dimension 2	Pearson correlation	0.611**
			Sig. (2-tailed)	0
		Dimension 3	Pearson correlation	0.349**
			Sig. (2-tailed)	0.004
		Dimension 4	Pearson correlation	0.517**
			Sig. (2-tailed)	0
		Dimension 5	Pearson correlation	0.648**
			Sig. (2-tailed)	0

(continued)

Table 5 (continued)

Model	Translation direction	Dimensions	Statistic type	Value
	Chinese to English	Total	Pearson correlation	0.281*
			Sig. (2-tailed)	0.021
		Dimension 1	Pearson correlation	0.400**
			Sig. (2-tailed)	0.001
		Dimension 2	Pearson correlation	0.232
			Sig. (2-tailed)	0.059
		Dimension 3	Pearson correlation	0.414**
			Sig. (2-tailed)	0
		Dimension 4	Pearson correlation	− 0.199
			Sig. (2-tailed)	0.106
		Dimension 5	Pearson correlation	0.231
			Sig. (2-tailed)	0.06
Gemini	English to Chinese	Total	Pearson correlation	0.726**
			Sig. (2-tailed)	0
		Dimension 1	Pearson correlation	0.510**
			Sig. (2-tailed)	0
		Dimension 2	Pearson correlation	0.530**
			Sig. (2-tailed)	0
		Dimension 3	Pearson correlation	0.430**
			Sig. (2-tailed)	0
		Dimension 4	Pearson correlation	0.479**
			Sig. (2-tailed)	0
		Dimension 5	Pearson correlation	0.548**
			Sig. (2-tailed)	0
	Chinese to English	Total	Pearson correlation	0.394**
			Sig. (2-tailed)	0.001
		Dimension 1	Pearson correlation	0.556**
			Sig. (2-tailed)	0
		Dimension 2	Pearson correlation	0.16
			Sig. (2-tailed)	0.196
		Dimension 3	Pearson correlation	0.128
			Sig. (2-tailed)	0.301
		Dimension 4	Pearson correlation	0.035
			Sig. (2-tailed)	0.777
		Dimension 5	Pearson correlation	0.559**
			Sig. (2-tailed)	0

Note Sample size for each model and translation direction is 68 showed a significant overall correlation ($r = 0.726$, $p < 0.001$), its correlation in Dimension 3 (intent and context) was relatively low at 0.430 ($p < 0.001$).

In the C–E translation tasks, the correlation patterns varied. Gemini showed a strong correlation in Dimension 1 (naturalness and clarity) at 0.556 ($p < 0.001$), but had no significant correlation in Dimension 4 (content and information) ($r = 0.035$, $p = 0.777$). Claude maintained a unique advantage in Dimension 3 (intent and context) ($r = 0.414$, $p < 0.001$), but showed a negative trend in Dimension 4 ($r = -0.199$, $p = 0.106$). ChatGPT's overall correlation declined to 0.339 ($p = 0.005$), with a breakdown in Dimension 2 (grammar and vocabulary), where the correlation dropped to 0.199 ($p = 0.106$).

Synthesizing results from the two-way mixed-effects model (ICC(3,1)) and Pearson correlation analysis, this study systematically verified the consistency and correlation patterns between LLM-generated scores and human evaluations. The key findings are as follows.

First, there were significant performance differences among the models. ChatGPT demonstrated overall superiority in the E–C tasks, with excellent overall consistency (ICC = 0.811, 95% CI [0.69, 0.88]) and the best performance in Dimension 5 (cultural and terminology accuracy) (ICC = 0.802). It also showed the most stable performance across dimensions, with all ICC values ≥ 0.255. Claude exhibited a localized advantage in grammar-related evaluation (Dimension 2, ICC = 0.567), but its overall consistency declined noticeably (ICC = 0.527), and its performance varied substantially across dimensions (ΔICC = 0.327). Gemini displayed task sensitivity: while it reached acceptable consistency in Dimension 1 (naturalness and clarity) for the C–E tasks (ICC = 0.638), its evaluation of content completeness (Dimension 4) was unreliable (ICC = 0.031).

Second, a clear directional effect was observed. Human–machine consistency in the E–C tasks (ICC = 0.358–0.811) was generally higher than in the C–E tasks (ICC = 0.123–0.257). Likewise, Pearson correlation coefficients for the E–C tasks ($r = 0.726$–0.800) were significantly higher than those for the C–E tasks ($r = 0.281$–0.394). This directional discrepancy was particularly evident in Claude's evaluation of cultural and terminology accuracy (Dimension 5), where its ICC dropped from 0.503 in the E–C task to just 0.099 in the C–E task, indicating an unstable application of culturally grounded evaluation criteria across translation directions.

Third, sensitivity varied across evaluation dimensions. Dimension 5 (cultural and terminology accuracy) showed the highest consistency (E–C ICC = 0.278–0.802; C–E ICC = 0.099–0.598) and maintained robust Pearson correlations (E–C $r = 0.548$–0.692; C–E $r = 0.231$–0.559). In contrast, Dimension 3 (intent and context) proved the most divergent, with the lowest ICC values in the E–C task (0.24–0.262) and negative consistency in the C–E task. For example, in the C–E task, ChatGPT's ICC in Dimension 3 dropped to –0.019, in sharp contrast to its stronger consistency in other dimensions, highlighting difficulty in evaluating cross-linguistic intent.

Finally, score trend alignment showed notable patterns. ChatGPT exhibited strong linear correlation in the E–C tasks (overall $r = 0.733$), but this correlation dropped markedly in the C–E tasks ($r = 0.339$). Claude achieved the best trend alignment (E–C $r = 0.800$), but due to its strict grammatical standards, certain dimensions deviated from human judgments—for instance, Dimension 4 in the C–E task showed negative consistency (ICC = –0.131).

4.3 *Discussion of Evaluation Results*

This study conducted a systematic analysis of LLM performance in the automated evaluation of student translations between Chinese and English, from the perspectives of scoring stability (RQ1), human–machine consistency (RQ2), and standard alignment (RQ3). The key preliminary findings are as follows.

The Influence of Model Architecture on Evaluation Performance. The evaluation performance of LLMs is closely related to their underlying architecture and training methodology. Claude, which is trained using a more rule–constrained approach (Anthropic, 2018), exhibited high scoring stability in the E–C tasks (overall ICC = 0.89, SD = 0.26), with low random variation. However, this highly stable scoring mechanism also has limitations, as it tends to concentrate scores in the high-score range (skewness = –0.32), revealing a strong reliance on standardized reference texts (Stureborg et al., 2024). In other words, while Claude excels in consistency, it lacks flexibility in accommodating varied translation styles and strategies, which may lead to divergence from human evaluations (overall ICC = 0.527), echoing concerns about the risk of "rigid scoring" from over-reliance on fixed standards.

ChatGPT, trained using reinforcement learning from human feedback (RLHF), displayed a dual nature in translation evaluation. For structured dimensions such as grammar and vocabulary (Dimension 2), it showed high scoring stability (ICC = 0.65–0.67) and strong correlation with human scores ($r = 0.512$), suggesting that its rule-based learning mechanism effectively enhances grammatical evaluation capability (Koo et al., 2023). However, for more interpretive dimensions like intent and context (Dimension 3), its consistency dropped significantly (ICC $\leq$ 0.26), and correlations weakened—indicating limitations in interpreting cross-cultural intentions, implicit information, and context adaptation (Wu et al., 2025). These findings align with Akpan (2024), who found that ChatGPT-4 underperformed Claude 3 in complex reasoning tasks. In short, ChatGPT is well-suited for evaluating quantifiable grammatical norms but remains inadequate in areas of cross-cultural adaptation and semantic understanding.

Gemini, due to its multimodal architecture, showed more instability in translation evaluation. This was particularly evident in Dimension 5 (cultural and terminology accuracy), where its score distribution was highly uneven, indicating inconsistent handling of culturally loaded items. This is consistent with findings by Chen et al. (2025), which showed that multimodal models still have relatively high failure rates (3–10%) in instruction-following tasks, suggesting a need for further optimization to enhance consistency in domain-specific evaluation. Although its hallucination rate has not been officially disclosed, related studies report that Gemini Advanced's hallucination rate in specific domains (76.7%) is significantly higher than that of ChatGPT-4o (20.0%), raising concerns about the accuracy of its outputs (Erdem et al., 2024).

While differences in model architecture account for variation in scoring behavior, a deeper challenge lies in the inherently opaque nature of LLM decision-making. Models such as Claude and ChatGPT are trained on vast, undisclosed datasets and rely on internal representations that are not accessible to users or researchers. This "black-box" nature limits interpretability and raises concerns in educational contexts, where transparency and accountability are critical. Educators and learners may hesitate to trust feedback that cannot be clearly explained or justified. One way to address this is through prompt engineering—structuring instructions to encourage clearer, more focused outputs. Additionally, integrating output rationales could help users better understand the basis of automated evaluations. Finally, involving teachers or trained evaluators in reviewing or adjusting the model's feedback can offer a balanced way to ensure both efficiency and trust.

Interaction Between Task Direction and Evaluation Dimensions. The study found significant differences in LLM evaluation performance between E–C and C–E tasks. The interaction between task direction and evaluation dimensions had a substantial impact on scoring stability and reliability. In E–C tasks, LLMs performed more consistently in structured dimensions such as terminology matching—likely due to the higher proportion of English data in their training corpora (Zhu et al., 2024). In contrast, in C–E tasks, the open-ended nature of English syntax (e.g., varied expressions of passive voice) and the relatively lower quality of student translations (mean score: 6.47 for combined C–E and E–C vs. 7.59 for E–C) significantly reduced the LLMs' stability in grammar evaluation and intent recognition. These findings support the quality threshold effect proposed by Takahashi et al. (2020), which posits that model scoring reliability deteriorates when input text quality falls below a certain threshold.

Limitations of the Structural–Semantic Dichotomy. Further analysis revealed that LLMs exhibit a "structural–semantic dichotomy" in translation evaluation: they perform reliably in dimensions governed by explicit rules but struggle with dimensions requiring semantic reasoning.

In structural dimensions such as grammar and terminology, discrete standards (e.g., term lists and syntactic rules) provide LLMs with clear criteria, resulting in relatively stable scores—particularly in the dimension of culture and terminology (Dimension 5), as emphasized in HTQE (Briva-Iglesias et al., 2024).

However, in semantic dimensions such as intent and content completeness, LLMs often exhibit instability in scoring—particularly when evaluating communicative intent, implicit meanings, and logical coherence in complex texts. For instance, Claude's confidence interval in Dimension 3 (intent and context) was notably wide (CI [–0.18, 0.55]), indicating limited contextual inference capacity and restricted scoring reliability in cross-cultural translation tasks. This inconsistency may stem from their reliance on heuristic strategies rather than true contextual understanding. That is, instead of interpreting meaning, these models approximate based on surface patterns and statistical associations learned during training (Wu et al., 2025). This reliance on heuristics may, in turn, be shaped by the composition of their training data. For example, if the distribution of language pairs is uneven—such as fewer high-quality C–E translation examples—models may exhibit directional differences when applying these strategies, contributing to the observed performance discrepancies between E–C and C–E tasks.

5 Pedagogical Implications

The results of this study indicate that while LLMs show promise in translation quality evaluation, their performance varies across evaluation dimensions. In particular, improvements are still needed in cross-cultural translation tasks and the translation of China-specific discourse. Therefore, LLM integration into translation pedagogy should be guided by well-informed strategies to harness their strengths while mitigating their limitations. The following recommendations address human–machine collaborative evaluation, assessment standard optimization, translator training, and China-specific translation strategies, aiming to enhance the effectiveness of LLM-based scoring and promote their meaningful application in translation education.

5.1 Building a Human–Machine Collaborative Evaluation Mechanism

LLMs demonstrate high efficiency in structural tasks such as grammar, vocabulary, and terminology norms, making them well-suited to serve as "baseline quality inspectors" in teaching. They can help instructors quickly identify basic issues in student translations and improve feedback efficiency. For instance, in specialized translation courses like science or law, instructors can use LLMs to check for terminological consistency, provide automated scoring linked to term banks, and assign post-editing tasks for students to revise LLM-generated outputs. This approach reduces teachers' workload for low-level error correction and fosters student awareness of terminology use and post-editing skills.

However, LLMs perform less reliably in Dimensions 3 (intent and context) and 4 (content and information), especially when dealing with metaphors, culturally loaded terms, or political discourse. Thus, in more advanced courses, it is recommended to integrate LLM-based and human evaluations, guiding students to analyze discrepancies between the two and understand the multi-dimensional nature of evaluation standards. These practices not only reveal the cognitive limitations of LLMs but also promote higher-order thinking by encouraging students to trace and interpret score differences (Zhang, 2024).

5.2 *Optimizing Translation Evaluation Standards*

Current HTQE standards are grounded in human scoring logic, while LLM scoring tends to favor formalized and structural aspects. This leads to instability when evaluating communicative function, cultural adaptation, and contextual reconstruction. In the future, dynamic weighting schemes could be explored to adjust the importance of different dimensions based on text types.

For instance, in a comprehensive translation course that includes diverse text types, individual sessions may focus on different genres. When working on manuals or patent documents, Dimension 4 (Content and Information) and Dimension 5 (Cultural and Terminology Accuracy) may account for 35% and 30% of the total score, respectively, prioritizing accurate information transfer and precise use of technical terminology. In these cases, the word list used to guide Dimension 5 evaluation would primarily consist of domain-specific terms. In contrast, when focusing on Chinese literary translation, more weight can be given to Dimension 3 (Intent and Context) and Dimension 5, at 35% and 30%, to better capture cultural contextual appropriateness and ensure appropriate rendering of culturally loaded words. For these sessions, the Dimension 5 word list would shift focus toward culturally embedded expressions and idioms. Dimensions such as naturalness, grammar, and vocabulary can be kept at lower fixed weights to maintain basic language quality without overshadowing the core evaluative focus.

Additionally, because LLMs usually rely on a single reference translation, they may overlook translation variability. In instructional settings, a multi-reference mechanism is recommended, especially in courses focused on China-specific discourse translation, where literal, domesticated, and free versions are provided for comparison. This helps improve the adaptability and flexibility of LLM scoring.

5.3 *Cultivating Students' Evaluation Literacy*

While LLMs can provide initial automated assessments, students should learn to analyze the rationale behind LLM ratings and reconcile them with human scores, rather than relying on them uncritically. Instructors can cultivate evaluation literacy by designing targeted activities that help students analyze the logic behind LLM ratings and recognize potential biases. For instance, students can conduct prompt-based variation exercises, adjusting instructions (e.g., "focus on grammar" vs. "check cultural term adaptation") and observing how scores shift. They can also engage in revision-and-resubmission tasks, submitting improved translations to see whether the LLM recognizes the changes and adjusts its ratings. Additionally, class discussions comparing LLM and human feedback on culturally loaded words or phrases can help students reflect on the challenges LLMs face in handling higher-order, context-sensitive translation dimensions, and deepen their understanding of cultural appropriateness in translation.

In China-specific translation courses, teachers can present texts containing political discourse, idioms, classical poetry, or four-character expressions. Students compare LLM scores with human ratings to examine how LLMs handle cultural imagery, ideology, and metaphor, thus fostering their understanding of context adaptation, cultural conversion, and communicative effect in China-specific translation. This approach not only sharpens students' evaluative thinking but also helps refine prompt engineering for future translation evaluation tasks aligned with the needs associated with the external dissemination of Chinese discourse.

5.4 Enhancing Technology-Enabled Translation Instruction

In institutions with technical capabilities, LLMs can be fine-tuned for instructional use. However, all technical improvements must center on enhancing teaching efficiency. For example, cultural understanding modules can be integrated into existing models to improve their comprehension of unstructured semantics, enabling more nuanced evaluations of metaphors, dialects, and culturally loaded terms.

Future systems could offer customizable multi-dimensional assessment plug-ins, allowing instructors to adjust HTQE weights based on course needs. Additionally, dashboards visualizing human–LLM scoring discrepancies could help teachers identify systematic errors in specific text types (e.g., idiom translation, dialect transfer, policy discourse export). These tools could include heatmaps of common misjudgments, guiding instructors to adjust focus areas and improve student comprehension of translation quality.

To facilitate human–AI instructional collaboration, relevant departments should offer technical training and specialized workshops on AI-based evaluation tools, helping instructors effectively apply and interpret intelligent evaluation systems.

To reduce optimization costs and broaden access, regional platforms can be used to foster collaboration among institutions, supporting the co-development and sharing of AI evaluation tools, corpora, and implementation experiences. This would lower technical barriers and enhance equity in translation education. For institutions with limited access to advanced LLMs, such collaborations are particularly valuable. Shared resources such as prompt templates, simplified evaluation frameworks, and open-source HTQE-compatible tools can help educators adopt LLM-supported evaluation without requiring high-end infrastructure. Regional educational networks can also organize joint training sessions and share practical case studies to guide implementation. By building a support system that emphasizes accessibility and modularity, human–AI collaboration in translation instruction can be meaningfully extended to less-resourced settings.

Importantly, the goal of technological enhancement is not to replace human evaluation, but to establish an intelligent loop of "AI scoring–difference analysis–pedagogical intervention," promoting a shift from experience-based to evidence-based translation instruction. By leveraging LLMs' data analysis capacity, instructors can refine evaluation standards, strengthen targeted instruction, and ensure that intelligent human–machine evaluation systems truly serve the evolving needs of translation education.

6 Limitations and Future Directions

While this study focused on expository texts with cultural content, future research should examine whether similar patterns hold across genres that emphasize different priorities—such as literary texts that value creativity or legal texts that demand strict precision. Generalizability remains a key concern, particularly in dimensions requiring nuanced semantic or stylistic judgment.

Future research should explore how LLMs perform across diverse translation types by incorporating varied corpora, including creative, legal, and scientific genres. One promising direction involves fine-tuning LLMs on domain-specific corpora to enhance their performance in higher-order semantic dimensions such as intent recognition or cultural adaptation. For example, a model exposed to diplomatic or policy-oriented translations may better capture tone sensitivity or geopolitical nuance.

Additionally, advances in multimodal LLMs offer new possibilities for translation evaluation. Models capable of processing not only text but also contextual audiovisual cues could help assess translations where nonverbal or visual context plays a key role—for instance, in subtitling or interpreting. These avenues would further expand the scope of LLM-based evaluation and support the development of more adaptable, context-aware systems.

Another promising direction involves longitudinal classroom integration of LLM feedback. Future studies could investigate how students' translation skills evolve when exposed to intelligent evaluation over an extended period. This would shed light on the developmental impact of LLM-assisted instruction and help determine how sustained use shapes students' awareness of translation quality, revision practices, and evaluative reasoning.

7 Practical Takeaways

7.1 Model Selection Recommendations

- Overall Recommendation: LLMs are more reliable for English-to-Chinese (E–C) tasks, especially in grammar and terminology. For Chinese-to-English (C–E) tasks, where intent and cultural nuance matter more, human or peer review is advised to supplement LLM scoring.

- Claude: Claude is the most stable, especially in E–C tasks, but tends to give mid-to-high, clustered scores. Best for consistent, low-stakes evaluation rather than fine-grained grading.
- ChatGPT: ChatGPT performs well in grammar and vocabulary and adapts to prompts, but is weaker in cultural interpretation. Best for linguistic accuracy tasks with prompt support.
- Gemini: Gemini's strength lies in multimodal tasks where visual or auditory context supports evaluation. For general translation, especially cultural texts, its inconsistency limits its usefulness.

7.2 Prompt Design Guide

- Step 1 Identify Scoring Priorities: Clarify which HTQE dimensions align best with your course objectives and text types (e.g., grammar for technical manuals, cultural context for literary texts).
- Step 2 Adjust the Rating Scale: Reweight HTQE dimensions accordingly. For example, increase weight on Dimension 5 (cultural/terminology accuracy) for technical texts or Dimension 3 (intent/context) for literary work.
- Step 3 Prepare Support Materials: Provide reference translations and targeted word lists (to support Dimension 5 evaluation). Use terminology lists for technical tasks, and culturally loaded word lists for texts with high cultural content.
- Step 4 Customize the Prompt: Use the template in Table 2 as a foundation. Modify the prompt as needed to request interpretable rationales, qualitative feedback, or specific focus areas in line with your learning goals.
- Step 5 Share Results and Guide Reflection: Provide students with LLM-generated scores and feedback. Facilitate guided discussion on rating rationales, discrepancies with human expectations, and the interpretive limitations of the model.
- Step 6 Support Revision and Iteration: Ask students to revise their translations based on the feedback. Optionally, they may resubmit the revised version for a second round of LLM evaluation, promoting iterative learning and self-assessment.

8 Conclusion

This study investigated the applicability of intelligent evaluation models, focusing on the use of Large Language Models (LLMs) in translation quality evaluation. Findings indicate that LLMs perform consistently in structured dimensions such as grammatical accuracy and terminology matching, and demonstrate a degree of alignment with human ratings, highlighting their potential for automated evaluation. However, in higher-order dimensions such as intent conveyance, cultural adaptation, and textual coherence, LLM-generated scores remain unstable and exhibit weaker alignment with human assessments. This reflects limitations in LLMs' capacity for contextual understanding and dynamic adjustment of evaluation criteria. Additionally, LLM-based evaluation mechanisms are constrained by the quality of training data and the opacity of scoring algorithms, remaining largely a "black box" and incapable of fully replicating the comprehensive evaluative judgment of human translators.

At present, the application of LLMs in translation education still requires human intervention to optimize human–machine collaborative evaluation systems. While LLMs are advantageous in detecting basic errors, providing multi-dimensional feedback, and improving evaluation efficiency, human judgment remains essential for handling complex contexts and cultural adaptation tasks. In instructional practice, adaptability can be enhanced by incorporating dynamic weighting schemes and multi-version reference translations. Furthermore, training activities such as score comparison, error analysis, and intelligent feedback optimization can help students develop stronger evaluation literacy.

The development of customizable evaluation plug-ins and visualization tools can also support instructors in fine-tuning evaluation criteria and improving feedback effectiveness. It is worth noting, however, that this study focused exclusively on expository texts with cultural themes. Future research should broaden the range of text types and datasets to further validate LLM performance across different genres and evaluative scenarios. To this end, future efforts should promote interdisciplinary collaboration between natural language processing and translation education, refine evaluation standards, and develop more targeted training corpora and domain-specific models, in order to improve the accuracy, stability, and pedagogical value of intelligent evaluation systems.

References

Akpan, M. (2024). *Have we reached AGI? Comparing ChatGPT, Claude, and Gemini to human literacy and education benchmarks*. https://doi.org/10.48550/arXiv.2407.09573

Anthropic. (2018). *Anthropic API fundamentals: Parameters*. https://github.com/anthropics/courses/blob/master/anthropic_api_fundamentals/04_parameters.ipynb

Briva-Iglesias, V., Camargo, J. L. C., & Dogru, G. (2024). *Large language models 'ad referendum': How good are they at machine translation in the legal domain?* https://arxiv.org/abs/2402.07681

Chatzikoumi, E. (2020). How to evaluate machine translation: A review of automated and human metrics. *Natural Language Engineering, 26*(2), 137–161.

Chen, A., Jia, J., & Su, H. (2024). Research hotspots, thematic development, and risk estimation in language assessment empowered by artificial intelligence. *Technology Enhanced Foreign Languages, 2*, 3–12.

Chen, A., Song, Y., Zhu, W., Chen, K., Yang, M., Zhao, T., & Zhang, M. (2025). *Evaluating o1-like LLMs: Unlocking reasoning for translation through comprehensive analysis*. https://arxiv.org/abs/2502.11544

Cicchetti, D. V. (1994). Guidelines, criteria, and rules of thumb for evaluating normed and standardized assessment instruments in psychology. *Psychological Assessment, 6*(4), 284–290.

Colina, S. (2008). *Functionalism in translation studies*. Continuum.

Colina, S. (2009). *Translation and text typology: Functional approaches*. Continuum.

Cui, Y., & Liang, M. (2024). Automated scoring of translations with BERT models: Chinese and English language case study. *Applied Sciences, 14*, 1925.
Erdem, O., Hassett, K., & Egriboyun, F. (2024). *Evaluating the accuracy of chatbots in financial literature.* http://arxiv.org/abs/2411.07031
Fernandes, P., Deutsch, D., Finkelstein, M., Riley, P., Martins, A. F. T., Neubig, G., Garg, A., Clark, J. H., Freitag, M., & Firat, O. (2023). The devil is in the errors: Leveraging large language models for fine-grained machine translation evaluation. In *Proceedings of the Eighth Conference on Machine Translation (WMT)* (pp. 1066–1083).
Gong, M. (2024). The neural network algorithm-based quality assessment method for university English translation. *Network: Computation in Neural Systems*, 1–13.
Han, C., & Lu, X. (2021). Can automated machine translation evaluation metrics be used to assess students' interpretation in the language learning classroom? *Computer Assisted Language Learning, 36*(5–6), 1064–1087.
Han, C. (2024). *Quality assessment in multilingual, multimodal, and multiagent translation and interpreting (QAM3T&I): Proposing a unifying framework for research.* https://doi.org/10.13140/RG.2.2.14066.62407
House, J. (1997). Contrastive discourse analysis and translation. In M. Baker (Ed.), *Routledge encyclopedia of translation studies* (pp. 121–124). Routledge.
House, J. (2015). *Translation quality assessment: A meta-theoretical framework.* De Gruyter Mouton.
Huang, X., & Guo, L. (2024). The application of large language models in formative assessment: In the case of the scoring and feedback in English writing. *Education Research Monthly, 7*, 74–80.
Huang, X., Zhang, Z., Geng, X., Du, Y., Chen, J., & Huang, S. (2024). Lost in the source language: How large language models evaluate the quality of machine translation. In *Proceedings of the Association for Computational Linguistics: ACL 2024* (pp. 3546–3562).
Jiang, J. (2013). An automatic approach to evaluating the linguistic quality of English-Chinese translations. *Modern Foreign Languages, 36*(1), 85–91.
Jiang, J., & Wen, Q. (2012). Computer scoring models for EFL learners' English-Chinese translation in large-scale tests. *Technology Enhanced Foreign Languages, 114*, 3–8.
Kocmi, T., & Federmann, C. (2023). *Large language models are state-of-the-art evaluators of translation quality.* https://arxiv.org/abs/2302.14520
Koo, T. K., & Li, M. Y. (2016). A guideline of selecting and reporting intraclass correlation coefficients for reliability research. *Journal of Chiropractic Medicine, 15*(2), 155–163.
Koo, R., Lee, M., Paheja, V., Park, J. I., Kim, Z. M., & Kang, D. (2023). *Benchmarking cognitive biases in large language models as evaluators.* https://arxiv.org/abs/2309.17012
Lavie, A. (2010). *Evaluating the output of machine translation systems.* AMTA tutorial.
Liu, J. (2024). Language assessment in the era of artificial intelligence: Opportunities and challenges. *Modern Foreign Languages, 47*(6), 859–869.
Lu, Q., Qiu, B., Ding, L., Xie, L., & Tao, D. (2023). *Error analysis prompting enables human-like translation evaluation in large language models: A case study on ChatGPT.* https://arxiv.org/abs/2303.13809
Nida, E. A. (1964). *Toward a science of translating.* Leiden: E. J. Brill.
Qian, S., Sindhujan, A., Kabra, M., Kanojia, D., Orăsan, C., Ranasinghe, T., & Blain, F. (2024). *What do large language models need for machine translation evaluation?* https://arxiv.org/abs/2410.03278
Reiss, K. (1971). *Über die Übersetzbarkeit.* Max Niemeyer Verlag.
Stureborg, R., Alikaniotis, D., & Suhara, Y. (2024). *Large language models are inconsistent and biased evaluators.* https://arxiv.org/abs/2405.01724
Takahashi, K., Sudoh, K., & Nakamura, S. (2020). Automatic machine translation evaluation using source language inputs and cross-lingual language model. In *Proceedings of the 58th Annual Meeting of the Association for Computational Linguistics* (pp. 3553–3558).
Wang, J. (2008). *A study and construction of a computer-assisted scoring model for Chinese–English translation by Chinese students* [Doctoral dissertation, Beijing Foreign Studies University].

Wang, L., & Chang, B. (2009). A preliminary study of computer-assisted scoring in college English translation tests. *Technology Enhanced Foreign Languages, 4*, 17–21.

Wang, W., Wang, K., & Zhang, Y. (2022). Exploring automatic scoring of interpreting based on the CSE interpreting scale. *Foreign Language World, 2*, 80–87.

Williams, M. (2004). *Translation quality assessment: An argumentation-centred approach*. University of Ottawa Press.

Wu, X., Saraf, P. P., Lee, G., Latif, E., Liu, N., & Zhai, X. (2025). *Unveiling scoring processes: Dissecting the differences between LLMs and human graders in automatic scoring*. https://arxiv.org/abs/2407.18328

Yang, H., Zhang, M., Tao, S., Ma, M., Qin, Y., & Wei, D. (2023). Teachersim: Cross-lingual machine translation evaluation with monolingual embedding as teacher. In *Proceedings of the ICACT 2023* (pp. 283–287).

Yang, L., & Li, R. (2024). ChatGPT for L2 learning: Current status and implications. *System, 124*, Article 103351.

Yang, Z. (2019). *Research on translation testing and assessment*. Foreign Language Teaching and Research Press.

Yuan, Y. (2016). A feature set for automated human translation quality estimation. *Foreign Language Teaching and Research, 48*(5), 776–787, 801.

Zhang, J. (2024). Constructing a teaching model for higher-order thinking in translation under the context of generative AI. *Chinese Translators Journal, 3*, 71–80.

Zhao, H., Liu, Y., Tao, S., Meng, W., Chen, Y., Geng, X., Su, C., Zhang, M., & Yang, H. (2024). *From handcrafted features to LLMs: A brief survey for machine translation quality estimation*. https://arxiv.org/abs/2403.14118

Zhou, M., Wang, B., Liu, S., Li, M., Zhang, D., & Zhao, T. (2008). Diagnostic evaluation of machine translation systems using automatically constructed linguistic check-points. In *Proceedings of the 22nd International Conference on Computational Linguistics (Coling 2008)* (pp. 1121–1128).

Zhou, X. (2020). Application and evaluation of AI technology in computer-assisted translation software. *Chinese Translators Journal, 5*, 121–129.

Zhu, W., Liu, H., Dong, Q., Xu, J., Huang, S., Kong, L., Chen, J., & Li, L. (2024). *Multilingual machine translation with large language models: Empirical results and analysis*. https://arxiv.org/abs/2304.04675

Sirui Peng is a Lecturer in the School of Foreign Languages at Chengdu Sport University, China. Her research primarily focuses on second language acquisition, with an emphasis on how emerging technologies can enrich language teaching and learning. She is particularly interested in the integration of artificial intelligence in higher education, exploring how large language models can be applied to translation evaluation and how AI-assisted tools may influence both learning processes and instructional practices. She has published on topics including project-based teaching and grammar acquisition, and her current projects continue to explore how technology can enhance language learning and evaluation by bridging insights from applied linguistics and educational technology.

Jing Zhang is an associate professor at Sichuan Normal University. Her research focuses on translation technology, translation education, and corpus translation studies. She has published a number of papers in these fields in CSSCI-indexed journals and contributed to edited volumes by internationally recognized publishers such as Routledge and John Benjamins. Her recent work has been published in journals including *Chinese Translators Journal, Foreign Language World, Shanghai Journal of Translators*.

Re-imagining the Classroom: Resources, Tasks, Engagement

Shifting the Translation Paradigm Through AI-Driven Approaches: A Case Study of Game Localization with LLMs

Lintao Han, Chongyu Chen, and Chuyi Zheng

Abstract As large language models (LLMs) expand their impact across various disciplines and industries, they have also found their way into translation. LLMs are now being utilized in multiple facets of translation practice and education, including the optimization of machine translation (MT), translation quality assessment, and translator training. While some view LLMs as potential replacements for traditional MT systems, existing research remains fragmented, predominantly addressing isolated aspects of the translation process. Critically, there is a corresponding gap in pedagogical guidance on how to holistically integrate these technologies into translator training. To address this insufficiency, our work presents a comprehensive approach to a case of game localization that leverages LLMs throughout the entire translation process, and explores its direct implications for translation education. In our work, we re-envision the traditional Computer-aided Translation (CAT) workflow for game localization through several key stages. We employ GPT-4o for automated terminology extraction, use OpenAI embedding models for semantic retrieval of translation memories, and apply GPT-4o for context-aware translation generation via structured prompts. Finally, we utilize COMET for quality assessment, with GPT-4o refining segments that fall below a set threshold. Beyond presenting a technical blueprint, this chapter critically examines the pedagogical value of this workflow. It illustrates how educators can structure project-based learning (PBL) activities around these stages to cultivate essential next-generation skills, such as prompt engineering, semantic resource management, and AI output validation. As a result, this workflow not only demonstrates a practical and holistic application of LLMs in a professional context but also provides a tangible framework for training future translators to thrive in an AI-driven industry.

Keywords Large language models · Game localization · Translation pedagogy · Computer-aided translation · Prompt engineering

L. Han (✉) · C. Chen · C. Zheng
Beijing Language and Culture University, Beijing, China
e-mail: hanlintao@blcu.edu.cn

T. Yin et al. (eds.), *AI Through LLMs*, New Frontiers in Translation Studies,
https://doi.org/10.1007/978-981-95-4798-2_8

1 Introduction

As artificial intelligence (AI) continues to expand its landscape in all walks of life, Large Language Models (LLMs) represent a particularly potent advancement. Trained on vast amounts of data under the Transformer architecture, LLMs are exerting profound changes across industries and academia, attributing to their state-of-the-art performance on typical NLP tasks (Liu et al., 2024; Peng et al., 2023; Qin et al., 2024) and, in particular translation (Hendy et al., 2023; Jiao et al., 2023). Empowered by LLMs, translation can now be progressed through a more flexible way with generally higher quality. This signifies new possibilities for how translation projects can be better completed, not only in terms of quality but also in the optimization of specific procedures and practices. Historically, the dominant digital translation assistant was machine translation (MT), which evolved from rule-based systems and statistical approaches to neural machine translation (NMT). This evolution, along with improvements in translation quality, has considerably increased efficiency and solidified the computer-aided translation (CAT) workflow—combining term management, translation memory, and quality assurance—as the industry standard.

While this established CAT workflow remains the current standard for translation and localization projects, the advent of LLMs introduces transformative opportunities. Despite a surge in research investigating LLMs' capabilities, a significant gap remains between demonstrating potential in isolated tasks and implementing these models in a cohesive, practical workflow. Current studies frequently focus on fragmented aspects, such as evaluating LLM raw translation output against NMT benchmarks (Jiang et al., 2024), exploring their potential for quality evaluation (Kocmi & Federmann, 2023b), and even fine-tuning them for domain adaptation (Moslem & Way, 2023). Critically, this fragmentation extends to translation pedagogy, where there is a significant lack of comprehensive models demonstrating how to systematically integrate these advanced LLM capabilities into a cohesive, project-based learning environment. Educators and trainers are often left without a clear roadmap for moving beyond isolated exercises (e.g., simple prompt translation) to teaching a holistic, industry-relevant workflow. A clear understanding of how LLMs can fundamentally reshape translation workflows, rather than merely improving individual steps, remains elusive for both industry practitioners and educators.

To address this need for both a holistic technical model and a practical pedagogical framework, this chapter focuses on a case study using GPT-4o for game localization. Localization, the adaptation of a product for foreign markets, involves translation as well as cultural and technical adjustments. Game localization amplifies this complexity with massive text volumes spanning dialogue, user interfaces, and narrative elements, all governed by specific terminology and creative constraints. This multifaceted nature makes it an exceptionally rigorous and engaging environment for training future translators, challenging them to master skills beyond literal translation, such as maintaining character voice and adapting to creative nuances—skills that are increasingly mediated by AI. It is, therefore, an ideal testbed for demonstrating the capabilities and practical feasibility of a comprehensive LLM-driven translation workflow and for deriving valuable educational insights.

A typical localization project follows three main phases: pre-production, production, and post-production. First, specialists analyze the product for necessary adjustments and extract translatable content. Second, the content is translated, often using a combination of human translators and machine translation, supported by style guides, glossaries, and translation memory. Third, the translated content is reintegrated into the product, followed by rigorous quality assurance checks.

This chapter examines the transformation of this process, specifically how incorporating LLMs marks a paradigm shift from conventional CAT tool usage to an LLM-driven approach offering enhanced automation, consistency, and quality assurance. The primary contribution of this study is twofold: first, to present a novel and holistic workflow that distinctively employs LLMs across the entire localization pipeline—from automated terminology extraction to intelligent memory retrieval and AI-driven quality refinement. Second, and more importantly, it aims to unpack the pedagogical implications of this workflow, providing a concrete example and actionable recommendations for how educators can adapt these advanced practices for the translation classroom. By doing so, we aim to demonstrate the practical architecture of this integrated system and provide a clear model for how LLMs can reshape both professional localization processes and the training of future translators.

2 Work Review

2.1 Traditional Computer-Aided Translation

It is generally recognized that the failure of machine translation in the 1960s led to the emergence of computer-aided translation (CAT) (Chan, 2015). Since then, it has spread from Europe to every corner of the world and, until now, has become the dominant workflow in translation and localization projects.

In a computer-aided translation (CAT) workflow, three core components collaborate to enhance efficiency: translation memory (TM), term base (TB), and machine translation (MT) engines. TM is a database that stores previous translations—varying from phrases and sentences to paragraphs—as source–target language pairs. With TM, translators can reuse existing translations for identical or similar segments in new projects, ensuring consistency and efficiency without starting from scratch. A TB is a structured database, essentially a glossary containing specialized words and domain-specific expressions with explanations relevant to a particular subject field. The TB is crucial for maintaining consistency, especially in large-scale or collaborative projects. Terminology management systems, such as SDL MultiTerm, facilitate the creation, management, and integration of this terminology within the CAT environment. MT engines are often integrated into CAT systems, where they can be employed for pre-translation, frequently working in conjunction with TM matches and TB suggestions. This generated output is then typically presented to human translators for review and post-editing.

In practice, a translation project in a CAT system proceeds through several standard steps. Before translation begins, translators or project managers prepare the linguistic assets. Terms can be extracted from source texts and organized into a TB. Relevant TM databases are also assigned to the project. Pre-translation then occurs by automatically populating segments with matches from the TM, TB, and MT engine. Translators then work through the pre-translated text, refining segments to meet the required standards. Subsequent steps typically include linguistic review, automated Quality Assurance (QA) checks, and the generation of the final target file. Throughout this process, the TM is updated upon segment confirmation, capturing new translations for future reuse.

2.2 Studies on LLMs in Translation Practice

As LLMs have brought new sights for translation, a series of studies focus on how LLMs perform on various tasks related to translation.

As translation engines, LLMs have demonstrated considerable effectiveness, both in comparative evaluations against competitors of NMT and human translators or in performance on standard translation benchmarks. GPT-4 delivers stronger capabilities over high-source European languages compared with commercial translation products (Jiao et al., 2023). Compared with human translators, leveled under junior, medium, and senior translators, GPT-4 produces better translation than junior translators, while lagging behind the medium and senior, and its translation capability gradually weakens from resource-rich to resource-poor directions (Yan et al., 2024). In domain-specific translation scenarios, LLMs can be used to enhance the translation process of rhymed and non-rhymed poetry, and it is found that LLMs can serve as valuable tools for literary translators, assisting with the creative process and suggesting solutions to problems that may not otherwise have been considered; however, it is less satisfied to use LLMs as a translation engine, and ask human translators to conduct post-editing (Resende & Hadley, 2024). Collectively, these findings illustrate that while LLMs like GPT-4 represent a significant advancement, their performance is nuanced: they can surpass benchmarks and junior translators in certain contexts but still lag behind expert humans and struggle with logical consistency or low-resource scenarios. This highlights their current role as powerful, yet context-dependent, tools whose optimal application requires careful consideration of task specifics and resource availability.

In light of viewing LLMs as translation evaluators, an equally remarkable performance is seen, aligned with the statement that the paradigm of LLM-as-a-judge shows a promising potential (Chiang & Lee, 2023; Zhang et al., 2023). GEMBA-MQM employs a fixed three-shot prompting technique, querying the GPT-4 model to mark error quality spans, showing a promising approach for quality evaluation through error analysis, which exhibits competitiveness over established metrics such as COMET and BLEURT-20 (Kocmi & Federmann, 2023a). From the perspective of agent, M-MAD develops a systematic LLM-based multi-agent framework for advanced LLM-as-a-judge MT evaluation and achieves a state-of-the-art performance over all existing LLM-driven evaluation methods (Feng et al., 2024). The success of frameworks like GEMBA-MQM and M-MAD underscores the growing potential of LLMs to not only generate translations but also to provide sophisticated, scalable, and potentially more insightful evaluations of translation quality, paving the way for new methodologies in MT assessment.

The application of LLMs in translation practices is not limited to purely translating or evaluating, and stretches to more dimensions. For example, LLMs show promise in outperforming traditional machine translation by augmented interactive concept-based instructions. In other words, LLMs are first used for target text analysis and produce a style report, and then supply this report in the prompt to produce translations (Qian & Kong, 2024). Focusing on post-editing, Raunak et al. (2023) reported that GPT-4 generally produced reliable, high-quality edits that aligned well with human judgment, pointing to a promising future for LLMs in improving APE (automatic post-editing) depending on its advanced multilingual capabilities. While a growing body of research underscores the considerable potential and utility of LLMs in the field of translation, much of the current literature adopts a somewhat fragmented approach. Studies frequently concentrate on evaluating LLMs' performance in discrete stages of the translation workflow, such as raw translation generation or quality evaluation, often in isolation. Consequently, there remains a relative paucity of research offering a holistic perspective that examines the integrated application and impact of LLMs across the entire translation process, from project preparation through to final delivery and feedback loops.

More importantly for the present volume, there is an even greater scarcity of literature that translates these fragmented technical advancements into structured, end-to-end pedagogical frameworks for training future translators.

2.3 The Emerging Role of LLMs in Translation Pedagogy

The rapid integration of LLMs into the professional translation landscape has created an urgent need for translation education to adapt its curricula. Consequently, a new body of research is beginning to explore how these powerful tools can be effectively incorporated into the classroom, not merely as replacements for older technologies but as catalysts for developing new competencies. A central theme in this emerging discourse is the shift from teaching students to use static tools to training them to collaborate dynamically with AI.

A primary focus of this pedagogical shift is the cultivation of prompt engineering as a core translator skill. Educators are moving beyond simple "translate this" exercises to designing activities where students learn to craft detailed prompts that control for tone, style, terminology, and context. This aligns with research demonstrating that the quality of LLM output is highly dependent on the quality of the input prompt. For instance, studies like Qian and Kong (2024) explore how concept-based prompting can guide LLMs to produce more human-centered translations, highlighting the sophisticated level of interaction that trainees must now master.

Furthermore, educators are leveraging LLMs to foster critical thinking and metacognitive skills. Instead of passively accepting AI-generated translations, students are tasked with critically evaluating, comparing, and refining them. LLMs are used as sparring partners for brainstorming alternative phrasings, as Socratic tutors for explaining linguistic choices, or as tools for generating deliberate "bad" translations that students must then analyze and correct. This approach reframes the translator's role from a simple producer of text to a strategic manager and validator of AI-generated content.

However, despite these promising developments, much of the current pedagogical application of LLMs remains as fragmented as the technical research. The challenge for educators is not just to teach individual skills like prompting or AI evaluation in isolation, but to situate them within an integrated, project-based workflow that mirrors contemporary professional practice. There is a clear need for holistic case studies and adaptable models that guide educators in designing curricula that prepare students for the end-to-end realities of an AI-driven translation project. This chapter aims to address that specific gap by presenting and deconstructing such a workflow.

3 Workflow Innovation

The advancement of AI, particularly LLMs with their strong multilingual capabilities, has enormously shifted how translation is completed by providing various techniques that enhance different procedures of a translation or localization project. Viewing translation from a project-based perspective, a typical chain involves term management, translation memory, translation, quality evaluation, and post-editing, which shares a common foundation with the traditional CAT workflow. When LLMs are thoroughly utilized, nearly every procedure can be enhanced with improved efficiency and intelligence. We are therefore motivated to conceive an innovative workflow that unleashes the potential of LLMs to the greatest degree and enhances every step of the traditional CAT workflow, while simultaneously providing a clear, adaptable model for translation educators.

3.1 Term Management

Building on the demonstrated effectiveness of LLMs for automatic extraction (Breton et al., forthcoming; Xu et al., 2023), their application across the broader scope of term management in a localization project, including extraction and matching, holds significant promise. Recent work has shown that combining traditional, feature-based candidate selection with contextual word-embedding features can substantially improve term extraction quality (Repar et al., 2025).

The proposed workflow commences with parsing existing Translation Memory eXchange (TMX) files to isolate plain texts from source and target segments, stripping away XML tags. An LLM, such as GPT-4o, is then integrated into the terminology lifecycle. By analyzing these bilingual segment pairs, the model identifies candidate term pairs, suggests relevant categorizations based on a predefined taxonomy, and can generate preliminary definitions. This approach leverages the deep semantic understanding inherent in LLMs, enabling the discovery of valuable domain concepts, even within novel contexts, surpassing the limitations of traditional manual curation or pattern-based methods.

Subsequently, translatable content, typically imported from formats like SDLXLIFF, is processed. The LLM analyzes the source text within these files to extract relevant terms, mirroring the structured output format used for the TMX-derived terminology. Following extraction from both sources, a matching process occurs. Terms identified in the SDLXLIFF source segments are compared against the source terms previously cataloged from the TMX. A successful match links the term in the current translation to its established, approved translation resident in the term base derived from the TMX. Terms lacking a match are flagged for subsequent resolution within the translation workflow.

Finally, all extracted and validated terminological data is consolidated for future reference and reuse. This integrated, LLM-augmented pipeline thus yields a continually evolving, high-precision terminology resource that streamlines translator workflows and enforces consistency across all localization assets.

Pedagogical Application and Classroom Activities:

This LLM-driven approach to term management transforms a traditionally laborious task into a dynamic learning opportunity focused on critical thinking and validation. Instead of manually compiling glossaries, students can be trained to act as "AI supervisors."

- Learning Objective: To develop students' ability to critically evaluate and refine AI-generated terminological data.
- Classroom Activity:

  1. **Extraction**: Provide students with a short, domain-specific text (e.g., a game's character description, a medical device manual). Task them with using an LLM (via a simple interface or API call) to extract key terms based on a predefined taxonomy (e.g., Character Names, Skills, Items).
  2. **Validation**: Students then compare the LLM-extracted list against an official glossary or their own manual extraction.
  3. **Discussion**: Facilitate a class discussion on the results. Where did the LLM excel? Where did it fail (e.g., extracting common words, missing nuanced terms)? This exercise teaches students that AI is a powerful but imperfect

assistant, reinforcing the indispensable role of human expertise in validating and curating linguistic assets.

3.2 Translation Memory

Translation memory traditionally relies on exact or fuzzy string matches. It finds prior source–target pairs where the overlap with a new sentence can be discovered. Embedding models and vector databases elevate this idea by enabling semantic research, so that even when phrasing changes, fragments can still be retrieved and reused once the meaning is detected to be equivalent.

On the one hand, as traditional databases are faced with challenges in dealing with high-dimensional data in terms of managing, retrieving, and real-time addition, vector databases have emerged as a specialized solution designed to manage high-dimensional vector embeddings effectively, optimized for the storage, indexing, and retrieval of vector data, providing advanced capabilities that traditional systems lack (Aradhya & Divya, 2024). On the other hand, LLMs with higher-dimensional embeddings have been reported to capture multi-faced semantic meanings (Tennenholtz et al., 2024). Concretely, OpenAI's text-embedding-3-small model produces embeddings with 1536 dimensions, and GPT-3-large model stands out as more powerful, offering embeddings with 3072 dimensions (Huang et al., 2025). Combining vector database and embedding models enables semantic similarity searches, moving beyond exact or fuzzy matching, which are frequent in traditional CAT systems. The process begins with embedding models, sophisticated neural networks trained to understand language nuances. These models convert text segments, typically source sentences from existing TM pairs, into high-dimensional numerical vectors, or embeddings. The crucial property is that sentences with similar meanings are mapped to vectors that are close to each other in the multi-dimensional vector space, regardless of exact wording.

Once generated, these vectors, along with their corresponding source and target text metadata, are stored in a vector database. Unlike traditional databases optimized for structured data or keyword search, vector databases are specifically designed for efficient nearest-neighbor searches in high-dimensional spaces. They use specialized indexing algorithms to quickly find vectors closest to a given query vector.

When a new sentence needs translation, it is first converted into a query vector using the same embedding model. This query vector is then used to search the vector database. The database returns the vectors and their associated term base entries that have the smallest distance to the query vector. These returned entries represent the most semantically relevant past translations, even if they differ significantly in phrasing from the new sentence. This allows translators or translation systems to leverage a much broader range of relevant past work, significantly enhancing consistency and efficiency.

Pedagogical Application and Classroom Activities:

While setting up a vector database may be too technical for many classrooms, the concept of semantic retrieval is a crucial competency for future translators. Educators can use simplified tools or pre-built demos to teach this principle.

- Learning Objective: To understand the difference between lexical (fuzzy match) and semantic retrieval and its impact on translation consistency (e.g., maintaining character voice).
- Classroom Activity:

  1. **Contrastive Analysis:** Provide students with a new source sentence and two sets of TM matches: one from a traditional fuzzy-match system and one from a semantic search demo (e.g., supported by OpenAI Embedding API).
  2. **Evaluation**: Ask students to evaluate which set of matches is more useful for translating the new sentence, especially when stylistic consistency is key. For example, a semantic search might retrieve stylistically similar lines for a specific game character, even if the wording differs.
  3. **Reflection**: Students write a short reflection on how semantic TM could help them maintain a consistent tone or character voice across a large project, a common challenge in game localization and literary translation.

3.3 Translation and Post-Editing

With everything prepared, translation begins. The LLMs, such as GPT-4o, act as the core translation engine, with historical data and specific terms involved, capable of generating fluent and contextually aware text. Translation memory, enhanced with vector embeddings, provides the LLMs with examples of how similar source sentences were previously translated. Whether through high-similarity fuzzy matches or semantically related segments recognition via vector search, segments in the translation memory base do great help to translation as hints. This guides the model to maintain consistency with past translations, adopt preferred phrasing, and correctly handle recurring structures or segments.

Meanwhile, terminology management ensures accuracy and brand consistency for specific keywords, product names, or technical jargon, and the integration of an approved domain terminology can improve the translation result (Moslem et al., 2023). A term base stores approved source–target term pairs. During translation preparation, the source text is scanned for recognized terms. These identified source terms, along with their prescribed target translations, are also included in the prompt given to the LLMs. The prompt explicitly instructs the LLMs to use the provided target terms whenever their corresponding source terms appear. The LLMs then synthesizes these inputs by processing the source sentence, adhering to the specific vocabulary mandated by the term base, referencing the translation memory base for the content that fails to discover a complete equivalent with previous translations, and applying its general linguistic knowledge to generate the final translation. This synergy ensures the output is not only fluent but also consistent with past work and adheres to specific project glossaries.

Beyond translation, LLMs are further employed for automated post-editing, aiming to refine translation output, particularly when initial quality metrics are subpar. After the designated LLMs generate the translation, it is followed by an automatic evaluation. If the score falls below a predefined quality threshold, an automated post-editing loop is triggered. Instead of immediately accepting the low-quality output, the system formulates a new prompt for the LLMs. This prompt typically includes the original source sentence, the initial translation generated earlier, the feedback from the evaluation metric, and specific instructions to improve the translation. The LLMs are essentially asked to critique and revise its own previous output. This iterative process might repeat a few times, with the goal of automatically elevating the translation quality to meet the desired standard with little immediate human intervention. This leverages the LLM's capacity for refinement and understanding quality-related instructions, automating a basic level of revision. Figure 1 shows an operational workflow of LLM-driven projects.

Pedagogical Application and Classroom Activities:

This stage is where students transition from being passive users of MT to active "AI directors." Prompt engineering and iterative refinement become the central skills.

- Learning Objective: To master prompt engineering for context-aware translation and to use AI for iterative quality improvement.
- Classroom Activity:
  1. **Prompt Design Challenge**: Divide students into groups and assign each a game character with a distinct personality (e.g., a wise old wizard, an energetic young hero). Their task is to design a detailed prompt to translate a

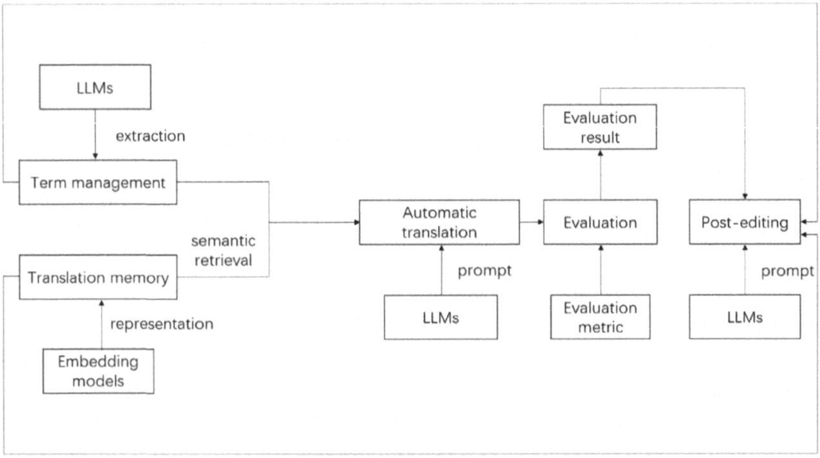

Fig. 1 Operational workflow of LLM-driven projects

set of neutral dialogue lines in the voice of their assigned character. The prompt should include personality descriptors, key terms (e.g., spell names), and stylistic examples.

2. **Iterative Refinement**: Give students an initial, mediocre LLM translation. Their task is to write a series of prompts to guide the LLM to improve it. For example: "Make this sound more archaic," or "Replace 'magic' with the approved term 'arcane arts'."
3. **Peer Review**: Students exchange their final, AI-refined translations and evaluate how successfully the target text captures the assigned character's voice, demonstrating the direct impact of their prompting strategies. This teaches them that translation quality in an LLM workflow is a direct result of their ability to provide clear and comprehensive instructions.

4 Case Study

Based on the conceptual workflow of the potential in enhancing term management, translation memory, machine translation, and post-editing with LLMs, this section presents a case study that demonstrates the operationalization of the workflow. The case of a game localization synthesizes every technological component with a LLM as the mainstay. In brief, it processes multiple external resources to create term base and translation memory, uses a LLM as the core translation engine altogether with the language assets for instruction, incorporates an automatic quality estimation metric for correction suggestion and a subsequent automatic post-editing loop to ensure the translation quality. This serves not only as a concrete example of an integrated, intelligent translation system but also as a detailed blueprint for a project-based learning module in a translation technology course.

4.1 Project Operation

The system designed for this project, realized in Python code, integrates several functional modules. The core components and their specific implementation details are elaborated below, with a consistent focus on their educational relevance.

4.2 Preparation Before Translation

In the preparation stage, the system first manages domain-specific terms and assembles a translation memory. Bilingual term lists are imported from Excel into a term base, with each entry pairing a source-language and its approved target-language equivalent. At the same time, all the TMX files are parsed into Chinese-English pairs ready for being extracted into a dictionary that maps each source-language segment to its corresponding translation. Table 1 shows part of parsed TMX files.

Next, we use GPT-4o, one of the most advanced models when we were doing this project, to extract terms from the dictionary. For each source–target pair, the model is prompted with a fixed taxonomy categorized into highly conceptual, universal game, activity, character attribute, skill, title, and other, and required to return JSON objects with parameters that specify the source term, the target term, the term type, and a brief explanation. Notably, if no terms of a given type are present, the model still emits an empty JSON structure to ensure output consistency. All JSON outputs are collected into a data frame with the columns mirroring the JSON fields shown in Table 2, ensuring that each extracted term is both structured and immediately retrievable in later stages.

Finally, we construct a translation memory base through vector database. Every source–target segment pair, already translated texts in the TMX files, is concatenated and embedded using OpenAI's text-embedding-3-large model for semantic representation, truncated to 768 dimensions, and L_2-normalized. These vectors are indexed so that any new segment can be matched precisely via cosine similarity to its nearest neighbors among previously translated segments. This vectorized memory ensures that the system can retrieve highly relevant past translations even when exact string matches are unavailable.

Pedagogical Takeaway and Classroom Activities:

This preparation phase provides a rich opportunity to teach students about the "front-end" of a modern localization project, focusing on resource management and critical evaluation of AI-generated data.

- Learning Objective: To train students to supervise and validate AI-driven linguistic asset creation.
- Classroom Activities:
    1. AI-Assisted Term Extraction: Provide students with a sample TMX file from a game. Task them with using a readily available LLM to extract terms based on

Table 1 Parsed TMX files

Source text	Target text
4件	4 pieces
受到致死攻击时立刻重置鬼之怒/隐形迷彩/水晶棺/回溯之光/金刚劲/绝镰之斩/千面诀/天选明星/漆甲/镜子戏法/移花接木/曲速跃迁/圣光荣耀/神隐之随/御震/无拘/烈风回旋的技能冷却时间，无敌6秒，且6秒内四元素伤害提高56%%。这个效果有80秒的冷却时间	when receiving a fatal attack, CD time for Demon Rage/Stealth Camouflage/Crystal Coffin/Recall Light/Giant Strength/Grim Scythe/Omni-Guard/The Chosen Star/Paint Armor/Mirror Trick/Disappear into the Flowers/Warp Speed Transition/Holy Glory/Spirit Follower/Quake/Unconstraint/Flame Whirlwind are reset, gain Invincible for 6 s and elemental DMG increases by 56%% for 6 s. This Effect has an 80 s CD time

Table 2 Data-framed terms

Number	term_cn	term_translation	term_frequency	term_type
0	鬼之怒	Demon Rage	0	技能名称
1	隐形迷彩	Stealth Camouflage	0	技能名称
2	水晶棺	Crystal Coffin	0	技能名称
3	回溯之光	Recall Light	0	技能名称
4	金刚劲	Giant Strength	0	技能名称
5	绝镰之斩	Grim Scythe	0	技能名称
6	千面诀	Omni-Guard	0	技能名称
7	天选明星	The Chosen Star	0	技能名称
8	漆甲	Paint Armor	0	技能名称
9	镜子戏法	Mirror Trick	0	技能名称
10	移花接木	Disappear into the Flowers	0	技能名称
11	曲速跃迁	Warp Speed Transition	0	技能名称
12	圣光荣耀	Holy Glory	0	技能名称
13	神隐之随	Spirit Follower	0	技能名称
14	御震	Quake	0	技能名称
15	无拘	Unconstraint	0	技能名称
16	烈火回旋	Flame Whirlwind	0	技能名称

a simple prompt. They must then review the AI's output, correcting errors and filling in omissions. This teaches them that LLMs are powerful for generating a first draft of a term base, but human oversight is essential for ensuring accuracy.

2. Exploring Semantic Search: Using a pre-configured demo (e.g., a simple web app showing semantic search on a small TM), ask students to input new game dialogue and analyze the retrieved results. They should compare these results to what a traditional CAT tool's fuzzy matching might provide. This helps them viscerally understand the practical value of semantic search for maintaining stylistic consistency, a concept that can be abstract otherwise.

4.3 Translation

As term base and translation memory base are prepared, the translation process is unfolded in three dimensions. The translation pipeline starts with identification and match of terms. The to-be-translated texts are read and then parsed into segments from SDLXLIFF files. Altogether we have 5,493 segments in this case. These segments are separately prompted with the aforementioned term base and translation memory. For each input source segment, it is operated in a term-lookup phase in which specialized vocabulary drawn from the established term base is applied. Whenever a match occurs, the approved target-language equivalent is recorded and flagged for preservation that these matched terms will subsequently be imposed unchanged in any candidate translation and be added in the translation prompt in order to guarantee consistency with established domain terms.

Once the work on term management has been settled, the pipeline immediately proceeds to the match of translation memory. The core in this step is to compare the to-be-translated source texts against previously stored bilingual pairs in the existing vector database. Before comparison, the source texts are separated into sentences and then are tokenized and stripped of punctuation and high-frequency function words. The exact or near-exact overlaps of at least two content words trigger retrieval of their stored translations. If none are found, the segment's embedding is computed and a nearest-neighbor search in the vector database using cosine similarity over L_2-normalized embeddings yields the most similar past segments. Any retrieved examples are then presented as reference translation memories, and their target-language renderings are preserved as strong suggestions for the final output.

When neither the term base nor the translation memory yields sufficient coverage does the system invoke GPT-4 to generate the translation sentence by sentence. At that point, the prompt is structured differently according to the result of term match and translation memory match, explicitly instructing the model to retain critical symbols and previously approved terms.

Pedagogical Takeaway and Classroom Activities:

This translation phase is the core of the pedagogical experience, designed to immerse students in an "AI-first" workflow and demonstrate the critical value of the "human-in-the-loop." The key takeaway for students is that in a modern, automated pipeline, their primary role shifts from manually translating text to strategically directing the AI. The majority of the process is automated by code, but the final quality hinges on the human's ability to inject nuanced, domain-specific knowledge (in this case, understanding the game's context, characters, and tone) at the most critical juncture: the prompt.

- Learning Objective: To master proactive prompt engineering by running a semi-automated translation script and iteratively refining the prompts to align the AI's output with specific stylistic and contextual requirements, thus embodying the "human-in-the-loop" principle.
- Classroom Activity: The "AI-First Translation Lab"
    1. Setup: Students are provided with a Python script (in this case a Python Jupyter Notebook file) that simulates the entire translation pipeline described. They are also given a scenario: "You are the lead localization specialist for a specific game. Your task is to translate the dialogue for two distinct characters: a wise, ancient Elf who speaks in a formal, archaic style, and a brash, young mercenary who uses modern slang." Students receive a character bio and a small, pre-loaded term base for each.
    2. Initial Run (The AI's First Pass): Students first run the script using a default, generic prompt. The script automatically handles the term lookups and

semantic searches, then generates a baseline translation. This output will be linguistically correct but stylistically flat, failing to capture the unique voices of the characters.

3. Human-in-the-Loop Intervention (The Core Task): The student's main task is not to post-edit the output directly. Instead, they must open the script and modify the prompt section. Based on their understanding of the character, they will craft a more sophisticated prompt.
4. Iterative Refinement and Evaluation: Students re-run the script with their new, refined prompt. They compare the new output with the baseline version. They are encouraged to repeat this process, continuously adjusting the prompt to see how different instructions affect the AI's tone, word choice, and overall style.
5. Peer Review and Reflection: Students submit their final, refined prompt and the AI-generated translation for one of the characters. In a peer-review session, the class evaluates which translations best capture the intended character persona. This directly demonstrates that the most successful outcomes were not the result of better post-editing, but of more insightful and skillful prompt engineering, solidifying their understanding of their new role as an AI director.

4.4 Post-Translation

Subsequent to the production of the translation, the pipeline enters the last phase centered on quality assessment and automatic post-editing to ensure its deliverability. In this project, COMET (Rei et al., 2020) is selected be the assessment model which returns a scalar quality score, ranging from 0 to 1, by feeding the GPT-4 produced translation without the intervention of reference translation. The raw GPT-4 output is packaged together with its source sentence and fed into a COMET regression model, which returns a scalar quality score. With a threshold of 0.7, those falling below it are placed into a list, waiting for an automatic correction.

After all translated sentences go through the COMET assessment, a new prompt is designed for GPT-4 aiming to edit the sentences in the list by incorporating the model's own previous output alongside the original instructions and any retrieved memory or term references, explicitly asking for an improved rendition. GPT-4 is then reinvoked up to three times in total to refine these unqualified translations until the COMET score climbs above 0.7 or the retry limit is reached. The flagged unqualified translations are stored for later manual edits.

Once a translated sentence is qualified with a score above 0.7, it is written back into the SDLXLIFF file where the target element is created or updated under the matching translation units. In parallel, all final result paired as source–target are collected into a data frame and exported to an Excel file for human review. Segments flagged as low-quality remain in their own spreadsheet, enabling a professional to precisely devote the efforts to where the automatic pipeline judged confidence to be insufficient. In this way, machine and human labor combine and the entire system guarantees that every segment has at least one high-scoring machine rendering, and the post-translation reports direct editors' attention to the subset that most needs human correction.

Pedagogical Takeaway and Classroom Activities:

This final phase introduces students to data-driven quality control and the concept of an iterative workflow, moving beyond the traditional one-pass "translate-and-edit" model.

- Learning Objective: To train students to interpret automated quality metrics and understand the principles of an iterative, AI-assisted revision process.
- Classroom Activity: The "Quality Gatekeeper" Exercise.

  1. Scenario: Provide students with a list of translated sentences and their corresponding (hypothetical or real) COMET scores.
  2. Analysis: Ask students to identify the correlation between low scores and specific error types (e.g., mistranslations, awkward phrasing). This develops their "data literacy" for translation quality.
  3. AI-Assisted Revision: For the low-scoring sentences, task students with writing a simple revision prompt for an LLM (e.g., "Correct the grammatical errors in this sentence"). They then compare the AI-revised output with their own manual revision.
  4. Discussion: Facilitate a discussion on when automated revision is "good enough" and when human intervention is non-negotiable. This teaches them to be critical and strategic users of AI post-editing tools, rather than blindly accepting their suggestions.

5 New Paradigm

The operational innovations detailed above—covering term management, translation memory, translation, and automated post-editing through LLMs—are indicative of an emerging paradigm shift. This shift moves away from the traditional CAT workflow toward an AI-driven approach characterized by a reoriented role for human translators, more dynamic resource management, and a more integrated, closed-loop process. Crucially, this new paradigm has profound implications for translation education, demanding a fundamental rethinking of what skills we teach and how we teach them.

5.1 The Evolving Role of the Translator: From Producer to AI Orchestrator

In the traditional CAT paradigm, the translator's role is primarily that of a producer and corrector of text. The machine provides suggestions (TM matches, MT output), and the human decides whether to accept, reject, or modify them. While collaborative, this interaction remains largely transactional.

The LLM-driven workflow redefines this role into that of a strategic orchestrator or AI director. The translator's primary value no longer lies solely in their ability to generate fluent target text, but in their capacity to expertly guide, manage, and validate an AI system to achieve a desired outcome. This shift imbues translators with significantly enhanced agency but also demands a more sophisticated engagement with technology.

As two of the significant functions of CATs are Translation Memory (TM) and Term Base (TB) (Karpińska, 2017), how the two can be approached innovatively renders a fundamentally shift of the human–machine collaboration. In the procedure of building term base, translators are exposed to various LLMs that can be used for term extraction. Those who have a strong mastery in deep learning can choose to fine-tune a model for higher extraction precision. Regarding translation memory, the key is to employ embedding models for semantic representation, a way to store previous translations and to facilitate their match with following translation segments. Compared to traditional CAT systems, more flexibility is given. Translators, based on various needs for match precision and cost, can select certain model for the project rather than a fixed way of establishing and using translation memory base.

The shift also occurs in automatic translation. Instead of embedding a machine translation engine, such as Google Translate or DeepL in a CAT system and calling it to translate the parsed file, we can now use LLMs for translation. The formula of instructing a LLM to translate typically involves crafting specific prompts that include the source text, the target language, and potentially terms and translation memory. Under this circumstance, translators are not limited to click the button of "translate" and then immediately get the product; they design a prompt in view of the specific requirements of the project, such as desired tone, language style and using scenarios, and feed the prompt to the selected LLM to have the translation complete. Essentially, prompt engineering, focusing on how to maximize the performance of LLMs through natural language, is added to the skill map of a translator.

Human-machine collaboration updates in post-editing. Similar to the advancements in automatic translation, the post-editing phase also undergoes a significant transformation. In the conventional CAT workflow, post-editing primarily involves the human translator reviewing and correcting the output generated by a machine translation engine, focusing on eliminating grammatical errors, improving fluency, and ensuring terminological consistency based on predefined quality metrics. The advent of LLMs refines this interaction. While the initial translation produced by a well-prompted LLM might require less correction due to potentially higher quality and better contextual adherence, the collaboration extends beyond simple error fixing.

using third-party APIs, a crucial consideration for any project involving sensitive content. These are real-world constraints that must be addressed to ensure equitable and secure access to such advanced training methods.

Looking ahead, this study opens several promising avenues for future work. A key direction is the development of simplified, user-friendly pedagogical tools that encapsulate the core functionalities of this workflow, allowing educators and students to engage with concepts like semantic search and prompt engineering without the need for complex technical setup. Further empirical research is also needed to assess the pedagogical efficacy of this model: do students trained within this project-based, AI-integrated framework demonstrate superior skills in critical thinking, technological adaptability, and quality management compared to those trained via traditional methods? Finally, this workflow can be adapted and tested in other specialized domains (such as legal, medical, or marketing translation) and with different language pairs to explore its versatility and scalability.

As artificial intelligence becomes inextricably woven into the fabric of the translation industry, our teaching paradigms must evolve in lockstep. By translating cutting-edge professional practices into structured, accessible, and critical pedagogical experiences, we can better equip the next generation of translators to not only navigate but thrive in the new era of human–machine collaboration.

References

Aradhya, K. C., & Divya, T. L. (2024). Vector databases. *Open Access Research Journal of Engineering and Technology, 7*, 96–104.

Breton, J., Billami, M. M., Chevalier, M., Nguyen, H. T., Satoh, K., Trojahn, C., & Zin, M. M. (forthcoming). Leveraging LLMs for legal terms extraction with limited annotated data. *Artificial Intelligence and Law*, 1–27.

Chan, S.-W. (Ed.). (2015). *The routledge encyclopedia of translation technology*. Routledge.

Chiang, C.-H., & Lee, H.-Y. (2023). Can large language models be an alternative to human evaluations? In *Proceedings of the 61st Annual Meeting of the Association for Computational Linguistics* (Vol. 1: Long Papers), 15607–15631. Association for Computational Linguistics.

Feng, Z., Su, J., Zheng, J., Ren, J., Yan, Z., Wu, J., Wang, H., & Liu, Z. (2024). M-MAD: Multidimensional multi-agent debate framework for fine-grained machine translation evaluation. arXiv preprint arXiv:2412.20127.

Hendy, A., Abdelrehim, M., Sharaf, A., Raunak, V., Gabr, M., Matsushita, H., Kim, Y. J., Afify, M., & Awadalla, H. H. (2023). How good are GPT models at machine translation? A comprehensive evaluation. arXiv preprint arXiv:2302.09210. https://doi.org/10.48550/arXiv.2302.09210.

Huang, Z., Long, Y., Peng, K., & Tong, S. (2025). An embedding-based semantic analysis approach: A preliminary study on redundancy detection in psychological concepts operationalized by scales. *Journal of Intelligence, 13*, 11.

Jiao, W., Wang, W., Huang, J., Wang, X., Shi, S., & Tu, Z. (2023). Is ChatGPT a good translator? Yes with GPT-4 as the engine. arXiv preprint arXiv:2301.08745. https://doi.org/10.48550/arXiv.2301.08745.

Jiang, Z., Lv, Q., Zhang, Z., & Lei, L. (2024). Convergences and divergences between automatic assessment and human evaluation: Insights from comparing ChatGPT-Generated translation and neural machine translation. arXiv preprint arXiv:2401.05176. https://doi.org/10.48550/arXiv.2401.05176.

Karpińska, P. (2017). Computer aided translation - possibilities, limitations and changes in the field of professional translation. *Journal of Education, Culture and Society, 8*, 133–142.

Kocmi, T., & Federmann, C. (2023a). Large language models are state-of-the-art evaluators of translation quality. In *Proceedings of the 24th Annual Conference of the European Association for Machine Translation*, (pp. 193–203). European Association for Machine Translation.

Kocmi, T., & Federmann, C. (2023b). GEMBA-MQM: Detecting translation quality error spans with GPT-4. In P. Koehn, B. Haddow, T. Kocmi, & C. Monz (Eds.), *Proceedings of the Eighth Conference on Machine Translation*, (pp. 768–775). Association for Computational Linguistics.

Liu, Q., He, Y., Lian, D., Zheng, Z., Xu, T., Liu, C., & Chen, E. (2024). UniMEL: A unified framework for multimodal entity linking with large language models. In *Proceedings of the 33rd ACM International Conference on Information and Knowledge Management* (CIKM 2024), 1909–1919. Association for Computing Machinery.

Moslem, Y., Haque, R., & Way, A. (2023). *Fine-tuning large language models for adaptive machine translation*. arXiv preprint arXiv:2312.12740. https://doi.org/10.48550/arXiv.2312.12740.

Moslem, Y., Romani, G., Molaei, M., Kelleher, J. D., Haque, R., & Way, A. (2023). Domain terminology integration into machine translation: Leveraging large language models. In P. Koehn, B. Haddow, T. Kocmi, & C. Monz (Eds.), *Proceedings of the Eighth Conference on Machine Translation*, pp. 902–911. Association for Computational Linguistics.

Peng, W., Li, G., Jiang, Y., Wang, Z., Ou, D., Zeng, X., Xu, D., Xu, T., & Chen, E. (2023). *Large language model based long-tail query rewriting in Taobao search*. arXiv preprint arXiv:2311.03758.

Qian, M., & Kong, C. (2024). Enabling human-centered machine translation using concept-based large language model prompting and translation memory. In *Artificial Intelligence in HCI: 5th International Conference*, AI-HCI 2024, (pp. 118–134). Springer.

Qin, L., Chen, Q., Feng, X., Wu, Y., Zhang, Y., Li, Y., Li, M., Che, W., & Yu, P. S. (2024). Large language models meet NLP: A survey. arXiv preprint arXiv:2405.12819. https://doi.org/10.48550/arXiv.2405.12819.

Raunak, V., Sharaf, A., Wang, Y., Awadalla, H., & Menezes, A. (2023). Leveraging GPT-4 for automatic translation post-editing. In H. Bouamor, J. Pino, & K. Bali (Eds.), *Findings of the association for computational linguistics: EMNLP 2023*, (pp. 12009–12024). Association for Computational Linguistics.

Rei, R., Stewart, C., Farinha, A. C., & Lavie, A. (2020). COMET: a neural framework for MT evaluation. In B. Webber, T. Cohn, Y. He, & Y. Liu, (Eds.), *Proceedings of the 2020 conference on empirical methods in Natural Language Processing (EMNLP)*, (pp. 2685–2702). Online: Association for Computational Linguistics.

Repar, A., Lavrac, N., & Pollak, S. (2025). *Extracting domain-specific terms using contextual word embeddings*. arXiv preprint arXiv:2502.17278.

Resende, N., & Hadley, J. (2024). The translator's canvas: Using LLMs to enhance poetry translation. In *Proceedings of the 16th conference of the association for machine translation in the Americas*, (pp. 178–189). Association for Machine Translation in the Americas.

Tennenholtz, G., Chow, Y., Hsu, C., Jeong, J., Shani, L., Tulepbergenov, A., Ramachandran, D., Mladenov, M., & Boutilier, C. (2024). Demystifying embedding spaces using large language models. In *Proceedings of the twelfth international conference on learning representations*. Vienna, Austria.

Xu, D., Chen, W., Peng, W., Zhang, C., Xu, T., Zhao, X., Wu, X., Zheng, Y., & Chen, E. (2023). Large language models for generative information extraction: A survey. *Frontiers of Computer Science, 18*, Article 186357.

Yan, J., Yan, P., Chen, Y., Li, J., Zhu, X., & Zhang, Y. (2024). *GPT-4 vs. human translators: A comprehensive evaluation of translation quality across languages, domains, and expertise levels*. arXiv preprint arXiv:2407.03658.

Zhang, R., Li, Y., Ma, Y., Zhou, M., & Zou, L. (2023). LLMaAA: Making large language models as active annotators. In *Findings of the 2023 conference on empirical methods in natural language processing (EMNLP)*, (pp. 13088–13103). Association for Computational Linguistics.

Lintao Han is an Associate Professor and the Deputy Dean of the School of English and International Studies at Beijing Language and Culture University. He also holds positions as Deputy Secretary-General of the International Service Committee of the Translators Association of China. His research focuses on translation technology, technology in translation education, and language intelligence and technology. He is the author of the book A Beginner's Guide to Programming for Translators (2020), published by Tsinghua University Press. This work was recognized as a Premium Undergraduate Textbook by the Beijing Municipal Education Commission in 2021. He has led several key research projects, including a project on AI translation based on large models with Baidu. Notably, in response to an earthquake in Myanmar, he led a team to rapidly develop a China-Myanmar-English trilingual translation system to support disaster relief efforts. He has published articles in academic journals such as Chinese Translation and Foreign Language Education Research Frontier and has received multiple teaching accolades, including the BLCU Teaching Excellence Award.

Chongyu Chen is a doctoral student in Translation Studies at Beijing Language and Culture University. His research focuses on the intersection of translation and AI technologies, with a particular focus on large language models and its applications in translation practice, translation evaluation, and translation training. By examining the evolving relationship between human translators and machine-assisted systems, he seeks to contribute to the development of innovative methodologies that enhance both the efficiency and quality of translation. He is currently working on investigating how advances in natural language processing and AI are reshaping translation studies and redefining the role of human expertise in multilingual communication.

Chuyi Zheng is an undergraduate student in Translation and Localization at the School of English and International Studies, Beijing Language and Culture University. Her research interests include large language model applications and localization.

Enhancing Translation Education with the AI-Integrated Corpus Platform: Design, Application, and Pedagogical Benefits

Simin Xu, Yanfang Su, and Kanglong Liu

Abstract The chapter introduces an AI-integrated corpus platform designed to enhance translation teaching by combining the strengths of corpora and Generative Artificial Intelligence (GenAI). The platform integrates AI capabilities with corpus resources to provide innovative functions such as corpus-based translation equivalence, reference translations, errors correction, translation feedback, and personalized AI assistant. A key feature is its ability to adapt to diverse instructional needs while supporting both learners and educators in task-based translation environments. The chapter discusses the platform's design and details the usages of each interface. Based on the framework of task-based learning cycle, the chapter demonstrates how the platform can be effectively applied into each phase of translation instruction: pre-task preparation, task execution, reporting, analysis, revision, and reflection. The AI-integrated corpus platform offers several key advantages for translation education in terms of instructional methods, learning objectives, and technological support. By analyzing both the pedagogical benefits and the broader implications of integrating GenAI with corpus resources, this chapter offers practical and insightful guidance for educators, aiming to enhance translation instruction in an evolving educational landscape.

Keywords AI-integrated corpus platform · Translation pedagogy · Task-based translation teaching · AI literacy · Learner engagement

S. Xu · K. Liu (✉)
The Hong Kong Polytechnic University, Hong Kong SAR, China
e-mail: klliu@polyu.edu.hk

S. Xu
e-mail: siminxu.xu@connect.polyu.hk

Y. Su
Lingnan University, Hong Kong SAR, China
e-mail: yanfangsu@ln.edu.hk

T. Yin et al. (eds.), *AI Through LLMs*, New Frontiers in Translation Studies,
https://doi.org/10.1007/978-981-95-4798-2_9

1 Introduction

With ongoing developments in technology, translation teaching has gained access to a wider range of resources and tools, including corpora and Generative Artificial Intelligence (GenAI). Corpora, in particular, provide extensive authentic language data and have become a well-established resource in translation studies. Their educational value has been increasingly acknowledged, especially through data-driven learning (DDL) approaches (Allan et al., 2023; Boulton & Cobb, 2017). These approaches support a gradual shift from traditional teacher-led instruction to more student-centered learning environments (Laviosa & Falco, 2023; Rodríguez-Inés, 2009).

Building on the foundation laid by corpus development, GenAI has recently gained attention as a promising resource for supporting translation and a variety of linguistic tasks (Kwok et al., 2025; Xu et al., 2025b). In contrast to corpora, which often involve large volumes of data and demand a certain level of technical expertise from users (Kennedy & Miceli, 2001), GenAI tools tend to offer more accessible interfaces and built-in analytical features that can help simplify complex linguistic information. Despite these advantages, the role of GenAI in education has sparked considerable discussion. As awareness grows around its potential limitations—such as hallucinations, concerns over data accuracy, and ethical considerations (Crosthwaite & Baise, 2023; Alasadi & Baiz, 2023)—educators and learners alike are approaching its use with increasing critical awareness. A balanced consideration of both corpora and GenAI suggests that their complementary strengths may be leveraged to enhance translation pedagogy in meaningful ways. In response to these developments, we have developed a corpus platform that incorporates GenAI functionalities such as summarizing corpus-based translation equivalence, suggesting reference translations, identifying potential errors, providing instant feedback, and enabling tailored human–AI interaction. The platform is intended to assist educators in enhancing translation instruction and to offer translation learners a supportive resource for more independent learning.

This chapter begins by examining the AI-integrated corpus platform, with attention to its theoretical underpinnings, design considerations, and core functionalities. It then discusses the platform's potential applications in classroom settings using the task-based learning cycle as an organizing framework, and how it contributes to the development of students' translation competences. In addition, the chapter discusses the pedagogical advantages and broader implications of incorporating such a platform into translation education. The aim is to contribute to ongoing developments in translation pedagogy by exploring how GenAI and corpus technologies may be thoughtfully integrated, while offering practical insights for language educators navigating today's evolving educational landscape.

2 Context and Background

2.1 Corpus-Based Translation Teaching

Developing translator competence entails the integration of multiple sub-competencies, including linguistic proficiency, intercultural awareness, and strategic problem-solving skills. Central to the translator's task is the ability to select contextually appropriate expressions across languages (Sonbul et al., 2022) and manage various textual and linguistic complexities (ISO, 2015). Facilitating the acquisition of such competencies constitutes a key pedagogical objective in translator training. Within this pedagogical framework, corpus-based resources offer promising affordances. By providing access to empirically derived patterns of language use, corpora can support learners in uncovering cross-linguistic patterns and communicative practices (Flowerdew, 2012).

Recognizing the pedagogical value of corpora, many educators have begun to incorporate them into translation teaching to support data-driven learning, which benefits both teachers and learners. This approach can offer a more informed and practical means of fostering key translation competences. For instructors, corpora provide a useful foundation for designing teaching materials based on authentic language patterns, rather than relying solely on intuition or prior experience (Li, 2013). For learners, working with real-world linguistic data may help them approach translation tasks more effectively across different contexts, contributing to improvements in accuracy, fluency, and overall language use (Liu et al., 2024). The use of corpora in translator education has also driven a pedagogical shift from traditional teacher-centered models to learner-centered approaches, where students are encouraged to take greater responsibility for their learning (Laviosa & Falco, 2023). Educators can select from various types of corpora—such as monolingual, comparable, and parallel—depending on their teaching goals. Among these, parallel corpora are often considered particularly helpful in translation education, as they allow learners to explore translation equivalents, terminology, collocations, and syntactic patterns that are directly relevant to translation practice (Santos & Frankenberg-Garcia, 2007). A growing body of research has explored the potential of corpus-based approaches in translation teaching from different perspectives. For instance, Yang (2023) discusses how corpora can assist learners in areas such as vocabulary selection, synonym differentiation, and translation quality assessment. Liu et al. (2024) examined students' use of a self-compiled parallel corpus during translation tasks and observed that such engagement may contribute to improvements in translation performance. These studies suggest that corpus-informed activities can offer practical support in developing translation-related skills, although further investigation is needed to better understand how learners interact with corpus tools in diverse pedagogical settings.

While corpus-based approaches offer a range of pedagogical benefits, their implementation in translation teaching also presents several challenges. One common issue concerns the technical demands associated with corpus use; effective use often requires skills in data querying and filtering, which not all students may possess

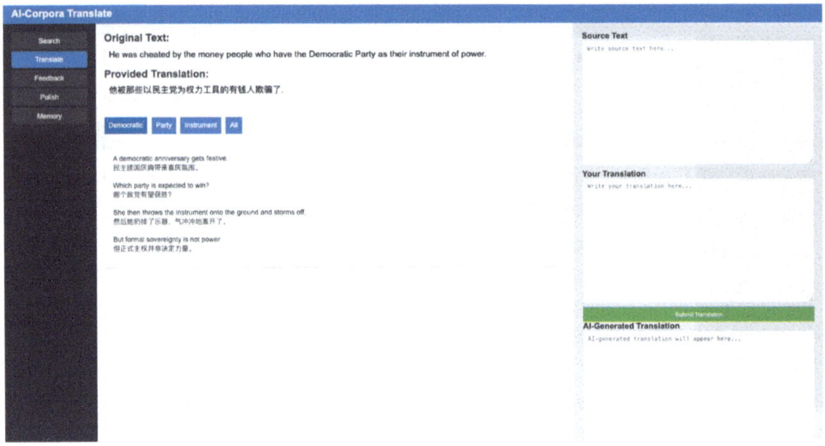

Fig. 2 Translate

into how to refine their translation strategies. Through this process, learners develop both linguistic skills and digital literacy, which are essential for translators working in a technology-enhanced environment.

3.4 Feedback

The "Feedback" interface enhances translation teaching by providing translation evaluation through two distinct types of feedback. When users submit both the source text and their translations, the platform processes the input using built-in prompts based on Hurtado Albir's (2015) translation assessment framework, along with prompt principles from Ekin (2023) and White et al. (2023). It evaluates the translation across multiple dimensions, including accuracy, composition, vocabulary, morphosyntax, cohesion, and coherence. Users can interact with the platform through custom prompts to ask follow-up questions about specific feedback points or request detailed explanations of particular translation issues. This function supports personalized learning by addressing individual needs and fostering deeper understanding.

In addition to providing a holistic evaluation, the system generates detailed sentence-level feedback on both meaning-related translation errors and contextual inaccuracies. To improve usability, the platform highlights errors within the translation and categorizes them by type, allowing users to quickly identify and address specific issues. Figure 3 illustrates this function with examples. When analyzing the sentence "He was cheated by the money people who have the Democratic Party as their instrument of power" and the user-submitted translation "他被那些使

Fig. 3 Feedback

用民主党作为金融仪器的银行家们多收了钱," the platform identified two terminology issues. It recommended replacing "仪器" with "工具" for "instrument" and suggested revising "多收了钱" to "被欺骗" to accurately capture the meaning of "cheated." In another example, the platform reviewed the sentence "Feeling betrayed and disillusioned, he began to question not only the motives behind their policies but also his own beliefs in the political system" alongside its translation "感到困惑和迷失, 他开始质疑他们政策背后的目标, 甚至质疑自己对政治系统的信念." Based on the context, the platform advised replacing "迷失" with "幻灭" as a more culturally and semantically appropriate translation of "disillusioned," and suggested using "动机" instead of "目标" to better reflect the meaning of "motives" in this context.

A unique feature of this interface is its integration of AI with corpus technology, addressing the limitations of AI-generated feedback, such as vagueness or generality (Su et al., 2023; Xu et al., 2025a). This integration helps users to build a deeper understanding of translation challenges across multiple linguistic levels, ranging from word choice and sentence structure to broader discourse-level considerations.

3.5 Polish

In professional translation projects, editing and revision are essential for ensuring translation quality (Mellinger, 2018). The "Polish" interface is designed to assist users during this stage by providing AI-powered refinement of translations. As shown in Fig. 4, users can submit both their original translation and the source text, enabling the platform to perform a side-by-side comparison and generate an improved version. To support learning and customization, the interactive chatbot allows users to request more detailed revisions, and ask specific questions about the polishing process. By interacting with the chatbot and comparing their work to AI-generated refinements, learners can have a better understanding of editing strategies.

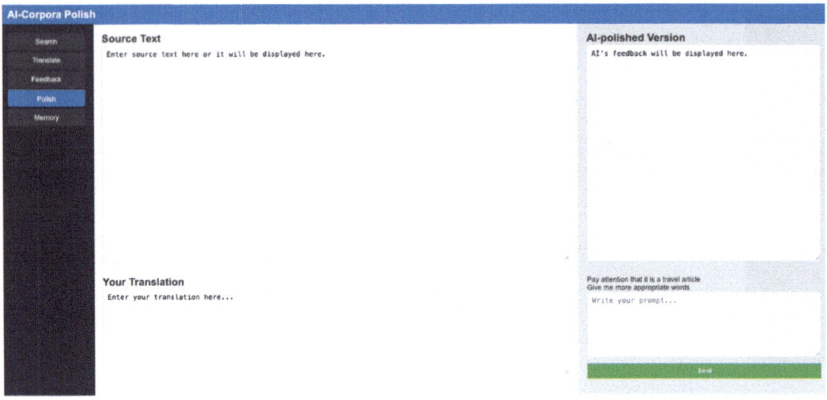

Fig. 4 Polish

3.6 *Memory*

After completing a translation task, systematic reflection on the knowledge gained during the process is essential for the continued development of translation skills. The “Memory” interface supports this process by serving as a personalized database where learners can collect and organize detailed feedback generated during their translation activities (Fig. 5). By regularly reviewing this accumulated feedback, users can identify recurring issues and gain deeper insights into the challenges they encounter over time. This interface not only contributes to the enhancement of translation competence but also supports professional growth by bridging the gap between individual practice and long-term skill development.

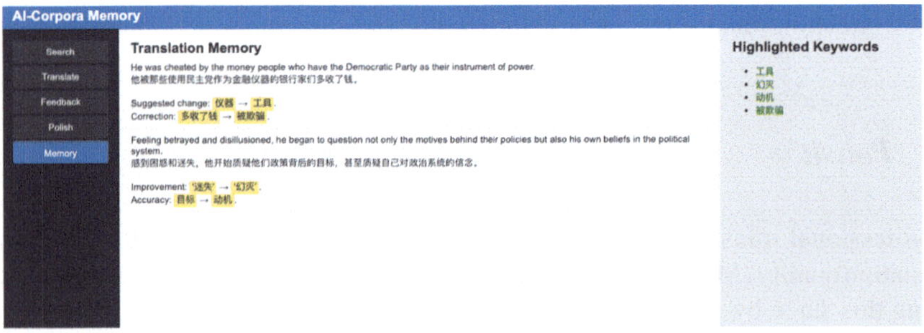

Fig. 5 Memory

4 Practical Application in the Teaching Process

This section examines how the AI-integrated corpus platform can be effectively incorporated into translation teaching practice. Previous studies have emphasized the importance of combining authentic translation tasks with process-oriented and task-based pedagogy to support effective translator training and consolidate competence (Li, 2013; Massey, 2005; Rini, 2024). Building on these insights, we evaluate how the platform's various functions can be strategically applied at different stages of a translation task, highlighting its potential to support both the procedural and reflective aspects of translation competence development.

Li's (2013) task-based translation teaching cycle includes six phases: pre-task, task, reporting, analysis, revising, and reflection. In this chapter, the Reporting and Analysis phases are merged into a single stage, Feedback, as both are intended to assess translation quality and process (Fig. 6). The following section bridges theory and practice by outlining how the AI-integrated corpus platform can be systematically implemented across all five phases of translation instruction. According to PACTE (2003), the translation competence model consists of six components, which are the bilingual sub-competence, extra-linguistic sub-competence, translation knowledge sub-competence, instrumental sub-competence, strategic sub-competence, and psycho-physiological competences. The following sections demonstrate how students' different sub-competences can be enhanced in each phase.

4.1 Pre-Task

The preparation stage emphasizes the comprehension of the source text and guidance of how to employ the platform in translation tasks. To start, teachers should introduce students to the AI-integrated corpus platform, explaining its core functions and demonstrating how it can be applied in translation practice. Since the platform's AI chatbot generates feedback based on user input (Knoth et al., 2024), a key component of this stage is instruction in prompt engineering, which refers to teaching students how to design clear and purposeful prompts to interact effectively with AI.

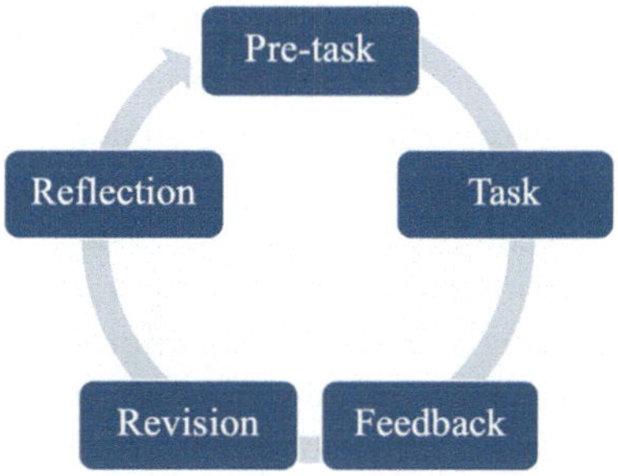

Fig. 6 Task-based cycle of teaching translation

Through demonstrations and guided practice, students gain a better understanding of how to interact effectively with GenAI, thereby maximizing the platform's potential. This process consolidates the development of instrumental sub-competence, which involves teaching students how to use relevant resources and tools effectively in the translation process (Albir et al., 2020; Li, 2013).

Furthermore, instructors should provide translation assessment rubrics aligned with the criteria used by the built-in prompts in the "Feedback" interface. It ensures coherence between classroom expectations and automated feedback, fostering transparent and consistent assessment practices. Equally important is students' understanding of the source text, including its contextual background, targeted readers, genre conventions, and potential translation challenges. It not only enhances their translation knowledge sub-competence, which refers to the ability to apply theoretical and practical knowledge about translation, but also enables them to formulate appropriate translation strategies and create a work plan for the task, developing the strategic sub-competence (Li, 2013).

Overall, this phase assists students not only to become familiar with the AI-integrated platform but also to learn the relevant knowledge and skills needed to complete translation tasks strategically and efficiently, which lays the foundation for later stages of the translation process.

4.2 Task

During this phase, students carry out translation tasks with the support of the AI-integrated corpus platform, while teachers serve primarily as facilitators, offering guidance on how to use the platform and responding to specific questions as they arise. The overall quality of students' translations depends on both accuracy and various linguistic factors, including lexical choice, sentence structure, and textual coherence, all of which can be addressed through the platform's "Search" and "Translate" interfaces.

A common challenge in translation is selecting vocabulary that appropriately fits the context. The "Search" interface helps address this issue by allowing students to look up terminology and filter results by part of speech and genre. Building on this, the "Translate" interface enables students to explore translation issues at a comprehensive level, including both linguistic accuracy and contextual relevance. Rather than offering simple definitions, the platform presents vocabulary in meaningful contexts, allowing students to observe how words function within sentences and broader discourse. By identifying keywords from the source text and suggesting translations based on their usage in similar contexts, the platform not only draws attention to terms that may lead to contextual translation errors but also supports students in making more informed and accurate lexical choices.

Beyond lexical concerns, the platform also supports students in addressing syntactic and textual challenges. Through AI-generated reference translations, students can compare their own work with AI-produced versions, which helps them recognize areas for improvement in sentence structure, coherence, cohesion, and overall textual quality. This comparative process also aids in detecting omissions in their translations, contributing to greater accuracy in the final version. The main benefit of the platform is to provide context-specific references in both source language and target language, which gradually strengthens students' bilingual subcompetence, the ability to communicate in two languages (Albir et al., 2020; Li, 2013). Additionally, it enhances students' understanding of cultural and domain-specific knowledge, contributing to the development of their extra-linguistic subcompetence, which encompasses awareness and knowledge of both the source and target cultures (PACTE, 2003).

4.3 Feedback

Once students complete their initial translations, they move on to the feedback phase, which focuses on evaluating the quality of their work. This stage involves two key components. First, students are required to perform a self-assessment using Hurtado Albir's (2015) evaluation rubric. This framework assesses translations across multiple dimensions, including accuracy, composition, vocabulary, morphosyntax, cohesion, and coherence. Through this self-assessment, students can identify the strengths and weaknesses in their work, evaluate how well they have addressed translation challenges, and pinpoint areas that need further improvement. Engaging in this reflective process not only strengthens students' capacity for independent learning (Ge & Pi, 2021) but also enhances their motivation for future translation tasks (Li, 2018). During this stage, teachers primarily act as facilitators, clarifying the objectives of the reporting process and offering guidance to help students complete the reflection effectively. Second, students use the platform's "Feedback" interface to receive targeted input on the strengths and weaknesses of their drafts. By submitting both the source text and their initial translations, they receive automated feedback that addresses issues at the word, sentence, and discourse levels, aligned with the criteria outlined in Hurtado Albir's (2015) evaluation rubric.

After receiving feedback, students are encouraged to review it carefully and make thoughtful decisions about which suggestions to incorporate into their revisions, which enhances their critical thinking, thereby developing psycho-physiological competences (Albir et al., 2020; Li, 2013). Students can communicate with the platform to request clarification or ask for more detailed explanations, which helps them better understand the feedback and apply it more effectively in their revisions.

During this stage, teachers provide support and guidance as students engage in both self-assessment and feedback interpretation. When students encounter uncertainty about specific feedback points, they are encouraged to reflect on their initial translations and seek teacher support to work through any difficulties. Peer discussions can also be integrated, offering opportunities for students to share perspectives and collaboratively determine how to revise their work based on the feedback received (Schillings et al., 2020).

Another key focus at this stage is fostering meaningful communication among students, the platform, peers, and teachers. Such interaction allows students to consider multiple viewpoints, deepens their engagement with the feedback process, and promotes more deliberate and informed decision-making during the revision phase (Wang & Xue, 2024; Smith et al., 2011). Through this collaborative approach, feedback shifts from a one-directional exchange to a dynamic, interactive learning experience.

4.4 Revision

Revision is a crucial component of the translation process and plays an important role in both translation pedagogy and the development of translation competence (Riondel, 2024). This phase is supported by the platform's "Polish" interface, which provides a structured environment for refining translation drafts using GenAI and corpus resources. After receiving feedback from the platform, students can revise, edit, and proofread their translations with reference to the AI-polished version. Once revisions are completed, students re-evaluate their updated drafts to ensure they meet the required standards.

Similar to the "Feedback" interface, students can interact with GenAI and critically adopt AI-polished versions to further improve their translations. During this process, teachers are responsible for guiding students through the revision stage and evaluating their final translation work. These are crucial for the development of psycho-physiological competences, which, according to PACTE (2003), include capabilities to analyze and think critically. Additionally, the revision process provides students with the opportunity to re-evaluate their translation strategies based on the issues identified by the platform, which helps consolidate their strategic sub-competence (PACTE, 2003).

4.5 Reflection

At this stage, students can collect feedback they find important or challenging. The "Memory" interface helps create a personalized learning record by drawing attention to vocabulary and issues that require further focus in future translation tasks. Repeatedly reviewing the mistakes and feedback helps students to refine their translation strategies, and strengthen procedural knowledge, which is an important component of the strategic sub-competence that enables students apply learned skills and knowledge effectively in future learning (Albir et al., 2020).

In addition, students are expected to reflect comprehensively on their entire translation experience, from the initial draft to the final revision. This reflection should address several key aspects: difficulties in understanding specific sentences and reformulating ideas (Gile, 1994), challenges encountered while using the platform, strategies developed to resolve translation problems, and the specific types of support provided by the platform. To deepen their reflection, students are encouraged to include concrete examples that illustrate how they tackled particular translation issues and leveraged technological tools to improve their work. They are also invited to compare their self-assessments with the feedback generated by the GenAI, a process that fosters critical thinking and supports the development of AI literacy.

Teachers play two important roles during this phase. First, they guide students through the reflection process, helping them analyze their translation experiences and identify areas for improvement. Second, teachers can reflect on the overall teaching activity by evaluating students' performance from a pedagogical perspective. Rather than simply correcting errors, they can use this reflection to offer targeted feedback on common issues and suggest effective translation strategies that address more complex challenges. This stage also provides teachers with valuable input for refining the curriculum and enhancing the integration of technology into the classroom, contributing useful empirical insights to the field of translation pedagogy.

5 Pedagogical Benefits

The effectiveness of corpus-based teaching and AI-assisted learning has received growing attention in translation pedagogy (Bowker, 2024; Fan et al., 2023). Considering the strengths and possible limitations of both approaches, the AI-integrated corpus platform offers several key advantages for translation education in terms of instructional methods, learning objectives, and technological support.

5.1 Instructional Approaches: Personalized and Task-Based Learning

The platform supports translation pedagogy by combining two instructional approaches: personalized learning and task-based teaching. This combination helps meet individual learner needs and supports the development of practical translation skills.

First, large class sizes in traditional classrooms often make it difficult for teachers to provide individual support or maintain regular communication with every student (Guo et al., 2024). The platform helps address this challenge by offering an AI-powered chatbot that gives personalized feedback based on each learner's input, rather than using one-size-fits-all instruction. This tailored support encourages students to take a more active role in translation activities and helps keep them motivated, which are both important for developing translation competence (Naik &

Kamat, 2018). It also reduces the workload for teachers by allowing GenAI to handle basic error correction, so teachers can focus more on supporting students' learning progress and individual needs.

Second, as a learner-centered teaching approach, task-based language teaching shifts the focus from "learning knowledge of language" to a pragmatic focus of "achieving communicative purposes" (Chong & Reinders, 2020). Since learning is an interactive, collaborative, and socio-personal process (Kiraly, 2003), giving students the chance to work on real translation tasks helps them develop specific skills at different stages of the translation process. This method not only improves their ability to communicate effectively but also helps prepare them for professional translation work. The AI-integrated corpus platform brings together tools that support each step of the translation workflow, including searching for equivalents, identifying keywords in context, generating AI reference translations, giving feedback, supporting revisions, and reviewing past learning. Students can practice with texts from different genres such as legal, news, financial, and business, which reflect real-world translation tasks. Through this kind of practice, students can gradually improve their translation skills and build a stronger foundation for future work.

For teachers, the platform allows a shift from being the main source of knowledge to taking on a more supportive role in student learning. It reduces the need for constant direct instruction, helping teachers focus on task-based instructional design and higher-level teaching goals. For example, to enhance students' AI literacy and critical thinking, reflective activities such as group discussions or peer review sessions can be conducted, where students analyze the platform's feedback, explain their revisions, and justify their decisions. In addition, task-based teaching provides useful information about how students learn, including common translation issues and skill gaps. These insights can help teachers make improvements to their teaching methods and course design.

5.2 Instructional Goals: Critical Thinking, AI Literacy, and Prompt Engineering Expertise

Traditionally, translation classrooms have focused primarily on developing students' linguistic competences. However, advances in technology call for a redefinition of instructional goals (Hurtado Albir, 2015). The integration of an AI-powered corpus platform expands the objectives of translation education.

GenAI, with its versatility, can be applied to carry out translation tasks across various genres. However, the quality of its output depends on the users' prompts (Knoth et al., 2024). Its generated results are sometimes inconsistent and unreliable (Su et al., 2023). In addition, ethical concerns arise when users' overreliance on AI leads them to accept AI-generated recommendations without question, resulting in errors during decision-making tasks (Zhai et al., 2024). Regarding both the potential and the limitations of GenAI, translator training should encourage professionals to reconsider their roles and adjust their professional mindset (Lee, 2023). It is essential for modern translators to develop competencies beyond basic translation skills, including critical thinking, AI literacy, and prompt engineering skills. These competencies are essential for evaluating, guiding, and making effective use of AI-generated content. Our platform addresses these needs by offering AI feedback, AI reference translations, and AI-polished translations. When integrated into classrooms, students should be guided to critically assess the reliability of AI feedback, compare AI-generated translations with their own work, and evaluate AI-polished versions before deciding whether to adopt them. Through these cognitively demanding activities, students learn to regard AI-generated content as a resource to be scrutinized rather than an authority to be trusted uncritically. This process can help strengthen students' critical thinking and AI literacy (Xu et al., 2025a), while fostering ethical awareness in AI-assisted learning.

In addition, through instructors' guidance on prompt writing and interaction with the platform's built-in chatbot, students can develop a practical understanding of how AI operates and learn how to craft precise prompts to generate high-quality AI output. This process not only enhances students' awareness of algorithmic bias in AI caused by training datasets (Zhai et al., 2024), but also supports the development of prompt engineering skills.

In sum, the platform connects theoretical understanding with practical application, preparing students for the changing demands of professional translation in an AI-augmented landscape.

5.3 *Instructional Tools: A Novel Platform Merging GenAI and Corpora*

Our platform brings together the strengths of corpora and GenAI to create an innovative instructional tool for translation pedagogy that enhances both teaching and learning in the translation classroom.

Translation involves transferring meaning between cultural and linguistic contexts, requiring translators to identify contextually appropriate language equivalents (Sonbul et al., 2022). To support the development of this essential skill, the platform integrates a parallel corpus (TR Corpus) that offers descriptive evidence of authentic language usage in both Chinese and English. These data serve as valuable reference materials for students as they work through translation challenges. For teachers, the diverse corpus resources across multiple genres and text types provide practical, evidence-based materials for use in translation instruction. In addition to corpus resources, the platform incorporates GenAI to take advantage of its advanced analytical and summarization capabilities. While corpus data can often overwhelm students due to its volume and complexity, GenAI helps address this challenge by efficiently filtering, organizing, and distilling the information into clear, contextually relevant outputs that students can apply directly to their translation work. This enables students to better understand how AI interprets corpus data, supporting their learning of both linguistic patterns and GenAI processes at the same time. This feature is particularly useful for students who have limited technical experience with corpus tools.

6 Concluding Remarks

This chapter has introduced an innovative AI-integrated corpus platform which assists translation education. Beyond the pedagogical benefits, the platform helps to address some challenges in translation practice caused by the rapid development of AI.

One challenge is about translation profession. Although GenAI enhances the efficiency of translation, its quality sometimes needs scrutinized (Zhai et al., 2024). Translators are expected to work with a wide array of digital tools while maintaining human creativity and contextual judgment. This shift drives the need to train translator trainees not only in language and cultural expertise but also in AI literacy, critical thinking, and post-editing skills (Guerberof Arenas & Moorkens, 2019). The platform responds to this challenge by providing students with hands-on experience in working with AI tools, enabling them to be familiar with the workflow of AI-assisted translation tasks.

From a broader perspective, the platform's integration of AI represents a transformative shift in translator training. It aligns with emerging trends that emphasize the importance of interdisciplinary skills, such as the ability to collaborate with AI, critically evaluate AI-generated outputs, and adapt to new workflows (Lai, 2025). By incorporating AI into the curriculum, the platform prepares students to take on different roles in the translation industry, from post-editing machine translations to managing AI-assisted projects and ensuring the ethical use of AI technologies. It helps translator trainees to thrive in a profession that is increasingly defined by its reliance on cutting-edge technology.

Additionally, the chapter has also outlined the practical application of the platform within a task-based teaching cycle and has provided implementation strategies for translation classrooms and clarified the respective roles of students and instructors in the instructional process. In addition, we have explored its pedagogical benefits in terms of instructional approaches, learning objectives, and tools, highlighting its broader significance for the future of translation education.

However, the chapter has several limitations. Although the chapter introduces how the platform can be used in the classroom, it is important to implement the platform in real-world teaching practices and research to systematically assess its impact on students' learning experiences and translation outcomes. Such studies could explore how learners with different levels of translation proficiency engage with the platform. Another area of investigation is the long-term effect of the platform on students' critical thinking skills and their ability to critically evaluate AI-generated content, which are essential competencies for translators in the era of AI.

In addition, the platform needs further enhancement. First, we plan to refine the platform's interface based on feedback from educators and learners to ensure it remains user-friendly and accessible to users with different needs and preferences. Second, the current scope of the tranining data is limited, which may affect the quality of AI-generated content. To address this issue, we aim to expand the TR Corpus by incorporating a wider range of authentic translation examples, covering additional languages, subject areas, and text types. Through continuous interface development and corpus expansion, we seek to build a flexible and effective tool that supports the evolving needs of translation education.

References

Alasadi, E., & Baiz, R. (2023). Generative AI in education and research: Opportunities, concerns, and solutions. *Journal of Chemical Education, 100*(8), 2965–2971. https://doi.org/10.1021/acs.jchemed.3c00323

Albir, P. Group. A. H., Galán-Mañas, A., Kuznik, A., Olalla-Soler, C., Rodríguez-Inés, P., & Romero, L. (2020). Translation competence acquisition. Design and results of the PACTE group's experimental research. *The Interpreter and Translator Trainer, 14*(2), 95–233. https://doi.org/10.1080/1750399X.2020.1732601

Allan, R., Walker, T., & Langum, V. (2023). Data-driven learning: Tools, approaches, and next steps. *Nordic Journal of English Studies, 22*(1), 1–12. https://doi.org/10.35360/njes.791

Amaro, I., Barra, P., Della Greca, A., Francese, R., & Tucci, C. (2023). Believe in artificial intelligence? A user study on the ChatGPT's fake information impact. *IEEE Transactions on Computational Social Systems.* https://doi.org/10.1109/TCSS.2023.3291539

Baghiat Esfahani, M. J., & Ketabi, S. (2024). The effect of corpus-assisted language teaching on academic collocation acquisition by Iranian advanced EFL learners. *Journal of Applied Research in Higher Education, 16*(4), 1188–1213. https://doi.org/10.1108/JARHE-05-2023-0199

Boulton, A., & Cobb, T. (2017). Corpus use in language learning: A meta-analysis. *Language Learning, 67*, 348–393. https://doi.org/10.1111/lang.12224

Bowker, L. (2024). Corpora and translator education. In D. Li & J. Corbett, *The Routledge handbook of corpus translation studies* (1st ed., pp. 369–382). Routledge. https://doi.org/10.4324/9781003184454-26

Chong S. W., & Reinders H. (2020). Technology-mediated task-based language teaching: A qualitative research synthesis. *Language Learning & Technology, 24*(3), 70–86. http://hdl.handle.net/10125/44739

Crosthwaite, P., & Baisa, V. (2023). Generative AI and the end of corpus-assisted data-driven learning? Not so fast! *Applied Corpus Linguistics, 3*(3), Article 100066. https://doi.org/10.1016/j.acorp.2023.100066

Ekin, S. (2023). Prompt engineering for ChatGPT: A quick guide to techniques, tips, and best practices. https://doi.org/10.36227/techrxiv.22683919.v2

Fan, P., Gong, H., & Gong, X. (2023). The application of ChatGPT in translation teaching: Changes, challenges, and responses. *International Journal of Education and Humanities, 11*(2), 49–52. https://doi.org/10.54097/ijeh.v11i2.13530

Flowerdew, L. (2012). *Corpora and language education.* Palgrave Macmillan.

Gao, Y., Wang, R., & Hou, F. (2023). *How to design translation prompts for ChatGPT: An empirical study* (No. arXiv:2304.02182). arXiv. http://arxiv.org/abs/2304.02182

Ge, S., & Pi, X. (2021). Research on construction of translation self-assessment activity for self-regulated learning in Chinese EFL context. In W. Jia, et al. *Emerging Technologies for Education.*

SETE 2021. Lecture Notes in Computer Science (Vol. 13089). Springer. https://doi.org/10.1007/978-3-030-92836-0_35

Gile, D. (1994). The process-oriented approach in translation training. In C. Dollerup & A. Lindegaard (Eds.), *Benjamins Translation Library* (Vol. 5, p. 107). John Benjamins Publishing Company. https://doi.org/10.1075/btl.5.17gil

Guerberof, A., & Moorkens, J. (2019). Machine translation and post-editing training as part of a master's programme. *The Journal of Specialised Translation*, (31), 217–238. https://doi.org/10.26034/cm.jostrans.2019.184

Guo, K., Pan, M., Li, Y., & Lai, C. (2024). Effects of an AI-supported approach to peer feedback on university EFL students' feedback quality and writing ability. *The Internet and Higher Education, 63*, Article 100962. https://doi.org/10.1016/j.iheduc.2024.100962

Hanna, M. G., Pantanowitz, L., Jackson, B., Palmer, O., Visweswaran, S., Pantanowitz, J., Deebajah, M., & Rashidi, H. H. (2025). Ethical and bias considerations in artificial intelligence/machine learning. *Modern Pathology, 38*(3), Article 100686. https://doi.org/10.1016/j.modpat.2024.100686

Hitsuwari, J., Ueda, Y., Yun, W., & Nomura, M. (2023). Does human–AI collaboration lead to more creative art? Aesthetic evaluation of human-made and AI-generated haiku poetry. *Computers in Human Behavior, 139*, Article 107502. https://doi.org/10.1016/j.chb.2022.107502

Hurtado Albir, A. (2015). The acquisition of translation competence. Competences, tasks, and assessment in translator training. *Meta, 60*(2), 256–280. https://doi.org/10.7202/1032857ar

ISO (2015). *ISO 17100 Translation services—Requirements for translation services* (1st ed.).

Kennedy, C., & Miceli, T. (2001). An evaluation of intermediate students' approaches to corpus investigation. *Language Learning & Technology*, *5*(3), 77–90. https://www.lltjournal.org/item/10125-44567/

Kiraly, D. (2003): "From teacher-centred to learning-centred classrooms in translator education: control, chaos or collaboration?". In A. Pym, C. Fallada, J. R. Biau & J. Orenstein (Eds.), *Innovation and E-learning in translator training: Reports on online symposia* (pp. 27–31). Universitat Rovira I Virgili.

Knoth, N., Tolzin, A., Janson, A., & Leimeister, J. M. (2024). AI literacy and its implications for prompt engineering strategies. *Computers and Education: Artificial Intelligence, 6*, Article 100225. https://doi.org/10.1016/j.caeai.2024.100225

Kruk, M., & Kałużna, A. (2025). Investigating the role of AI tools in enhancing translation skills, emotional experiences, and motivation in L2 learning. *European Journal of Education, 60*(1), Article e12859. https://doi.org/10.1111/ejed.12859

Kwok, H. L., Shi, Y., Xu, H., Li, D., & Liu, K. (2025). GenAI as a translation assistant? A corpus-based study on lexical and syntactic complexity of GPT-post-edited learner translation. *System, 130*, Article 103618. https://doi.org/10.1016/j.system.2025.103618

Lai, H. (2025). Using Critical posthumanist methods to navigate human translators' roles in the AI era. *INContext: Studies in Translation and Interculturalism, 5*(1). https://doi.org/10.54754/incontext.v5i1.113

Laviosa, S., & Falco, G. (2023). Corpora and translator education: Past, present, and future. In J. Pan, & S. Laviosa (Eds.), *Corpora and translation education. New Frontiers in Translation Studies*. Springer. https://doi.org/10.1007/978-981-99-6589-2_2

Lee, T. K. (2023). Artificial intelligence and posthumanist translation: ChatGPT versus the translator. *Applied Linguistics Review*. https://doi.org/10.1515/applirev-2023-0122

Li, D. (2013). Teaching business translation: A task-based approach. *The Interpreter and Translator Trainer, 7*(1), 1–26. https://doi.org/10.1080/13556509.2013.10798841

Li, X. (2018). Self-assessment as 'assessment as learning' in translator and interpreter education: Validity and washback. *The Interpreter and Translator Trainer, 12*(1), 48–67. https://doi.org/10.1080/1750399X.2017.1418581

Liu, J., Liu, K., & Su, Y. (2023). Corpus-assisted translation learning: Attitudes and perceptions of novice translation students. In K. Mak (Ed.), *Advances in techno-humanities: Case studies from culture, philosophy and the arts* (pp. 76–92). (Routledge Studies in Translation Technology and Techno-Humanities). Routledge. https://doi.org/10.4324/9781003376491-7

Liu, K., Su, Y., Lai, C., & Jin, T. (2024). How do students engage with parallel corpora in translation? A multiple case study approach. *International Journal of Applied Linguistics (United Kingdom), 34*(4), 1746–1766. https://doi.org/10.1111/ijal.12594

Massey, G. (2005). Process-oriented translator training and the challenge for E-learning. *Meta, 50*(2), 626–633. https://doi.org/10.7202/011006ar

Mellinger, C. D. (2018). Re-thinking translation quality: Revision in the digital age. *Target. International Journal of Translation Studies*. https://doi.org/10.1075/target.16104.mel

Memon, S. A., & West, J. D. (2024). *Search engines post-ChatGPT: How generative artificial intelligence could make search less reliable* (No. arXiv:2402.11707). arXiv. https://doi.org/10.48550/arXiv.2402.11707

Naik, V., & Kamat, V. (2018). Analyzing relation between response time, engagement and performance. In *2018 IEEE Tenth International Conference on Technology for Education (T4E)* (pp. 110–113). https://doi.org/10.1109/T4E.2018.00030

PACTE Group. (2003). Building a translation competence model. In F. Alves (Ed.), *Triangulating translation: Perspectives in process oriented research* (pp. 43–66). John Benjamins.

Rini, J. E. (2024). Text and practice in teaching translation: Documenting the process. *K@ta, 26*(00), 45–52. https://doi.org/10.9744/kata.26.00.45-52

Riondel, A. (2024). How to teach revision: Tips from an interview study. *The Interpreter and Translator Trainer, 18*(3), 507–522. https://doi.org/10.1080/1750399X.2024.2372916

Rodríguez-Inés, P. (2009). Evaluating the process and not just the product when using corpora in translator education. In A. Beeby, P. RodríguezInés, & P. Sánchez-Gijón (Eds.), *Corpus use and translating: Corpus use for learning to translate and learning corpus use to translate* (pp. 129–149). John Benjamins Publishing.

Sahari, Y., Al-Kadi, A. M. T., & Ali, J. K. M. (2023). A cross sectional study of ChatGPT in translation: Magnitude of use, attitudes, and uncertainties. *Journal of Psycholinguistic Research, 52*(6), 2937–2954. https://doi.org/10.1007/s10936-023-10031-y

Santos, D., & Frankenberg-Garcia, A. (2007). The corpus, its users and their needs: A user-oriented evaluation of COMPARA. *International Journal of Corpus Linguistics, 12*(3), 335–374. https://doi.org/10.1075/ijcl.12.3.03san

Satake, Y. (2024). Expanding L2 learners' essay topic ideas with ChatGPT and DDL. In *Proceedings of the International CALL Research Conference, 2024* (pp. 247–252). https://doi.org/10.29140/9780648184485-37

Schillings, M., Roebertsen, H., Savelberg, H., van Dijk, A., & Dolmans, D. (2020). Improving the understanding of written peer feedback through face-to-face peer dialogue: Students' perspective. *Higher Education Research & Development, 40*(5), 1100–1116. https://doi.org/10.1080/07294360.2020.1798889

Smith, M. K., Wood, W. B., Krauter, K., & Knight, J. K. (2011). Combining peer discussion with instructor explanation increases student learning from in-class concept questions. *CBE—Life Sciences Education, 10*(1), 55–63. https://doi.org/10.1187/cbe.10-08-0101

Sonbul, S., El-Dakhs, D. A. S., & Al-Otaibi, H. (2022). Translation competence and collocation knowledge: Do congruency and word type have an effect on the accuracy of collocations in translation? *The Interpreter and Translator Trainer, 16*(4), 409–427. https://doi.org/10.1080/1750399X.2022.2084251

Su, Y., Lin, Y., & Lai, C. (2023). Collaborating with ChatGPT in argumentative writing classrooms. *Assessing Writing, 57*, Article 100752. https://doi.org/10.1016/j.asw.2023.100752

Su, Y., Xu, S., & Liu, K. (2025). Adapt or adopt? Examining the Efficacy of ChatGPT in providing translation feedback. *The Interpreter and Translator Trainer*. https://doi.org/10.1080/1750399X.2025.2541486

Tsai, Y.-C. (2024). Empowering students through active learning in educational big data analytics. *Smart Learning Environments, 11*(1), 14. https://doi.org/10.1186/s40561-024-00300-1

Wang, Y., & Xue, L. (2024). Using AI-driven chatbots to foster Chinese EFL students' academic engagement: An intervention study. *Computers in Human Behavior, 159*, Article 108353. https://doi.org/10.1016/j.chb.2024.108353

White, J., Fu, Q., Hays, S., Sandborn, M., Olea, C., Gilbert, H., Elnashar, A., Spencer-Smith, J., & Schmidt, D. C. (2023). *A prompt pattern catalog to enhance prompt engineering with ChatGPT* (No. arXiv:2302.11382). arXiv. http://arxiv.org/abs/2302.11382

Xu, S., Su, Y., & Liu, K. (2025a). Investigating student engagement with AI-driven feedback in translation revision: A mixed-methods study. *Education and Information Technologies*. https://doi.org/10.1007/s10639-025-13457-0

Xu, S., Sun, Y., Su, Y., & Liu, K. (2025b). Translation pedagogy in the AI Era: Design and application of a ChatGPT-powered platform for training and feedback. In S. Sun, K. Liu, & R. Moratto (Eds.), *Translation studies in the age of artificial intelligence* (pp. 100–124). (Routledge Studies in Translation Technology and Techno-Humanities). Taylor and Francis Ltd. https://doi.org/10.4324/9781003482369-6

Xu, Z. (2025). *The intersection of corpus-based and AI-assisted second language education: An overview of current trends and reflections*. SocArXiv. https://doi.org/10.31235/osf.io/ax7uv_v1

Yang, G. (2023). The application of the combined corpus in C-E translation teaching. *International Journal of Languages, Literature and Linguistics, 9*(4), 445–450. https://doi.org/10.18178/IJLLL.2023.9.6.448

Yao, Y., Han, T., & Li, D. (2025). Measuring translation trainees' effort in AI-assisted post-editing: A multi-method approach. *The Interpreter and Translator Trainer*. https://doi.org/10.1080/1750399X.2025.2535239

Yu, Y. (2024). Application of translation technology based on AI in translation teaching. *Systems and Soft Computing, 6*, Article 200072. https://doi.org/10.1016/j.sasc.2024.200072

Zhai, C., Wibowo, S., & Li, L. D. (2024). The effects of over-reliance on AI dialogue systems on students' cognitive abilities: A systematic review. *Smart Learning Environments, 11*(1), 28. https://doi.org/10.1186/s40561-024-00316-7

Simin Xu is a Ph.D. student in the Department of Language Science and Technology, The Hong Kong Polytechnic University. Her research interests include translation pedagogy, corpus-based translation studies, and computer-assisted language learning.

Yanfang Su is an Assistant Professor in the Department of Translation, Lingnan University. Her research interests include corpus linguistics, corpus-based translation studies, and computer-assisted language learning.

Kanglong Liu is an Associate Professor in the Department of Language Science and Technology, Hong Kong Polytechnic University. He specializes in corpus-based translation studies and his main interests include empirical approaches to translation studies, translation pedagogy, and corpus-based translation research.

Exploring Learner Engagement in AI-Assisted Interpreting Training: A Multiple Case Mixed-Methods Study

Ting Yin and Ling Xu

Abstract Research on GenAI-assisted language learning has grown, yet learner engagement in GenAI-assisted interpreting training remains underexplored. This exploratory study examined how nine participants engaged with GenAI across behavioural, cognitive, and emotional dimensions in an 8-week training program. Data were collected through an engagement scale, video recordings, open-ended questionnaires, and reflective diaries. Results show that GenAI fostered emotional engagement, particularly enhancing confidence and self-efficacy. At the cognitive level, it reduced note-taking load, allowing participants to focus on evaluating AI-generated output. Behaviourally, participants invested effort in post-editing to improve language quality. Given the small, all-female sample, findings provide preliminary evidence rather than generalisable conclusions. The study suggests potential for integrating GenAI into interpreter training while highlighting the need for further large-scale research.

Keywords GenAI-assisted · Interpreting training · Engagement · Post-editing

1 Introduction

With the ongoing digital transformation fundamentally reshaping educational ecosystems, learning engagement—recognised as a core indicator of deep learning—has garnered growing attention in the field of technology-enhanced education (Yuan & Liu, 2024). Consecutive interpreting instruction, which aims to cultivate globally competent language service professionals, fundamentally depends on sustained, deliberate practice and expert feedback (Gile, 2009). However, traditional pedagogy faces structural limitations. Restricted contact hours (typically 2–4 h per week) are often insufficient for developing interpreting competence (Moser-Mercer,

T. Yin (✉) · L. Xu
Guangdong Polytechnic Normal University, University of Macao, Guangdong, China
e-mail: yinting@gpnu.edu.cn

FAH, University of Macau, Macau, China

T. Yin et al. (eds.), *AI Through LLMs*, New Frontiers in Translation Studies,
https://doi.org/10.1007/978-981-95-4798-2_10

2008), while self-directed after-class practice frequently stagnates due to a lack of timely and meaningful feedback mechanisms (Wang, 2017). Although computer-assisted interpreting tools provide some technological interventions (Alaskar, 2024; Chen & Kruger, 2023), their reliance on specialised equipment and instructor support hinders scalable implementation in out-of-class settings. These pedagogical constraints highlight the need for innovative and scalable approaches that can effectively sustain student engagement beyond the classroom.

Generative artificial intelligence (GenAI) offers a promising avenue for after-class interpreting training. By generating instant translations that function as feedback, GenAI has the potential to address the aforementioned challenges. Nevertheless, the dynamics of how GenAI influences student engagement, particularly in interpreting training, constitute a critical knowledge gap.

Drawing on the framework of self-regulated learning (SRL) (Zimmerman, 2000) and socio-technical interaction theory (Rogers, 2004), this study aims to provide empirical insights into the role of GenAI in sustaining learner engagement in consecutive interpreting instruction. The findings contribute to both theory and pedagogy by illuminating how AI-mediated feedback can support autonomous, high-quality practice in professional language training.

2 Literature Review

This review establishes the theoretical foundation for the study by exploring two interconnected streams of literature. While substantial research has documented the benefits of technological tools in interpreter education, less is known about how learners psychologically and behaviourally engage with these innovations. Therefore, we begin by surveying the landscape of technology-assisted interpreting training before focusing specifically on the critical role of learner engagement in AI-mediated learning environments.

2.1 Previous Study on Technology-Assisted Interpreting Training

Interpreting demands the complex real-time integration of discourse processing, memory management, and target language production—a cognitive architecture that requires pedagogical approaches to automate these procedures through deliberate practice (Pöchhacker & Schaffner, 2004; Moser-Mercer, 2008; Gile, 2009). Dai (2019) fundamentally reconceptualised this pedagogical paradigm, positing that effective practical interpreter training necessitates smart, innovative learning ecosystems where students, instructors, and institutional resources interact dynamically. Early technological interventions centred on computer-assisted tools (CAI), which enabled audio segmentation and transcription for consecutive interpreting rehearsal but relied on instructor-mediated feedback, thereby constraining the efficacy of autonomous learning (Alaskar, 2024; Lee, 2014; Lim, 2013).

The advent of artificial intelligence catalysed a paradigm shift. Deng and Zhong (2019) demonstrated how technology reshapes the core dimensions of interpreting pedagogy, redefining what to teach through human-AI collaboration frameworks, transforming how to teach via simulation-based methodologies, and expanding holistic learning objectives towards adaptive skill transfer. This evolution precipitated calls for curriculum reforms emphasising specialisation and industry alignment (Zhang, 2020). Empirical validations subsequently emerged, with Hu and Xia (2023) establishing VR simulations' capacity to reduce anxiety while improving accuracy, Chen and Kruger (2023) quantifying CAI tools' supplementary value in classroom settings, and Zhang (2025) designing blended models that optimise cognitive-behavioural-emotional synergy through AI agents. Yang et al. (2025) extended this trajectory through a six-competency framework—encompassing cognitive adaptability, emotional resilience, and technological literacy—wherein AI personalisation enhances multidimensional engagement.

Persistent barriers nevertheless undermine these advances. Hardware limitations and accessibility challenges restrict post-class application (Alaskar, 2024), failing to support the high-frequency, high-intensity deliberate practice essential for acquiring consecutive interpreting skills—particularly for developing working memory capacity and stress resilience (Gile, 2009; Moser-Mercer, 2008). Recent innovations address this research gap: Ni (2025) operationalised Zimmerman's self-regulated learning theory into an AI-integrated framework combining automatic speech recognition and machine translation to enhance autonomous practice; concurrently, Su and Li (2024) empirically validated how natural language processing technologies reduce cognitive load during simultaneous interpreting.

Crucially, this research trajectory remains disproportionately system-oriented. The behavioural, cognitive, and emotional engagement dynamics that mediate self-regulated practice in generative AI-assisted interpreting contexts constitute a significant area requiring further investigation—one that impedes the design of pedagogically sound training programs. This study, therefore, investigates how GenAI tools, through their capacity for contextualised feedback and web-based accessibility, can sustain multidimensional engagement in post-class interpreting training.

2.2 Prior Study on Learning Engagement in AI-Assisted Interpreting

Learning engagement is a core predictor of deep learning outcomes (Fredricks et al., 2016). Although scholars hold diverse perspectives on this construct, it is widely recognised as a multidimensional and multilevel concept, typically encompassing three dimensions: behavioural engagement, cognitive engagement, and emotional engagement (Hiver et al., 2021). Behavioural engagement refers to students' observable participation in learning activities, such as asking questions, taking notes, and sustaining attention. Cognitive engagement involves the application of cognitive strategies and the mental effort required to accomplish learning tasks. Emotional engagement reflects learners' affective responses, such as interest, enjoyment, or anxiety, associated with learning tasks (Philp & Duchesne, 2016).

Engagement is particularly salient in the context of interpreting training. It has been shown to significantly influence the development of interpreting competence, with student interpreters typically exhibiting high levels of behavioural and cognitive engagement, as well as moderate levels of emotional engagement (Zhang & Wang, 2022). In interpreting practice, strong engagement is evidenced by increased training intensity and persistence (behavioural), the refinement of note-taking logic and memory strategies (cognitive), and the maintenance of a positive learning attitude (emotional) (Chen, 2022; Zhan & Huang, 2024). These findings underscore the pivotal role of learning engagement in enhancing students' interpreting performance.

With the emergence of generative AI, AI-assisted interpreting—characterised by its generative capabilities, interactivity, and accessibility—is reshaping language learning paradigms. To date, most research on learner engagement in educational linguistics has focused on writing (Koltovskaia et al., 2024; Yeung, 2025; Zhan & Yan, 2025), reading (Jafarian & Kramer, 2025; Martucci et al., 2025; Shafiee Rad, 2025), and speaking (Fathi et al., 2024; Huang et al., 2025; Huang, 2025). These studies have shed light on how students engage with AI-assisted tasks across these modalities.

However, learner engagement in AI-assisted interpreting remains an under-researched area. Only a few studies have addressed this issue. For example, Yu et al. (2025) compared students' engagement with peer feedback and AI-generated feedback in interpreting tasks, reporting that learners were more willing to challenge or critique AI than their peers. Similarly, Xu et al. (2025) examined student engagement with AI-generated feedback during translation revision. They found that students invested greater cognitive effort in the revision process when interacting with AI-generated suggestions. These pioneering studies offer valuable insights into engagement dynamics within AI-assisted interpreting and translation contexts, contributing to a deeper understanding of how AI can facilitate active learning.

Nonetheless, current research focuses mainly on classroom-based learning. Few studies have explored how generative AI might support post-class, self-directed interpreting practice, particularly in terms of how it shapes learner engagement across cognitive, behavioural, and emotional dimensions. This gap in the literature underscores the need for further investigation into the mechanisms by which AI empowers learner engagement in out-of-class interpreting training contexts.

2.3 Research Gap and Question

Although prior research has demonstrated the potential of technological interventions in interpreting training—such as computer-assisted or AI-enhanced tools (Alaskar, 2024; Chen & Kruger, 2023)—most studies have focused on the effectiveness or usability of these tools, with limited attention to learners' multidimensional engagement. In particular, how students engage cognitively, behaviourally, and emotionally with GenAI in out-of-class, self-directed interpreting practice remains poorly understood.

Moreover, many existing solutions rely on classroom-specific infrastructure and instructor mediation, which limits their scalability and accessibility for autonomous learning. Given that interpreting competence requires high-frequency deliberate practice beyond scheduled class time, there is a pressing need for accessible, feedback-rich environments that sustain learner engagement.

This study responds to this need by investigating the research question:

How do students behaviourally, cognitively, and emotionally engage in AI-assisted consecutive interpreting practice?

3 Methodology

This study employed a mixed-methods multiple-case study design, deemed appropriate for exploring how students engage with AI-assisted interpreting in small-scale contexts, such as classrooms. The mixed-methods approach enables researchers to leverage the strengths of both quantitative and qualitative methods (Plano Clark, 2019), allowing for methodological triangulation and enhancing the depth and breadth of insights into students' engagement in AI-assisted interpreting.

3.1 Participants

Participants were recruited from a cohort of third-year undergraduate English majors at a university in Guangdong Province. During the Fall 2024 semester, volunteers were solicited from this cohort for participation in supplementary machine-assisted interpreting training sessions. All participants were female, reflecting the gender distribution of English majors in this regional context. Prior to the experiment, participants were informed about the purpose of the AI-assisted interpreting training program and the procedures involved. They were assured that all data collected during the study would be anonymised to protect their privacy. Written informed consent was obtained from all participants before their participation commenced. A total of nine students volunteered and completed the 8-week intervention. The training regimen comprised two 2-h sessions per week. All participants were native

Table 1 Background information of nine participants

Participant ID	Gender	TEM-4 score (CEFR Level)	Prior interpreting experience
P01	Female	77 (C1)	No
P02	Female	67 (B2)	No
P03	Female	78 (B2)	No
P04	Female	84 (C1)	No
P05	Female	75 (B2)	No
P06	Female	72 (B2)	No
P07	Female	76 (B2)	No
P08	Female	61 (B2)	No
P09	Female	83 (C1)	No

Mandarin speakers with L2 English proficiency ranging from CEFR B2 to C1 levels (see Table 1 for TEM-4 score conversion). The detailed background information is presented in Table 1.

3.2 Interpreting Materials

All experimental tasks employed consecutive English-to-Chinese interpreting passages drawn from the 2019–2020 National Interpreting Competition (NIC) archives. Materials were selected based on four rigour criteria to ensure representativeness, comparability, and scoring reliability across interpreting tasks.

(1) Topical representativeness, with balanced coverage across political (30%), economic (25%), cultural (25%), and technological (20%) domains;
(2) Difficulty calibration at the CEFR B2–C1 levels, independently verified by three expert raters to align with participants' TEM-4 proficiency;
(3) Length standardisation, with each speech segment comprising 120–150 words to ensure task equivalence;
(4) Scoring consistency is ensured through the use of the competition's validated analytic rubric, which weights accuracy (40%), fluency (30%), and delivery (30%).

To mitigate potential practice effects and control for text-type order effects, the sequence of interpreting materials was counterbalanced across sessions using a Latin square design, which ensured that each topic domain appeared equally across all presentation positions.

3.3 The AI-Assisted Training Process

The eight-week intervention implemented a structured protocol comprising bi-weekly training sessions. Training sessions followed a fixed 45-min sequence twice weekly. Each session began with a 5-min theme briefing, during which researchers disclosed key topics and distributed background glossaries tailored to participants' TEM-4 proficiency levels. Then, participants listened to source speeches while creating handwritten notes. Simultaneously, Kimi AI's real-time transcription was displayed textually on isolated monitors. Finally, participants synthesised their human-generated notes with AI outputs to produce target interpretations. Sessions concluded with 15-min reflective journaling using structured prompts derived from the engagement questionnaire. We also designed the interpreting materials with the following methods: (1) Source speeches standardised to 120 words per minute (WPM), matching NIC's delivery rate for consecutive interpreting tasks; (2) version-freezing of the Kimi API (2024.06 release) throughout the training program.

3.4 Scale for Measuring Engagement

This study employed a validated questionnaire to assess participants' engagement in AI-assisted interpreting. The 13-item learning engagement scale was adapted from Sun and Qi's (2025) technology-enhanced learning framework and Fredricks et al.'s (2016) multidimensional engagement model. The adaptation followed a rigorous four-stage process. First, the original instruments were translated using a forward-backwards method, with semantic equivalence confirmed by two certified linguists. Second, domain-specific revisions were made, including the incorporation of AI-assisted interpreting scenarios and the removal of three contextually irrelevant items. Third, content validity was evaluated by a panel of five experts: two certified interpreters, two educational psychologists, and one CALL specialist. Finally, cognitive interviews with 15 non-participant students led to wording refinements to ensure conceptual clarity.

The finalised scale adopted a 5-point Likert format (1 = Strongly Disagree to 5 = Strongly Agree) and assessed three overarching dimensions of learning engagement: behavioural, cognitive, and emotional. These were further divided into five subconstructs (see Table 2), providing a more nuanced understanding of participants' engagement in the AI-assisted interpreting context.

We piloted the study with 121 students in an AI-assisted interpreting training program. A confirmatory factor analysis (CFA) was conducted to examine the construct validity of the scale. The results indicated a good model fit ($\chi^2 = 82.213$, $df = 58$, $RMSEA = 0.059$, $CFI = 0.932$, $TLI = 0.909$). Reliability analysis based on Cronbach's alpha showed that each subconstruct demonstrated satisfactory internal consistency ($\alpha > 0.70$). These findings suggest that the scale used to measure engagement possesses sound psychometric properties.

Table 2 Questionnaire for measuring engagement

First layer	Second layer	Content
Cognitive engagement	(1) Processing	During practice, I can quickly comprehend and process source language information and effectively convert it into the target language
	(2) Strategies	While practising, I consider the use of different interpreting strategies and choose the most suitable translation method
	(3) Solution	When practising with AI assistance, I often identify and resolve issues encountered during the translation process
	(4) Attention	My attention usually remains highly focused during interpreting practice, and I am less prone to distraction
Behavioral engagement	(1) Frequency	I spend time every week on AI-assisted interpreting practice, both inside and outside the classroom
	(2) Proactiveness	I actively seek extracurricular AI interpreting materials or opportunities to improve my interpreting skills
	(3) Note-Taking	During AI-assisted interpreting practice, I diligently take and analyse my interpreting notes
	(4) Management	In AI-assisted interpreting practice, I experiment with various interpreting strategies to enhance fluency and accuracy
	(5) Reflection	After AI-assisted interpreting practice, I reflect on my performance and summarise my translation process
Emotional engagement	(1) Interest	I am highly interested in AI-assisted interpreting practice and willing to dedicate time and effort to training
	(2) Challenge resilience	I find AI-assisted interpreting practice challenging and am motivated to overcome these challenges
	(3) Enjoyment	During AI-assisted interpreting practice, I enjoy the learning and translation process
	(4) Grit	When facing difficulties in interpreting tasks, I do not give up easily but instead persist in my efforts

3.5 Data Collection and Analysis

To address the research question, both quantitative and qualitative methods were employed. First, the proportion of response options selected by the nine participants was calculated, providing quantitative indicators of behavioural, emotional, and cognitive engagement.

To complement the quantitative findings, qualitative data were also collected through video recordings, open-ended questionnaires, and interpreting diaries to explore further how students engaged with AI during AI-assisted interpreting. These qualitative data were analysed using NVivo 12, following the thematic analysis framework proposed by Braun and Clarke (2006).

Several procedures were adopted to enhance the transparency and credibility of the qualitative analysis. The second author first familiarised herself with the data.

Subsequently, the second author conducted initial coding using NVivo 12. Based on these codes, she identified preliminary themes and systematically analysed the relationships among them to construct a cohesive thematic framework. The first author then reviewed and verified this process. Any discrepancies were resolved through negotiation until consensus was reached regarding the reporting of qualitative findings.

4 Results

Guided by our research question, the following results delineate how the nine participants engaged with the AI-assisted interpreting training across behavioural, cognitive, and emotional facets. The presentation of findings mirrors this structure, first outlining patterns of behavioural interaction, then delving into cognitive processes, and finally exploring affective responses, with integrated evidence from both quantitative and qualitative datasets.

4.1 Behavioural Engagement

Table 3 presents students' self-reported behavioural engagement with AI-assisted interpreting. Notably, none of the nine participants selected "strongly disagree" or "disagree" for any item. The majority chose either "agree" or "neutral," indicating a generally proactive behavioural engagement with AI-assisted interpreting.

Qualitative data corroborated these quantitative findings. Several participants reported increased motivation to engage in self-directed learning activities such as internalising and interpreting materials and undertaking additional practice to enhance their skills. For instance, Student 1 stated:

> I would like to spend more time on AI-assisted interpreting. I can acquire more vocabulary by marking down the new words I encounter during the interpreting process.

Table 3 Students' behavioural engagement

First layer	Second layer	Strongly disagree	Disagree	Neutral	Agree	Strongly agree
Behavioural engagement	(1) Frequency	0.00 (0)	0.00 (0)	0.33 (3)	0.67 (6)	0.00 (0)
	(2) Proactiveness	0.00 (0)	0.44 (4)	0.56 (5)	0.00 (0)	0.00 (0)
	(3) Note-Taking	0.00 (0)	0.00 (0)	0.00 (0)	0.78 (7)	0.22 (2)
	(4) Management	0.00 (0)	0.00 (0)	0.89 (8)	0.11 (1)	0.00 (0)
	(5) Reflection	0.00 (0)	0.00 (0)	0.00 (0)	0.89 (8)	0.11 (1)

Note The numbers in Table 3 represent the proportion, and the numbers in the brackets represent the number of students

Further insights were drawn from participants' interpreting diaries, which revealed shifts in behavioural engagement patterns compared to traditional interpreting training. In conventional settings, students typically relied on manual searches for unfamiliar words or expressions. However, with AI-assisted interpreting, students reported that AI-generated feedback reduced the need for such lookups, allowing them to reallocate time towards evaluating and refining AI outputs. As Student 2 reflected:

> In traditional interpreting practice, when encountering unfamiliar words or sentences, we need to look them up ourselves. However, in AI-assisted interpreting, AI can provide instant translations, saving us the time spent on looking up new words or expressions.

Observational data from recorded sessions further supported these findings. Behavioural engagement was primarily distributed across two focal points: (1) students' notebooks and (2) the AI interface. This distribution reflects the distinct interaction patterns in AI-assisted versus traditional interpreting modes.

In addition to these engagement behaviours, post-editing emerged as a critical component of students' interaction with AI. Evidence from semi-structured interviews and interpreting diaries indicated that students actively engaged in post-editing to address limitations inherent in AI outputs. For example, seven out of nine participants noted that AI often failed to perform sentences properly and lacked sensitivity to emotional nuance. Student 5 commented:

> When translating from English to Chinese, Sentence segmentation often fails in the AI output, which leads to discrepancies between machine translation and human translation.

Other students highlighted challenges related to automatic speech recognition, including recognition errors and interference from background noise. Student 8 observed:

> Machine translation sometimes has time limitations and occasional recognition errors. It also often picks up background sounds, which increases the workload for text processing.

To address these issues, students employed a variety of post-editing strategies to overcome the limitations of the AI-generated translation, including (1) correcting lexical or grammatical errors, (2) adjusting word order, (3) adding sentence segmentation, (4) enhancing textual coherence, and (5) refining stylistic expression. These strategies represent key dimensions of students' behavioural engagement in AI-assisted interpreting. As Student 1 noted:

> I found that AI-assisted interpreting has some problems. I would adjust the word order and enhance the coherence of the sentence based on the output of AI.

4.2 Cognitive Engagement

Table 4 presents students' cognitive engagement with AI-assisted interpreting. Notably, a majority of students selected the "agree" option in the *solution* dimension, indicating that they perceived AI as helpful in addressing interpreting challenges.

Table 4 Students' cognitive engagement

First layer	Second layer	Strongly disagree	Disagree	Neutral	Agree	Strongly agree
Cognitive engagement	(1) Processing	0.00 (0)	0.11 (1)	0.67 (6)	0.22 (2)	0.00 (0)
	(2) Strategies	0.00 (0)	0.11 (1)	0.33 (3)	0.56 (5)	0.00 (0)
	(3) Solution	0.00 (0)	0.00 (0)	0.11 (1)	0.78 (7)	0.11 (1)
	(4) Attention	0.00 (0)	0.00 (0)	0.22 (2)	0.56 (5)	0.22 (2)

Note The numbers in Table 4 represent the proportion, and the numbers in the brackets represent the number of students

Qualitative data offer further insights into these quantitative findings. Students reported in their interpreting diaries that AI contributed to (1) enhancing interpreting efficiency and (2) expanding lexical variety. These perceptions explain the high agreement rates observed in the *solution* dimension. For example, Student 3 remarked:

> AI can interpret the information simultaneously, which helps us increase efficiency. It also provides more natural expressions with fewer grammatical errors. In addition, it offers examples of how to interpret unfamiliar words or phrases.

Another noteworthy finding regarding cognitive engagement was that participants reported that AI can help interpreters record all key and detailed information during the interpreting process, thereby reducing their cognitive load when taking notes. For instance, student 4 wrote in her interpreting diary:

> During the AIGC-assisted interpreting practice, my favourite feature was listening to the source material. The AI technology was able to comprehensively capture the speech content, including all the key points and details.

However, cognitive engagement was not uniformly positive across all participants. As indicated in Table 4, one student selected "disagree" in the *processing and strategies* dimension, reflecting challenges related to task difficulty and individual differences in learning experience. This suggests that while AI can support cognitive processes, its benefits may not be equally accessible to all learners. For instance, Student 8 commented:

> After using AI-assisted interpreting, I found interpreting to be extremely tough for me. My engagement did not increase.

These findings indicate that students' cognitive engagement is shaped not only by the affordances of AI but also by their perceived task difficulty and self-efficacy in managing the interpreting process.

4.3 Emotional Engagement

Table 5 summarises students' emotional engagement with AI-assisted interpreting. Compared to behavioural engagement, a greater number of students selected "agree" or "strongly agree" across the measured dimensions. Only one student chose "neutral" in the first four dimensions, and three students selected "neutral" in the grit dimension. Overall, these findings indicate generally positive emotional engagement among the nine participants.

Qualitative data further elucidate these quantitative results. Seven out of nine students reported that AI-assisted interpreting increased their interest in the task. For example, Student 1 remarked:

> If I were to practice interpretation through traditional methods, I would lose interest and motivation because interpretation itself is quite challenging for me. In conventional practice, I constantly encounter complex words and sentences that I do not know how to translate, which weakens my enthusiasm. However, with AI-assisted interpretation, I find the process much more engaging. The AI provides real-time translations and helps me translate unfamiliar words and sentences.

However, two students indicated that their interest did not improve after using AI-assisted interpreting, highlighting notable individual differences in emotional engagement. Student 5 expressed:

> After using AI-assisted interpreting, I have a clearer understanding of the difficulty of interpreting: it is tough. My interest did not change.

Notably, eight of nine students reported that AI-assisted interpreting brought them enjoyment. The qualitative data reveal a possible mechanism behind this enjoyment: AI's ability to mark key information during the interpreting process alleviates students' cognitive load related to memorisation and note-taking, thereby reducing anxiety and enhancing enjoyment. For instance, Student 3 commented:

> AI can avoid the loss of information during the interpreting process, which greatly reduces the pressure and anxiety of interpreters.

Additionally, students reported increased confidence and self-efficacy, which aligns with the quantitative findings, shown in Table 5. This boost in confidence is attributed

Table 5 Students' emotional engagement

First layer	Second layer	Strongly disagree	Disagree	Neutral	Agree	Strongly agree
Emotional engagement	(1) Interest	0.00 (0)	0.00 (0)	0.11 (1)	0.89 (8)	0.00 (0)
	(2) Challenge resilience	0.00 (0)	0.00 (0)	0.11 (1)	0.78 (7)	0.11 (1)
	(3) Enjoyment	0.00 (0)	0.00 (0)	0.11 (1)	0.89 (8)	0.00 (0)
	(4) Grit	0.00 (0)	0.00 (0)	0.33 (3)	0.44 (4)	0.22 (2)

Note The numbers in Table 5 represent the proportion, and the numbers in the brackets represent the number of students

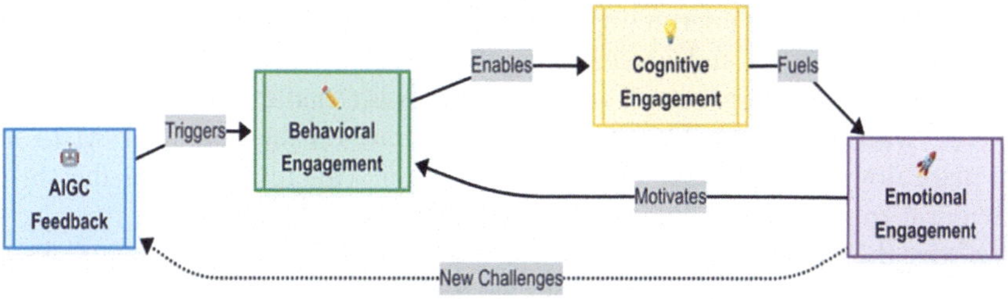

Fig. 1 AI-powered learning engagement circle

to AI's scaffolding role, helping students by (1) taking notes of key information and (2) providing interpretation examples, thereby substantially reducing working memory demands. As Student 9 noted:

> I think AI-assisted interpreting can promote my confidence in interpreting. I can feel a sense of achievement using AI-assisted interpreting to complete more challenging interpreting tasks.

The above findings on the three types of engagement in AI-assisted interpreting can be synthesised into a conceptual framework illustrating how students interact with AI to enhance their interpreting skills. As depicted in Fig. 1, AI provides instant feedback, highlights key information, and offers examples of how to interpret unfamiliar words or expressions. These examples help reduce students' cognitive load during interpreting, thereby alleviating anxiety and boosting confidence. Crucially, the feedback scaffolds students in completing interpreting tasks that exceed their current competence level, enabling them to achieve a sense of accomplishment (emotional engagement) through tackling more challenging tasks. Enhanced emotional engagement, in turn, motivates students to persist with increasingly complex interpreting activities. This conceptual framework elucidates the mechanisms through which AI supports the development of interpreting subskills, carrying significant pedagogical implications for interpreter trainers.

5 Discussion

This study aimed to investigate students' engagement with AI-assisted interpreting using a mixed-methods, multiple-case design, examining three aspects: behavioural, cognitive, and emotional engagement.

Behaviourally, students reported that in AI-assisted interpreting, they can draw on the output of AI, which can help them save time on looking up new words and expressions. This finding was consistent with the result reported by Lu (2025), who found that ChatGPT can be used to improve students' lexical and syntactic flexibility in the Chinese-to-English interpreting process. This finding highlights the role of AI output as feedback for students in AI-assisted interpreting. This function is handy for students with lower interpreting competencies. The reason is that this function (feedback) can scaffold students, enabling them to complete the interpreting task.

In the traditional interpreting mode, taking notes is a challenging task for students. However, with the aid of AI, interpreters can draw on the output of AI to help them mark down and organise the key information. This result reflects the shift in behavioural engagement of interpreting in the AI-assisted interpreting. It is also the reason why their behavioural engagement was distributed into both notebooks and the screen (AI), as reported in the results section.

The findings revealed that students actively engage with AI through post-editing in AI-assisted interpreting, marking a novel discovery in this field. Participants reported employing several strategies during post-editing to address shortcomings in AI-generated output, including (1) adjusting word order, (2) segmenting sentences, and (3) refining expressions to sound more natural. One potential reason for these limitations is that the prevailing large language models are primarily trained on English data, resulting in relatively weaker performance in Chinese. Consequently, the English-to-Chinese translation quality is affected. Future research is therefore encouraged to develop and train models based on Chinese corpora to improve AI's capability in processing Chinese language tasks.

Previous research has also noted a shift in the role of interpreters in the context of AI-assisted interpreting (Yin, 2025), emphasising the growing importance of post-editing in this emerging paradigm. This observation aligns with findings from the current study, which revealed that interpreters are no longer required to devote as much effort to information recording. Instead, their focus has shifted towards refining linguistic output and engaging in post-editing processes.

This finding has important implications for teaching and training interpreting in AI-assisted interpreting. The competence of post-editing has emerged as an indispensable interpreting subskill in AI-assisted interpreting. Beyond course design, this shift towards post-editing also underscores the need to develop students' AI literacy. For example, courses related to post-editing should be incorporated into the training program, helping students enhance their skills in post-editing for AI-assisted interpreting.

Furthermore, researchers (Yu et al., 2025) stated that AI literacy, including the critical thinking of AI output, is crucial in AI-assisted interpreting mode. The reason is that current language models inevitably have some inherent shortcomings, which should be improved during the process of interpreting. Therefore, as a legitimate interpreter, he or she should be able to evaluate the output of AI critically, correct the mistakes of AI, and refine the output of AI. This finding also prompts us to rethink the shift in interpreting competence in the AI-assisted interpreting context.

Cognitively, students reported that AI-assisted interpreting can empower them to complement more challenging interpreting tasks by providing examples. This finding underscores the potentially useful educational functions of AI in scaffolding students to higher levels of tasks. This finding was consistent with the result reported by Zhong and Ma (2025), who reported that speech recognition AI technologies are perceived to be helpful to enhance students' intention to adopt AI in practising interpreting. However, this finding does not imply that students in AI-assisted interpreting would accept all the materials generated by AI without any critical analysis during the cognitive process. Most participants reported that they would critically analyse the output. This finding was inconsistent with the finding reported by Lo et al. (2024), who reported that the use of AI might incur some side effects, such as reducing critical thinking.

However, we also found that one participant reported that AI could not improve her cognitive engagement in interpreting. The interpreting diary provides insight into this issue. The participant noted that she thought the interpreting task was far beyond her interpreting competence. She failed to complete the task even though she put all her effort into the interpreting task.

One possible explanation for this result is that the interpreting materials used in the training program were not well aligned with this participant's current level of competence. This finding underscores the importance of matching the difficulty level of interpreting tasks with learners' proficiency. It also resonates with Vygotsky's (1978) theory of the Zone of Proximal Development (ZPD), which posits that optimal learning occurs when instructional tasks fall within a learner's ZPD. In this context, appropriately challenging materials are essential for facilitating the development of interpreting competence.

Therefore, future studies should ensure that the interpreting materials selected for students are compatible with their interpreting ability. One possible solution is to measure students' interpreting ability before recommending interpreting materials. The reason is that the result can inform interpreting trainers how to set the speed of interpreting materials for students. Additionally, future studies can also develop an AI recommendation system for interpreting training programs, which can provide more adaptive materials for students, thereby promoting their cognitive engagement.

Emotionally, the finding revealed that AI-assisted interpreting can promote their confidence and self-efficacy in interpreting, which is an encouraging finding. This result was consistent with findings reported by Zou et al. (2025), who reported that ChatGPT can improve interpreters' gisting skills. This result was also in line with the finding reported by Zhong and Ma (2025), who reported that technology anxiety hinders the acceptance of technology in computer-assisted language learning.

The plausible reasons for the increasing emotional engagement are discussed below. Interpreting is demanding and challenging for interpreters, as they must accurately record all the information. Therefore, anxiety is inevitable during the interpreting process. With the aid of AI, this problem can be significantly mitigated. AI can help students take note of the key information and provide examples of translations. This scaffolding function can release students' tension during the interpreting process.

As reported in Table 5, eight out of nine students perceived that AI-assisted interpreting can bring them a sense of achievement. This finding suggested that the AI-assisted interpreting mode can increase students' well-being during the process of learning interpreting. The finding can also be discussed from the perspective of positive psychology in language learning (Macintyre et al., 2019). As indicated by Li (2020), promoting students' well-being can provide sustainable driving forces to enhance their learning motivations. Therefore, adopting AI to bring happiness to students during interpreting training is an interesting and inspiring finding.

This finding has important implications for interpreting training as well. To be specific, it is well-recognised that interpreting (both consecutive interpreting and simultaneous interpreting) is challenging or even daunting for beginner learning interpreting. Therefore, students usually feel anxious or afraid of losing face during the practice of interpreting. Their willingness to continue would diminish when their emotional engagement is low. In this sense, AI-assisted interpreting has one unique advantage over traditional training methods: enhancing their interest and confidence in interpreting. This function might be beneficial for novice learners in interpreting and constructing their self-efficacy to complement the interpreting tasks.

Finally, although several previous studies (Yu et al., 2025) have been conducted to investigate students' engagement in AI-assisted interpreting, few have systematically examined how students engage with three dimensions (namely behavioural, cognitive, and emotional). This study differs from previous studies in AI-assisted interpreting (Zou et al., 2025) by uncovering the underlying mechanism of AI-interpreting, as illustrated in Fig. 1. Building on the findings of previous studies on engagement in AI-assisted interpreting (Xu et al., 2025; Yu et al., 2025), this study extends our understanding of how each type of engagement is interconnected to shape students' experiences and cognitions during AI-assisted interpreting. This conceptual system can advance our understanding of students' engagement in AI-assisted interpreting, providing important theoretical implications for future researchers and interpreting trainers on how to promote students' engagement and learning effects in AI-interpreting training.

6 Implications

These findings have important pedagogical and practical implications for AI-assisted interpreting and language teaching.

Pedagogically, the following implications are summarised for interpreter trainers who would like to adopt AI in interpreting. (1) Language teachers can adopt AI to provide timely feedback to students during the interpreting process, which can help them lower the learning threshold. (2) Besides, AI-assisted interpreting can promote students' emotional engagement and enhance students' confidence, serving as a scaffolding tool. (3) It is necessary to choose the proper interpreting training materials that align with students' interpreting competence to promote their cognitive engagement. The interpreting materials would overwhelm students if the interpreting task is far beyond their interpreting competence. (4) Post-editing behavioural engagement has become increasingly important in the context of AI-assisted interpreting, as it enables interpreters to refine and improve the output generated by AI tools. Given its growing relevance in practice, targeted training in post-editing strategies should be integrated into interpreting curricula to better prepare students for real-world interpreting scenarios involving AI support.

Practically, the following implications are summarised for interpreter trainers who would like to adopt AI in interpreting. (1) Language model trainers can fine-tune a new model for educational purposes, which can maximise the educational functions of AI in training students' interpreting competence. (2) Human–machine collaboration is essential in AI-assisted interpreting. Therefore, interpreters should utilise the advantages of machine learning (AI) in interpreting, such as taking note of information, and the subjective initiative of humans to help them better complement the interpreting task.

7 Conclusion

This study investigated students' engagement in AI-assisted interpreting from behavioural, cognitive, and emotional perspectives. The findings revealed that participants would like to utilise the scaffolding function of AI, such as marking down information and providing translation examples, to enhance their interpreting skills during the AI-assisted interpreting process. Students also reported that they would engage in post-editing in AI-assisted interpreting, refining the output of AI to enhance the language quality in interpreting. The scaffolding functions of AI can also ease students' cognitive load and enable them to complete more challenging tasks, which has a positive impact on their emotional engagement. The interconnected system among students' behavioural, cognitive, and emotional engagement deepens our understanding of the mechanisms by which students' cognitive and emotional states shape their behavioural engagement.

However, this study also has some limitations that deserve further investigation. First of all, the relatively small, preliminary sample size and the all-female participant group may limit the extent to which the findings can be generalised to broader populations. Hence, future studies can replicate this study with a larger sample size from diverse backgrounds. Moreover, this study measured students' engagement using only scales, open-ended questionnaires, and interpreting diaries, which may not fully capture the complexity of engagement in AI-assisted interpreting. Future research is therefore encouraged to incorporate additional methods, such as eye-tracking (Hu & Xia, 2023), to provide a more comprehensive understanding of student engagement. Additionally, this study employed a cross-sectional design, whereas students' engagement with AI technologies may evolve. Longitudinal studies are recommended to track such changes and offer deeper insights into the dynamics of engagement in AI-assisted interpreting.

Acknowledgements This work was supported by the General Project of Guangdong Province Philosophy and Social Sciences Planning 2023 Annual Foreign Languages Discipline Specific Project "Research on the Intervention Model of Learning Engagement for Foreign Language Learners Empowered by Digital Technology" (Grant No.: GD23WZXC01-03).

Appendix: The Content of Open-Ended Questions for Students

1. In the process of AI-assisted interpreting practice, what are your favourite functions? And why?
2. Before and after using AI-assisted interpreting practice, how has your engagement in interpreting learning changed?
3. What specific improvements in your interpreting skills do you think AI-assisted practice has helped you achieve?
4. What are your opinions on traditional interpreting practice versus AI-assisted interpreting practice? Which one do you find more effective?

References

Alaskar, H. (2024). Examining the effectiveness of employing CAI tools in English/Arabic consecutive interpreting class. *International Journal of English Language and Literature Studies, 13*(3), 369–385.

Braun, V., & Clarke, V. (2006). Using thematic analysis in psychology. *Qualitative Research in Psychology, 3*(2), 77–101.

Chen, S. (2022). The process and product of note-taking and consecutive interpreting: Empirical data from professionals and students. *Perspectives, 30*(2), 258–274.

Chen, S., & Kruger, J. L. (2023). The effectiveness of computer-assisted interpreting: A preliminary study based on English-Chinese consecutive interpreting. *Translation and Interpreting Studies, 18*(3), 399–420.

Dai, C. (2019). Exploring college English interpreting teaching from the perspective of smart education. *Shanghai Journal of Translators, 3*, 67–73.

Deng, J., & Zhong, W. (2019). Integration of information technology and interpreting teaching: Levels, mechanisms, and trends. *Chinese Translators Journal*, *40*(6), 88–95, 192.

Fathi, J., Rahimi, M., Derakhshan, A. (2024). Improving EFL learners' speaking skills and willingness to communicate via artificial intelligence-mediated interactions. *System, 121*, 103254. https://doi.org/10.1016/j.system.2024.103254

Fredricks, J. A., Filsecker, M., & Lawson, M. A. (2016). Student engagement, context, and adjustment: Addressing definitional, measurement, and methodological issues. *Learning and Instruction, 43*, 1–4.

Gile, D. (2009). *Basic concepts and models for interpreter and translator training*. John Benjamins.

Hiver, P., Whiteside, Z., Sánchez Solarte, A. C., & Kim, C. J. (Eds.). (2021). *Student engagement in the language classroom*. Multilingual Matters.

Hu, P., & Xia, R. (2023). Research on the effectiveness and influencing factors of VR-assisted interpretation teaching. *Computer-Assisted Foreign Language Education in China*, (3), 86–92, 125.

Huang, F., Peng, D., & Teo, T. (2025). AI affordances and EFL learners' speaking engagement: The moderating roles of gender and learner type. *European Journal of Education, 60*(1), Article e70041.

Huang, M. (2025). Student engagement and speaking performance in AI-assisted learning environments: A mixed-methods study from Chinese middle schools. *Education and Information Technologies, 30*(6), 7143–7165.

Jafarian, N. R., & Kramer, A.-W. (2025). AI-assisted audio-learning improves academic achievement through motivation and reading engagement. *Computers and Education: Artificial Intelligence, 8*, Article 100357.
Koltovskaia, S., Rahmati, P., & Saeli, H. (2024). Graduate students' use of ChatGPT for academic text revision: Behavioral, cognitive, and affective engagement. *Journal of Second Language Writing, 65*, Article 101130.
Lee, T. (2014). Using computer-assisted interpreter training methods in Korean undergraduate English classrooms. *The Interpreter and Translator Trainer, 8*(1), 102–122.
Li, C. (2020). A Positive Psychology perspective on Chinese EFL students' trait emotional intelligence, foreign language enjoyment and EFL learning achievement. *Journal of Multilingual and Multicultural Development, 41*(3), 246–263.
Lim, L. (2013). Examining students' perceptions of computer-assisted interpreter training. *The Interpreter and Translator Trainer, 7*(1), 71–89.
Lo, C. K., Hew, K. F., & Jong, M. S. (2024). The influence of ChatGPT on student engagement: A systematic review and future research agenda. *Computers & Education, 219*, Article 105100.
Lu, X. (2025). The effectiveness of ChatGPT-assisted lexical-syntactic flexibility practice for interpreting competence and quality: The case of Chinese-to-English consecutive interpreting. *The Interpreter and Translator Trainer*.
Macintyre, P. D., Gregersen, T., & Mercer, S. (2019). Setting an agenda for positive psychology in SLA: Theory, practice, and research. *The Modern Language Journal, 103*(1), 262–274.
Martucci, A., Graziani, D., Bei, E., Bischetti, L., Bambini, V., Gursesli, M. C., Guazzini, A., & Pecini, C. (2025). Emotional engagement in a humor-understanding reading task: An AI study perspective. *Current Psychology*, 1–14.
Moser-Mercer, B. (2008). Skill acquisition in interpreting: A human performance perspective. *The Interpreter and Translator Trainer, 2*(1), 1–28.
Ni, N. (2025). The role of artificial intelligence in autonomous learning of simultaneous interpretation. *Advances in Education, 15*(1), 627–633.
Plano Clark, V. L. (2019). Meaningful integration within mixed methods studies: Identifying why, what, when, and how. *Contemporary Educational Psychology, 57*, 106–111.
Philp, J., & Duchesne, S. (2016). Exploring engagement in tasks in the language classroom. *Annual Review of Applied Linguistics, 36*, 50–72.
Pöchhacker, F., & Schaffner, C. (2004). I in TS: On partnership in translation studies. *Translation Research and Interpreting Research: Traditions, Gaps and Synergies*, 104–115. Multilingual Matters.
Rogers, E. M. (2004). *Diffusion of innovations* (5th ed., pp. 1–38). Free Press.
Shafiee Rad, H. (2025). Reinforcing L2 reading comprehension through artificial intelligence intervention: Refining engagement to foster self-regulated learning. *Smart Learning Environments, 12*(1), 23.
Su, W., & Li, D. (2024). Cognitive load and output quality in technology-assisted new forms of simultaneous interpreting. *Foreign Language Teaching and Research, 56*(1), 125–135, 161.
Sun, S., & Qi, T. (2025). Classroom assessment in interpreting courses based on Teacher-AI-student collaboration. *Modern Foreign Languages*.
Vygotsky, L. S. (1978). *Mind in society: The development of higher psychological processes*. Harvard University Press.
Wang, W. (2017). Development and application of the Chinese Interpreting Proficiency Scale: A case study of formative assessment in interpreting teaching. *Foreign Language World, 6*, 2–10.
Xu, S., Su, Y., & Liu, K. (2025). Investigating student engagement with AI-driven feedback in translation revision: A mixed-methods study. *Education and Information Technologies*.
Yang, C., Chen, J., & Zou, D. (2025). Artificial intelligence in interpreting education curriculum: A Delphi study for interpreter competencies. *International Journal of Education and Humanities, 5*(3), 387–403.
Yeung, S. (2025). University students' engagement with generative AI-supported automated writing evaluation (AWE) feedback. *Journal of Second Language Writing, 68*, Article 101203.

Yin, T. (2025). Has the use of AI-translated live captions in simultaneous interpreting changed the role of the interpreter? A study based on professional interpreters' perceptions. *The Translator, 31*(2), 214–231.

Yu, Y., Wei, W., & Chen, Z. (2025). Comparing learners' engagement strategies with feedback from a generative AI chatbot and peers in an interpreter training programme: A quasi-experimental study. *The Interpreter and Translator Trainer.*

Yuan, L., & Liu, X. (2024). The effect of artificial intelligence tools on EFL learners' engagement, enjoyment, and motivation. *Computers in Human Behavior, 162*, Article 108474.

Zimmerman, B. J. (2000). Attaining self-regulation: A social cognitive perspective. In M. Boekaerts, P. R. Pintrich, & M. Zeidner (Eds.), *Handbook of self-regulation* (pp. 13–39). Academic Press.

Zhan, C., & Huang, J. (2024). Interpreting learning engagement based on corrective feedback. *Foreign Language Education Research Frontiers, 7*(3), 76–83, 96.

Zhan, Y., & Yan, Z. (2025). Students' engagement with ChatGPT feedback: Implications for student feedback literacy in the context of generative artificial intelligence. *Assessment & Evaluation in Higher Education*, 1–14.

Zhang, J. (2020). The concept and strategy of constructing a golden course in interpretation for English majors. *Foreign Language and Literature, 36*(3), 130–137.

Zhang, J. (2025). AI intelligent agent-assisted blended foreign language autonomous learning model: Design, implementation, and optimization. *Foreign Language World, 3*, 29–37.

Zhang, Q., & Wang, J. (2022). The influence mechanism of learning engagement on interpreting competence under the IEO framework. *Foreign Language World, 4*, 88–96.

Zhong, L., & Ma, X. (2025). Investigating student interpreters' use of automatic speech recognition in China: Insights from the extended technology acceptance model. *Computer Assisted Language Learning.*

Zou, D., Zhang, H., Zhao, Y., & Xu, P. (2025). Unleashing the potential: How ChatGPT improves gisting skills in student interpreters. *The Interpreter and Translator Trainer*, 1–25.

Ting Yin is an Associate Professor and Head of the English Department at Guangdong Polytechnic Normal University. She is currently pursuing her Ph.D. in Linguistics at the University of Macau. Her research focuses on computer-assisted language learning.

Ling Xu is a Professor and Dean of the School of Foreign Languages at Guangdong Polytechnic Normal University. She is currently pursuing her Ph.D. in Linguistics at the University of Macau. Her research interests lie in the areas of language teaching and teacher training.

The manufacturer's authorised representative in the EU is Springer Nature Customer Service Centre GmbH, Europaplatz 3, 69115 Heidelberg, Germany. If you have any concerns regarding our products, please contact ProductSafety@springernature.com

Printed and bound by CPI Group (UK) Ltd, Croydon, CR0 4YY
07/10/2026
02229349-0005